# CRISIS IN CAR INSURANCE

# CRISIS IN CAR INSURANCE

*Edited by*
**Robert E. Keeton**
**Jeffrey O'Connell**
**John H. McCord**

**UNIVERSITY OF ILLINOIS PRESS**

*Urbana Chicago London 1968*

# FOREWORD

Controversy swirls about automobile insurance and automobile accident claims. The topic is as current as this morning's headlines and the excitement which it generates is much hotter than this morning's coffee. It is probably no exaggeration to state that automobile insurance is—or, at any rate, soon will be—the number one consumer issue in the United States. The controversy does not merely involve the insurance industry and an increasingly restive public. The legal profession is deeply involved. State and federal government officials, academicians, members of the press, and representatives of consumer groups have also been caught up in the debate. Scarcely a week goes by without a major newspaper or periodical devoting substantial space to this topic. Similarly, many state and federal government investigations, as well as insurance industry studies, are proceeding apace.

Perhaps the fundamental question being raised about automobile insurance is whether payment of automobile accident claims should continue to be based on a finding of fault or whether, instead, automobile insurance might be paid without reference to anyone's fault—as in the case of accident and health insurance, for example. It is often argued that adherence to fault as the criterion of payment is the source of many of the deficiencies of the present system. Many accident victims, particularly the more seriously injured, are unpaid or paid only a fraction of their losses, while many who have suffered trivial injuries are overpaid. Delay in payments, court congestion, and an inordinate invasion of the premium dollar by insurance overhead and attorneys' fees are also laid to the fault criterion.

On the other hand, it is argued that paying automobile insurance victims on the basis of who was at fault in the accident is only fair—and worth what it costs in time and money, both of which costs, it is said, are in any event, often exaggerated.

In addition to controversy about the fault concept and the cost of automobile insurance to the consumer, other problems are often cited: The availability of automobile insurance to the consumer in light of "creaming" of the market by insurers anxious to write more insurance for so-called preferred risks, with concomitant cancellations, failures to renew policies, and shifting of other customers into high-risk categories is a matter of sore concern. The insolvency of many automobile insurers, particularly those writing high-risk business, is an increasing and most distressing condition. Many question the reasonableness of rates allowed insurers by state insurance commissioners, while insurers complain that their underwriting losses —or at least thin margins of profit—unfairly hamper the business. As an outgrowth of these factors, the continued advisability of state—as opposed to federal—regulation of insurance is being hotly debated.

v

Many different proposals for change in automobile insurance and in the way automobile claims should be handled are being made and studied. Some changes are already being instituted and further changes of one kind or another seem inevitable.

In light of all the controversy, on October 2-3, 1967, the University of Illinois College of Law, assisted by grants from Consumers Union and the Walter E. Meyer Research Institute of Law—Program of Research on Auto Accident Reparation, held a conference to consider "Changes for Automobile Claims?" Leading figures from all segments of the insurance industry, from the plaintiffs' and defense bars, from federal and state governments, from universities, and from consumer groups took part in a wide-ranging discussion of the merits both of present methods of handling automobile claims and the various changes being proposed by many different individuals and groups.

This volume is an outgrowth of that conference, containing the papers delivered during the two days of the meeting.

We are very grateful to the many individuals who helped make the conference—and the volume—possible. Space allows mention of only a few. They include Colston Warne, President, and Walker Sandbach, Executive Director of Consumers Union; Maurice Rosenberg, Director, and the trustees of the Walter E. Meyer Research Institute of Law; Dean John E. Cribbet and the staff of the University of Illinois College of Law; Norman W. Johnson, Director, and the staff of Short Courses and Conferences, Division of University Extension, University of Illinois; Zelda T. Derber, Associate Editor of the University of Illinois Law Forum; and the Board of Student Editors of the University of Illinois Law Forum.

One final word of caution: Many of those writing in this volume discuss or refer to the Basic Protection plan for reforming automobile insurance and claims which was authored by Professors Keeton and O'Connell. As editors, we have not felt free to suggest changes in descriptions and characterizations by other contributors, given the controversy surrounding the proposal and the understandable differences of opinion concerning it. As a result, readers should not necessarily assume that as editors we have tacitly agreed to any characterization concerning the plan by others in the course of their remarks as printed in this volume.

ROBERT E. KEETON
JEFFREY O'CONNELL
JOHN H. McCORD

January 1968

# CONTENTS

# CHANGES FOR AUTOMOBILE CLAIMS?

*BY DANIEL P. MOYNIHAN\**

THE ISSUE HERE BEING DISCUSSED is change in automobile insurance. The question is: will there be any change, and if so, in what direction? I think at a time such as this that we ought to be aware that we may not know precisely what will be the direction of events—to be aware that there are alternatives and that none of the varying alternatives is necessarily clear. President Johnson tells the story about the unemployed school teacher who in the very depths of the depression arrived in a small town on the Texas plains where there was a job open. He applied for it, and halfway through the interview by the school board, a puckered old rancher looked over at him and asked, "Do you teach that the world is round or that the world is flat?" The teacher looked up and down the board but didn't get any clue whatever from the other members; finally he swallowed hard and said, "I can teach it either way." Similarly, I think that with respect to the subject here being discussed you can see two very real alternative possibilities— neither very difficult to imagine—(1) that there will be a change or (2) that there will not be.

The argument that there will not be a change is a respectable one. Many of the essential issues concerning "Changes for Automobile Claims" were raised in 1932 in the *Report by the Committee To Study Compensation for Automobile Accidents*, published by the Columbia University Council for Research in the Social Sciences.[1] This was a civilized country in 1932 and there were a lot of automobiles around. The Committee came out very explicitly on behalf of scrapping the concept of tort liability in automobile accidents in favor of a non-fault, workmen's compensation-like solution for such accidents. That was 35 years ago. And yet the proposal which the researchers at Columbia University so confidently recommended to a rational nation made no impression whatsoever, save perhaps on the impressionable minds of Robert Keeton and Jeffrey O'Connell and their occasional followers. Things do not change that simply.

The undeniable fact seems to be that built into the American system is a predisposition to keep things as they are in this and other respects. Anybody would be ill-advised to suppose that the American society changes

\* *DANIEL P. MOYNIHAN. B.A. 1948, Tufts College; M.A. 1949, Ph.D. 1961, Fletcher School of International Law & Diplomacy; Assistant Secretary of Labor for Policy Planning and Research, 1963-65; Director, Joint Center for Urban Studies of the Massachusetts Institute of Technology and Harvard University.*

---

[1] COLUMBIA UNIVERSITY COUNCIL FOR RESEARCH IN THE SOCIAL SCIENCES, REPORT BY THE COMMITTEE TO STUDY COMPENSATION FOR AUTOMOBILE ACCIDENTS (1932).

very rapidly when it shows itself able to resist for so long such proposals for reform. Remember that one of the things that really matters about this country is that this is an extremely stable country. There are no more than nine nations in the United Nations today whose government has persisted without change since 1914. We are one of them. We live in a society established in the 18th century, with the second oldest written constitution in the world. We are one of the most stable on-going societies on earth. This is a thought not hard to contemplate on the Illinois prairie and one which should make anyone who foresees great transformations a little humble.

On the other hand, one might ask, if there has been such extraordinary, sudden, unexpected, and very radical change with respect to the whole area of automobile safety, does it not follow that this related area of automobile insurance will also change? I think it does not follow. One reason—and it is my second reason against expecting change—is that the American bar is on a different side with respect to change in insurance. One cannot understand the extraordinary willingness of the United States Congress to adopt the National Traffic and Motor Vehicle Safety Act of 1966,[2] save in the context that both of its chambers are preponderantly made up of lawyers, and that lawyers were among the first and most articulate group to see the need for changes concerning automobile safety. On the other hand, perhaps a third of the legal fees of the United States bar come from litigation over automobile accidents. The simple fact is the American bar has no interest whatever in getting rid of the source of so much of its income.

And, in addition to the bar, whose interests happen to predominate in many legislatures, there are approximately 600,000 persons who make their livelihood through property and casualty insurance in one way or another. And their interests are not only real and powerful, but—like the bar's—legitimate.

The third factor arguing against any expectation of great change is the fact that the automobile insurance industry—the casualty insurance industry and its firms—are much more diverse than was the case with automobile manufacturers. There are, after all, only three and one-half automobile companies, and really only one, or maybe two, the others being tributes to the anti-trust laws. In a curious way concentration deprives an industry of sympathy and, at the least, it certainly deprives it of many home towns. There is only one home town for the three and one-half automobile companies. But clearly the automobile insurance industry is much more diversified and has many more sources of political strength and interest in many more states of the nation—with the normal consequences of political influence.

The fourth, and a very important factor militating against change in automobile insurance and claims is that this is a system which is now deeply

---

[2] Law of Sept. 9, 1966, 15 U.S.C.A. §§ 1381-1425 (Supp. 1967).

embedded in state government and state politics. Insurance companies are regulated by state governments, and this has led to that whole network of relationships, lobbying, debts, counter-debts—not to speak of skeletons, and all that misery—accompanying such a relationship. Many people make their living out of all this. On the other hand, in the case of automobile safety, the federal government, in imposing regulation of the design of the automobile, did so in an empty field, or on a *tabula rasa*, as the lawyers say; it interfered with no one else's bailiwick. But for the federal government to step in with respect to automobile insurance will require interfering with existing on-going activities of state governments in a form that will necessarily be resisted. At the same time, for any state to take the initiative itself will require it to change an existing structure of relationships and power which is a very different and normally a more difficult thing than simply establishing something *de novo*. (Do you notice the Latin influence of the legal surroundings?)

What are the arguments that there will be a change? The present system seems about to enter a period of revision—even of revolution. I think probably the most important reason for this is the fact that the issue of change has been raised. Nothing is as powerful as a new idea in a vibrant and intelligent society such as the United States today. You know the classic remark of the great mountain climber in the 19th century who was asked why he climbed mountains and who replied, "Because they're there." Why do you solve problems? Because they are there. The world is full of problems that aren't being solved because we don't know they are there.

But suddenly the problem of automobile insurance is a problem we *do* know is there. It's not something like the weather which you can't change; indeed it is increasingly like the weather which you *can* change; and if you can change it, why don't you? People up until now have simply put up with the misery of it. Now they are asking themselves, *need* they put up with the misery of it? This is a tremendously important event— when suddenly people say, "Must this happen?" "Is this necessarily the condition that must prevail?" And then they may answer themselves, "Well, no, it isn't. There are alternatives. There are better ways of doing it." It is a great moment in American life when this happens. You can trace through two centuries when certain conditions—certain parts of the sin and suffering of mankind—which had appeared immutable, turn out to be something you can get rid of. Thanks very much to the mischief of some of the persons contributing to this symposium, the thought is that automobile insurance doesn't have to be so expensive, cases don't have to take so long, and settlements don't have to be so unjust.

Two things have happened.

The first is very dangerous for American business—in this case, insurance executives: there are intellectuals interested in their problem. That almost always turns out to be to the disadvantage of businessmen. Alas, that's their fault—not that of the intellectuals. Intellectuals are willing to be agreeable, but nobody is ever willing to be agreeable to them. One small anecdote from the history of the automobile safety experience will suffice. (The automobile safety experience, incidentally, is one that ought to be very much on the minds of insurance executives.) The anecdote concerns listening to people who give free advice. I happen to be a neighbor of the American writer, Justin Kaplan, whose wife, Anne Bernays, is also a writer. Her father is Edward L. Bernays, one of the great pioneers of public relations in American business. One of his clients had been Alfred P. Sloan, the man who invented General Motors—to his considerable profit. Bernays is an old gentleman now, in his late 70's, and he comes to his son-in-law's parties on occasion. I found myself with him on a Sunday afternoon last year and began recounting some of my involvements with automobile safety. I described how I had found myself going around to one automobile industry representative after another, trying to convey the nature of the industry's dilemma. I had told industry representatives that if the railroad experience of the 19th century was of value as a precedent, the likelihood was either that the automobile industry would have to do something about safety on its own or it would end up working for a bureaucrat in Washington. (I might note that one of my associates in those days was Dr. William Haddon, Jr., who has ended up as that bureaucrat! In this respect the automobile industry has had more luck than it deserved. He is that rare combination of public administrator and scientist that has begun to make its appearance in American public life, to our very great advantage.) I asked Bernays why couldn't anybody in the industry heed what was a correct—and predictable—turn of events. It wouldn't have taken a graduate student much to figure all this out. All we had said, really, was that what had happened before would happen again. That's not always true, of course, but in this case it was. Why didn't anyone believe us? Bernays replied: "Oh, that's very easy. They weren't paying you. My Uncle Freud," he continued, "made it one of the first principles of psychoanalysis that patients must pay. You can never take advice from someone you aren't paying. It's just an unequal exchange; you resist it."

He was right. The automobile industry went right on ignoring good—but free—advice, while taking the advice of public relations counsel they were paying huge sums every year to march them off the cliff. Insurance executives should not be misled by the fact that, because all they have to do to find out what Keeton and O'Connell think is to buy a $5 book, that their advice is only worth $5. I say no more than that, and don't mean to be specific about them. But, generally speaking, one of the real problems with most industries is that they pay large sums to people who correctly suppose that what industry wants to hear is nice things, knowing that most executives are not really very good at hearing bad news. Remember, though, the sign that Boss Kettering of General Motors put up on his door: "Only Bring Me Bad News, Good News Makes Me Sick."

A second reason that change might be in order is one that occurred with traffic safety—namely the problem is beginning to be severe. It has begun to impress itself on the popular mind as a problem. Rates go up everywhere. People complain. Insurance commissioners get in trouble over it. It seems to have been going on too long. Patience begins to be exhausted.

Probably the best test of when something is a popular issue—and really popular—is when the trade unions discover it. It takes them a long time to figure out what their membership is thinking. That American trade unions are now finding out that automobile insurance is something that their members care about suggests that for at least 15 years their members have already been thinking it is pretty serious. And do not underestimate that dinosaur when its tail begins to sweep across the plains.

The third piece of evidence that change may be in order is that the United States Congress has become involved. This is another sign that there is a very considerable level of public interest. The insurance industry is about to face a series of Congressional hearings. They won't necessarily have immediate consequences, but nobody in Detroit thought that much of consequence would emerge from Congressman Roberts' hearings on automobile safety which began in 1956. It took 10 years almost to the day for Detroit's mistake to mature. Ten years is a rather short time for the diffusion of an idea as important as regulating an industry as large and formidable as the automobile industry but that's all it took. Once Congress begins to be interested, Congressional reputations will legitimately be made on pursuing the issue and producing some result; and the characteristic result of Congressional efforts is federal legislation.

So hearings will be starting soon. And note that they will not be starting *de novo*, but rather in the context of Congressional decisions made a generation ago. The McCarran-Ferguson Act of 1945,[3] was, in a certain sense, a tentative decision to see what would happen if regulation of insurance were to remain in state hands. That tentative decision in the United States Congress has lasted 22 years. But it seems perfectly possible that Congress will decide it's time to revise the McCarran Act. Remember that Congress was willing enough to revise another McCarran Act.

The fourth—if much the most uncertain but possibly the most important—sign that change is coming is one I don't know how to put in any very confident terms. Let me raise it simply to share as an idea. I think the United States is emerging from a period of about two decades—almost three—of great political stability. However much one may have liked or disliked Presidents Truman, Eisenhower, Kennedy, or Johnson, the extent to which we acted out our likes and dislikes was fairly restrained. The general nature of our domestic society was pretty calm and insurance men, among others, had a pretty good life; the most many of us had to think about was being over-

[3] Insurance Regulation Act, 15 U.S.C. § 1011 (1964).

weight. I think we're coming out of that. I think we're entering a period of political turbulence. You mustn't mistake turbulence for decline. The 1930's were a period of political turbulence and yet a creative period for American life. The 1950's were a period of calm—some would say somnolence. The fact is that a great many people today are withdrawing their consent from society. People are making stronger and stronger demands and expressing their discontent in increasingly radical terms. This is a contagious thing—it tends to spread. It may emerge that there is a large body of American opinion, one of whose principal complaints is automobile insurance. While some are demanding escalation or withdrawal in Vietnam, others may be demanding that something be done about automobile insurance. Do not suppose these things are not related, because they are. At times when certain groups are expressing grievances, other people tend to find their own to express as well. (Alas, there are those whose lives are sufficiently placid that this indeed is as much as they can call to mind in the way of injustice.) A political scientist, then, would tend to say, "Yes, there is going to be change." Many taking part in this conference do so in the expectation that there will be change; indeed, with the thought that there ought to be change.

I would like to offer, then, four guidelines with which this change should be managed. Keep in mind that those of you concerned with this problem are nothing if not managers; it is your profession; it is an honorable profession, and it is one that has to proceed from notions of what are one's larger interests and what are the contexts in which those interests operate with other interests. In this spirit, I offer four guidelines for change.

The first is that the problem of automobile insurance must be seen simply as one of several social costs of the automobile. Not to see it first in this context is to miss its meaning. This is particularly important to those who come to the subject of the automobile from other worlds entirely. Many insurance executives in this country work for firms that began insuring ships in the tea trade with China, or whatever; then came fire insurance and now automobile insurance. Such companies came out of an established insurance world, and extended its principles in the most normal course of events to the work of insuring automobiles. But they must see that the problems that they now face do not come so much from the insurance world as from the automobile world. These problems, in turn, are characteristic of a larger problem of American life today—namely, the aftereffects of the introduction of technology. We are a society—a capitalist society—wherein persons who successfully introduce new technology reap very high rewards. By the same token, our society is not very much restrained by the less attractive second, third, and fourth order of effects stemming from new technology. We put all the incentive on the plus or minus of the first order. That means we are a very innovative society; that means people are always thinking up things; that means people are getting rich returns for being inventive and for taking risks. It also means that some years later it can turn out that those pills make babies turn blue, or everybody's got cancer, or those cars kill a lot of people, or the courts get clogged with automobile claims. All these are the second, third, and fourth order of effects which we are not very good at controlling. Air pollution is certainly one of the most common examples.

In another society—not one I would particularly want to live in, but many people have opted for it—whenever someone comes along with a new idea, they say, "What are the second, third, fourth, and fifth order of effects?" And if these latter don't look very promising, one is not allowed to undertake the first one. A dull way of life. American life, on the other hand, is full of chances, full of rewards. It's very exciting, because you never know what's going to happen next, even whether or not you're going to be killed. But the fact is that we are beginning to see that we are going to have to be a little more orderly. We are going to have to begin to ask, what are the second, third, and the fourth order of effects of proposed changes?

One of the tertiary effects of the automobile has been this tremendous problem of insurance, which, in turn, involves problems that manifest themselves in costs; not only in direct costs to individuals, but in social costs. A good example is the effect of automobile insurance on our legal system, which turns out to be very seriously affected. Somehow, those who are trying to deal with the automobile from another world, such as insurance, are going to have to understand that they are dealing with a prototypical problem of our society—how to deal with the effects of technology, in this case the automobile. This is fascinating territory—and if insurance men and tort lawyers don't find it so, they ought to be doing something else.

The second guideline for change that I would lay down is that before we move forward, it's time for everybody—conservatives more than liberals—to examine the whole question of our experience with government regulation of industry. By and large, this has not been a very good experience. Conservatives characteristically say that it has been a bad experience because it has hamstrung industry. That's not so. What really happened is that it has corrupted government. Milton Friedman, an economics professor at the University of Chicago, has described this very accurately in an article in *Newsweek*.[4] Friedman, an advisor to Presidential candidate Goldwater and certainly a man with conservative credentials, was discussing the new federal bureau that has been set up to regulate the automobile industry. According to Friedman, the automobile industry will corrupt this new bureau just as industry corrupted the Interstate Commerce Commission (I.C.C.), the Federal Communications Commission (F.C.C.), and every other agency that has been set up to regulate business. Industry populates them and infiltrates them, in one way or another, and pretty soon industries are regulating themselves. The railroad industry regulates itself through the I.C.C., the communications industry regulates itself through F.C.C., and so on down a dreary list of liberal

---

[4] Friedman, *Auto-Safety Standards*, Newsweek, June 5, 1967, at 80.

dreams turned into nightmares. Although I am sure the bureau's director, Dr. William Haddon, will demur, Friedman predicts that, sure enough, the automobile industry will end up owning the National Highway Safety Bureau, thereby regulating itself—and, at long last, drive the Volkswagen out of the American market. I really do think we should think twice about going through this particular bad drama over again.

If the government were to make a rational decision, it would choose not to regulate the insurance industry, but simply to put it out of business. It would be a much wiser thing to have government insurance than to have federal regulation of insurance with all the misery of low-grade corruption involving all those three-martini lunches with GS 11's in Washington. That just isn't fair to mankind, and we don't need any more of it. If the federal government is going to get involved, then it should simply put the insurance companies out of business, run automobile insurance as another form of social insurance, and be done with it.

The alternative is a system which runs itself and does not require government regulation. Such is their perversity that Professors Keeton and O'Connell have thought up one such scheme.[5] I am not so much interested in the details of their proposal because as a political scientist I have the luxury of focusing only on tendencies. Their scheme is obviously workable: what will be the reaction to it? In that respect, the tendencies of the insurance industry at this point will probably be to resist this kind of reform. And that tendency will probably be detrimental to the industry's own interest, because it will mean that the industry will tend to be negative; will tend not to make the effort to provide alternatives; will indeed tend not to be very intelligent. I don't know why it is that businesses get this way. But look at the automobile industry. One would be hard put to find as large a collection of dunderheads as Detroit had managing its interests in Washington in the 1950's and 60's. And we all saw what Detroit got, didn't we? The tendencies of the insurance industry—certainly if they are exemplified by the Insurance Institute for Highway Safety—could be even worse.

The third general guideline for reform that I would like to establish is that in considering this whole area, we ought at all times to be thinking of one really important issue—much more important than profits, much more important than private enterprise, much more important than the self-esteem of professors: and that is the functioning of our legal system. We are dealing here with one of the central aspects of sovereignty, one of the fundamental bases of social stability. The perception of the larger society that justice is being done is sacred. And justice is possible only when it is done quickly and reflects the community sense of what is right and what is wrong. This tran-

[5] KEETON & O'CONNELL, BASIC PROTECTION FOR THE TRAFFIC VICTIM: A BLUEPRINT FOR REFORMING AUTOMOBILE INSURANCE (1965) [hereinafter this book is often cited as Basic Protection]. *See also* Keeton & O'Connell, *Basic Protection Automobile Insurance*, p. 40 *infra*.

scends the issue of government regulation or non-regulation, transcends the issue of how you distribute or don't distribute the wealth, transcends the issue of whether or not certain groups are discriminated against or not discriminated against. This has to do with the stability of our society. We are dealing, then, with something fundamental, and if those concerned with automobile claims cannot produce solutions that preserve the viability of the American legal system, then they fail. And not just they fail—after all, none of us matters that much—America fails, and that does matter. That is what is at issue here. The present system of automobile insurance is preventing the American legal system from functioning properly, and no more solemn issue could be put before the American citizenry. The insurance industry and the bar either have to rebut that proposition or change the present system because their interests are as nothing compared with this interest.

The last guideline I would offer is also a very serious one. In the resolution of this issue—in what is likely to be a fairly conspicuous arena—the reputation and the standards of two great American callings are at stake. First, the ethics of the American bar are at stake. If the bar cannot do anything but proceed with the squalid concerns that have characterized its dealing with this issue for the last 20 years, then the bar is sicker than anyone knows, and we are in deeper trouble than we know. But I don't think that's the case. The American bar led this nation to confront the problem of automobile safety and wrote in that moment a commendable chapter in our history. And the bar can respond to this allied challenge as well—despite its self-interest.

Secondly, and probably of even more concern to a person such as myself, in the liberal end of American politics, the viability of American business to conduct its own affairs is involved. The insurance companies are acting, by and large, like people who want to be run by bureaucrats. It's as if they had a pseudo-masochistic relationship with the Civil Service Commission. They really ought to think twice about it. Do they want to be run by a bureau in Washington? Do they really think that's going to make matters better? Will it help them to give up all their decisions? Does that express the virility of the American business community? I don't think so. And yet, we said to automobile executives, year in and year out, "For heavens sakes, who needs another bureau in Washington? Listen to us, we're trying to say something. We're not that smart, but you have to be stupid not to see what we're saying." And they said, "You really are a bunch of nuts, aren't you? Probably socialists, too." And now they're working for a bureau in Washington. They will corrupt it, don't doubt that; they will corrupt it. And we will all get a little more rigid, a little less able to respond to our problems. That's not good enough for America. It isn't good enough for the insurance industry and its leaders. It's not the record they want to write in their time. They have it in their capacity to respond to this problem, and they wouldn't want it said—three generations from now—that they weren't up to it.

I don't think it will be said.

# AUTOMOBILE ACCIDENT COMPENSATION SYSTEMS— OBJECTIVES AND PERSPECTIVES

*BY SPENCER L. KIMBALL**

## I. INTRODUCTION

THIS PAPER WILL NEITHER PRESENT a new plan for handling automobile accident compensation, nor discuss in detail any plan already proposed. Rather, it will try to suggest, and to sharpen as much as possible, some major considerations in the discussion of any system for dealing with automobile claims. If the objective is put somewhat pretentiously, it is to suggest criteria for evaluating any automobile claims system.

The topic assigned to me for this symposium was "Automobile Claims Systems." The change from the assigned title rests on a notion that discussion should not focus on "claims." It should concentrate attention not on what people demand, nor even on what they get, but on what they need or deserve or, given the larger goals of the legal and political system, on what they should get.

The dichotomy of the assigned topic, "objectives *and* perspectives," is preserved, and the discussion is correspondingly divided into two parts, though much more attention is given the former. These categories represent two stages, or at least two levels, of thought, involving different questions and considerations. For objectives, we ask: "What are the ultimate goals we seek (or *should* seek) in dealing with automobile accident compensation problems?" We must also ask: "If goals conflict, how shall they be reconciled?," which necessitates either setting up a hierarchy of values, or giving appropriate weights to conflicting values. For perspectives, we ask quite different questions, such as "What limitations do the environment, the political and legal system, and economic reality place upon us in seeking to achieve the goals we seek?" "What conflicts are there in fact among the goals accepted as valid?" And "Through what means can we best achieve maximum implementation of all the goals, or at least those placed highest in the hierarchy of values?"

Failing to separate the two levels of thought, or at least to keep them in mind throughout the discussion, has a special danger—that what are in reality only necessities may be treated as if they were ultimate goals. Our propensity to be political animals leads us to make compromises before (1) deciding what it is we really would seek if we could have our "druthers", and (2) finding out what are the minimum number of inevitably necessary

*SPENCER L. KIMBALL. B.S. 1940, University of Arizona; B.C.L. 1949, Oxford University (England); S.J.D. 1958, University of Wisconsin; Professor of Law, University of Michigan.*

compromises. Our wish to be considered political realists, rather than visionaries, leads us toward anticipatory capitulation, which is rationalized by treating as ultimate goals what are only intermediate ones, or even worse, what are merely necessities and not goals at all. Once a necessity comes to be seen as a goal it acquires an aura of sanctity that prevents its abandonment when circumstances change and it is no longer a necessity.

Ranking, or giving appropriate weight to the objectives, is difficult. In the nature of the case, the emphasis to be placed on various goals cannot be verified as objective truth. It can be reasoned about, but at bottom it rests on unverifiable subjective judgment. The weight to be attached to the various considerations here called perspectives, on the other hand, depends on an evaluation of factual considerations that in theory can be performed scientifically, even if in practice the problems are so complex that subjective judgment plays a great role and consensus is not to be anticipated.

Satisfactory treatment of this problem makes it necessary to keep in mind many inconsistent or intricately interrelated considerations, however intellectually taxing. We can not always indulge ourselves in oversimplification. Even the lesser objectives of the legal order, which must not determine the basic direction in which we go, may sometimes be effectuated without loss to the major objectives of the system.

## II. Objectives

It is important to achieve the largest possible consensus in a subject requiring extensive legislative intervention. It is doubtful whether it can be obtained best at the level of abstract principle, or at the level of specific rule. An articulated view holds that common sense men of good will are likely to find it easier to reach agreement on specific rules than on general philosophical positions—that men will fight vigorously about abstractions who would have the good sense to agree on particulars. This proposition contains much of the truth, but not all of it. On this subject, common sense is inordinately uncommon and interests that are not legally vested but are felt to be vested hold sway. It would not be amiss, therefore, to try to suggest a general principle on which reasonable consensus might be reached, in the hope that it will illuminate the more specific levels of the discourse.

Taken in this context alone and not necessarily generally, a frankly utilitarian approach is likely to produce fairly wide consensus. On such a view, the ultimate objective of the law is and should be to maximize human satisfactions, or to put it in the crassest Benthamite terms, to minimize pain and maximize pleasure for the totality of persons for whose happiness the legislature is in some sense responsible. Consistent with modern thought about the implementation of a utilitarian goal, this should be a modified utilitarianism which decides individual cases in accordance with rules, tests the rules in terms of broader principles, and the principles against the general standard, rather than evaluating each specific legislative or judicial action directly against the ultimate standard. Stating this utilitarian goal will not satisfy everyone, but in this field it may go a long way toward doing so. In any event if will be possible to gain some insights by testing specific rules or practices against this general goal.

It may be of some use to sketch some of the analysis through which one might test the existing tort liability-liability insurance system by a utilitarian standard. One apologist—one might almost say a quasi-official apologist—for the existing system seems to see a single basic argument for the preservation of the existing fault-oriented system. He begins with the unquestioned premise that unless there is good reason to shift loss from where it happens to fall, the initial victim should be left to bear it. The argument then becomes a moralistic one. The only justifications that are regarded as sufficient for shifting the loss must be based on moral wrongdoing by the defendant. The fact that injured people are left in desperate straits does not offend this morality. The position of the apologist is that the concept of liability based solely upon fault is "a crowning triumph of reason and morality."[1] It is based upon the notion that the individual "is responsible to his God for his own conduct,"[2] and should have to suffer the consequences if he is negligent (either as wrongdoer or victim). Individual immorality and thus responsibility is the sufficient, and ordinarily the necessary, reason for shifting the loss from its adventitious initial resting place. Any reform such as the Basic Protection plan[3] would "inevitably put an end to the moral and legal responsibilities of individuals who inflict injuries upon their fellows. The regimentation of all injured persons in 'basic protection' without regard to guilt or innocence would certainly lead to the simultaneous destruction of the dignity of the individual and the evenhanded justice of the common law."[4]

It is difficult to argue with this notion, which puts fault doctrine on a transcendent moral or religious plane where it is an article of faith and not an assertion of fact. As formulated, it is clearly nonutilitarian, and treats the maximizing of satisfactions, even in the long run, as totally irrelevant—too irrelevant even to mention. Faced with a clear choice between preserving the purity of the moral (or religious) concept of fault and the equally moral (or religious) precept that one should "visit the fatherless and widows in their affliction,"[5] the former choice would be made. It should be noted that the argument is not that a particular rule encourages specific conduct widely

[1] Knepper, *Alimony for Accident Victims?*, 15 Defense L.J. 513, 530 (1966), *also printed in* Institute of Continuing Legal Education, Protection for the Traffic Victim: The Keeton-O'Connell Plan and Its Critics 179, 199 (Mich. 1967).

[2] *Id.*

[3] Keeton & O'Connell, Basic Protection for the Traffic Victim: A Blueprint for Reforming Automobile Insurance (1965) [hereinbefore and hereinafter this book is often cited as Basic Protection]. *See also* Keeton & O'Connell, *Basic Protection Automobile Insurance*, p. 40 *infra*.

[4] Knepper, *supra* note 1.

[5] *James* 1:27.

considered immoral, such as malingering or feigning of injury or even in-gratitude. Such arguments, put at a level that would permit factually oriented discussion of the relations between legal rules and human conduct, would be most welcome. Indeed it would be utilitarian, since most if not all "im-moral" conduct does have utilitarian consequences. But at the level on which the moralistic position is presented, the arguments cannot be met. But neither can they be understood and they certainly do not persuade. They are quite irrelevant to the discourse suggested here. To the extent that there is agree-ment on a utilitarian goal, keyed to the maximizing of human satisfactions, the religious footing for fault doctrines must be disregarded unless it can be brought out of the clouds and put in understandable utilitarian terms. To turn a regrettably common *ad hominem* argument around, it must be ob-served that in this instance it is not an academic lawyer who is operating at a level so remote from reality.

Even in a utilitarian system, fault is sometimes a useful criterion. But when it is, it is because it achieves concrete results, such as deterring wrong-ful conduct. But the ultimate criterion is not fault, as is shown by the fact that a fully utilitarian system could not deal in all-or-nothing solutions. To impose the whole loss on either party is antiutilitarian. If the wrongdoer is made thus to suffer a crushing blow it will destroy or greatly diminish not only his own happiness but his usefulness to society. This is not ordinarily justified, even to deter him.

An argument for the fault doctrine which is a frankly utilitarian argu-ment is its deterrent effect. Deterrence has been one of the most commonly offered justifications for the present system in the rhetoric about automobile accident compensation. We refer here to what Calabresi terms "specific" deterrence in his articles that have become "must" reading for all students of the subject.[6] Deterrence of negligence is an objective with which there can be no disagreement, apart from recognition of the difficulties and costs of implementation. Deterrence would reduce the human wastage consequent on automobile accidents and would lessen pain. Nevertheless, serious difficulties arise. In the first place, the uncertainties of the trial process, following hard upon the manifestations of human frailty in the investigation of the accident, ensure that only the roughest kind of justice can ever be done and deterrence achieved in doing it. The figures that Marryott presents[7] make it clear that we have focused too much on appellate court opinions, and in consequence have underestimated the quality of the judgment of which the trial process is capable. This we have always known abstractly. But whatever the con-clusion about the accuracy of jury verdicts, there is little if any evidence

[6] *See especially* Calabresi, *The Decision for Accidents: An Approach to Nonfault Allocation of Costs*, 78 HARV. L. REV. 713 (1965); *Some Thoughts on Risk Distribu-tion and the Law of Torts*, 70 YALE L.J. (1961). *See also* Calabresi, *Views and Overviews*, p. 240 *infra*.

[7] Marryott, *Remarks*, pp. 30-32 *infra*.

that the fault concept is a significant deterrent. Fear of injury to oneself, habits of caution, concern for the trouble one might have if he is involved in an accident, even innocently, simple human decency are all deterrents far more potent than potential liability for fault but only for fault. Moreover, the deterrent effect is greatly lessened by the relative infrequency of accidents—at least serious ones. Each person can say: "It can't (or won't) happen to me."

On the other side, potential liability based on fault can seldom be in the consciousness of the man in a hurry, the show-off, the person with a death-wish. Fault doctrines are deterrents so trivial that they can be safely ignored in any utilitarian evaluation. Moreover, such deterrence as liability might achieve is lessened because the essential causal connections are obscured by the need in the economy of the human psyche for each person unfortunately involved in an accident to remain convinced that not he, but someone or something else, was at fault. The normal person is easy to convince that there has been a miscarriage of justice if he is found at fault. Moreover, that effect is prospective as well as retrospective. For each of us the extra skill with which he drives, his extra perceptiveness and knowledge of the road and his car render the deterrent effect problematical.

Even if one could assume frictionless and impeccably accurate operation of the fault-ascertaining machinery, together with a predictable and substantial awareness by potential fault-doers of what constitutes faulty conduct, one could still not hope for a great deal of deterrence from a system that measured liability by fault. Whatever deterrent effect the present system otherwise might have had is hopelessly compromised by the very existence of liability insurance. Except at the extreme, where insurance becomes either unavailable or so costly that it amounts to the same thing, insurance removes nearly all specific deterrent effect. If we wanted deliberately to maximize deterrence through compensation rules, insurance would have to be made illegal. The consequences of that move would be disastrous, for while fully solvent automobile drivers might then be more substantially deterred than now, the majority who are practically judgment proof would not, and when accidents did happen, far more pain would be suffered in the aggregate than now because injured persons would have no source of reimbursement. "Specific" deterrence is a goal that is unobtainable in significant measure through accident compensation law, except by making changes that are quite unacceptable for other reasons. To the extent that specific deterrence is to be sought (and it surely should be in all reasonable ways), it can best be sought outside the compensation system, by the more vigorous enforcement of the criminal law, for example. Accident compensation law, which has quite enough to do, should not be made to bear primary responsibility for specific deterrence as well, particularly since deterrence conflicts in a fundamental way with other important objectives when it is sought in this way.

Deterrence need not be abandoned altogether, however. One may be very skeptical about specific deterrence but hopeful that what Calabresi has termed "general" deterrence will make a useful contribution. As he has so perceptively pointed out, we have made a "decision for accidents" as a normal and acceptable part of human life. Accidents involve cost, and a decision to permit conduct that produces accidents is a decision that the activity is worth the cost of the accidents. The decision involves a determination of the number and severity of accidents to be permitted, which is determined in part by the way the costs of the accidents are allocated. If they are allowed to lie where they first fall, there is little or no "general" deterrent effect on the conduct that causes accidents, in this case the use of automobiles, except to the extent that fear of harm to oneself is a deterrent. If, on the other hand, the full cost of the accidents were to be imposed on the activity that caused them, one might expect a whole series of market or quasi-market decisions that would naturally and organically, if not altogether rationally, affect the extent to which people engaged in the activity. The full cost of accidents is very substantial. It would be an extremely effective deterrent if it were actually imposed. Some persons who now drive cars would not be able to afford to drive; some who now have two cars might choose to have only one; some who could afford to drive would choose instead to depend on public transportation.

The full cost of accidents is not now imposed on the activity that causes them, of course, and the general deterrent effect is much less than it could be. Since most defendants are judgment proof beyond a modest threshold, imposing the full cost of accidents on the use of automobiles would involve either compulsory insurance without limits in the amount of the coverage or some mechanism for getting substantially complete insurance coverage of the same kind. The customary limits of $10/20,000 restrict seriously the general deterrent effect of imposing the cost of accidents upon the activity that produces them.

Of course, the degree of general deterrence could be either increased or reduced by interfering with the market operation through deliberate or unconscious political decisions of various kinds. For example, deterrence might be lessened by paying part of the cost of accidents in another way, such as through tax revenues. It could be lessened even more by not compensating for them at all, just as infant industry in the nineteenth century is said to have been subsidized by the rules restricting compensation to injured employees—the fellow servant rule, the assumption of risk doctrine, etc. This is what happens now to a major share of the cost—it simply remains where it happens to fall; the automobile's use is heavily subsidized by its victims. Conversely, justified by a view that the automobile is strangling us, and destroying the human qualities of life, some might like to increase the deterrent effect beyond what a free market would produce. This could be done by imposing a tax for general revenue purposes either on automobiles or on the activity of driving, in addition to the full burden of compensation. No proposed system has gone so far; perhaps one should do so to test the public sentiment on the question. But our society is more likely to subsidize than to tax driving.

On utilitarian grounds there is much to be said for making maximum use of a market or quasi-market mechanism to settle the extent of use of the automobile. Then the people affected may quantify their own satisfactions or pains, and compare them with other satisfactions and pains, through the pricing mechanism. No other method can reduce incommensurables to common terms for comparison. In a sense Calabresi's general deterrence with a market mechanism for settling the costs is another way of putting the general utilitarian standard—or it would be if one could assume (1) universal rationality, and (2) that every one had a sufficient economic stake for the economic considerations to be decisive.

Of course, if full costs are charged back after sophisticated cost measurement or through the market, some collateral problems would arise. Many persons would be priced out of the activity who for sound social reasons need to be engaged in it, and subsidies might need to be provided. On the other hand, payment of full costs by automobile users would give a boost to the restoration of the public transportation system, lessening the need for automobiles. Many of us who now afford a second car, and perhaps could still afford it even if it paid its full costs, would nevertheless prefer to utilize public transportation more if it were more adequate. The market choice is often inaccurate, unfortunately, because the heavy investment and long-range postponement of profit involved in rebuilding the public transportation network, and the subsidies to automobiles and burdens on railroads, deprive the voter of his ballot.

The general utilitarian objective also leads directly and easily to a proposition with which few could quarrel: any system devised should be as efficient as possible in the transfer of money, and should have an expensive mechanism only when important objectives cannot be achieved at lesser cost. Avoidable cost is pure "pain." If it is not balanced by additional satisfactions it is indefensible. Conard's study[8] has demonstrated the great waste in the system as it now exists. The operating costs of the tort liability-liability insurance system are substantially greater than the amount of money that finds its way into the pockets of persons receiving compensation for injury.[9] That fact alone is enough to condemn the system, unless the product is the achievement of such important goals that it is worth a very high cost. Such excellence is not to be found in the system. It produces only crude frontier justice, and for that we pay a very high price. The price would even be high if it resulted in discriminating and precise justice. Even if Marryott is right

---

[8] A. Conard, J. Morgan, R. Pratt, C. Voltz & R. Bombaugh, Automobile Accident Costs and Payments—Studies in the Economics of Injury Reparation (1964).
  [9] *Id.* at 59.

that the uncertainty of the fault doctrine is exaggerated, the cost is still too high.

In a real sense a utilitarian system is a cost-oriented system. The entire analysis is a comparison of the costs incurred with the benefits conferred. To the extent that the analysis can be made scientific, it becomes a statement of a simple algebraic inequality. If the benefits conferred exceed the costs the system is a good one, if not it is bad. If the margin of benefit over cost is greater in one system than in another, then the first system is preferable to the second. The difficulty, quite obviously, is that many of the factors on both sides of the equation are not really susceptible to any kind of quantification, and the clarity of the verbal formulation is obscured when one reaches the stage of applying it to the facts.

The frequent suggestion that dignitary or psychic damages, or damages for pain and suffering, should no longer be awarded reflects in part great concern with the problem of cost. Partly because it is very expensive to ascertain this element of damages and partly for other reasons, suggestions are frequently made for eliminating such recovery. When fault is clearly established in a fully solvent or insured defendant, with no contributory fault in the plaintiff, recovery of psychic damages on something like the present basis seems very attractive, especially to the person who approaches the problem from a moralistic viewpoint. But it is costly—since both fault and damage are difficult to determine, often leading to the full jury trial procedure and in any case to payment of a large contingent fee to the plaintiff's attorney. When the burden of automobile insurance premiums seems great, a natural reaction is to propose elimination of this kind of damages.

An often stated objective in reforming the compensation system, on which far too much emphasis has been placed, is that of speeding up the trial process and relieving the congestion in the courts by changing the method of handling personal injury cases. It is true that delay is "pain" to claimants awaiting the solace of compensation, and either the delay should be eliminated or its consequential harms mitigated in some other way, if it can be done at reasonable cost. It is noteworthy, therefore, that in the Ann Arbor conference[10] on this subject two years ago, Maurice Rosenberg suggested that this objective was a red herring. If it is important enough for the proper settlement of important issues to have the elaborate trials we now have, we should and can afford to supply adequate judicial machinery for them. We now spend very little on the judicial system itself relative to the other factors of cost in the compensation system. It follows that at little cost, relatively, court congestion could be relieved. It is not judicial salaries, but lawyers' fees, that put heavy cost burdens on the system. Of course the

[10] The Ann Arbor conference was a very small invitational conference. The proceedings were not published as such but one or two of the papers were published separately.

objective of speeding up the trial process is neither unreal nor irrelevant to the present discussion, but it should not be elevated to an important position.

The rule that compensation is on a lump-sum basis presents an interesting problem in a utilitarian calculus. Periodic payments would often improve the human result. It would come closer to reflecting with reasonable accuracy the damage suffered as well as meeting better the true needs of the victim. On the other hand, administrative cost would be added to the system. These are highly utilitarian considerations. What the proponents of periodic payments may really want most is early partial payment. The permanent continuation of payments may be less important than avoidance of the necessity for waiting for any payment at all until the entire matter can be settled for a single lump sum. Perhaps without adding excessive administrative cost to the system, much improvement could result. Thus current proposals—and changes in insurer practice—providing rehabilitation, even before considering fault, is a long step in the right direction.

In discussing the fault doctrines, I criticized the moral judgments made about responsibility, whether to God or to man. Sweeping assertions of that kind have neither meaning nor persuasive power. But at a different level, the consequences of the system for the individual morality of participants is of considerable importance. The consequences only need to be brought down to size in terms sufficiently concrete to have meaning and to become susceptible to valuation and, theoretically at least, even to quantification. No contribution is made to the dialogue by grand clichés about moral values. But the system should be so structured as to improve the human result—to enrich rather than to impoverish the quality of human life. Subconscious malingering, for example, is an unfortunate consequence of some aspects of the compensation rules in the opinions of respected psychiatrists. Malingering, whether it be of the conscious or the unconscious kind, surely should be discouraged when possible, not only because it adds appreciably to the costs of the system and lessens the productive potential of the persons guilty of it, but because it also is damaging to the person involved. It does not produce a net increase in satisfactions to malinger, however common it may be, especially among people who try to satisfy their own inner needs and solve their psychological problems by staying away from work rather than by returning. When it is pecuniarily profitable to do so, as it is very often when payments from several sources combine to make illness pay, it can occur without any conscious wrongdoing. It usually happens more subtly than that.

But conscious wrong is sometimes involved. Even the basic notion of the system—that it depends on fault—has subtle power to corrupt. The system encourages fraud, subornation, perjury, and malingering. Several aspects of the system induce it. Not only is the possibility of awarding damages for pain and suffering a substantial cost factor in itself, but it has untoward consequences in encouraging conscious or unconscious exacerbation of loss. Moreover, it encourages exaggeration of loss in proof, amounting at times to outright fraud. The collateral-sources rule is a prime cause, and lump-sum settlement is not guiltless.

The whole tort system leads people to play games with compensation. The "gamesmanship" of the litigation process is at its worst in the automobile compensation field. The name of the game is money, obtained or retained in any way one can. Whether any other system would do better is a fair question, but one surely must start with abundant recognition of the immoralities produced and exacerbated by the present system, and with full awareness of the cost of such immoralities under even the crassest utilitarian system focussed on pains and pleasures.

The collateral-sources rule comes in for evaluation in any utilitarian or cost-centered analysis. It is curious that the assertions about the high morality of the present tort liability system—of the nobility of the moral plane achieved by the common law—do not hesitate to include the collateral-sources rule within the sweep of the statement. However, not only is the collateral-sources rule one which leads to much waste in the system but it is also one, as suggested above, that has great potential for producing what every one would consider immoral conduct. Duplication of payments, even frequently triplication of payments, can hardly avoid leading to conscious or subconscious malingering. Even with honest people, subconscious malingering is common.

As also suggested above, the inclusion of full and doctrinally unlimited damages for pain and suffering introduces enormously ramified immoralities and difficulties into the system, on the part of litigant and lawyer alike. This is not to say that there is not a legitimate case for damages for pain and suffering—psychic damages are potent and poignant whenever they are real. It is only to suggest that fraud, dissimulation, malingering and subornation inevitably arise in any system that not only permits pain and suffering as a category of damages but encourages large jury awards under that heading. One need not characterize the whole personal injury bar as unscrupulous, as some undiscriminating critics do, to recognize that it is a segment of the bar with many unscrupulous members.

Lump-sum settlement, as we have seen, is a basic tenet of the present system which has both costs and advantages in a cost-focussed analysis; it also produces a variety of immoralities. It encourages insurers to scale down claims in return for quick settlements, relying on the pressing need of the litigant. It encourages claimants to refuse rehabilitation and to malinger until the lump-sum settlement has been reached. It leads lawyers to engage in sundry unsavory practices, and it tends to turn the court room into a circus. It has made it necessary for us to accept the contingent fee system, not because it is good but because it is the least among evils. And it is an evil. The lump-sum settlement system encourages the poker table mentality—the treatment of the tort liability-liability insurance system as a game played for high stakes in which the only objective is winning as much as possible or losing as little as possible, not of achieving justice. Early partial payments and the freer use of expenditures for rehabilitation, as suggested above, would help to minimize the difficulties; they could be and have been worked out satisfactorily in certain compensation regimes.

### III.   DIVERSITY OF OBJECTIVES AND PROGRAMS

Conard and his fellow workers have brought some novel insights[11] to the subject, or insights which at least have now been brought home clearly to the rest of us, even if they were dimly appreciated before by some. They have illuminated the complexity of the problems, and showed us how much the interplay of the objectives to be sought varies with the nature of the accident and the changing circumstances of the people involved. Conard has also shown us how important it is to examine some quantitative information about the subject, so we can learn what the really significant problems are.[12] That knowledge may lead us to refrain from seeking a simplistic solution, and to seek for many partial solutions on a broad front. To speak in a facile way of justice is not only antiutilitarian, but also it absurdly oversimplifies the problem.

In his own scale of values, Conard puts rehabilitation first. "Wounds should be healed, bones set, prostheses supplied, psychic readjustment achieved, and occupational retraining provided when needed." [13] These things are so important, he thinks, that we should implement the objective however the money is found, even though he would put the burden on automobiles if possible to carry out the general deterrence objective.[14] It is hard to argue with either part of his proposition, on utilitarian grounds. Maximizing of satisfactions is his implicit ultimate goal.

Conard then moves to a discussion of income replacement, talking first of the provision of subsistence.[15] This is, he thought, no different than any other cause of poverty and, arguably, can most cheaply be handled as a part of that general problem. As with rehabilitation, however, a desire to allocate costs appropriately to implement the objective of general deterrence should lead us, he thinks, to find the money in a way that will place the cost on the use of automobiles. That is less crucial, however, since the goal of ensuring subsistence is more important than that of general deterrence. Conard thinks

---

[11] CONARD, *et al.*, *supra* note 8; and *see particularly* Conard, *The Economic Treatment of Automobile Injuries*, 63 MICH. L. REV. 279 (1964).

[12] See an interesting recent paper by Conard, *The Quantitative Analysis of Justice*, 20 J. LEGAL ED. 1 (1967), devoted to showing the importance of jurimetrics. He quotes with obvious relish the statement of an econometrician, that "the purpose of econometrics is to keep economists from wasting their time on unimportant questions." *Id.* at 17. It is quite obviously his view that lawyers (and even jurists and jurisprudes) need to be taught a similar lesson.

[13] Conard, *The Economic Treatment of Automobile Injuries*, 63 MICH. L. REV. 279, 294 (1964).

[14] *Id.* at 299-300.

[15] *Id.* at 300-05.

that one of the consequences of automobile accidents, in case of serious accident or of particularly susceptible circumstances in the lives of the persons injured, can be such serious poverty and suffering that the money should be found irrespective of fault in any degree and irrespective of where it can be found. Compensation should be unqualified and comprehensively supplied. Disagreement with him is difficult, either on utilitarian or purely moral and humanitarian grounds.

It is less clear that Conard is right when he proposes maintenance of basic income up to a somewhat larger limit.[16] If his second goal is an aspect of the war against poverty, this one is more like the goal of the workmen's compensation system—to make an activity that puts burdens on members of society bear at least part of that loss up to decent limits of income. Again, he thinks the source of funds is not crucial. The affirmative utilitarian grounds for the proposal are clear; less clear are the costs. A utilitarian system must inevitably pay great attention to marginal benefits and costs, and the further one moves away from severe deprivation, the less significant are the benefits in relation to the costs.

Conard would not give full recompense to an injured person without the satisfaction of criteria other than mere ascertainment of the loss. At levels above decent minima there is merit, on various grounds, in leaving some of the burden on the sufferer, unless some such reason as the existence of traditional fault justifies shifting all of it to the wrongdoer or his insurer. He suggests retention of the tort system as it now stands at that level.[17] The question may fairly be raised whether complete reimbursement serves utilitarian goals at all. Perhaps substantial satisfaction is given by full recovery when one has a sense of outrage because of harm negligently inflicted, but the likelihood of self deception inclines one to be very suspicious of the reliability of that sense. The cost of salving the sense of outrage may be very high when one takes into account the high probability that for nearly every successful claimant who is sure he has received justice by recovering his loss in full there is an adjudged tortfeasor who is subjected to the pain not only of the damages imposed on him but also of the assessment of blame he does not accept.

In order for recovery at any of these levels to produce its maximum effect, any theoretical liability would have to be backed up by collectible insurance with high limits or no limits. Probably this means compulsory insurance, with much higher limits than anyone has suggested in this country, or altogether without limit, as occasionally exists elsewhere.[18]

16 *Id.*

17 *Id.* at 306-08.

18 The West German minimum limit is 250,000 DM for each accident for personal injury which, when one takes into account different standards of living, is a very large sum. It is three times as large as the normal corresponding minimum limit in this country. *Gesetz über die Pflichtversicherung für Kraftfahrzeughalter (Pflichtversicherungsgesetz),* Law of April 5, 1965, [1965] I BGBl. 213, § 4 Abs. 2, at 215, Anlage zu § 4 Abs. 2.

At all the levels of potential recovery, Conard has made it clear to us how many programs other than tort liability-liability insurance must be considered in determining what is now done and what remains to be done to maximize satisfactions. Life and disability insurance, non-profit medical and hospitalization plans, social security coverage whether for old age or retirement benefits or for disability, all contribute in a major way to the total compensation for accidents. His subtle and discriminating approach to the subject has contributed many penetrating insights.

## IV. Perspectives

The goals sketched above, with some suggestions about the way in which they interact and sometimes conflict, will not startle anyone and may not even produce much disagreement. More disagreement, certainly, will be felt about the matters now to be suggested.

Historically insurers and lawyers have had a great deal to do with the management and administration of automobile compensation systems. Obviously they would like to continue their participation, on as extensive and profitable a basis as possible. Insurers, latterly with very good reason, have some queasy feelings about the system;[19] lawyers can less easily support a complaint about the profitability of their involvement, which has generally been very lucrative to the more successful of them. One can concede the fact of the interests of these two groups and the legitimacy of reasonable efforts on their part to protect their interests, within limits of propriety not always strictly observed, without regarding the interests as in any sense vested. If the services of personal injury lawyers and the insurance enterprise can be utilized consistent with the public interest, they provide a pool of experienced and talented people to perform the new tasks. But they have no inherent claim nor color of vested interest in the existing system. If it would serve the public interest to dispense with them, they should be dispensed with. Probably no technological unemployment need be feared, but even if it should, that is no ground for hesitation. On the other hand, at another level of discourse, it may not be politically possible to dispense with these classes of people, even if it would be desirable to do so.

To the extent that either class is utilized in any system that is devised, however, they should be compensated commensurate with their contribu-

---

at 221. In Belgium there is no limit. *Loi relative à l'assurance obligatoire de la responsabilité civile en matière de véhicules automoteurs*, Law of July 1, 1956(1), art. 3, para. 4, II Les Codes Belges (Matières Pénales) (1965).

[19] News releases in October 1967 revealed the defection of one major automobile insurer, Insurance Company of North America (INA), from the hitherto closed ranks of the defenders of the existing system. There was even some suggestion that perhaps the Keeton-O'Connell plan would be a good point of departure for a new way of dealing with claims. N.Y. Times, Oct. 9, 1967, p. 51, cols. 2-8. For another advertisement from another company, The Glens Falls Group, endorsing the INA ad, *see* N.Y. Times, Oct. 17, 1967, p. 34, cols. 5-8.

tion. There is an unfortunate disposition to impose on insurers a duty to serve the needs of the market without providing adequate compensation. Rates are restricted under a regulatory regime that gives significant effect to political pressures to keep rates down. Somehow insurers, who have not always been fairly treated in this field, need to get compensation that is adequate for the risks they run. If they had been, many of the present problems of the insurance market would not exist or would be less severe. It is anomalous and even scandalous, in this connection, that plaintiffs' lawyers, who otherwise would seem to have a community of interest with insurers so far as continuation of the system is concerned, at one and the same time press with a vigor not always kept within ethical bounds for the "more adequate award," and lead the populace in objection to rate increases. In this story, there is something redolent of the goose that laid the golden egg.

Plaintiffs' lawyers, too, should receive compensation commensurate with the skill with which they perform. Outside the personal injury bar, it is widely thought that they now get too much, but the opposite mistake of unduly restricting their rewards should not result. They should be adequately rewarded, or the skills needed to ensure that plaintiffs get their just deserts will be applied to other tasks. Adequacy of compensation is not a matter of morality, but of utilitarian considerations—of the efficiency of the system.

Neither insurers nor lawyers have any special claim to be heard. Each must play the role assigned him by the legal order, not dictate that role. Only as individual private citizens do members of either group have any "right" to be heard. More than that, their claim to speak as experts is a doubtful one. Their biases are too evident and their perspectives too limited to give their views undue weight. Their relatively modest competence to speak authoritatively is in striking contrast to their immodest claim to be almost the only ones qualified to do so, which usually appears in customary form as an attack on the academic authors of plans because of their lack of "practical" knowledge.

Further, if major changes are proposed, the existing "expertise" of lawyers and insurers may be a liability because it will serve as a brake on the process of change. More than once lawyers' skills and habits have delayed the full impact of accomplished reform of the legal system at even its most technical and professional levels. That fact argues both ways. If a change is large enough to permit (or require) dispensing with the pool of talent altogether, the loss of the pool must be accounted a cost. Marryott has used a similar perception to produce a conclusion that change should be gradual and evolutionary.[20] Perhaps an alternative proposition is more fully justified: change must either be evolutionary or quite drastic. Nothing intermediate is prac-

---

[20] Marryott, *A Practical Framework for Examining Proposals for Changes in the Tort System for Handling Automobile Accident Cases*, 33 Ins. Counsel J. 432, 434 (1966).

ticable. But in any event, evolutionary change is at most a necessity, not a duty nor a goal. It is a limit on what we can do, not on what we should.

Insurer and lawyer claims, while not valid as vested interests, must be recognized as important facts in the political situation conditioning passage of any proposed bill. They may be able to block legislation, even when they can not get it passed. However, they are much prone to overestimate their own strength, and other people tend to take them at their own value. Lawyers are traditionally suspect in state legislatures, despite their presence there in numbers, and personal injury lawyers are perhaps more suspect than others of the species. Whether this is with or without good reason is not relevant. The insurance business too now has a tarnished image, only partially justified. Even the full and vigorous opposition of both insurers and personal injury lawyers may not be fatal, if a plan can be devised that is attractive to other powerful and vocal elements in the community. Testing the Basic Protection plan against this notion, it comes out badly, however. Its authors compromised much to avoid lawyer and insurer opposition, but seem to have obtained from the one at most a neutrality produced less by the concessions than by other factors like repeated underwriting losses. From the other they are getting opposition no less bitter, unrestrained, and full of invective because of the concessions. Much can be said for making concessions only when they have to be made—for refraining from anticipatory capitulation.

This is the time to devise and present the best possible system, without undue regard for political considerations. Even the professional politician is a notoriously bad guesser. Political acceptability in such a tortured and difficult subject is no goal, however much it may ultimately prove to be a necessity. But necessity can be tested further than Keeton and O'Connell tested it. Their judgment on the question is rendered suspect by their results—by the failure to acquire powerful friends for their proposal despite the significant concessions they made but *might* not have made except for assumed necessity.

A legitimate question is whether economic necessity places any limits on the solution of the automobile problem. The notion that cost is an important factor in deciding what program we want is deeply ingrained. There is a strong feeling that we cannot afford any proposed system, unless it costs little more than the existing one. (The point that the cost should be predictable is quite a different point, and clearly valid.)[21] Keeton and O'Connell have been going to great lengths to demonstrate that their plan will cost less than the present one. And the program of this conference includes a whole session devoted to the question of cost. Most of the discussion of cost completely misses the point, however, by failing to distinguish several quite different kinds of "cost," and two ways of measuring it. Cost can be taken

[21] *Id.* at 435.

as referring to the amount paid to claimants, or as the administrative costs of the system, or as the two taken in combination. It can be measured in dollars or in pains, through some felicific calculus.[22]

It should be noted that, assuming a frictionless system, there is no monetary cost at all in the first sense of cost. The full "cost" of automobile accidents is being paid already, unavoidably. The only question is whether and how far the costs should be transferred from where they first happen to fall. Inasmuch as most shifting of cost takes place by taking small amounts from many people without losses to buy insurance which pays to a few people with fairly serious losses enough to approximate their losses, the transfer may actually enhance aggregate satisfaction tremendously, while changing dollar costs not at all. In that sense a frictionless system for transferring and spreading already incurred costs would actually create value. It wouldn't create wealth, but it would increase satisfactions and diminish pains in the deployment of that wealth. Such a system would have negative cost in a Benthamite sense.

Of course no system is frictionless. More, it is doubtful if the tort liability-liability insurance system, operating at an administrative cost of well over half the premiums paid, does not actually diminish aggregate satisfactions. Altogether too much is lost in the machinery. It is the amount lost in the machinery that is a real net loss to the community. If regimes as efficient as social security would put money in the right places, the whole cost problem could be ignored. Thus the cost question can be better put than it usually is, for the meaningful question is concerned with the cost of shovelling money, or administrative costs, not the amount to be transferred, nor the sum of the two. That kind of cost is relevant to the choice of regimes. This does not say that the cost problem is of no importance, but that it has been put in altogether inappropriate terms in the dialogue about the Basic Protection plan.

The cost objective should be stated as one of devising a system as efficient and cheap as possible in transferring money consistent with the achievement of other objectives. Cheapness in the amounts to be transferred is not a suitable criterion. The cost of compensation regimes varies so much and is so large that the cost of shovelling money becomes a consideration of great importance, sometimes enough to shift choice from one regime to another. At the higher levels of compensation beyond rehabilitation and continuation of subsistence, it could be argued, if it were not for overhead costs, that the traditional fault doctrines should govern compensation. The inordinately great administrative cost of the tort regime suggests, however, that a shift to other forms might be desirable, even in the areas where discriminat-

---

[22] Bentham's felicific calculus, or analysis in terms of pleasures and pains, will be found elaborately worked out in J. BENTHAM, AN INTRODUCTION TO THE PRINCIPLES OF MORALS AND LEGISLATION (1789).

ing judgments might theoretically be desirable. Consideration of costs, whether purely monetary or measured in pains or reduced satisfactions, is thoroughly utilitarian.

Another question of economic "reality" does raise questions about levels of compensation, or cost in the first or third senses. Is there economic need for a society that depends so heavily on motorized transport to subsidize that essential activity by levying tribute against its hapless victims? Would such a subsidy contribute to economic development that is enough faster to make benefits from the development outweigh the high cost to individuals who are left destitute? Or conversely, can a society with a need for economic expansion afford to concern itself with the satisfactions of the victims, or must the interests of some be sacrificed for the longrun benefit of the economic system and of the whole community? This can also be framed more simply: "How far does the interest of all necessitate the sacrifice of some?" Perhaps, paradoxically, the exponents of responsibility and justice are in the end the great utilitarians—in the crassest possible sense—sacrificing completely the interests of the few for the benefit of the many.

Only an economist could hope to answer these questions definitively. To the layman, however, there seems little reason to think that a society as affluent as ours is in midtwentieth century, need give any thought to whether it can afford to compel motorized transportation to pay its full social cost, down to the last farthing. The activity as a whole does not need subsidy, though some individuals in the society may need to be subsidized in its use if the full cost is imposed on the activity. But that can be done in better ways than by distorting the legal system through having the victims provide a subsidy to the users. Economics puts no limits on us and if the questions are properly framed we may get even more striking and "revolutionary" proposals than Keeton and O'Connell have made.

# REMARKS

*OF FRANKLIN J. MARRYOTT**

ONE OF THE CRITICISMS of the tort system is that the question of fault is difficult to determine. This difficulty, it is said, causes unjustified expense and results in too many wrong determinations. It is argued that accidents happen so quickly and arise from such complex circumstances that the people involved really do not know what happened. We should, I suggest, not accept such assertions without a reasonable effort to test their validity. One of the purposes of this paper is to tell you about our efforts to perform such a test.

But before I discuss our own research, let us consider the material presented on this point in the Keeton-O'Connell book.[1]

One item is a fanciful description of the act of driving an automobile by Professor Leon Green.[2] It is not, and does not pretend to be, a precise or accurate description based upon scientific analysis; it is merely one man's effort to state in colorful language all the things a person needs to do under all the circumstances that might present themselves. (I think that I could write a description of a man eating a plate of spaghetti or of a group of dancers doing the twist, that would sound much like Professor Green's description, such as the need to observe the presence of other "operators"—front, rear and to the sides, the necessity for near perfect muscular reactions, the delicate coordination required, and the subtle judgments of speed, motion and space.) Professor Green concludes, and Professors Keeton and O'Connell seem to adopt this conclusion as a cornerstone for their case, that it would be unlikely that the accident facts could be accurately stated and even more unlikely that anyone could apply rational judgment in allocating responsibility between the parties on the basis of fault.

Professors Keeton and O'Connell also rely upon an analysis of the average number of "probable occurrences" while driving a car. This begins with an estimate of the number of "observations" per mile (200—why so low?), and ends with an estimate of the number of personal injuries (1 per 430,000 miles) and the number of fatal accidents (1 per 16,000,000 miles).[3] But these facts, if they are facts, challenge the idea that driving an automobile is a very complicated job.

**FRANKLIN J. MARRYOTT.* Litt. B. 1925, Rutgers University; LL.B. 1928, New Jersey Law School; Vice President and General Counsel, Liberty Mutual Insurance Company, Boston.*

[1] KEETON & O'CONNELL, BASIC PROTECTION FOR THE TRAFFIC VICTIM: A BLUEPRINT FOR REFORMING AUTOMOBILE INSURANCE 15-22 (1965) [both hereinbefore and hereinafter the book is often cited as Basic Protection].

[2] Id. 16-17, quoting from L. GREEN, TRAFFIC VICTIMS—TORT LAW AND INSURANCE 66-68 (1958).

[3] Basic Protection 16.

We all know that about 101 million people now have drivers licenses. Most of them have learned to drive very well, usually without formal instruction of any kind. Whether the general level of such skills can be much improved by formal training, and whether those not up to the job can be identified more promptly and precisely are questions that should have been more fully answered long ago. But my point now is that driving a car is not such an esoteric skill as Professor Green would have us believe and the decisions as to who was at fault are, in a great majority of all the cases, not very difficult to make.

Professors Blum and Kalven also challenge the thesis that effective recreation of traffic accidents is too difficult. Their point is that these difficulties are "manageable" and are not greater than we deal with in many other phases of our lives.[4] Professors Keeton and O'Connell's answer is that events preceding an accident are too commonplace to receive close attention from the participants. In support they cite (1) Attorney Lawrence H. Eldredge's description of his personal inability to give a good account of an accident in which he was involved, and (2) a fictional account, printed in the *New Yorker* magazine,[5] of a motorist's confusion in the face of questioning. The section concludes with the suggestion that automobile accidents are unique in human experience in the "intractability" of the facts.

Professors Keeton and O'Connell are careful to point out that they are not trying to say that there never are cases in which fault is easily determined.[6] They do say that there are "many more" accidents in which fault is difficult to determine and that very often fault is an unrealistic, expensive and frustrating criterion.[7]

I doubt that these conclusions can be supported. Our studies indicate that a large proportion of all automobile accidents are uncomplicated events in which the fault determination is very easy and that many of the more complex accidents can be accurately analyzed by people trained to do such work on the basis of the physical facts, even when the impressions of the witnesses are confused. The final positions of the cars, the tire marks, the location and extent of the damage, frequently established very clearly how the accident happened and who was at fault.

Other points emphasized by Professors Keeton and O'Connell are that witnesses are likely to be (1) unable to remember, (2) too full of pride to admit that they are wrong, (3) deliberate liars, or (4) hopelessly confused.[8]

---

[4] Blum & Kalven, Public Law Perspectives on a Private Law Problem—Auto Compensation Plans 9 (1965), *published earlier as an article*, 31 U. Chi. L. Rev. 641, 647 (1964).

[5] *Potter, Finding by Referee*, New Yorker, Nov. 7, 1964, at 204.

[6] As examples of easy fault determinations, they cite speeding, weaving, following too closely, passing in a no-passing zone, and failing to stop at a stop sign. Basic Protection 21.

[7] *Id.*

[8] *Id.* at 15-24.

Again there is almost total reliance upon personal opinion rather than any sort of factual studies.

The honest witness who never does manage to tell his story, because cross-examination caused him to become hopelessly confused, is probably more common in literature than he is in real life. That the "Memorable Trial of Bardell v. Pickwick" is the underlying foundation for the school of thought that assumes that witnesses are chronically befuddled and juries are usually misled, I can only suspect. In my own experience I never did encounter a cross examiner as successful as Mr. Serjeant Buzfuz nor a plaintiff's witness so well prepared as Mrs. Bardell. As Dickens himself foresaw "the license of counsel and the degree to which juries are ingeniously bewildered" have been moderated over the years.

Another Keeton-O'Connell point is that the trial of a case is a poor way to determine fault because, among other difficulties, the jury is apt to be confused or misled. It is said that the theatrical tricks of the plaintiff's lawyer, or sympathy or other emotional factors unduly influence the jurors. Lawyers, it is said, are more and more making trials into theatrical productions and are deliberately searching for and using techniques designed to appeal to bias, credulity and gullibility and to "cash in" by exploiting the human weakness of jurors.[9]

Surely here again we need more than mere assertion. Have we gotten to the point when judges generally have lost control of the conduct of the trial? Most of the judges I know are skilled at quashing such conduct and some can turn it against the practitioner who has the bad taste and poor judgment to attempt such tactics in their courtrooms. If this situation is out of control it had better be brought under control regardless of the ultimate form of the injury reparation system.

In fact, however, there is a formidable body of expert opinion, well supported and documented, that juries are rarely bewildered or deceived. I accept the Blum and Kalven comment that "It is thus difficult to make any special argument about the failure of the negligence criterion to control the jury."[10]

[9] *Id.* at 22.

[10] Blum & Kalven, *supra* note 4, at 11, 31 U. CHI. L. REV. at 649. In the 1920's the Hon. Philip J. McCook, Justice of the Supreme Court of New York City, stated that from Oct. 1, 1924 to June 30, 1925 he disagreed with the jury in only 66 of 1,532 verdicts. McCook, *The Jury*, 49 N.J.L.J. 102, 111 (1926).

In 1933, Judge Joseph N. Ulman of the Supreme Court of Baltimore said that jury verdicts were "practically identical with the verdicts I should reach in over 75 per cent of the cases." ULMAN, A JUDGE TAKES THE STAND 22 (1933).

In 1949, Judge Richard Hartshorn of the Common Pleas Court, Essex County, New Jersey, reported his agreement with 85% of the jury verdicts in his court in the 12-year period from 1947 to 1949. His conclusion was that, on the whole, jury verdicts amounted to "realistic justice." Hartshorn, *Jury Verdicts: A Study of Their Characteristics and Trends*, 35 A.B.A.J. 113, 117 (1949).

In a progress report on the jury project of the Law School of the University of Chicago, Professor Kalven reported: [I]f we consider separately cases where the jury

This brings me to the point of describing our little bit of research. I wanted to find out, if I could, what proportion of automobile liability cases reported to Liberty Mutual Insurance Company were such that a decision of who was at fault was easy and uncomplicated. The experiment consisted of two parts. First we took the "file" on each of 229 accidents reported to our Andover, Massachusetts office beginning on March 1, 1967 and examined the reports in numerical sequence. Then we did the same thing with 123 cases in our Natick, Massachusetts office—beginning with April 1, 1967. The total is 352. In some cases the "file" consisted of an accident report alone. (These were the cases in which the accident was so insignificant, or in which the facts, as originally reported, so clearly indicated who was at fault, as to justify a decision that no further investigation need be made.) In the other cases an appropriate investigation had been made.

This is what we found:

In 25 cases the policyholder struck a stationary object other than a parked car.

In 64 cases parked cars were involved. In 24 of these the policyholder backed into the other car. In 21 cases our policyholder struck the parked car in some way other than by backing into it.

In 16 cases the other car struck our parked car other than by backing into it.

In one case the policyholder said he was struck in the rear by the other car. In the same case the claimant said the policyholder backed into him while he was parked. We recorded that case as "fault questionable."

In 29 other cases backing into a moving car was involved. In 18 of these our policyholder backed into the claimant and was clearly at fault. In 9 other cases the other car backed into ours and was clearly at fault.

There were 79 "rear enders" other than those included above. In 44 of these the policyholder struck the other car from the rear and was judged to be clearly at fault. In 35 of these the claimant struck our car from the rear and was judged to be clearly at fault.

found for the defendant we find the judge in agreement 82% of the time, whereas in cases where the jury found for the plaintiff the judge is in complete agreement only 18% of the time. However, in some 69% of such cases the judge differed from the jury only in the amount of damages and not on liability." Kalven, *A Report on the Jury Project of the University of Chicago Law School*, 24 Ins. Counsel J. 368, 380 (1957). In a later progress report, Professor Broeder reported agreement in 83% of the cases involved: "The personal injury questionnaires found the judge and jury agreeing on the question of liability in eighty-three percent of the cases." Broeder, *The University of Chicago Jury Project*," 38 Neb. L. Rev. 744, 750 (1959). Eighty per cent agreement in personal injury cases was found in Blum & Kalven, *supra* note 4, at 11, 31 U. Chi. L. Rev. at 649.

There were 78 intersection cases—22 per cent of the total number. Of these the policyholder was judged clearly at fault in 16 cases, and probably at fault in 19 cases. The claimant was thought to be clearly at fault in 22 cases and probably at fault in 10 cases; 11 were "questionable."

Only one pedestrian case showed up and in this one the policyholder was judged to be clearly at fault.

Six cases involved a car that was pulling out from a parked position. The policyholder was judged clearly at fault in four, the claimant in one, and one was "questionable."

There were 14 "sideswipe" cases, *i.e.*, the cars were going in the same direction. Our policyholder was held clearly at fault in six. The claimant was held to be clearly at fault in five. Three cases were "questionable."

In 32 cases the cars were going in opposite directions. In 16 of these the policyholder's car crossed the center line and was judged to be clearly at fault. In 12 the claimant crossed the center line and was held to be clearly at fault. Four cases were classed as "questionable."

Twenty-three cases fell into the "miscellaneous" slot. The policyholder was clearly at fault in three, and probably at fault in four. The claimant was held clearly at fault in eight and probably at fault in five. Three were "questionable."

Three cases were found that involved a question of being "under the influence."

One case involved a defect in the vehicle.

No cases attributable to road defect (other than ice and snow) were found.

No cases involving speeding in excess of 10 miles over the limit were found.

The summary is:

| | | |
|---|---|---|
| Policyholder clearly at fault | 201 | 57.1% |
| Claimant clearly at fault | 125 | 35.5% |
| Fault questionable | 26 | 7.4% |
| | 352 | 100.0% |

The results in the two samples were consistent with each other.

We didn't stop with a sample of all the cases. Obviously such a sample contains many minor accidents which, as one might expect and as the results show, can be analyzed very easily and reliable fault determinations made with very little trouble. The next part of our experiment involved 106 bodily injury cases, taken as they came, from several hundred files shipped to the home office from our East Orange, New Jersey office. Here we were looking at a group of files that involved more serious and more complex accidents.

We found the "insured at fault" or "not at fault" determination was clear in 90.4 per cent of the accidents.

> There were 44 instances of "rear ending." Two of these involved de-fects—brake failure in one and in the other the pedal cover fell off. There were three cases in which one car backed into the other.

> Of the 17 pedestrian cases the insured was judged at fault in 7, not at fault in 6 (in one of these the pedestrian was drunk). Four were "ques-tionable."

> Of the 28 intersection cases the insured was at fault in 18. In five of these he "ran the light." In nine cases the insured was judged not at fault; the other party "ran the light." Only one of the intersection cases was viewed as "questionable."

> Of the eight head-on collision cases one was caused by a heart attack; one when an unknown car forced the insured over the center line.

We also interviewed, separately, six claims men who were at the man-ager or supervisor level. We did not tell them what our figures showed. All six stated that in their opinion, as to the whole run of cases that they were responsible for, about 75 per cent were susceptible of clear determinations on the original reports, and about 90 per cent upon the completion of the initial investigation.

If these tests are reliable enough to indicate anything it is that in most cases fault is not difficult for trained claims men to determine. In the small cases the ease is somewhat greater than it is in the serious case. I suspect that we hear much more about the hard cases than we do about the easy ones. Judges, and the lawyers too, are apt to be exposed to a relatively small num-ber of most troublesome cases. Personal impressions are apt to be based on very biased samples.

Obviously, at least some of the Liberty Mutual claims men are having much less trouble with the fault criterion than the professors. Nor are they anywhere near as pessimistically cynical about the shortcomings of society. With some exceptions they, I am happy to say, still believe that a very large segment of the public is basically honest, and that the moral standards of our society have not yet deteriorated to the point that the survival of insurance is in serious doubt.[11]

I think it is fair to conclude, with appropriate reservations, that the

---

[11] *See* Professor John D. Long's Presidential Address to the American Risk and Insurance Association, *as reported in* The National Underwriter, Sept. 8, 1967, at 1.

argument that the fault system should be abolished because negligence is too difficult to determine or because it is too difficult to learn how the accidents happen is probably invalid. If there has been any effort made by those who think the fault concept is unworkable (because automobile accidents can't be related to the customary standards of conduct) or who believe it to amount to little more than an "immoral lottery,"[12] to support their conclusions by research into claims files or court records or any other original sources, it has escaped my attention. Since no such research is reported by Professors Keeton and O'Connell, I am strengthened in my impression that none exists.

Obviously our sample was rather small. Obviously another man's judgment might not yield exactly the same results. But the indicated fact is that in over 90 per cent of all cases sampled the question of fault was clear. In many of these the physical facts tell the story. In most of these the conduct of the driver is the significant factor rather than road design, car design or equipment.

I am not willing to accept, without critical examination, broad assertions about automobile accident cases clogging court calendars. How much judge time is actually being devoted to the trial of automobile cases? Recently Chief Justice Tauro reported that in Suffolk County Superior Court, Massachusetts, it is only 13 per cent and that one of the main reasons for the congestion there is the upsurge of criminal cases.[13]

Criticisms of the doctrines of contributory negligence, of charitable or governmental immunity, do not lead to the conclusion that the tort system itself should be substantially abolished.

Nor am I ready to accept the assertion that "the present system is marred by temptations to dishonesty that lure into their snares a stunning percentage of drivers and victims."[14] The support for this shocking statement seems to be in the following passage:

"If one is inclined to doubt the influence of these debasing factors, let him compare his own rough-and-ready estimates of the percentage of drivers who are at fault in accidents and the percentage who admit it when the question is put under oath. Of course the disparity is partly accounted for by self-deception, but only partly. And even this self-deception is an insidious undermining of integrity, not to be encouraged."[15]

In our Massachusetts experiment we found that our policyholders were reporting facts clearly indicating that the policyholder himself was at fault

[12] Franklin, *Replacing the Negligence Lottery: Compensation and Selective Reimbursement*, 53 Va. L. Rev. 774, 778 (1967).

[13] Letter from the Hon. G. Joseph Tauro to Gov. John A. Volpe of Massachusetts, dated Aug. 29, 1967, reprinted in *Automobile Torts Not Cause of Court Congestion*, 8 For the Defense .. 57, 59 (1967).

[14] Basic Protection 3.

[15] *Id.*

in about 57 per cent of the cases.[16] In many of these the policyholder stated a conclusion that he was at fault, along with his statement of the facts. Surely these facts do not support free-swinging statements about dishonesty and self-deception.

I cannot accept as clearly correct the oft-repeated assertions that the possibility of being held at fault has little or no value as a deterrent to bad driving. Where is the evidence? How can anyone feel confident that such an expansion of the "permissive" attitude as would be reflected by a decision to abandon the fault concept won't result in a very great increase in irresponsible attitudes on the part of drivers?

I do not wish to retract my several earlier statements that the tort system needs to be modernized, improved, and in some respects reformed. I have made some specific suggestions as to how this can be done.[17] But I do say that the factual support for some (not all) of the criticisms of the tort system is weak indeed and does not justify such drastic changes as are being proposed.

As often noted, most of the proposal for change in the tort system comes from the "intellectuals" rather than from those actually working at the day by day conduct of the system. Indeed, the past several years have been marked by a great upsurge in the influence of the intellectual in many aspects of American political and economic life.

I do not deplore this emergence of the intellectual. But with this new power should come a deeper responsibility. A college or law school professor, who has no direct participation in the final decisions that must be made, is expected to challenge, to dissent, and to raise questions about the validity of conventional wisdom. But when the professor moves from the classroom to legislative halls, or to the executive offices of government, some changes must occur. In this new environment there are new responsibilities. In the past this has sometimes served to change a radical professor into a conservative judge. This is because the judge has a direct responsibility.

Direct responsibility is lacking when the proposals originating with the intellectuals depend upon legislative or executive action for their implementation. When academic scholarship becomes the source of action proposals, the criteria of excellence take on some new dimensions. When scholarship alone is involved originality is important. The scholar is in his natural role when he is directing minds toward new patterns of thought, and when truth is sought for its own sake. The price for being wrong need not

---

[16] The claims people who worked on our experiment believe that there are a significant number of cases in which the policyholder is so obviously free from fault that he does not feel it necessary to make any report to his insurer and that usually no claim is made on such cases.

[17] Address by F. J. Marryott to the American Management Association Fall Insurance Conference, *A Response to the Critics of the Automobile Insurance-Tort System: New Concepts To Protect Traffic Victims*, Nov. 9, 1966.

be paid at once or may be avoided entirely as the continued search produces revisions of the concepts. But the role of harbinger of change is not the same thing as being actually involved in the political maneuvering that is so often associated with the accomplishment of change. When the intellectual becomes the man of political action, or the zealous advocate of "a cause," he takes on some attributes that do not coincide with those of a scholar and he is apt to find himself involved in the sort of rough and tumble debate apt to produce overstatements and distortions.

The political man appreciates that there should be some pauses along the road to consensus so that the concepts may be learned, understood, and accommodated to the needs of the various elements in the body politic. Even the most unassailable logic needs to be imposed, if it is to be imposed at all, at a pace measured by the ability of the people to comprehend what the leaders are doing.

There is something incongruous, perhaps even damaging to both the scholars and to the rest of the population, when the scholars become drawn into the political machine rather than remaining as members of the general community of scholars. Whether both roles can be successfully occupied simultaneously is, I suggest, at least open to doubt.[18]

There is one further point I would like to make. If the professors wish to be listened to more routinely by the insurance community they should assume some part of the responsibility for using communication media that will do the job. The *Virginia Law Review*[19] is a fine publication but it is not read by very many insurance executives. I would guess that the *Monday Evening Papers* has such a restricted circulation as to almost guarantee that Dr. Moynihan's paper "Traffic Safety and the Health of the Body Politic"[20] is not on very many desks in home offices of insurance companies.

This is very sad. Perhaps it's even worse that I would be unable to assure the people who are writing these articles that they would have a large, perceptive and receptive readership even if such publications came along in regular course. But at least the opportunity should be provided, and if the action intellectual is here to stay—as I think he is—my closing words are aimed at my fellow insurance executives—start listening to what is being said.

[18] *See Symposium—Intellectuals and Just Causes,* Encounter, Sept. 1967, at 3-16.

[19] *See especially A Symposium in Honor of Charles O. Gregory,* 53 Va. L. Rev. 774-923 (1967).

[20] Monday Evening Papers: No. 10 (1966), published by the Center for Advanced Studies, Wesleyan University. A version of this paper also appeared in The Public Interest, No. 3, Spring 1966, at 10.

# REMARKS

*OF ROBERT I. MEHR\**

THE PRIMARY MEANING OF CLAIM is to demand recognition of a right. Any formulated, regular, or special method or plan of procedure designed to facilitate the recognition of a right is a claims system. When the right relates to compensation for injuries suffered in an automobile accident, the system is an automobile claims system.

What is the proper objective of an automobile claims system? What useful and logical goal can be set up that can be both practical and consistent with all perspectives? The following statement of objective is offered as being both adequate and adaptive to all philosophies: The objective of a claims system is to maximize the efficiency with which rights are recognized.

Much of the adaptability of this statement of objective lies in the multitude of possible interpretations of the concept of "efficiency." Clearly it refers to the relationship between benefits and costs, but there are many ways to measure benefits and costs. The usefulness of stating the objective of an automobile claims system as "maximization of efficiency" is its independence of any particulars regarding what benefits and what costs are or should be used to measure efficiency. Therefore, generalizations about claims systems appropriate to achieving this objective are applicable regardless of the benefits or costs considered in a given situation.

While the objective of a claims system is independent of a particular attitude toward benefits and costs, interested parties seeking to measure the efficiency of a system do not find all attitudes toward benefits and costs equally useful, desirable or acceptable in approaching the problem. The particular benefits and costs and the relative values assigned to them are a function of perspective. A perspective is a mental image and relates to the faculty of seeing all the relevant data in a meaningful relationship. Because the facts known and the state of the ideas held vary so widely among people, a meaningful interrelationship for one viewer might be quite different from that of another.

Perspective is frequently a function of emotional attitudes. When we become emotionally involved in an issue we become slaves to our biases and prejudices. What is so unfortunate about an emotionally-conditioned perspective is that even rational and learned men are not free of it. Rational men present arguments in logical form when they are defending their unreasonable positions and learned men use their intelligence to support untenable views rather than to defeat them. And because of their perspective,

\* *ROBERT I. MEHR. B.S. 1938, M.S. 1939, University of Alabama; Ph.D. 1943, University of Pennsylvania; Professor of Finance, University of Illinois.*

they believe that their opinions are held entirely on rational grounds. They are not hypocrites but self-deceivers.

Perspective also is conditioned by reverence for traditional methods of doing things, or by loyalty to established institutions and customary ways of thinking. A different perspective can be accomplished only by a re-evaluation of old thought habits. When one reads or hears something that breaks his thought barriers, he often plays the role of the "shocked disbeliever" rather than questioning his old belief and preparing himself for examination of what might turn out to be new but unfamiliar approaches to problems.

Writing about the property and liability insurance business in the *Journal of Insurance*, Professor Ingolf H. E. Otto commented on what he called the pathological sensibility of its practitioners[1] and what Professor Ralph Blanchard called the "almost religious worship of its machinery."[2] "An institution which does not seek out, encourage, and reward criticism condemns itself to obsolescence, inefficiency and deterioration."[3]

The perspectives are varied among those attending this national conference to consider changes in automobile claims. This makes for a stimulating exchange. The one point on which all of us can agree is the observation made by the seventeenth century English author Owen Felltham: "Perfection is immutable, but for things imperfect, to change is the way to perfect them. Constancy without knowledge cannot be always good; and in things ill, it is not virtue but an absolute vice."

Some of us use polar concepts in viewing the current automobile claims system. We view it as either perfect or ill. Many of us, however, do not apply polar concepts. We view it as neither perfect nor ill, and are willing to accept the thesis that constancy with knowledge is acceptable though not necessarily virtuous. Aside from our disagreement over whether the current automobile claims system is imperfect or whether the degree of its imperfection is serious enough to warrant change, we also disagree on whether a proposed change is an improvement over the present system. Some of us are willing to debate *ad infinitum* on just what should be done. For the latter group, to paraphrase the words of the contemporary Irish poet, William R. Rodgers, perhaps our doubts are the private detectives employed by our dislike to make a case against change or choice.

Because of our varying perspectives, we assign different values to the benefits and costs of the tort system of automobile claims. We have different concepts of social welfare and are willing to pay different prices for it. Professor Henry C. Wallich in his book *The Cost of Freedom* argues that maximum efficiency of our economic system cannot be demanded if we also

[1] Otto, *A Review Article on* Insurance Statistics, 1961, 30 J. INS. 295, 304 (1963).

[2] Blanchard, *The Lawyer and Insurance*, 277 INS. L.J. 66, 67 (1946), *quoted in* Otto, *supra* note 1, at 304.

[3] Otto, *supra* note 1, at 304.

value individual freedom. It seems that the value placed on individual freedom and the cost of relinquishing this freedom should be variables to be considered in measuring the efficiency of the system rather than something added later to tilt the scale in favor of a less efficient system.

I would like to make a few comments on Mr. Marryott's paper. He challenges the assertion that the tort system causes unjustified expenses and results in too many wrong determinations being made. But what is a wrong determination and how many of them make too many?

In a book published by *The Spectator*, an insurance publisher, a claims consultant and trial counsel with years of experience in "intellectually attractive" claims work wrote:

> "Thus, it must be evident that any claim is basically a contest of facts and assertions of fact. Sometimes the assertions of facts are true; sometimes they are false. This feature is one that adds interest to the battle, . . . because some claimants, as well as some claims managers and defendants' lawyers, are occasionally so misled about true facts as to work tenaciously to establish facts that are not so. In the main, however, the victory usually goes to the better thinker and the one who makes the better use of the available true facts. Lest the reader be astonished at this suggestion that facts can be anything but true, he must realize that in a lawsuit the facts that are ultimately decided to be true, are the ones adopted by the jury. The truth is what the jury believes to be the truth. It is common knowledge that this belief is, upon occasion, as different from the actual truth as night is from day."[4]

He goes on to say that "we cannot escape the conviction that one of the best sources of proper technique with which to resist a claim can be found in our oldest and most scientific pastime, the game of chess."[5]

To return to the question of what is a wrong determination. Consider the following proposition. If claims-waging is to be compared to the game of chess, are we prepared to say that there can be *any wrong* determinations? Is it wrong for the party that makes the least costly mistakes to be declared the winner? If the concept of wrong is defined to mean not in accordance with what is morally right or good, then a claims system that rewards the better thinkers can be open to challenge. While the determinations under this system might not be said to be wrong, the system that leads to some of the determinations might be considered to be wrong.

How many so-called wrong determinations can be tolerated before they are judged to be many? In answer to that question, I can say without hesitation that if I am the wronged party, then one is too many. Beyond that I have no basis for making any meaningful estimates.

Mr. Marryott raises some provocative questions about the role of the

[4] F. REES, CLAIMS PHILOSOPHY AND PRACTICE 2 (1947).
[5] *Id.* at 2-3.

college professor in American political and economic life. We no longer contend that the woman's place is in the home. Time marches on. We do not believe that the professor's place is only in the classroom, library, and laboratory. His public responsibility is not confined to the creation, whole-saling, and retailing of knowledge but extends to making his influence felt through playing an active role in matters of public interest. His status as a scholar does not require of him any form of celibacy.

# BASIC PROTECTION AUTOMOBILE INSURANCE†

## BY ROBERT E. KEETON* AND JEFFREY O'CONNELL**

### I. The Need for Reform

EVERY TIME AN INSURANCE COMPANY FAILS there is a hue and cry of scandal. In this respect recent years have surpassed others because of the failure of an alarming number of companies specializing in automobile insurance for high-risk drivers who cannot get their insurance through ordinary channels.[1] Legislatures and commissioners of insurance have already tightened surveillance of such companies, and other remedial measures are under consideration in Congress and in the states. Meanwhile, far more serious shortcomings of our automobile insurance system go unchecked, and they cost the public hundreds of times more, year after year, than the combined sum of unpaid obligations of the few automobile insurance companies that fail. These are the evils of inadequacy, delay, injustice, waste, and corruption in the present system of handling claims of traffic victims.[2]

Measured as a way of compensating for personal injuries suffered in automobile accidents, the present system is a dismal failure. Many injured persons receive nothing at all. Many others receive far less than their out-of-pocket losses.[3] This discrepancy between loss and compensation is due, in part, to the financial irresponsibility of a substantial percentage of drivers. The owners of somewhere between 10 and 15 per cent of the cars on our nation's highways have failed to obtain insurance to cover the operation of their vehicles.[4] However, the gap between loss and compensation is due primarily to the role of fault in the system.

In general, an injured person must seek compensation not from his own insurance company but from the other driver's insurance company. To get a

---

\* ROBERT E. KEETON. B.B.A. 1940, LL.B. 1941, University of Texas; S.J.D. 1956, Harvard University; Professor of Law, Harvard University.

\*\* JEFFREY O'CONNELL. B.A. 1951, Dartmouth College; LL.B. 1954, Harvard University; Professor of Law, University of Illinois.

---

† The Basic Protection Automobile Insurance Plan is set forth more fully, along with documentation for its pressing need, in KEETON & O'CONNELL, BASIC PROTECTION FOR THE TRAFFIC VICTIM: A BLUEPRINT FOR REFORMING AUTOMOBILE INSURANCE (1965) [both hereinbefore and hereinafter this book is often cited as Basic Protection]. See also KEETON & O'CONNELL, AFTER CARS CRASH—THE NEED FOR LEGAL AND INSURANCE REFORM (1967), a version written for the general reader.

[1] 113 CONG. REC. 978, 1017-19 (daily ed. Jan. 26, 1967). See also N.Y. Times, April 4, 1965, § 3, p. 1, col. 4; Wall St. J., May 6, 1965, p. 1, col. 6.
[2] Basic Protection 1-5, 13-34.
[3] Id. at 34-69.
[4] See id. at 65-66.

hearing in court, or even in the insurance office from which he hopes to receive an out-of-court settlement, an injured person must assert that he was blameless and that the "other driver" was at fault—that is, was negligent. If this theory were in fact faithfully administered, most traffic victims would go uncompensated. Happily this is not the case. Insurance companies are ever mindful of the cost of litigation and fearful of a jury verdict that disregards the judge's instructions on fault and awards something anyway. Thus, insurance companies settle with a very high percentage of the traffic victims who make claims—reliably estimated in some quarters to be as high as 85 per cent.[5]

Fault nevertheless plays its role for it is still sometimes faithfully applied in cases actually tried. And in virtually every case the threat that the fault criterion will defeat the claim looms as a factor in the settlement negotiations. In cases of severe injury it helps to produce settlements in which compensation is far less than the victim's out-of-pocket loss, even though in theory if he is entitled to anything at all he is supposed to receive, in one lump sum, enough to compensate him fairly and reasonably not only for all his past and future out-of-pocket loss but for his past and future pain and suffering as well.[6]

The present system is cumbersome and slow. It delivers its benefits too late. Prompt payment of compensation is rare. According to a study published in 1966, the flood of automobile accident litigation has produced an *average* delay of 31.1 months for personal injury trials in metropolitan areas. The longest average delay was 69.5 months in Chicago, followed by periods ranging downward from 51.5 to 46.8 months in Westchester, Kings, Suffolk, and Queens Counties in New York and 50.8 months in Philadelphia.[7] These delays pile up while the parties and their lawyers bicker about who was at fault and what lump sum of damages they suppose a jury would allow if the case were tried. Moreover, because of their overwhelming number and time consuming nature, these automobile cases are choking the court calendars and delaying the administration of justice in other types of cases as well. Automobile accident cases are typically two-thirds or more of a court's civil jury docket.[8]

Injustice is rampant in the present system. Of course injustice in some individual cases is bound to occur in any system administered by human beings. But automobile insurance is plagued by inherent injustices that occur even when everybody is doing his assigned task faithfully and efficiently. The long delays characteristic of the system produce a cruel injustice that strikes harder as injuries are more severe, and hardest at those most in need—

[5] *See id.* at 35, 55.

[6] *Id.* at 45-46.

[7] Institute of Judicial Administration, Calendar Status Study—1966: State Trial Courts of General Jurisdiction—Personal Injury Jury Cases v.

[8] Basic Protection 14.

the disabled breadwinners and their families. A hard-bargaining insurance company can buy the claim of such a person with a penurious settlement offer that capitalizes on his pressing needs in the face of the long wait for trial. According to a recent study of traffic accidents in Michigan, "the man who has a severe injury is likely to settle for it quickly only if he settles for a relatively small amount."[9]

This harsh treatment of the deserving, severely injured person is only one aspect of a whole pattern of unfair allocation of the total pool of insurance money available from automobile insurance premiums. The present system, while awarding far too little or even nothing to some victims, makes generous and even profligate awards to others—especially to the trivially injured.[10] This pattern of generous treatment of those with relatively little injury has led one observer, describing the process of compensating for traffic injuries in New York City, to exclaim, "From wrecks to riches!"

There is injustice, too, in the way the present system allocates the burden of paying for traffic injuries. Motoring should pay its way in our society.[11] Injuries are part of the inevitable toll of using as many cars as we choose to use in the hands of as many drivers as we choose to license on the kinds of roads we choose to provide. Yet the present system says to the victim of an unavoidable accident—one in which nobody was at fault—"You pay for your own injuries, and pay in poverty and deprivation if you happen not to have other means of providing for yourself."

Curiously, this system is ardently defended under the banner of the morality of basing compensation on fault—under the banner, that is, of forcing one to make payment only if he is in the wrong and only to those in the right. Such a system, if faithfully applied, would pay a few victims in full for all loss and would pay all others nothing. And these payments would be made by the individual wrongdoers. Those who defend the *status quo* on this moral theory seem strangely unaware of the inconsistency between their theory and what actually happens under the present system in which most victims are paid a fraction of their losses, and are paid not by the wrongdoers but by the wrongdoers' insurance companies using mostly money paid in by many others who have done nothing wrong at all.

The present system is also appallingly wasteful. Nationwide, less than 50 cents of the automobile liability insurance dollar ever reaches the hands of any injured person.[12] The rest goes to agents, adjustors, investigators, lawyers, overhead, and profit. This is not to say that these people are being overpaid. Fighting over who was at fault in an accident, over translating a day of

---

[9] A. Conard, J. Morgan, R. Pratt, C. Voltz, & R. Bombaugh, Automobile Accident Costs and Payments—Studies in the Economics of Injury Reparation 222 (1964) [hereinafter this book is often cited as Conard, et al.].

[10] Basic Protection 36-37.

[11] *Id.* at 256-72.

[12] Conard, *et al.* 59.

pain and suffering into dollars, and over how soon and how fully an injured person will recover takes the time and skill and effort of many different people. Inevitably this costs money. Most disputed cases—by far the greater percentage—involve injuries that are not severe, and in these small cases it often happens that more is spent in fighting a claim than it would be worth if valid. Added to this, of course, is a fortune in tax dollars used to maintain the courts whose time is consumed by these cases.

The system is topped off with powerful temptations to dishonesty. To the toll of physical injury is added a toll of psychological and moral injury resulting from pressures for exaggeration to improve one's case or defense, and even for outright invention—or perjury—to fill any gaps and cure any weaknesses. These inducements strike at the integrity of driver and victim alike, all too often corrupting both and leaving the latter twice a victim—physically injured and morally debased. If one is inclined to doubt the influence of these pressures, let him compare his own estimates of the percentage of drivers who are at fault in accidents and the percentage who admit it under oath. Of course the disparity is partly accounted for by self-deception, but only partly. And even the explanation of self-deception does not justify a system which demands that parties and witnesses reconstruct accidents with split-second accuracy, when no man's powers of observation and memory are that good.

We propose a basic reform to correct the evils of the present system. We propose fundamental changes in the laws and insurance policies applying to the claims of traffic victims.

The proposed reform, called the Basic Protection plan, has two main features.

The first is to develop a new form of automobile insurance, called Basic Protection insurance. It is an extension of the idea of the medical payments coverage—a supplemental coverage one can buy in an automobile insurance policy today. Medical payments coverage reimburses actual medical expenses up to a stated limit, say $500, regardless of who was at fault in the accident. Basic Protection insurance would do the same for all out-of-pocket loss—wage loss, for example, as well as medical expense—up to a limit of $10,000 per person.[13]

As in the case of medical payments coverage, one would buy this coverage for himself, his family and guests, and he would make his claim and recover his benefits from his own insurance company.[14] The insurance company would be required to pay month by month, as doctors' bills, hospital bills, or lost wages occurred, rather than delaying as under the present system until the injured person and the company could agree on a lump sum or have their disagreement resolved in a long-delayed trial.[15]

[13] Basic Protection 276-77, 280, 283.
[14] *Id*. at 274.
[15] *Id*. at 277-78.

The second main feature of the plan is that Basic Protection insurance would be coupled with a new law that would do away with claims based on negligence unless the damages were higher than $5,000 for pain and suffering or $10,000 for all other items such as medical expense and wage loss.[16] This would mean that all but a very small percentage of the claims for injuries in automobile accidents would be handled entirely under the new Basic Protection coverage. The wasteful expense of bickering over fault—with all the cost of the time of investigators, lawyers, and courts spent on these questions—would be eliminated except in the few cases in which injuries were quite severe. This would reduce sharply the overhead of the present system and thus lead to lower insurance costs. Also, eliminating in the multitude of small cases the arguments that now occur over fault, lump-sum awards, and damages for pain and suffering would remove the chief opportunities for fraud and exaggeration existing under the present system. Although no one should expect that this would eradicate fraud completely, at least a substantial reduction would be achieved. This would not only help reduce costs but would be a good thing in itself.

Another reduction of waste and of insurance costs would be gained by paying a victim only to the extent that he had an actual out-of-pocket loss. If he received payment for his loss from some other source, such as sick leave pay or Blue Cross benefits, Basic Protection insurance would not pay him again for that loss.[16a] At the present time, an injured person can often make a profit by incurring extra medical expense. For example, if he has automobile medical payments insurance and Blue Cross coverage (in a common form under which Blue Cross does not get its payment back from the negligent party), he may make $40 by having a set of X-rays for which the charge is $20, since he gets $20 from his medical payments insurance company, $20 from his Blue Cross, and another $20 when he settles with the insurance company covering the other driver's negligence. In addition he might even make $40 to $60 more since payments for pain and suffering are often settled on the basis of an unofficial rule of thumb allowing $2 to $3 for every dollar expended or lost by the victim.

Another way in which the Basic Protection plan permits one to reduce his automobile insurance cost—is through a new method of handling payments for pain and suffering. At present, the compulsory insurance laws (in Massachusetts, New York, and North Carolina) require one to buy insurance that pays pain and suffering damages to the other persons he carelessly injures. The financial responsibility laws of the other 47 states, though not requiring such insurance, strongly encourage it. In contrast, the new plan provides that Basic Protection benefits be paid by one's own insurance company rather than the other driver's insurance company. Thus, under the Basic Protection plan it becomes feasible to give a policyholder a choice

[16] *Id.* at 274-76.
[16a] *Id.* at 275-79.

whether he wants coverage for pain and suffering—a choice that no one has under the present system, because obviously we cannot allow people a choice *not* to pay others. Under the Basic Protection plan, a policyholder may buy what is called Added Protection coverage providing payments for his pain and inconvenience up to the amount of $5,000.[17] (This is the amount of the Basic Protection exclusion of pain and suffering damages from negligence trials. Above that amount one can still claim for his pain and suffering in a negligence suit.) But he is free to decline pain and inconvenience coverage for the first $5,000 if he prefers to reduce his insurance costs.

As originally drafted, the Basic Protection plan did not cover property damage.[18] Recently, however, we have drafted a change under which a motorist has a two-fold choice about property damage insurance. (1) He can choose to include damage to his own car under a new coverage like Basic Protection coverage, along with a corresponding exemption from tort liability like that applying to personal injury under Basic Protection. (2) Or, instead, he can choose to omit this non-fault coverage for damage to his own car, carry coverage for damage he negligently causes to the cars of others who make this choice, and also be assured that he can recover for damage to his car, provided he can prove a negligence claim against some other driver. This would eliminate most of the negligence suits over damage to cars, because most people would make the first choice, under which negligence claims no longer arise. This would mean further premium savings at least to the policyholder who now carries both collision coverage (for damage to his own car) and liability coverage (for damage to other cars)—as most policyholders do.[19]

The savings under Basic Protection would be striking. An independent actuary has calculated that if Basic Protection were enacted in New York State, not only would about 25 per cent more people be paid than under the present system, but also automobile insurance costs would drop from 15 to 25 per cent with coverage up to a higher per-accident limit under Basic Protection ($100,000 rather than $10,000). Nine per cent more savings (for a total of 24 to 34 per cent) would be achieved if coverages of the same per-accident limit were compared. And all these savings are, according to the actuary, a *conservative* estimate.[20]

Daniel Patrick Moynihan, a distinguished observer of many facets of American life, points in a recent *New York Times* article to the analogy

17 *Id*. at 285-86.
18 *Id*. at 280-81.
19 *See* paras. 23-26 *infra*.
20 Harwayne, *Insurance Cost of Automobile Basic Protection Plan in Relation to Automobile Bodily Injury Liability Costs*, 53 PROCEEDINGS OF THE CASUALTY ACTUARIAL SOCIETY 122 (1966). *See also* Keeton & O'Connell, *Basic Protection and the Costs of Traffic Accidents*, 38 N.Y.S.B.J. 255, 256, 257 (1966). For another actuarial report by Harwayne indicating that automobile insurance costs in a midwestern state—Michigan— might be reduced from 19 to 28% if that state enacted the Basic Protection system, *see* Harwayne, *Insurance Costs of Basic Protection Plan in Michigan*, p. 119 *infra*.

between the controversy surrounding the inadequacies of the automobile *insurance* industry and the recent controversy surrounding the inadequacies of the automobile *manufacturing* industry:

"Starting in 1964, Congress began enacting legislation having to do with safety features for Government-purchased vehicles, tire standards, automotive exhaust controls and the like.

"No great notice was taken until President Johnson in the 1966 State of the Union message proposed a general measure providing for safe cars. Then in a rush of events ending in a Rose Garden ceremony nine months later on Sept. 9, 1966, the decisive battle was fought and won. The largest manufacturing complex on earth, which into the sixth decade of the 20th century had persisted as an utterly unregulated private enterprise, was all of a sudden subjected to detailed and permanent Government regulation.

. . . .

"Nothing comparable has occurred since the establishment of railroad regulation in the late 19th century. . . .

. . . .

"The problem [with automobile insurance] is precisely parallel to that of automobile safety. The system is not working well as such, and its secondary effects are wasteful and expensive. On either ground change is in order, and given both, change is as near to urgent as a world of competing sorrows will permit."[21]

For years, the insurance industry bitterly fought any suggestion of change in automobile insurance. Even today, the response to a proposed change such as the Basic Protection plan is often one of grudging interest at best. But, as suggested in further remarks by Moynihan in the same article, some voices within the insurance industry are responding to calls for significant change.[22] It remains to be seen whether the industry will actively help to bring about change of real significance, or instead will stand neutral, or even counter with a futilely cautious patchwork on the present ailing system.

In contrast to signs from the insurance industry that can be viewed with some hope, the response of some segments of the bar to proposals for reform is cause for deep concern. Speaking of this response, Illinois Supreme Court Justice Walter Schaefer told a meeting of the Chicago Bar, "Too much of [a negative] . . . attitude permeates our bar, and, . . . , the very segment of the bar that has the biggest stake in the existing [automobile claims] procedure."[23] But, as Martin Mayer, a nonlawyer surveying the whole legal profession, has remarked, "[W]ith injuries from automobile accidents running at a rate of more than four million a year, the problem is too large to

[21] Moynihan, *Next: A New Auto Insurance Policy*, N.Y. Times, Aug. 27, 1967, § 6 (Magazine), at 26, 76.

[22] *Id.* at 82-83.

[23] *Remarks of Hon. Walter V. Schaefer*, 39 Chi. B. Record 265, 267 (1958), *also quoted* in M. Mayer, The Lawyers 270 (1967).

be dealt with as a question of what might be best for lawyers."[24] Moreover, from the long-range point of view, the present system defeats the best interests of the bar as well as the public. Disrespect for the system is inevitably translated into disrespect for law, and lawyers as well. Yet impassioned defense of the present system continues. For example:

¶ Spokesmen for trial lawyers wax eloquent in their objections to any encroachment on jury trials, but somehow cannot see in the same light the practical encroachment on the right to jury trial that occurs as the norm in a system requiring a litigant to wait years for a jury to be available to him.

¶ Defenders of the status quo insist that the problem of court congestion can be solved simply enough by just appointing more judges. But they offer no answer to the problem of costs—the fact, for example, that the cost to New York City of maintaining its trial courts (which are so largely devoted to traffic cases) is approximately 20 million dollars annually.[25] And each new judge means an increase in cost of a quarter of a million dollars annually by the time he is provided with a courtroom, a salary, clerks, bailiffs, and other supporting personnel and property.[26] It is small wonder that most states balk at such costs. Keep in mind, too, that even if appointing many more lawyers as judges would solve the problem of court congestion—and it might very well not[27]—it still would not solve the problems of unfair payment, high costs, and wasteful expenses under the present automobile claims system.

¶ Partisans of negligence law continue to insist that if traffic victims are paid without reference to fault, deterrence of unsafe driving will be seriously undermined. But if fear of injuring oneself and if fear of criminal sanctions and losing one's driver's license will not deter unsafe driving, surely fear of the outcome of civil litigation months or even years after the accident will have little effect.

¶ In an ultimate appeal defenders of the present system insist that it is *immoral* to make innocent motorists pay insurance premiums to cover traffic losses and equally immoral to award insurance benefits to motorists guilty of wrongdoing—even benefits from their own insurance companies to whom they have paid premiums. Yet these same defenders contend that non-fault insurance, such as Basic Protection, is not needed because other non-fault insurance—accident and health insurance and even the supplementary medical payments coverage under the automobile liability policy—is already available to motorists. They cannot have it both ways.

[24] *Id.*
[25] N.Y. Times, March 13, 1967, p. 42, col. 1.
[26] *Id.*
[27] Basic Protection 15.

Consider this argument of immorality more closely. Is it really immoral to pay insurance money to people who suffer in accident regardless of fault? If it were, most insurance would have long since been outlawed. The very availability of accident and health insurance, medical payments insurance, fire insurance, and collision insurance mocks such an argument of "immorality." And so does liability insurance itself, since the insurance company is paying damages *on behalf* of the party at fault.

The availability of other kinds of non-fault insurance, however, is no defense for maintaining automobile liability insurance unchanged. Automobile insurance itself can and should be structured to cover losses from automobile accidents adequately and fairly. The only question now is whether organized opposition to change will extend to the point that—as happened with Medicare—there emerges a federal solution, perhaps involving federal insurance.

Those who really believe in the efficacy of state government and private enterprise should join with us in urging use of the means at hand to preserve them in the important area of automobile insurance. In the words of Daniel Patrick Moynihan, "Some small part of the future of American private enterprise will be determined by the response to that [opportunity]. . . ."[28]

## II.   Summary of the Basic Protection Plan with Property Damage Option[29]

The Basic Protection system is a proposal for a fairer, simpler, and more efficient way of treating the vast number of claims arising from the annual toll of traffic accidents. It is based on two major principles—first, paying losses regardless of fault up to a moderate limit and, second, eliminating small negligence claims for injuries suffered in traffic accidents.

Initially, as stated above, we proposed a system of Basic Protection insurance to cover bodily injury claims only. These are the claims that present potentially the most severe problems both to the individual victim and to the community, and therefore constitute the most pressing need. Discussions of the Basic Protection proposal, however, have often turned to the question whether the two basic principles underlying the plan—paying insurance benefits without regard to fault up to a moderate limit and doing away with small negligence claims—ought not to be extended to vehicle damage as well as personal injury. From an early point in our study, which began in 1963, we were searching for some practical way of including damage to vehicles in the Basic Protection system. The problem has been to find a way to accomplish this while at the same time achieving three other important objectives, namely, (1) leaving each car owner free to carry insurance against damage

[28] Moynihan, *supra* note 21, at 83.
[29] Copyright 1967 by Robert E. Keeton and Jeffrey O'Connell. Published with permission.

to his own car or not as he prefers, (2) avoiding complicated options that would be difficult to explain to the public in terms such that they could understand the way the system affected their individual interests, and (3) maintaining fair differentials in insurance rates charged to those electing different options.

In early 1967, as efforts to resolve this dilemma continued, we finally succeeded in working out methods for including an optional property damage coverage in the Basic Protection system.[30] We believe these methods are workable, and we recommend this addition to the Basic Protection system with enthusiasm.

The purpose of the remainder of this paper is to present a summary of the full Basic Protection system as modified to include this optional property damage coverage.[31]

1. NEW FORM OF COVERAGE.—*Basic Protection coverage is a new form of automobile insurance; most of its features, however, are derived from types of insurance already in use, medical payments coverage of current policies being the closest analogy.*

The proposed reform retains many elements of the system existing in the United States but offers increased benefits to victims through improved insurance arrangements. It is, in essence, an extension of the principles of medical payments coverage to all out-of-pocket net losses, including wage losses, with modifications designed to reimburse losses month by month as they accrue rather than by lump-sum payments.

2. PARTIAL REPLACEMENT OF NEGLIGENCE LIABILITY INSURANCE WITH LOSS INSURANCE.—*The new coverage partially replaces negligence liability insurance and its three-party claims procedure with loss insurance, payable regardless of fault, and a two-party claims procedure under which a victim ordinarily claims directly against the insurance company of his own car or, if a guest, his host's car, or, if a pedestrian, the car striking him.*

Under our present negligence and negligence liability insurance system, there are ordinarily three parties to a claim: the victim, a motorist, and the motorist's negligence liability insurance company. In form and theory the victim makes his claim against the motorist, asserting that the latter negligently caused the injury. In practice, however, the victim presents his claim to the motorist's insurance company, which owes nothing to the victim unless the negligence liability of its insured is established. Under the proposed

---

[30] *See* paras. 23-26 *infra.*

[31] A more detailed explanation of the initial plan appears in Basic Protection and a summary presentation for the general reader appears in KEETON & O'CONNELL, AFTER CARS CRASH—THE NEED FOR LEGAL AND INSURANCE REFORM (1967). Further explanation of the property damage option appears in Keeton & O'Connell, Basic Protection and Property Damage Dual Option Coverage (mimeo. ed. 1967). The following numbered paragraphs and discussion in the text of this article are adapted from Basic Protection ch. 6.

system, on the other hand, the insurance coverage for the first $10,000 of loss is of a type commonly referred to as loss insurance; that is, Basic Protection benefits depend not on liability for negligence but only on whether an insured car has been involved in an accident that resulted in loss to the claimant. In form, in theory, and in practice there will ordinarily be only two parties to a Basic Protection claim—the victim and a company insuring an involved vehicle. Moreover, in most instances the victim's claim will be presented to an insurance company from which he himself, or a member of his family, or his host driver, has previously obtained an insurance policy covering the injury.[32] This contrasts with negligence liability insurance under which the claim is ordinarily against the other driver's insurance company —or, in more precise terms, against the company insuring another car involved in the collision.

3. EXEMPTION FROM NEGLIGENCE LIABILITY TO SOME EXTENT.—*If damages for pain and suffering would not exceed $5,000 and other bodily injury damages, principally for out-of-pocket loss, would not exceed $10,000, an action for Basic Protection benefit replaces any negligence action against an exempt person (that is, a Basic Protection insured) for bodily injuries suffered in a traffic accident; in cases of more severe injury, the negligence action for bodily injuries is preserved, but the recovery is reduced by these same amounts.*[33]

The exemption of Basic Protection insureds from negligence liability applies to (1) the first $5,000 otherwise recoverable as negligence damages for pain and suffering and (2) the first $10,000 otherwise recoverable for other elements of negligence damages, which in general compensate for out-of-pocket loss such as for wage loss and medical expenses. In the cases of less severe injury, this exemption is full protection against liability based on negligence, and the victim is compensated instead under Basic Protection insurance. For the relatively small percentage of cases in which negligence verdicts exceed either $5,000 for pain and suffering or $10,000 for other damages, this exemption serves to reduce the negligence judgment for the plaintiff. The fact finder in these cases (whether judge or jury) is required to state pain and suffering damages separately from other damages in order that this reduction can be properly calculated.[34] In both large and small cases the exemption serves to avoid overlap between Basic Protection and negligence liability payments.

The negligence exemption is also important because it precludes litigation over negligence in a great mass of cases involving less severe injuries. If the damages in a claim based on negligence could not possibly exceed

[32] Basic Protection Act § 2.6. In the footnotes that follow, citations of sections and subsections are references to this Act, the full text of which appears in Basic Protection 302-39.

[33] Sections 4.1-.4.

[34] *See* § 4.3 and comments thereto, Basic Protection 445-62.

either $5,000 for pain and suffering or $10,000 for other damages, it would be futile for the victim to assert such a claim. His remedy would be entirely under Basic Protection coverage. On the other hand, if the victim could establish liability based on negligence and damages in excess of either of these limits, his negligence claim would be available to him if he wished to assert it. Thus, the exemption drastically reduces the number of cases in which the expense of litigation and preparation for the prospect of litigation will be incurred, since the percentage of injuries so severe as to go above the negligence exemption is small.[35] The effect on both court congestion and on the administrative overhead of the automobile claims system will be distinctly beneficial.

In the Basic Protection plan as initially proposed, there was no comparable provision for doing away with negligence actions for damage to vehicles. In the form now proposed, however, the great majority of such negligence actions for damage to vehicles will be eliminated by the arrangement described in paragraphs 25 and 26 below.

One other feature of the negligence exemption requires explanation. Since the exemption does not apply to the first $100 of net loss from personal injury, the right to a negligence claim for the first $100 of net personal injury loss is preserved.[36]

Although this arrangement has the disadvantage of permitting negligence claims for small sums in which insurance and legal costs tend to dwarf the compensation involved, we have concluded that it would be unwise to attempt extension of the Basic Protection system to such small losses. As a corollary we have also concluded that to deprive victims of the right to recover for such small losses through a negligence claim when they are not covered by Basic Protection would be impractical and perhaps unfair. The disadvantages of preserving this small negligence litigation may easily be exaggerated. It seems unlikely that victims will press claims for this $100 in any substantial number of cases, or that the cases that do arise will consume much court time. Unless the loss has occurred under peculiarly aggravating circumstances, a victim will ordinarily choose to bear the first $100 of loss himself. This result could be defended as a reasonable deductible even if it were imposed upon the victim unconditionally; it is more supportable when the victim has the choice of either prosecuting the claim or bearing the loss.

4. BASIC PROTECTION FOR BODILY INJURIES ONLY.—*Basic Protection insurance applies to bodily injuries only. Property damage, including damage to vehicles, is covered by a separate new form of insurance called Property Damage Dual Option coverage.*[37]

---

[35] *See* Keeton & O'Connell, *Basic Protection: A Rebuttal to Its Critics*, 53 A.B.A.J. 633, 634 n.6 and accompanying text (1967).

[36] *See* para. 9 *infra* concerning the $100 deductible from Basic Protection benefits.

[37] *See* paras. 23-26 *infra*.

Extending Basic Protection insurance—which is compulsory[38]—to vehicular damage would deprive the car owner of the option he now has to do without insurance against damage to his own car. A motorist's choice whether or not to obtain insurance against damage to his own car can be viewed as almost exclusively his own business. But a motorist's decision as to insurance covering personal injury is a very different one because it is so much more likely to involve substantial interests of other people, as well as interests of society in general.

A very substantial percentage of all car owners—over one-third in many states—choose not to carry the coverage now available for damage to their own vehicles (collision coverage). A person with an older car is especially likely to make this choice. He may consider it cheaper to cover the risk of damage to such a car himself, thus avoiding the relatively high cost of collision insurance on a relatively low value car. Persons electing not to carry collision coverage may also be influenced by the fact that they could take as an income tax deduction casualty losses of this type. This motivation may be even stronger for the affluent owner of a car of high value than for the less affluent owner of a used car of low value. Thus, our decision not to include damage to one's own vehicle in the compulsory Basic Protection insurance is based on the undesirability, as well as the impracticality, of trying to force each car owner to insure against damage to his own vehicle. Including damage to vehicles in the over-all plan on an optional basis, as described in paragraphs 23-26 below, avoids these difficulties.

5. BENEFITS NOT BASED ON FAULT.—*In general, a person who suffers injury arising out of the ownership, maintenance, or use of a motor vehicle is entitled to Basic Protection benefits without regard to fault,*[39] *though one who intentionally suffers injury does not qualify for benefits.*[40]

---

[38] *See* para. 14 *infra.*

[39] Sections 2.1-.2.

[40] Critics of the Basic Protection plan often complain that Basic Protection, by paying on a nonfault basis, will reward the wrongdoer, citing particularly the drunken driver. (Our reasons for covering even drivers who have been drinking are set forth in Basic Protection 396-97.) In fact, if the objection to reimbursing losses of drunken drivers is genuine and not simply a debater's point, the solution is very simple under first-party—or related-insurer—coverage such as Basic Protection (under which you claim against your own insurance company rather than some other—see para. 2). Just allow an optional exclusion for benefits to a person whose conduct such as drunken driving contributed to his injury. Thus, nobody is forced to pay premiums to cover injuries to someone else who was guilty of drunken driving, but if a person prefers to include coverage for himself in case he happens to be involved in an accident after some drinking, he may pay whatever premium is needed and have this coverage in his policy. A provision for such an option was incorporated into the Basic Protection bill filed in Massachusetts for the 1968 session to be inserted as part of § 2.4 (numbered 113-2.4 in the Massachusetts bill) of the Basic Protection act. The revised section will then read in part as follows:

"Section 113-2.4. Coverage less than standard prohibited except for optional deductibles *and optional exclusions.—Every insurer writing basic protection insurance*

That another person may have caused a victim's injury intentionally does not defeat the victim's claim against the appropriate Basic Protection insurance company;[41] but the company, after paying the victim, is entitled to complete reimbursement from one who intentionally injures a victim.[42]

Benefits extend to injury in an accident involving only one vehicle,[43] as well as to an accident in which two or more vehicles are involved. Thus, the driver of a vehicle striking a utility pole is entitled to benefits if he does not intentionally cause his own injury. This is an application of the insurance principle used in numerous other forms of non-fault insurance, including fire insurance, health and accident insurance, and even the supplementary medical payments coverage in automobile insurance policies. An injured person other than the driver is entitled to benefits even if the driver intentionally causes the injury, unless the injured person intentionally suffers the injury.[44]

One who is claiming loss through the death of another in an automobile collision is denied benefits if he himself intended to injure the decedent or if the decedent intended to commit suicide or to injure himself less seriously. But the fact that someone else intended to injure the decedent, by means of the automobile collision, does not disqualify the claimant. Similarly, a parent claiming benefits because of injury to his child in an automobile collision is barred if the parent intentionally caused the injury or if the child intentionally suffered it, but he is not barred by the fact that a third person intentionally injured the child by means of the automobile collision.[45]

*within the state shall offer optional exclusions as described in this section, at appropriately reduced premium rates, and* [basic protection insurers] *may offer singly or in combination, and at appropriately reduced premium rates, any of the types of optional deductible provisions described in this section, in lieu of the standard deductible. With this exception, insurance providing benefits less in any respect than under standard provisions does not qualify as basic protection insurance.*

. . . .

*"(c) Optional exclusion of persons committing specified offenses.—Each insurer shall offer an optional exclusion denying benefits to each injured person, whether the policyholder or some other person, whose conduct in any of the following ways contributed to the injury because of which he claims benefits: operating a motor vehicle while under the influence of intoxicating liquor or narcotic drugs; using a motor vehicle without authority knowing that such use is unauthorized; operating a motor vehicle after suspension or revocation of his license or right to operate without a license; operating a motor vehicle upon a bet or wager or in a race; refusal to stop when signaled by a police officer. A person who is disqualified from receiving benefits because of this exclusion in a policy otherwise applying to his injury is also disqualified from receiving benefits under the assigned claims plan established pursuant to section 9.1 of this Act."* (Bracketed matter omitted; italicized matter added.)

41 Sections 1.6-.7.
42 Section 2.8.
43 Sections 1.4, 1.11.
44 Sections 1.6-.7.
45 Section 1.7.

6. PERIODIC REIMBURSEMENT.—*Basic Protection benefits are payable month by month as losses accrue, subject to lump-sum payments in special circumstances.*[46]

Basic Protection payments are designed to reimburse losses as they occur, rather than by the lump-sum payment customary in settling or paying a negligence damages judgment or claim. Provision is made, however, for lump-sum awards by court order if the present value of all benefits expected to come due in the future does not exceed $1,000 or if a court makes a finding supported by medical evidence that a final disposition will contribute substantially to the health and rehabilitation of the injured person. This may be done, for example, if there is persuasive medical testimony that, because of a "compensation neurosis," the injured person will not get well before final disposition of his claim. Furthermore, a claim is subject at any time to final settlement (as opposed to an award by court decision) for benefits claimed to be due for future loss, by an agreement for a lump-sum payment not exceeding $1,000 or by an agreement for future payments not exceeding $1,000 per month. With judicial approval, upon a finding that the form of settlement is in the best interests of the claimant, a claim may be settled for a larger lump sum or larger installments.[47] Since the disposition is here being made by agreement, the standard is more permissive than when it is being ordered by a court over opposition.

7. REIMBURSEMENTS LIMITED TO NET LOSS.—*Basic Protection benefits are designed to reimburse net out-of-pocket loss only; overlapping with benefits from other sources is avoided by subtracting these other benefits from gross loss in calculating net loss.*[48]

Gratuities are disregarded, but with few exceptions benefits from other sources, such as payments from a sick leave program, Blue Cross, or an accident insurance policy, are subtracted from loss in calculating the net loss upon which Basic Protection benefits are based.

Basic Protection benefits in all likelihood will not be treated as taxable income. The victim with lost wages, however, will ordinarily claim as out-of-pocket loss a sum that would be taxable if received as wages in the ordinary course. In such a case it is fair to limit the victim's award to the amount he would have received after the tax due had been paid. As an administrative convenience, it is presumed, subject to proof of a lower value by the claimant, that the value of this tax advantage equals 15 per cent of the loss of income.[49] Thus, a person losing $100 gross wages is presumed to suffer an $85 loss of take-home pay.

[46] Sections 1.9(d), 3.1, 3.3.
[47] Section 3.3.
[48] Section 1.10.
[49] Section 1.10(d). Because administrative problems and costs outweigh the advantages of allowing the insurance company the converse right of proving that the tax advantage has a higher value, the statute does not afford the insurer that right. *See* Basic Protection 408.

Special provisions are made for negligence claims based on an injury for which Basic Protection benefits are also claimed. These provisions draw a distinction between a negligence claim against one who is an exempt person under applicable Basic Protection coverage and a negligence claim against one who is not such an exempt person (for example, a railroad company whose locomotive struck a car occupied by the victim). An exempt person is an "owner, driver, or other person . . . out of whose ownership, maintenance, or use of a motor vehicle" arises an insurance company's liability for payment of Basic Protection benefits.[50] In calculating Basic Protection benefits, the value of a victim's claim against such an exempt person is disregarded. Overlapping of benefits is avoided in this instance by the exemption reducing negligence damages for pain and suffering by $5,000 and other negligence damages by $10,000.[51]

When a negligence claim is lodged against one who is not an exempt person under applicable Basic Protection coverage, a somewhat different procedure is followed. Overlapping of benefits is again avoided but only by steps taken after the individual has recovered under his negligence claim. For example, consider a case in which a passenger in a car insured for Basic Protection coverage is injured when the car is struck by a train at a railroad grade crossing. The victim may claim Basic Protection benefits against the Basic Protection insurer at the outset. If the victim also elects to press his negligence claim and recovers, the expenses he incurs in this litigation, such as attorneys' fees, are subtracted from the gross recovery based on negligence in order to determine his net recovery based on negligence. If the victim has already received Basic Protection benefits he must at this point reimburse the Basic Protection insurance company in the amount of such benefits received. Rarely will his net recovery based on negligence be less than the Basic Protection benefits already received. Should this occur, however, the obligation of reimbursement is limited to the amount of the net recovery based on negligence. Ordinarily the reimbursement of the Basic Protection insurance company will exhaust only part of the net recovery based on negligence. In such a case, as further losses are incurred, the victim has no claim to Basic Protection benefits until he has depleted the net recovery based on negligence by setting it off against losses as they accrue.[52] If the net recovery based on negligence is exhausted in this way and he continues to suffer loss from the injury, he again becomes eligible to receive Basic Protection benefits and will continue to do so until losses cease or the limit of $10,000 is reached. The earlier payments of Basic Protection benefits are not charged against the limit in this calculation since they were fully reimbursed. For example, suppose Basic Protection benefits of $4,000 have been paid before a negligence judgment of $20,000 is obtained. Suppose also the claimant's ex-

[50] Section 1.3.
[51] Sections 1.10(c)(1), 4.3.
[52] Section 1.10(c)(2).

penses in the negligence action, including attorneys' fees, amount to $7,000, leaving a net recovery based on negligence of $13,000. The claimant is obligated to repay $4,000 to the Basic Protection insurance company immediately. The remaining $9,000 is credited against further losses as they occur, so the Basic Protection insurance company will not be obligated to pay further benefits unless and until further losses exceed this $9,000 balance. At that point it will be subject to liability up to the $10,000 limit if additional losses occur.

8. Loss Consists of Expenses and Work Loss.—*Out-of-pocket loss for which Basic Protection benefits are payable consists of reasonable expenses incurred and work loss. Work loss consists of loss of income from work (for example, wages) and expenses reasonably incurred for services in lieu of those the injured person would have performed without income. For example, the expenses of hiring household help to do work a housewife had been doing before being disabled by injury are reimbursable.*[53]

Allowable expenses consist of reasonable charges for reasonably necessary products and services. Generally, the proposed act establishes no standard for what is an allowable expense beyond the requirement of reasonableness, but there are a few exceptions. First, to the extent that a charge for a hospital room is in excess of a reasonable and customary charge for semiprivate accommodations it is not an allowable expense.[54] Second, the maximum allowable charge for expenses in any way related to funeral and burial is $500.[55] These two provisions do not prohibit higher charges; they simply exclude the excess amount from Basic Protection coverage.[56] The criterion of reasonableness is also supplemented by another specific provision making it unlawful to charge for medical or hospital services rendered, or for rehabilitative occupational training, any amount in excess of that customarily charged for like services in cases involving no insurance.[57] In other words, it is unlawful to charge extra just because Basic Protection insurance is applicable.

9. Deductible Losses.—*The standard deductible of Basic Protection coverage excludes from reimbursable losses the first $100 of net loss of all types or 10 per cent of work loss, whichever is greater.*[58]

The term "deductible" has customarily been used to signify the provision in present-day collision coverage under which the insured owner of the vehicle is himself expected to bear the loss from damage to his vehicle up to a specified amount (commonly $50) and his insurance company reim-

[53] Section 1.9.
[54] Sections 1.9(a).
[55] Section 1.9(a).
[56] Section 1.9(a).
[57] Sections 6.7, 7.2.
[58] Section 2.3(a).

burses him for loss in excess of that amount. In small cases the standard deductible of Basic Protection coverage operates in the same way; the insured himself bears the first $100 of his net loss of all types. The purpose of this provision is to hold down the cost of Basic Protection by excluding the very small claims as to which the modest benefits of reimbursement are outweighed by the relatively high costs of processing. As originally drafted, the deductible applied on a per person basis. This could cause hardship, however, in the case of, say, a family of five, each injured while traveling in the family car to the extent of nearly $100 of loss or more. In such a case, the family, as a unit, would have to bear a deductible of about $500. To correct such a potential hardship, we recommend that the provision concerning the deductible be changed to apply on a per family—as opposed to a per person—basis.[59]

A second feature of the standard deductible comes into operation only in the larger cases when 10 per cent of the work loss proved exceeds $100. In that event, the only applicable deductible is 10 per cent of the work loss proved; the remainder of all net loss is covered up to the limits of Basic Protection coverage. This 10 per cent deductible does not apply to medical and hospital expenses, which are the principal out-of-pocket expenses arising from injuries sustained in automobile accidents. It does apply not only to work loss of a wage earner or a self-employed person but also to the expenses incurred in replacing the services of an injured housewife. Since the principal work loss caused by automobile accidents is wage loss, this deductible in practice will ordinarily amount to roughly 10 per cent of wages lost due to accident. In addition to directly reducing the cost of Basic Protection coverage to this extent, this deductible will reduce costs indirectly by diminishing the likelihood that the reimbursement allowed will induce malingering. A wage earner injured in a traffic accident might be tempted to stay out of work beyond any period of genuine disability if by doing so he could receive exactly the same income as work would bring. To the extent that staying out of work results in a decrease in income, the inducement to return to work is greater. We have chosen 10 per cent of gross work loss as a deductible that will reduce the temptation to malinger while providing nearly full reimbursement of wages lost by a genuinely disabled victim. The

[59] Thus § 2.3 (a) should be changed to read as follows:

"*Standard deductible*. The greater of the following amounts otherwise qualifying for reimbursement under this insurance is to be excluded in calculating benefits to each claimant arising from one accident: (i) the first one hundred dollars ($100) of net loss or (ii) ten per cent (10%) of all work loss. *Provided, however, that if two or more persons who are relatives residing in the same household are injured in one accident, the deductible shall be one hundred dollars ($100) for all such persons combined or ten per cent (10%) of all work loss, whichever is greater.*" (Italicized matter added.)

Concerning the $100 deductible in general, as is now true under collision coverage, if the victim can prove the necessary facts to support a negligence claim he can recover this first $100 of loss through such a claim. Section 4.2(b).

combined effect of deducting this 10 per cent and further reducing the claim by an amount equal to the tax advantage of a nontaxable award produces benefits totaling about 75 per cent of gross wages, or a little less than 90 per cent of take-home pay. For example, suppose during the third month of disability gross wage loss was $500 and no proof was offered contrary to the presumption that the tax advantage equals 15 per cent of income lost. In this case the standard deduction is $50—10 per cent of $500; the tax advantage is $75—15 per cent of $500; and the benefits received total $375.

There is little need to apply a deductible provision to out-of-pocket losses, since even full reimbursement of such losses produces no profit for the victim. He pays the doctor or other person serving his needs—for example, a taxi driver or a temporary domestic employee—and then receives as a benefit precisely the same amount. The problem of excessive charges for out-of-pocket loss is better dealt with by other devices, such as a provision allowing the expenses only if reasonable in amount and comparable to charges in cases not involving insurance.[60] Such statutory controls will be supplemented in practice by the considerable power of the insurance industry to resist being overcharged.

10.   STANDARD LIMITS OF LIABILITY.—*The standard maximum liability of an insurance company on any Basic Protection policy is $10,000 for injuries to one person in one accident and $100,000 for all injuries in one accident; an additional limitation prevents liability for payments of more than $750 for work loss in any one month.*[61]

The maximum limitation on liability applies to benefits for all types of loss within Basic Protection coverage. The per month limit applies to benefits for work loss only. Thus, during a single month one may recover benefits totaling $750 for work loss and in addition receive compensation for any out-of-pocket expenses that he has incurred.

The purpose of the per month limit is, first, to reduce somewhat the over-all cost of Basic Protection coverage and, second, to achieve a more equitable allocation of the costs of motoring accidents than would otherwise occur. Since most persons suffer no appreciable work loss beyond wage loss, ordinarily this $750 limit, like the 10 per cent deductible, applies only to wage loss. This arrangement is founded on the belief that it is desirable for the high earner whose monthly income exceeds $750 to obtain for an added premium charge whatever added coverage he wishes, rather than for it to be included within the compulsory Basic Protection coverage. In the absence of such an income limit, it might appropriately be argued that a very high earner should be required to pay a very much higher premium for Basic Protection coverage than average or low earners. Adjusting premiums all along the income scale, however, would be a complicated and administra-

[60] Sections 1.9(a), 6.7, 7.2.
[61] Sections 2.3 (d) and (e).

tively expensive process. It seems wiser and fairer to adopt a limitation on the amount of compensable work loss. Under this arrangement the argument that a very high earner should pay a very much higher premium because his loss per unit of time is much higher is counterbalanced by the likelihood that he will cease to draw benefits and will return to work as soon as it is possible to do so. This early return of the very high earner is induced both because he receives no reimbursement for loss in excess of the work-loss limit and because generally his work is more stimulating than that of the average or low earner. This latter factor, of course, would operate with or without a work-loss limit.

This is not to say that there will be no variations in Basic Protection premiums depending on, for example, the amount of the policyholder's income and other insurance covering wage loss and medical expenses available to him and his family. On the contrary, a big advantage of the Basic Protection proposal is that since an insurance company pays its own insured and members of his family, it can, in setting rates for individuals and classes, take account of its advance knowledge of the likely loss of the people to be paid. Under the negligence liability system, on the other hand, no account can be taken, in rating a policyholder's premiums, of the income and collateral sources available to the policyholder and his family since the insurance company will be paying not them but the occupants of the *other* car whom it cannot identify in advance.[62]

Nevertheless, it still makes sense to limit the standard income coverage under Basic Protection to $750 per month in order (1) to limit the variety of different amounts of lost income so that it will not be necessary to have an inordinate number of premium classifications for the standard coverage, and (2) to carry out the central theme connoted by the name *Basic* Protection.

11. OPTIONAL MODIFICATIONS OF COVERAGE; ADDED PROTECTION BENEFITS.— *Coverage with the standard limits (see paragraph 10), exclusion (see paragraph 17), and deductible (see paragraph 9) is the minimum that qualifies as Basic Protection coverage except that larger deductibles, which result in reduced benefits, are offered on an optional basis at reduced premiums.[63] Policyholders are also offered on an optional basis enlarged coverage, called Added Protection coverage. (See paragraphs 12 and 13.)*

The optional deductibles give the vehicle owner an opportunity to choose coverage somewhat more limited in scope than standard coverage, at appropriately reduced premium rates. There are two types of such optional deductible provisions. First, an individual may choose a provision that

---

[62] *See* KEETON AND O'CONNELL, AFTER CARS CRASH—THE NEED FOR LEGAL AND INSURANCE REFORM 85-96 (1967). *See also* Keeton & O'Connell, *Automobile Insurance Underwriting Through the Perspective of the Basic Protection Plan*, 60 Best's Ins. News, No. 1, p. 22 (Fire & Cas. Ed. 1967).

[63] Section 2.4.

substitutes a figure not exceeding $300 for the figure of $100 in the standard deductible. This modified figure applies to any claim of the named insured, or of a relative residing in the same household, for Basic Protection benefits under the insured's policy. His election does not, however, affect the right of other persons, such as pedestrians or passengers in the insured's car, who are not relatives residing in the same household. Second, one may choose a provision that substitutes for the 10 per cent work-loss deductible a larger work-loss deductible not exceeding 30 per cent, or a deductible not exceeding 30 per cent of all loss. Thus, the policyholder is given an option to apply the deductible to out-of-pocket losses as well as to work loss. This option, if elected, is like the dollar modification in that it does not affect the claim of unrelated third parties.

Added Protection coverage serves a converse need. The Basic Protection package is limited in scope, as is appropriate for minimum coverage. It seems desirable, therefore, to make available broader protection on an optional basis. The opportunity to purchase broader protection might be made available even if the Basic Protection statute said nothing about extra protection and left insurance companies free to develop coverage as they wished. This approach, however, would leave problems with respect to the relationship of the additional coverage to negligence claims. Also, it would not provide for the statutory sections on administering claims to be applied to claims brought under voluntary coverage. Therefore, the Basic Protection statute provides especially for optional Added Protection coverage.

The optional coverages, at increased premium cost, include provisions for Pain and Inconvenience benefits, Catastrophe Protection benefits and benefits for all or any part of any loss excluded from Basic Protection by the several limits, the standard deductible, and the standard extraterritorial exclusion (which excludes out-of-state injuries to persons other than the insured, relatives residing in the same household as the insured, and occupants of the insured vehicle).[64] For example, Added Protection coverage might provide benefits for work loss exceeding the $750 monthly limit. Overlapping between Added Protection benefits and other sources of compensation is avoided by provisions similar to those operating under Basic Protection, especially those preventing duplication of benefits from collateral sources, such as sick leave and Blue Cross,[65] and those that subtract net amounts realized from negligence suits against persons or companies, such as railroads, that are not exempt from negligence claims under applicable Basic Protection insurance.[66]

[64] *See* para. 17 *infra.*

[65] Section 1.10 and 2.5 (b)(2)-(3).

[66] A victim receiving Added Protection benefits is able to claim against someone else's liability insurance company, on the basis of negligence, for amounts already paid as Added Protection benefits, but if successful he then must repay to the Added Protection insurance company. Such a victim would retain any surplus. As the text suggests, this is the same situation that prevails when a traffic victim is paid Basic Protection benefits

Though insurance companies are authorized to offer other types of Added Protection coverage, the only type they are required to offer is a coverage, optional to the insured, providing pain and inconvenience benefits to the insured and members of his family. Insurance companies may offer this or other types of Added Protection coverage in independent policies to persons not owning motor vehicles, as well as to vehicle owners.[67]

12. OPTIONAL ADDED PROTECTION BENEFITS FOR PAIN AND INCONVENIENCE.— *Basic Protection benefits are limited to reimbursement of out-of-pocket losses and provide no compensation for pain and suffering; a policyholder may purchase optional Added Protection coverage for pain and inconvenience benefits.*

Although Basic Protection does not provide compensation for pain and suffering, it does provide compensation for any resulting out-of-pocket loss, such as loss of wages due to severe pain that prevents work. The special provisions concerning optional benefits for pain and inconvenience go beyond this coverage of out-of-pocket losses. Insurance companies are authorized, but with one exception are not required, to offer pain and inconvenience coverage in any reasonable form they wish to develop. They are required to offer coverage providing such benefits at a selected monthly rate to an injured insured, or an injured relative residing in the same household, during any period in which the injured person is completely unable to work in his occupation. The benefits may range from $100 to $500 per month. This statutory form of coverage also provides for payment proportional to partial inability when the injured person is able to do some but not full work in his occupation. Under this statutory form of coverage the limit of liability for combined benefits during both complete and partial disability is 25 times the amount stated as the monthly benefit for pain and inconvenience during complete disability. Thus the maximum amount of pain and inconvenience benefits that can be paid to one victim under this statutory form of coverage is $12,500 ($500 x 25).

13. CATASTROPHE PROTECTION.—*One optional form of Added Protection coverage is Catastrophe Protection, which provides benefits up to $100,000 in addition to Basic Protection benefits.*[68]

after being injured by the negligence of someone, such as a railroad, not among those who are exempt persons under applicable Basic Protection insurance. Sections 1.10(c)-(1)-(2). *See also* Basic Protection 279-80, 402-03, 404-06. In addition, whenever Added Protection payments are made, the insured of the policy under which the payments are made is exempt from any liability for negligence to the payee to the extent of the Added Protection payments. Often this additional negligence exemption is not significant since most Added Protection payments go to the insured's relatives residing in the same household, and the intrafamily immunity in effect in many jurisdictions (see Basic Protection 26) would probably bar negligence claims by such persons anyway. Section 4.3(c)-(d).

[67] Section 10.3.
[68] Section 2.5(b)(3).

Catastrophe benefits come into operation only above Basic Protection benefits, rather than overlapping them. Through a combination of Basic Protection and Catastrophe Protection, a policyholder may insure against all net losses up to $110,000: the first $10,000 is paid as Basic Protection and the remainder as Added Protection benefits. Or, if he chooses, a policyholder may obtain Catastrophe Protection with a deductible of no more than the standard catastrophe deductible, under which 30 per cent of all loss is excluded in calculating benefits. If an individual chooses the standard catastrophe deductible without modification, he will be reimbursed for 70 per cent of his loss above the Basic Protection limits and will bear the other 30 per cent himself.

14.  BASIC PROTECTION COVERAGE COMPULSORY.—*Basic Protection coverage is compulsory in the sense that it is a prerequisite to registering or lawfully operating an automobile.*[69]

We have considered four possible methods of inducing motorists to obtain Basic Protection coverage. The first, which we recommend strongly, is that Basic Protection coverage be made compulsory. If a legislature adopts this recommendation, the compulsory feature of Basic Protection coverage will be quite similar to that of negligence liability insurance coverage in Massachusetts, New York, and North Carolina. The second method requires that a motorist carry either Basic Protection insurance *or negligence* liability insurance. The resulting competition between the two types of insurance might be adopted as a way of testing the new coverage in practice.[70] The principal disadvantages of this course are two: In significant measure, all the inadequacies of the present negligence system would continue; and it would be difficult at best, and perhaps impossible, to assure an evenhanded trial for the Basic Protection system if it were administered by insurance personnel also operating a competing system. Having an investment of experience in the present system, they could not be expected to embrace the novel, competitive system with equal enthusiasm. Furthermore, the handling of negligence liability insurance claims is built on the assumption of lump-sum settlement after considerable delay; unthinking extension by claims personnel of this assumption to Basic Protection claims would impair the effectiveness of the Basic Protection system. Such difficulties might be avoided if a state fund for Basic Protection were established that would compete with private insurance companies also authorized to write this coverage. This route, however, also has its difficulties. On the whole, it seems preferable to make a clean break with the past.

The third method also gives motorists an election about Basic Protection coverage but not an election between Basic Protection and negligence

[69] Sections 5.1-.4, 7.1.

[70] For a method under which property damage insurance of the Basic Protection type exists alongside and competes with property damage liability insurance, *see* paras. 23-26 and Exhibits A and B *infra*.

liability insurance. Rather, each motorist is given the choice of buying automobile insurance for losses up to $10,000 under Basic Protection or not buying it, but under terms that tend to encourage most motorists to buy it, much as a motorist under present financial responsibility laws has the choice of buying negligence liability insurance or not. Under this third method, if a motorist chooses not to buy Basic Protection coverage, he has to pay a substantially higher automobile registration fee than an insured motorist. The extra payments are used to finance a fund, analogous to an unsatisfied judgment fund, that makes Basic Protection benefits available to all victims not otherwise covered, including the uninsured himself and his family. This type of procedure is incorporated in Ontario's negligence liability program.[71] The fourth method is identical to the third except that the special fund does not provide Basic Protection benefits for the uninsured motorist himself or his family. The excess registration fee the uninsured motorist pays is consequently not as far in excess of the fee paid by the insured motorist as is the fee required by the third plan. New Jersey's negligence liability program exemplifies this fourth method.[72]

These third and fourth methods of inducing motorists to obtain Basic Protection coverage are identical in several respects: (1) They leave the motorist free to obtain Basic Protection coverage or not as he wishes; (2) they induce the motorist to purchase this coverage so users of his car will receive a partial exemption from negligence liability; and (3) as suggested above, they establish essentially the same relationship between Basic Protection coverage and financial responsibility legislation that present statutes establish between negligence liability coverage and financial responsibility legislation. A legislature disapproving the principle of compulsory insurance might appropriately adopt the Basic Protection plan with one of these latter two noncompulsory modifications.

15. AN ASSIGNED CLAIMS PLAN.—*Through an assigned claims plan, Basic Protection benefits are available even when every vehicle involved in an accident is either uninsured or a hit-and-run car.*[73]

Sometimes a victim is legally entitled to payment of his claim yet is unable to recover any form of compensation because there is no financially responsible person against whom he can proceed. In this event, there exists a gap between the amount awarded by the system and the amount actually received. In Massachusetts, for example, accidents involving hit-and-run vehicles, stolen vehicles, and out-of-state uninsured vehicles may produce this result. Legislation has been adopted in several states that attempts to close

---

[71] The Motor Vehicle Accident Claims Act of 1962, 10 & 11 Eliz. 2, ch. 84, § 2(2) (Ontario). In 1965 Michigan adopted a vehicle accident claims act patterned after the Ontario act. MICH. STAT. ANN. §§ 9.2801-.2831 (Supp. 1965).

[72] *See generally* N.J. STAT. ANN. §§ 39: 6-61 to -104 (1961), amended by §§ 39: 6-64.1 to -79 (Supp. 1963).

[73] Sections 9.1-.8.

this gap. Three legislative methods have emerged: (1) establishing an unsatisfied judgment fund; (2) requiring that insurance companies offer to include uninsured motorist coverage in all liability policies; and (3) establishing a combination of uninsured motorist coverage and a special fund that provides benefits even in those cases to which no insurance coverage applies.

Unsatisfied judgment funds have been established in North Dakota,[74] New Jersey,[75] Maryland,[76] and Michigan,[77] involving several features of particular significance. The statutes create a state fund rather than relying on private insurance. Under most of these acts the fund is financed in part by a charge upon liability insurers doing business in the state, allocated according to volume of business, and in part by automobile registration and operator's license fees. Costs are held down by provisions for recoupment, to the extent practicable, from uninsured motorists guilty of negligence. The special procedures for processing claims against the funds are generally less favorable to the claimant than those applicable to the ordinary automobile case; for example, special notice is sometimes required.

Of more recent origin are the second and third methods of closing the gap. The second, which merely requires that insurance companies include (or, in some states, offer to include) uninsured motorist coverage in negligence liability policies they issue,[78] makes no provision for compensating the victim who is not himself an insured, a member of an insured's family, or an occupant of an insured vehicle. The third method, developed in New York, relies heavily upon compulsory uninsured motorist coverage in privately written motor vehicle liability policies. Provision is made for payments by the insurance company to satisfy the claims of these insureds and members of their households against uninsured or unidentified drivers, thereby closing most of the gap. The small gap that remains is composed of claims by persons who are neither named insureds of automobile liability policies nor members of the households of such insureds against uninsured or unidentified drivers. This gap too is closed by provision for payments to such persons by the Motor Vehicle Accident Indemnification Corporation (MVAIC), financed by charges on motor vehicle insurance companies based on their volume of business.[79]

One objection to MVAIC, which applies with even greater force to unsatisfied judgment funds, is the dependence upon a state fund. This char-

---

[74] N.D. Cent. Code §§ 39-17-01 to -10 (Supp. 1967).

[75] N.J. Stat. Ann. §§ 39:6-61 to -104 (1961), as amended, §§ 39:6-64.1 to -79 (Supp. 1963).

[76] Md. Ann. Code art. 66½, §§ 150-79 (1967).

[77] Mich. Stat. Ann. §§ 9.2801-.2831 (Supp. 1965).

[78] *E.g.,* Cal. Ins. Code § 1158.0.2 (West Supp. 1966) (authorizing a supplemental agreement waiving this coverage); N.H. Rev. Stat. Ann. § 268.15-a (Supp. 1967); Va. Code Ann. § 38.1-381(b) (Supp. 1966). *See* Basic Protection 111.

[79] *See* Basic Protection 113-15.

acteristic has been viewed by the insurance industry not only as an evil in itself but also as the dangerous "entering wedge" of government-written insurance. We propose to avoid this objection by adapting the principle of assigned risk plans to the problem of the gap.

Assigned risk plans have been developed to meet the need of the undesirable applicant for insurance protection without resort to a state insurance fund,[80] and a similar device might be used to close the gap in financial responsibility. Under the plan proposed, uninsured motorist coverage is automatically included in Basic Protection insurance. This closes a major part of the gap, since most of the victims injured in accidents involving no insured vehicle will be either named insureds or relatives residing in an insured's household and will be able to proceed against their own insurance companies. The remaining claims are those relatively few claims asserted by persons who are neither named insureds nor relatives residing in an insured's household against uninsured or unidentified drivers. These are to be handled through an assigned claims plan to be organized and maintained by Basic Protection insurance companies under rules and regulations approved by the insurance commissioner.[81] The claimant is to file his claim with the bureau of assigned claims,[82] which is to assign the claims in rotation, allocating them to insurance companies on the basis of volume of Basic Protection insurance written in the state.[83] An insurance company is responsible for investigation and defense, as well as payment, of any award recovered on a claim.[84] All insurance companies writing Basic Protection insurance in the state are required to participate.[85] Because of the possible inequality of claims assigned, insurance companies are permitted to create a fund, administered by the bureau, from which the companies can obtain reimbursement of a specified percentage of their outlay incident to this participation. This fund might be financed out of payments from participating insurance companies of an appropriate percentage of the premiums collected for Basic Protection coverage.

If a motorist causing an injury does not carry Basic Protection insurance, he remains subject to liability for negligence, and any negligence recovery of a victim against such an uninsured motorist is subtracted in calculating net loss for which Basic Protection benefits are paid. This arrangement serves both to reduce the cost of the assigned claims plan and to preserve the liability of the uninsured motorist for his negligence.

16.  INJURIES INVOLVING NONRESIDENTS.—*Motoring injuries that occur within the state enacting the plan and are suffered or caused by nonresidents are*

[80] *See, e.g.*, MASS. ANN. LAWS ch. 175, §§ 113H-I (1959).
[81] Section 9.1.
[82] Section 9.7.
[83] Sections 9.5-.6.
[84] Section 9.5.
[85] Section 9.3.

*covered by Basic Protection;*[86] *when no policy in effect applies to such injuries, they are handled through the "assigned claims plan."*[87]

Basic Protection benefits are available when a nonresident, driving alone within the state, runs into a tree, and also when a nonresident is injured through the negligence of another nonresident driving in the state. This inclusive protection is accomplished, however, without requiring a nonresident who is in the state for only a short period to obtain Basic Protection coverage.[88] Such a requirement would be difficult to enforce and perhaps an undesirable restraint on tourism. Instead, coverage of all in-state injuries is assured through the assigned claims plan. For example, a resident pedestrian who is neither a named insured nor a relative residing in an insured's household and is struck by a nonresident motorist may present his claim through the assigned claims plan. The same is true for the injured nonresident driver and for passengers in his motor vehicle. Even though the victim's claim is processed through the assigned claims plan, the nonresident negligent driver causing injury—like the uninsured resident driver who is negligent[89]—remains liable for his negligence, and the victim's net recovery based on negligence is subtracted in calculating net loss for which Basic Protection benefits are due.[90] If the nonresident wishes to avoid liability for his negligent driving, he may obtain Basic Protection coverage for the operation of his vehicle within the state, and he may exercise the option for Added Protection benefits when doing so. Of course, he is less likely than the resident to have the possibility of covering himself for Basic and Added Protection called to his attention.

17. EXTRATERRITORIAL INJURIES.—*Motoring injuries suffered out of state by a person who is an insured, or is a relative residing in the same household, or is an occupant of a vehicle insured for Basic Protection, are covered by Basic Protection;*[91] *except for this provision, no attempt is made to extend the plan to injuries occurring outside the state enacting it.*

It seems wise not to grant the insured an exemption from liability for negligence even in the limited group of cases in which Basic Protection benefits are payable to victims of out-of-state injuries. This is so even though in some instances both the insured and the victim will be residents of the legislating state. If the plan provided that the exemption from liability for negligence applied to extraterritorial injuries and suit were brought in another

---

86 Sections 1.4, 2.2, 2.9.

87 Section 9.4.

88 Section 5.3 requires that a nonresident owner of a vehicle not registered in the enacting state obtain Basic Protection coverage in order lawfully to operate the vehicle in the enacting state for more than 30 days in any calendar year.

89 *See* para. 15 *supra.*

90 Section 1.10(c) (2).

91 Section 2.10.

state in which the accident occurred, probably that state would not be required to give full faith and credit to the exemption.[92] Thus assume that Massachusetts enacts the proposed statute and a Massachusetts insured has an accident in Connecticut in which a passenger of the insured is injured and incurs losses totaling $5,000. In such a situation the victim can both claim Basic Protection benefits and sue the insured for negligence subject to provisions against overlapping benefits. Under this arrangement the Basic Protection policyholder will need negligence liability insurance coverage for out-of-state driving, but both the need for and cost of negligence liability coverage will be less substantial than under the present system.

18. MULTIPLE POLICIES AND MULTIPLE INJURIES.—*Provisions are made for allocating and prorating coverage when two or more policies or two or more injured persons are involved.*[93]

Frequently more than one policy of Basic Protection will be invoked by a single accident. This will be the case, for example, if two cars collide and each is an automobile described in some policy including Basic Protection coverage. If the injured person is a passenger in one of the vehicles involved, ordinarily he must proceed against the insurer or insurers of this vehicle. A pedestrian, or any other injured person not occupying a vehicle involved in the accident, is entitled to make his entire claim against a Basic Protection insurer of any involved vehicle, and, if he claims against only one, that insurer is entitled to contribution from the other insurers to achieve proration of the loss.

19. DISCOVERY PROCEDURES.—*Special provisions are made for physical and mental examination of an injured person at the request of an insurance company and for discovery of facts about the injury, its treatment, and the victim's earnings before and after injury.*[94]

The provisions of the Federal Rules of Civil Procedure concerning physical and mental examination, though controversial when initially adopted, have come to be generally recognized as both equitable and effective. The sections of the Basic Protection Act concerning these subjects are consequently adapted from the Federal Rules.[95] Other provisions for discovery,

[92] *Cf.* Pacific Employers Ins. Co. v. Industrial Accident Comm'n, 306 U.S. 493, 59 S. Ct. 629 (1939). The statute could properly extend the exemption to negligence actions arising from out-of-state injuries that were brought in the legislating state by a resident of that state. Probably the exemption could also be extended to negligence actions on out-of-state injuries brought in the legislating state by a resident of the state in which the accident occurred. Despite the possibility of such extensions, we have chosen to allow the victims of out-of-state accidents that give rise to claims for Basic Protection benefits the right to sue for negligence in the courts of the legislating state. The victim's negligence claim is preserved regardless of whether the state in which the accident occurred, if the negligence claim had been brought there, would have applied its law or the law of the legislating state.

[93] Sections 2.6-.7.

[94] Sections 6.1-.3, 6.8.

[95] See Fed. R. Civ. P. 35 and 37(b).

though generally patterned after the Federal Rules, are more explicit in authorizing discovery of facts about the injury, its treatment, and the victim's earnings before and after injury.[96]

20.   REHABILITATION.—*Special provisions are made for paying costs of rehabilitation, including medical treatment and occupational training, and for imposing sanctions against a claimant when an offer of rehabilitation is unreasonably refused.*[97]

The provisions imposing sanctions authorize court orders reducing or cutting off benefits when a victim unreasonably refuses to submit to rehabilitation.

21.   CLAIMS AND LITIGATION PROCEDURES.—*In general the Basic Protection system preserves present procedures, including jury trial, for settling and litigating disputed claims based on negligence; modifications adapt these procedures to the Basic Protection plan and particularly to periodic payment of benefits.*[98]

A claimant's attorney is entitled to a reasonable fee for his services. In cases involving overdue benefits, this fee, as well as 6 per cent interest on overdue benefits,[99] is ordinarily paid by the insurer in addition to benefits.[100] In cases involving no overdue benefits, half of this fee is ordinarily chargeable against the claimant's benefits and the other half is paid by the insurer in addition to benefits. Provisions are made, however, for allowing part or all of the fees for attorneys on both sides to be charged to a claimant who has asserted a claim that was in some respect fraudulent or so excessive as to have no reasonable foundation.[101]

An adjudication concerning future benefits is not conclusive as to benefits coming due more than five years after the date of the judgment. If the court considers that the evidence of future losses even within five years is unreliable, the judgment is to be conclusive only as to the shorter period for which the court finds the evidence to be reliable.[102]

The right of jury trial extends to claims for Basic and Added Protection benefits if the amount in controversy is at least $5,000, exclusive of interest, and attorneys' fees not chargeable as benefits, and costs.[103] Claims for Basic Protection in lesser amounts are subject to nonjury trial. No administrative board is established. The right of jury trial in negligence suits, as distinguished from suits for Basic Protection benefits, is unaffected in all situations in which negligence claims are preserved.

[96] *See* Basic Protection 469-70.
[97] Sections 6.4-.6.
[98] Sections 3.1-.10.
[99] Section 3.4.
[100] Section 3.8(b).
[101] Sections 3.8-.9.
[102] Section 3.7.
[103] Section 3.10.

22. RULES APPLICABLE IF A VICTIM DIES.—*The benefits of Basic Protection extend to survivors when an automobile accident causes death;*[104] *the exemption (see paragraph 3) applies and special provisions treat the problem of overlapping benefits.*[105]

If a widow or the surviving children of the deceased can prove the facts necessary to support negligence suits under either a typical survival statute or a typical wrongful death statute[106] they are entitled to the benefit of either or both of these suits and to Basic Protection coverage as well. The provisions of the Basic Protection system prevent the overlapping of Basic Protection benefits payable to survivors and recovery in a suit for wrongful death. Basic Protection benefits paid to the decedent or to his estate, however, do not affect the wrongful death claim of the survivors; the possibility of overlapping between these two sources of compensation is so remote that the advantage of providing against it is outweighed by the administrative cost of doing so.[107] Any such Basic Protection payments made to the decedent are, however, credited against the Basic Protection insurer's maximum liability for injury to one person. Consequently, the combined Basic Protection payments to the decedent and his surviving widow and children cannot exceed the per-person limit of liability.[108]

23. PROPERTY DAMAGE DUAL OPTION COVERAGE COMPULSORY.—*Property Damage Dual Option coverage is compulsory in the sense that it is a prerequisite to registering or lawfully operating an automobile.*

Though each policyholder is given an option with respect to property damage coverage, he must carry one or the other of the two types of coverage explained in paragraph 25. This does not force him to carry nonfault coverage for damage to his own vehicle, however. He may, if he prefers, elect instead the negligence liability option, as explained in paragraph 25.

24. COVERAGE FOR DAMAGE TO PROPERTY OF OTHERS.—*Under the Property Damage Dual Option coverage, each policyholder has protection against liability for damage that he negligently causes to others.*[109]

25. COVERAGE FOR DAMAGE TO THE POLICYHOLDER'S VEHICLE.—*The Property Damage Dual Option coverage can apply also to damage to the policy-*

---

[104] Sections 1.9, 1.11.

[105] Sections 1.10(c)(2), 4.3(e).

[106] In general—but not without confusion and overlapping, for discussion of which *see* 2 F. HARPER & F. JAMES, THE LAW OF TORTS § 24.2 (1956)—wrongful death statutes and survival statutes cover different losses. Wrongful death statutes usually allow a suit for the recovery of out-of-pocket loss resulting to the surviving members of a family after the death of one of its members; thus a widow and children may recover for the loss accruing to them after the death of their breadwinner. Survival actions, on the other hand, allow a suit on behalf of the estate of a deceased person for harms he himself suffered *before* death (including medical expenses, pain and suffering, etc.).

[107] *See generally* Basic Protection 382-86.

[108] Section 2.3(e).

[109] *See* para. 25 and discussion thereunder.

*holder's own vehicle, and it is in this respect that the policyholder has a dual option. If he elects what is termed the "Added Protection Option," he is paid for damage to his own car regardless of fault. If he elects what is termed the "Liability Option," he is paid for damage to his own car only if he can prove a valid claim based on the negligence of another person—for example, the other driver in the typical two-car accident.*

The property damage phase of the Basic Protection system is a dual option arrangement in the sense that it includes, operating side by side, Property Damage Liability insurance similar to that now available and a new Property Damage Added Protection insurance, each policyholder being allowed to elect, at the time he applies for his policy, whichever of these he wishes to have applied to damage to his own car.

If one elects the Property Damage *Added Protection* Option when buying automobile insurance, he will receive payment from his own insurance company regardless of fault to cover damage to his own vehicle. Also, in making this election he thereby joins with his insurance company in an agreement doing away with all negligence claims for such loss against every insured under other Dual Option policies, regardless which of the two optional coverages the other policyholder has elected. Thus, if one elects the Property Damage *Added Protection* Option and he has a collision with a motorist who has elected either the Property Damage *Added Protection* Option or the Property Damage *Liability* Option, there would be an agreement among both parties to the collision and their insurance companies mutually exempting each driver from liability for vehicular damage based on negligence.

If on the other hand, one elects the Property Damage *Liability* Option, he will still have his claim, based on negligence, for damage to his car—that is, a claim under which he can recover only by asserting that another driver was at fault and he was not. If the other driver had also elected this *Liability* Option, payment would still be made by the other driver's liability insurance company, just as it is today. But if that other driver had elected the *Added Protection* rather than the *Liability* Option, the mutual exemptions referred to previously (as applying in a collision between two policyholders with Property Damage Dual Option coverage, one of whom had elected the Property Damage Added Protection Option) would also apply to this accident. Thus, if an insured—with Property Damage *Liability* coverage—collided with a policyholder who had elected the Property Damage *Added Protection* Option, he would have no valid claim against the other party or his insurance company for vehicular damage. Rather his claim for the damage to his vehicle would be paid by his own insurance company.[110] He would be en-

---

[110] Note that all the foregoing applies only to vehicular damage. Every policyholder under the Property Damage Dual Option coverage (regardless of whether the *Added Protection* or *Liability* type) would remain liable for damage to property other than vehicles (*e.g.* ruined clothing or a smashed fence) in the same manner as under

titled to payment, however, only if he had a valid negligence claim against the other driver since we are now assuming he elected the *Liability* system rather than the nonfault system.

This device of having a traffic victim claim against his own insurance company on the basis that some other driver was negligent has been in use for many years. It is the key idea of Uninsured Motorist coverage, the very common supplementary coverage in most automobile insurance policies sold today under which the insured's own company pays him for his personal injury losses caused by an uninsured motorist *if* the latter was negligent and the insured was free from negligence.[111] Indeed the analogy between Uninsured Motorist coverage and the Property Damage *Liability* Option is strengthened by the fact that if the other driver was an uninsured motorist, the insured would still be covered under the Property Damage *Liability* Option. Again, having elected the *Liability* system, the insured would have to prove that the other driver was at fault. But having done so, he would be entitled to payment by his own insurance company under what amounts to the uninsured motorist feature of the Property Damage *Liability* Option.

What all this means is that unless neither party to an accident had elected the nonfault *Added Protection* Option, the mutual exemptions provided for in their policies would do away with all claims of each against the other and the other's insurance company for damages to the vehicles. Each car owner would recover, instead, from his own insurance company, according to whichever option he had elected. That is, one who had elected the Property Damage *Added Protection* Option would recover without regard to fault. And one who had elected the Property Damage *Liability* Option would recover only if he could prove that he had a valid negligence claim against the other driver. But, to repeat, in this latter instance, his claim for property damage to his own vehicle would be made against his own insurance company under a new "exempt motorist coverage," analogous to uninsured motorist coverage in the present negligence liability system.

Under this dual option system, if one elected the Property Damage *Liability* Option he would pay virtually the same premiums he would have to pay under the present system for Property Damage Liability Insurance

the present negligence liability system. The Property Damage Dual Option coverage would also cover this liability.

Note, too, that all the foregoing in the text applies only when both cars are covered by the Property Damage Dual Option coverage (whether of the *Added Protection* or *Liability* type). Since the dual option coverage is compulsory this will include almost every car in the legislating state, but it will not include out-of-state cars, nor the few in-state cars illegally uninsured. For those cars, as for property other than vehicles, the old liability system remains in effect, and the policyholder with Property Damage Dual Option coverage will have coverage for his liability for damaging such cars.

111 Commonly, uninsured motorist coverage covers only personal injury losses, not property damage. But some companies do, in some states, include property damage in their Uninsured Motorist coverage.

of the same limits plus that portion of his uninsured motorist coverage applicable to property damage only.[112]

Today, if one wants nonfault coverage for damage to his own car, as well as property damage liability coverage for damage he negligently causes to other vehicles and property, he must purchase both Collision Coverage and Property Damage Liability Coverage, the latter usually with a limit of $5,000 per accident. Under the new plan, if the motorist wanted to cover damage to his own car, he would elect the Property Damage *Added Protection* Option, which would cover all the benefit he can receive under both the Collision and Property Damage Liability Coverages he carries under the present system. His premiums would be a little higher than he now pays for Collision Coverage, but not nearly as high as the *combined* premiums for Collision Coverage and Property Damage Liability Coverage. Among other savings realized would be a sum equal to nearly all the wasteful administrative cost that now goes into subrogation claims whereby one insurance company (a collision insurance company, paying its insured regardless of fault and thereby succeeding to his fault claim) presses its claim against another insurance company (the Property Damage Liability insurance company of the other driver). Also saved is the cost of investigations concerning fault in a great mass of minor accidents involving only vehicular damage.

As indicated in paragraph 23, property damage coverage under the revised Basic Protection plan is compulsory, though it allows each policyholder a choice about which type of property damage coverage he carries. The property damage phase of the system, however, could be implemented on a noncompulsory basis. It might even be possible, at least in some states, to implement the property damage phase without either the associated bodily injury coverage or legislation. In other words, a company could today simply begin offering any policyholder the choice of (1) buying either Property Damage *Added Protection* Coverage or Property Damage *Liability* Coverage with the waivers in such policies operating whenever cars covered by either coverage collide, or (2) buying the type of Property Damage Liability Coverage extant under the present negligence system, with no exemptions. If the second option were selected, the insured's insurance company would always pay others, as it does today, for any property damage he negligently caused them. He would also always have a claim, as he does today, against anyone (or his insurance company) negligently damaging his car.[113] In other words,

---

[112] *See* note 111 *supra* and accompanying text. "Would have to pay," if the present system were continued, rather than "does pay," is a deliberately chosen phrase. Rates will probably continue to rise, of course, with rising repair costs and increasing congestion on the streets and highways.

[113] The Property Damage Dual Option coverage would then protect against negligence claims by those covered under the old form of Property Damage Liability coverage (without any exemption) just as it protects against other claims not covered by exemptions. *See* note 110 *supra*.

companies could simply begin offering the Property Damage Dual Option to those who want to buy it regardless of whether Basic Protection applicable to personal injuries had been instituted by legislation. Consequently, we have prepared policy coverage forms that are designed for use either with or without the supporting legislation.[114] We urge, however, that the Property Damage Dual Option be implemented by legislation because the advantages gained by its introduction will depend in considerable measure on widespread use of the new coverage. This is true because the great savings of the dual option plan occur when both cars in a two-car collision are covered by insurance providing for the mutual exemptions from negligence claims. Thus, to the extent that motorists continue to carry the old-fashioned kind of Property Damage Liability insurance rather than Dual Option coverage, negligence suits for property damage—with all the investigations over fault and subrogation claims by one insurance company against another—will remain to take their wasteful toll. Also, a system in which some policies are still written in the old form while others are written in the new form would be troublesome because of the added complications of meshing not two but three different types of property damage coverage applicable to vehicles—Property Damage Added Protection and the two different forms of Property Damage Liability insurance.

26. MOST NEGLIGENCE CLAIMS FOR PROPERTY DAMAGE ELIMINATED.—*In order to avoid administrative waste that occurs in the present system, the new Property Damage Dual Option coverage, through its system of mutual exemptions, does away with most claims by which one driver's insurance company, after paying for a loss, tries to get its money back from the other driver's insurance company.*[115]

27. THE INSURANCE UNIT AND MARKETING ARRANGEMENTS ARE NOT ALTERED.—*The insurance unit under the Basic Protection plan is the same as under the present system; ordinarily a policy will be issued on a vehicle described in the policy to the owner of that vehicle. It is expected that the new coverage will be marketed in the same way as automobile negligence liability insurance.*

With the marketing arrangements and contracting parties remaining similar to those of existing practice, what will the typical automobile insurance policy contain if the overall Basic Protection system is adopted?

The only compulsory features will be Basic Protection coverage and Property Damage Dual Option coverage. Each of the other features hereafter noted is an optional coverage that we would expect most motorists to purchase. Thus, ordinarily a policy will include: (1) Basic Protection cover-

---

[114] *See* Exhibit A *infra.* For the statutory provisions implementing the Property Damage Dual Option, see Exhibit B *infra.*

[115] *See* discussion under para. 25.

age with limits of $10,000 per person and $100,000 per accident, subject to the standard provisions, including the standard deductible;[116] (2) Liability coverage for bodily injury with whatever limits the policyholder chooses, protecting the policyholder (and others driving the car with permission) against liability for negligent driving in any other state[117] and for liability above the exemption from liability for negligent driving in the legislating state;[118] and (3) Property Damage Dual Option coverage.[119] (This package of insurance does not include Added Protection coverage for pain and inconvenience. Most policyholders will probably forego this coverage in order to save the additional premium cost.)

Note that the Basic Protection coverage will include practically all that is ordinarily included under the present system's (a) negligence liability coverage for in-state accidents up to $10,000 for any person's out-of-pocket loss and $5,000 for any person's pain and suffering;[120] (b) Medical Payments coverage for both in-state and out-of-state accidents;[121] and (c) uninsured motorist coverage for in-state and out-of-state accidents.[122]

The Property Damage Dual Option coverage would include all that is ordinarily included under the present system's (a) Property Damage Liability coverage for damage to other property (including other cars);[123] (b) Collision coverage for damage to the insured vehicle;[124] and (c) Comprehensive coverage for loss by fire, theft and various other risks.[125] One would be free

[116] Paragraphs 9-10 *supra.*

[117] Paragraph 17 *supra.*

[118] *See* paras. 2-3 *supra.*

[119] Paragraphs 23-26 *supra.*

[120] Basic Protection will not cover liability for out-of-state accidents. See paragraph 3 and paragraphs 16-17 *supra. See also* Basic Protection 429-30. It should be noted too that Basic Protection does not include the cost of defending against a liability claim (lawyers' fees, court costs, etc.) which *is* included under present liability coverage. Such defense costs will be covered under the optional bodily injury liability coverage most drivers will purchase, covering liability above the negligence exemption and for out-of-state driving.

[121] Because under Basic Protection, one's own insurance company pays for medical expenses (as well as wage loss) up to $10,000 for accidents both in-state and out-of-state (see paras. 16-17, *supra*) without reference to fault, this will eliminate the need for the medical payments coverage under present insurance under which one's own company pays for medical expenses up to a stated limit of from $500 to $5,000, depending on the insured's option.

[122] Under Basic Protection, one will always be eligible for payment for any accident occurring in-state or out-of-state without reference to fault (see note 121 *supra*) and thus will not need an uninsured motorist coverage to pay for damage done to him by a negligent uninsured motorist.

[123] Paragraphs 23-26 *supra.*

[124] *Id.*

[125] *See* Appendix A, and more particularly the coverage entitled, "Damage to the Insured Vehicle—Added Protection Option," which provides for coverage for "accidental loss of or damage to the insured vehicle regardless of fault," which would include loss by fire, theft, and various other risks. (For an indication that this phrase covers damage by fire, theft, and various other risks, see the next clause in Appendix A entitled, "Damage to the Insured Vehicle—Liability Option," indicating by negative implication that the

to elect the form of Dual Option coverage that omits that part of the new coverage corresponding with Collision coverage under the present system; in other words, to select only the Property Damage Liability coverage. Also, he would be free to elect exclusion of that part of the new Property Damage Added Protection coverage corresponding with the Comprehensive coverage under the present system, though few policyholders would be likely to do so.

## APPENDIX A

### Policy Form[1]

#### Coverage PDDO—Property Damage Dual Option

*Damage to Other Vehicles and Property.* The company will pay on behalf of the insured all sums the insured shall become legally obligated to pay as damages because of property damage caused by accident and arising out of the ownership, maintenance or use, including loading and unloading, of any motor vehicle, subject to the limits stated on the face of the policy. The company shall have the right and duty to defend any suit against the insured seeking damages on account of such property damage, even if any of the allegations of the suit are groundless, false or fraudulent, and may make such investigation and settlement of any claim or suit as it deems expedient.

*Damage to the Insured Vehicle—Added Protection (Non-Fault) Option.* If the insured elects this option, the company will pay for accidental loss of or damage to the insured vehicle regardless of fault, subject to the deductible and limits stated on the face of the policy. In consideration of exemptions under other policies containing options and exemptions consistent with those of this policy, the company and the insured of this policy agree that every insured under either the Property Damage Liability Option or the Property Damage Added Protection Option of every such policy shall be exempt from all claims the company and the insured might otherwise have to recover, by subrogation or otherwise, for such damage accidentally caused to the insured vehicle. To the extent of its payment, however, the company shall be subrogated to the tort claim of the insured for such damage against any person to whom this exemption does not extend.[2]

*Damage to the Insured Vehicle—Liability (Fault) Option.* If the insured elects this option, the company will pay for all accidental loss of or damage to the in-

company under this clause will pay, as it will under the prior clause, for "all accidental loss of or damage to the insured vehicle not caused by collision of the vehicle with another object or by upset of the vehicle . . ." In other words, under the *Liability* Option of the Property Damage Dual Option, the insurance company will pay for all the damage that it pays for under the *Added Protection* Option with the important exception that it will not cover loss of or damage to the insured vehicle caused by collision or upset unless the insured has a valid negligence claim against someone else.)

[1] Copyright 1967 by Robert E. Keeton and Jeffrey O'Connell. Published with permission.

[2] This would apply, for example, to any car not covered by either the Property Damage Liability Option or the Property Damage Added Protection Option. Even if it was compulsory to have one or the other, this provision would apply to out-of-state cars, for example, or cars on the road without insurance, though illegally so.

sured vehicle not caused by collision of the vehicle with another object or by upset of the vehicle, but as to loss of or damage to the insured vehicle caused by collision or upset the company will pay only if the insured has a valid claim in tort against another person in one of the following two classes of persons.

(i) *Exempt motorists.* If such other person is an insured under a policy offering options and exemptions consistent with those of this policy and such other person has elected the Property Damage Added Protection Option, the company will pay to the insured, on behalf of such other person, the sum for which the other person has become legally liable to the insured because of damage to the insured vehicle. The company shall have the right and duty to defend any suit by the insured against such other person seeking damages on account of such property damage, even if any of the allegations of the suit are groundless, false or fraudulent, and may make such investigation and settlement of any claim or suit as it deems expedient. Subject to the exception stated in the next sentence, the company and the insured of this policy, in consideration of exemptions under the Property Damage Added Protection Option of other policies, agree that such other person and his insurer shall be exempt from all claims the insured and the company might otherwise have to recover, by subrogation or otherwise, for such damage accidentally caused to the insured vehicle. If, however, such other person fails to give reasonable assistance and cooperation to the company in defending against a claim that he is liable in tort to the insured of this policy, this exemption, though otherwise still effective, shall not apply in his favor against the company, and the company, if held liable to the insured upon the insured's claim that such other person tortiously caused damage to the insured vehicle, shall be entitled to indemnity from such other person.

(ii) *Uninsured motorists.* If such other person is an uninsured motorist, the company will pay to the insured a sum equal to that for which such other person is legally liable, and to the extent of its payment the company shall be subrogated to the tort claim of the insured against such uninsured motorist as well as any other person liable for such damage and not exempt.

## APPENDIX B

Statutory Provisions Implementing Property Damage Dual Option Insurance[1]

The Commonwealth of Massachusetts
In the Year One Thousand Nine Hundred and Sixty-Eight

### AN ACT PROVIDING FOR COMPULSORY PROPERTY DAMAGE DUAL OPTION INSURANCE FOR ALL REGISTERED MOTOR VEHICLES AND AMENDING AND REPEALING LAWS RELATED THERETO

*Section 1.* Chapter 90 of the General Laws is hereby amended by inserting the following new sections and headings:—

*Section 1B. Exceptions from requirement of Property Damage Dual Option coverage.* With the exceptions provided in section one A,[2] no motor vehicle

---

[1] This draft was designed for use in Massachusetts, along with a bill based on the draft act appearing in chapter 7 of Basic Protection. With slight modifications, it can be adapted to use in other states.

[2] Section one A, which is not herein reproduced, provides that all motor vehicles

shall be registered under sections two to five,[3] inclusive, unless the application therefor is accompanied by proof of security as required by section one C.

*Section 1C. Requirements for registration of motor vehicles.*

(a) *Continuous security*. Except as otherwise provided in section one B, no motor vehicle shall be registered in this state unless the application for registration is accompanied by proof of security for payment of benefits as provided in this section, such benefits to be paid by an insurance company or by other means consistent with the terms of section one D. The owner of each motor vehicle registered in this state shall maintain such security continuously throughout the registration period. If security is terminated for any cause, the owner shall surrender forthwith the registration certificate and number plates of the vehicle to the registrar of motor vehicles unless other security in compliance with this section has been placed in effect.

(b) *Property damage dual option insurance*. To comply with this section insurance must contain provisions as follows, among such others consistent with the terms and objectives of this section as the commissioner of insurance may approve:

(1) *Damage to property other than the insured vehicle*. The company will pay on behalf of the insured all sums the insured shall become legally obligated to pay as damages because of property damage caused by accident and arising out of the ownership, maintenance or use, including loading and unloading, of any motor vehicle, subject to a limit of not less than ten thousand dollars because of damage to or destruction of property of others in any one accident. The company shall have the right and duty to defend any suit against the insured seeking damages on account of such property damage, even if any of the allegations of the suit are groundless, false or fraudulent, and may make such investigation and settlement of any claim or suit as it deems expedient.

(2) *Damage to the insured vehicle—added protection (non-fault) option*. If the insured elects the property damage added protection option, the company will pay for accidental loss of or damage to the insured vehicle regardless of fault, subject to any deductible stated on the face of the policy and to a limit not less than the actual cash value of the vehicle, and subject to any exclusion as to damage caused otherwise than by collision or upset. In consideration of exemptions under other policies containing options and exemptions consistent with this section, the company and the insured of this policy agree that every insured under either the property damage liability option or the property damage added protection option of every such policy shall be exempt from all claims the company and the insured might otherwise have to recover, by subrogation or otherwise, for such damage accidentally caused to the insured vehicle. To the extent of its payment, however, the company may be subrogated to the tort claim of the insured for such damage against any person to whom this exemption does not extend.

(3) *Damage to the insured vehicle—liability (fault) option*. If the insured elects the property damage liability option, the company, subject to any deductibles, will pay for all accidental loss of or damage to the insured vehicle not caused by collision of the vehicle with another object or by upset of the vehicle,

shall be insured (or covered by a substitute form of security) except for certain vehicles, such as those owned by the Commonwealth of Massachusetts or a political subdivision thereof. MASS. ANN. LAWS ch. 90, § 1A (1967).

[3] Not herein reproduced. (The section two *infra* is section two of this enabling legislation.)

except to the extent that damage not caused by collision or upset is excluded, but as to the loss of or damage to the insured vehicle caused by collision or upset the company will pay only if the insured has a valid claim in tort against another person in one of the following two classes of persons. (i) *Exempt motorists.* If such other person is an insured under a policy offering options and exemptions consistent with this section and such other person has elected the property damage added protection option, the company will pay to the insured, on behalf of such other person, the sum for which the other person has become legally liable to the insured because of damage to the insured vehicle. The company shall have the right and duty to defend any suit by the insured against such other person seeking damages on account of such property damage, even if any of the allegations of the suit are groundless, false or fraudulent, and may make such investigation and settlement of any claim or suit as it deems expedient. Subject to the exception stated in the next sentence, the company and the insured, in consideration of exemptions under the property damage added protection option of other policies, agree that such other person and his insurer shall be exempt from all claims the insured and the company might otherwise have to recover, by subrogation or otherwise, for such damage accidentally caused to the insured vehicle. A policy may provide, however, that if such other person fails to give reasonable assistance and cooperation to the company in defending against a claim that he is liable in tort to the insured of the policy, this exemption, though otherwise still effective, shall not apply in his favor against the company, and the company, if held liable to the insured upon the insured's claim that such other person tortiously caused damage to the insured vehicle, shall be entitled to indemnity from such other person. (ii) *Uninsured motorists.* If such other person is an uninsured motorist, the company will pay to the insured a sum equal to that for which such other person is legally liable, and to the extent of its payment the company may be subrogated to the tort claims of the insured against such uninsured motorist, as well as any other person who may be liable for such damage and not exempt.

Section 1D.  *Proof of security.*

(a)  *Certificate of insurance.* Proof of security for compliance with the requirements of section one C concerning payments, options, and exemptions may be provided, with respect to any motor vehicle, by filing with the registrar of motor vehicles a certificate of insurance, by or on behalf of an insurer duly authorized to transact business in this state, of a policy including the insurance required by section one C.

(b)  *Other proof of security.* Proof of security for compliance with the requirements of section one C concerning payments, options, and exemptions may be provided, with respect to any motor vehicle, by any other method approved by the commissioner of insurance as affording security substantially equivalent to that afforded by a certificate of insurance.

Section 1E.  *Proof of security of non-residents.* A non-resident owner of a motor vehicle not registered in this state shall not operate or permit such vehicle to be operated in this state for an aggregate of more than thirty days in any calendar year unless he has on file with the registrar of motor vehicles proof of security for compliance with the requirements of section one C concerning payments, options and exemptions.

Section 1F.  *Applicability of laws governing insurance.* The following laws of the Commonwealth shall apply also to insurance certified as proof of security under paragraph (a) of section one D and, when appropriate, other proof of security approved under paragraph (b) of section one D: The Laws of the Commonwealth regarding assigned risk plans, rate making, policy cancellations and renewals, refusals to issue policies, the regulation of insurance companies, company officers and employees, and agents and brokers, and the illegal operation of motor vehicles. The property damage liability insurance required by subparagraph (1) of paragraph (b) of section one C shall also be subject to the Laws of the Commonwealth that apply to motor vehicle liability insurance generally and are consistent with the provisions of this section and section one C.

Section 2. This act shall take effect on January first, nineteen hundred and seventy, except that insurers authorized to write motor vehicle liability insurance in this state may offer insurance consistent with the terms of section one C at any time after the date of enactment of this bill.

# REMARKS

## OF ALFRED F. CONARD*

I WILL TRY to state briefly something about how the Basic Protection plan[1] will probably affect automobile accident victims.

It is hard for most of us to visualize the consequences of legal norms in the area of injury reparation because the pattern of facts is so unlike that to which we are accustomed. Most of the social facts with which we are familiar can be summarized by a curve in the shape of a bell. Sometimes the bell is skewed to the left or to the right, but whether it is skewed or symmetrical, the great bulk of the cases are clustered around the "typical" case. When you visualize the effect of a proposal on a "typical" case, you are approximating its effect on most of the cases that will exist.

But accident losses fall into a very different pattern. Figure 1 represents economic losses, meaning chiefly medical and hospital expense, damage to motor vehicles, and loss of wages. It is not bell-shaped. It is downhill all the way.

## I. THE CURVE OF ACCIDENT LOSSES

If we presented the statistics in Figure 1 on an arithmetic scale, the slope would be too steep to read, and we still couldn't get very much of the statistics on the chart. In order to get a look at it, we present it in logarithmic intervals, which reach from $10 to $100, from $100 to $1,000, from $1,000 to $10,000, and from $10,000 to $100,000.

The first column, representing losses from $10 to $100 would involve cases where the car bumper was bent and the driver's head was bumped, so that he put an ice-pack on it and was late to work the next morning. Under the current system, these cases are often very generously compensated. If the injury victim collects damages at all, he is likely to collect them for several times the amount of his dollar loss. For instance, the accident costs him $75, but he collects $350 to cover his out-of-pocket loss plus his pain and suffering, plus any chance of future complications.

The second column represents losses from $100 to $1,000. Typically this would mean someone out of work for a week or two, possibly two or three days in a hospital, and a smashed front end of his car. Many of these cases also are compensated by a good deal more than the dollar loss. For instance, a man suffers dollar losses of $300, and collects $750.

* ALFRED F. CONARD. B.A. 1932, Grinnell College; LL.B. 1936, University of Pennsylvania; LL.M 1939, J.S.D. 1942, Columbia University; Professor of Law, University of Michigan.

---

[1] KEETON & O'CONNELL, BASIC PROTECTION FOR THE TRAFFIC VICTIM: A BLUEPRINT FOR REFORMING AUTOMOBILE INSURANCE (1965) [hereinbefore and hereinafter this book is often cited as Basic Protection]. *See also* Keeton & O'Connell, *Basic Protection Automobile Insurance*, p. 40 *supra*.

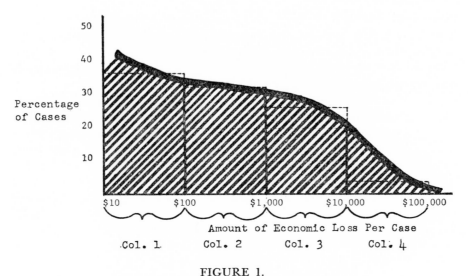

FIGURE 1.

AMOUNTS OF ECONOMIC LOSS SUFFERED BY INJURY
VICTIMS COMPENSABLE UNDER TORT LAW

The third column represents losses of $1,000 to $10,000, suggesting a case where a car is demolished, the victim spends two months in a hospital, and is out of work for half a year. These cases are most likely to be paid, at the most, in rough equality to the dollar losses suffered; but sometimes they are not paid at all, or are paid very much less than is lost, with the result of extreme hardship to the injury victim and his family. However, assuming that the injury victim returns to work, he will probably eventually recover economically as well as medically from his misfortune.

The fourth column represents losses from $10,000 to $100,000. These are the stories of men killed or totally and permanently disabled. The car is demolished, there are fearful hospital bills, and wages are lost for the 10 or 20 or 40 years which remain in the injury victim's life expectancy. These cases are hardly ever overcompensated, and are usually compensated, if at all, by a minute fraction of the economic loss, to say nothing of the pain and suffering. Though the wage losses in such cases naturally run up into the hundreds of thousands of dollars, the prevailing limit on automobile liability insurance means that very few victims ever collect more than $10,000 for an automobile accident. As a result, a disabled individual, or the survivors of a fatality victim, may live in poverty and destitution for the rest of their days.

Now notice the relation of these four columns. Each one is smaller than the one before. There are less victims in the class from $100 to $1,000 than in the class from $10 to $100; and still less in the class from $1,000 to $10,000. If this surprises you at first glance, just think about it, and see if it doesn't correspond precisely to your own observation. For every fatality that you have known, have you not known at least two cases of prolonged hospitalization, but eventual rehabilitation? For every two cases of prolonged hospitalization and eventual recovery, have you not known at least three cases where the victim was back at work in a week? For every three cases of short-term disability, haven't you known at least five cases of loss with no real disability but only some discomfort, torn clothes, and scraped paint?

In short, there are a tremendous number of trivial losses, and a trivial number of tremendous losses. Under tort law, in theory, all of these losses are compensable in full in the presence of primary negligence and in the absence of contributory negligence, and not compensable at all under other conditions. Partly because of the negligence situation, and partly because tactical problems like availability of witnesses and varying skill of lawyers, a great many people in all categories receive no negligence damages. Among those who do recover, the small losers get relatively high reparation, and the relatively large losers get relatively low reparation.

## II.    The Effect of Basic Protection on Reparation for Economic Losses

What we want to know is, how will the Basic Protection plan affect the reparation of these losses? Figure 2 suggests an answer.

The plan will divide them into three classes. First, there are the small losses, under $100. They will be left under the tort law, in which injuries are compensable or noncompensable according to the negligence and tactical balance.[2] But they will no longer be covered by the insurance which every autoist is directly or indirectly bound to carry. Consequently, they will not be paid unless the defendant has bought extra insurance coverage, or can be forced to pay them out of his own pocket. We all know how difficult it is to enforce payment of a small claim by an individual uninsured defendant. The effect of the plan will be to reduce very radically the number of these claims that are paid.

The significance of this change is very great in view of the fact that, remembering the distribution curve, this is the most numerous class of claims. The saving in insurance costs might be very large, considering not only the reduction in total payouts, but also in the expense of administering all these claims.

The second class of losses under the Basic Protection plan embraces the column from $100 to $1,000 and also the column from $1,000 to $10,000, shown in Figure 2 as solid black. These claims will be paid under Basic Protection insurance regardless of fault.[3] This means that a very large number of losses which now go uncompensated under tort law will get compensated under Basic Protection. For the $5,000 losses, meaning a year's wages for a

[2] Keeton & O'Connell, *Basic Protection Automobile Insurance*, p. 51 *supra*.
[3] *Id*. at 52-53, 58-59.

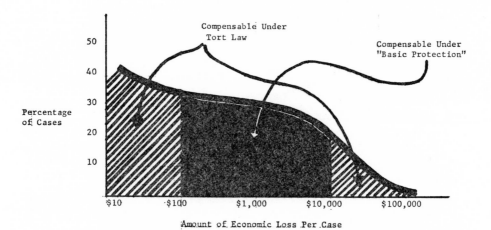

FIGURE 2.

EFFECT OF BASIC PROTECTION PLAN ON REPARATION

working man, there is no doubt in my mind that this is a splendid step. For the $150 to $200 losses, I am not so sure. Is it better for people to have their $200 claims paid by someone else or to take care of them out of their own pockets? It is not without significance that already many motorists choose to buy $200 deductible collision insurance, and to omit collision insurance entirely on cars worth less than $500. You may well ask whether Keaton and O'Connell have drawn this $100 deductible limit at the right place.

With regard to the losses from $10,000 and up, the Basic Protection plan will pay the first $10,000 (less the $100 deduuctible) regardless of fault. After that, the injury victim is on his own under tort law, just as he is today.[4] That is, in theory. In practice, I think lawyers will find it harder to gamble on a $50,000 claim, when they know that if it falls under $10,000, they get nothing by their suit. So I think the net effect of this is to help catastrophic injury victims get their first $10,000, but to make it a little tougher to collect any more than that. Since very few get more than $10,000, the catastrophic injury victims who will benefit by the Basic Protection plan outnumber those who will lose.

This is the heart of the Basic Protection plan, but it is only part of the story, because I have presented only the effects on economic—or out-of-pocket—losses. What about pain and suffering, or "psychic loss"?

### III. REPARATION OF PSYCHIC LOSS

On the reparation of psychic loss, we are really in the dark. We know a lot about the curve of economic loss, because it has been surveyed in Michi-

[4] *Id.* at 50-51.

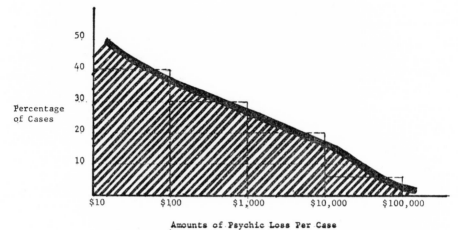

FIGURE 3.

Amount of Psychic Loss Suffered by Injury
Victims Compensable Under Tort Law ? ? ?

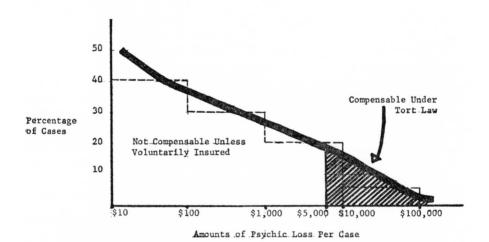

FIGURE 4.

Effect of Basic Protection on Reparation for Psychic Loss

gan,[5] in Philadelphia,[6] and in New Jersey.[7] But what is the shape of the curve for payment for psychic loss? A realistic estimate would assume that it is shaped just like the economic loss curve, as suggested in Figure 3. On this assumption, Figure 4 shows what the Basic Protection plan would do to it. Psychic losses under $5,000 would not be compensated at all. Over $5,000, tort law would allow recovery as before, subject to negligence and tactical contingencies.[8] But the compulsory insurance under the overall Basic Protection plan would not cover these losses,[9] and it would be risky to gamble on a $10,000 claim when you get nothing if it falls under $5,000, unless juries change their ways. However, is it fair to assume that juries would keep bringing in verdicts under $5,000 most of the time which would be nullified by the effect of the Basic Protection plan? Or will the word get around that the plaintiff only gets the amount over $5,000, so that the jury would say, "Well, we think the plaintiff ought to have $1,000, let's award him $6,000"? Lawyers and insurance personnel know juries better than I do. I hope they will figure it out and let me know.

### IV. Time of Payment

Next I would like to tackle the problem of time—the time of losses and the time of payment. This has commonly been called the "delay" problem. Figure 5 indicates the time when losses are incurred, rising very rapidly and very high immediately after the accident, when the victim may be running up a bill of $50 a day for medical and hospital services. Gradually these expenses peak and drop off. After one or two years, the victim is usually either cured, so that he ceases to incur loss, or he is dead or totally disabled, so that loss goes on for the rest of his life or life expectancy at a stable rate.

Figure 6 suggests that under current negligence law, if these losses are paid at all, they are paid in a lump sum, usually close to the time of recuperation, or when the character of the injury becomes stabilized.

This lump sum is very nice when it arrives. But if the injury victim has been lucky enough to receive medical and hospital treatment, and to eat, and to keep a roof over his head during the intervening year or two, it is certainly not because of the tort payment. The tragic fact is that people often fail to get the medical care which they should get, they fail to get the food and shelter which they should get, and they suffer both materially and

---

[5] A. CONARD, J. MORGAN, R. PRATT, C. VOLTZ & R. BOMBAUGH, AUTOMOBILE ACCIDENT COSTS AND PAYMENTS—STUDIES IN THE ECONOMICS OF INJURY REPARATION (1964).

[6] Morris & Paul, *The Financial Impact of Automobile Accidents*, 110 U. PA. L. REV. 913 (1962).

[7] Adams, *A Comparative Analysis of Costs of Insuring Against Losses Due to Automobile Accidents—Various Hypotheses—New Jersey 1955*, Temple U. Econ. & Bus. Bull., March 1960.

[8] Keeton & O'Connell, *supra* note 2, at 50-51.

[9] *Id.* at 62-63.

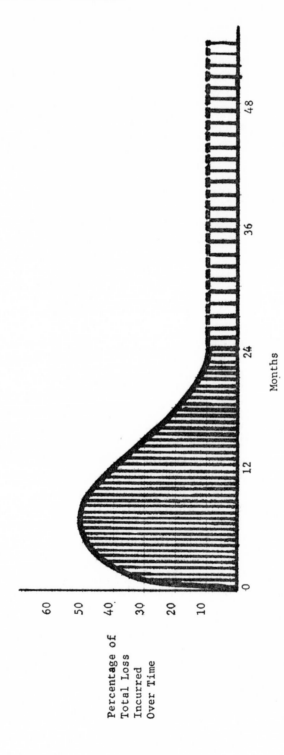

FIGURE 5.
INCIDENCE OF LOSS OVER TIME

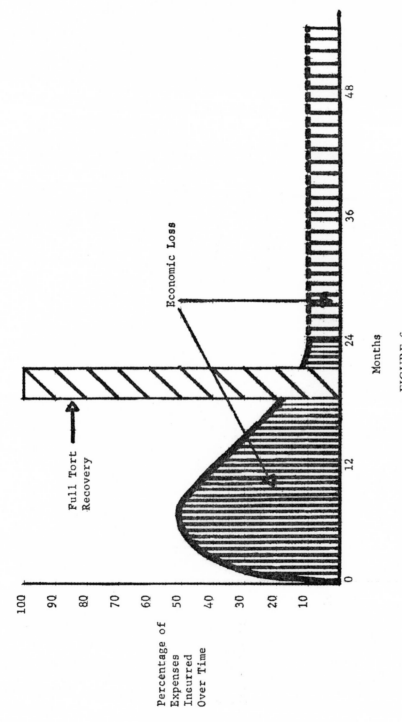

FIGURE 6.

INCIDENCE OF LOSS OVER TIME IN RELATION TO RECOVERY IN TORT

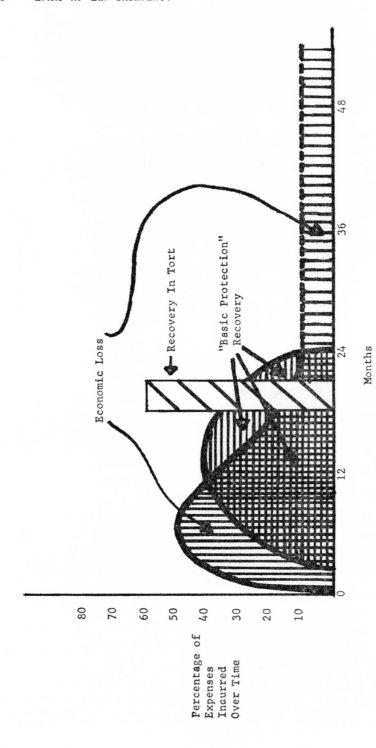

FIGURE 7.

Incidence of Loss Over Time in Relation to Recovery Under Basic Protection and Tort Law

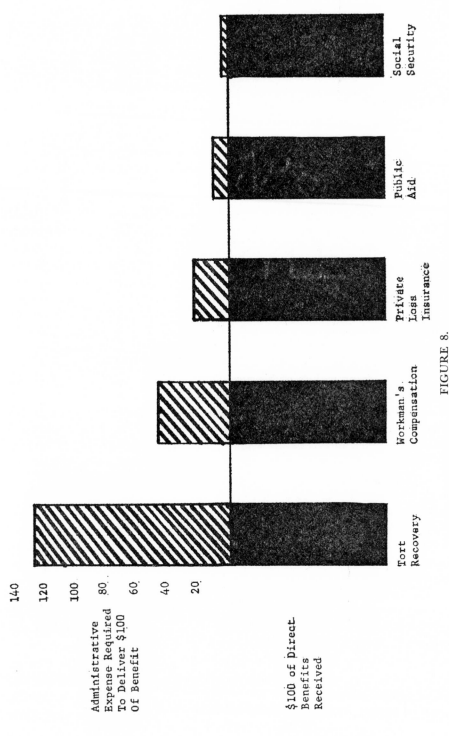

FIGURE 8.

COMPARATIVE ADMINISTRATIVE COSTS OF REPARATION MEASURES

psychically in a heartrending way during the long period while they wait for tort reparation.

Here, the Basic Protection plan proposes a very simple reform, suggested by Figure 7. The horizontally barred hump, which overlaps the vertically barred hump, suggests the incidence of reparation, which would follow very shortly the incurring of losses. Usually, the Basic Protection coverage would run out in a year or two, because it is subject to a $10,000 limit. If the victim has prospective losses after that, he might receive under negligence law a lump sum for the difference between his total loss and his Basic Protection benefits. That would be contingent, of course, upon the negligence situation, and upon collectability.

## V.  Costs of Administration

Another important phase of the reparation picture is the cost of administration, and here we find the most amazing differences among the various systems which are at work on accident cases. At the present time, as Figure 8 indicates, an accident victim may receive reparation from many sources. If the negligence situation is favorable, he may receive reparation from a tort claim, represented by the first column. If the accident happened in connection with his work, he may also receive workmen's compensation benefits, represented by the second column. If he was seriously hurt, some kind of private loss insurance such as life, disability, or health and medical will probably pay something to him or his survivors; that is the third column. If the family is rendered destitute by the accident, it will receive public aid or relief (the fourth column), and if death or total disability ensues, social security benefits will become payable for most of the working population (the last column). In this graph, each solid column indicates $100 of benefit to the injury victim or his survivors. The striped column indicates the administrative expense which is required to deliver that benefit. Starting from the right we see that to deliver $100 of benefit through social security costs about 3 administrative dollars; through public aid about 4 administrative dollars; through private loss insurance about 20 administrative dollars; through workmen's compensation about 50 administrative dollars; and through insured automobile liability about 125 administrative dollars for every 100 benefit dollars.

This analysis of the cost of reparation under tort law is so startling that I think I should give you a little breakdown to indicate how it is made up. Figure 9 indicates that of the total social cost for payments on account of negligence liability for automobile injuries, about one per cent goes to maintain the courts. It seems odd that society cannot afford to supply a few more of them. The next 40 per cent goes to administer the cost of handling liability insurance—selling expense, rating expense, adjustment expense, and the return on capital. There is no room for debate about these figures; they are

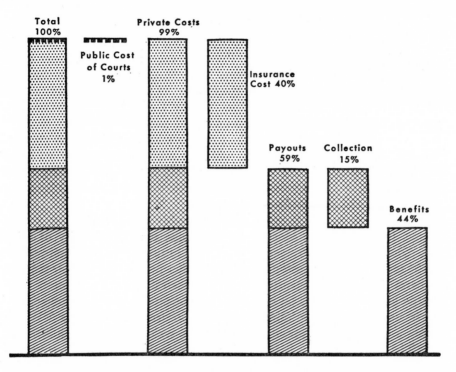

FIGURE 9.
Costs and Benefits of Tort Reparation 1960

discoverable in the casualty aggregates which the insurance industry publishes every year.

You will note that after taking out one per cent for the courts and 40 per cent for the insurance industry, we have 59 per cent left which represents pay-outs for liability. But the victims don't get the entire pay-outs. They have collection expenses, which amount to about a quarter of the pay-out, in the aggregate. In the cases where they hire lawyers, the lawyers collect an average of about 35 per cent of the pay-out. But many victims collect without lawyers, so that the overall collection expense is about a quarter of the pay-out, or another 15 per cent of the total social bill. This leaves about 44 per cent of the total social cost for net benefit.

Now the 64 million dollar question is, how will the Basic Protection plan rate among the others in relation to administrative expense? To condense a long story, it seems to me that the insurance expense will be almost the same as it is under automobile liability. Lawyers' fees may be a little less, either because the court is given express control of them, or because more people will collect without going to lawyers. Thus it is possible that the Basic Protection plan would be efficient enough to incur only $100 of administrative expense for every $100 of net benefit. I think that is the best that could be hoped for.

## VI. Relations with Insurers

A final phase of the Basic Protection plan is its effect on the relations between injury victims and insurers. Presently each automobile owner insures against liability. If an accident occurs between Car 1 and Car 2, the occupants of Car 1 try to collect from the insurers of Car 2 and the occupants of Car 2 try to collect from the insurer of Car 1. The Basic Protection plan would reverse the pattern. The occupants of each car would try to collect from the insurer of that car.[10] The primary advantage from this change is that the insurer and the insureds will deal more harmoniously with each other. The insured will not want to spoil his insurability by making an outrageous claim, and the insurance company will not want to treat claims contemptuously, and thereby lose its customers.

In addition to this benefit, there is possibly another, cited by my colleague, Professor James Morgan, an economist at the University of Michigan. Under the Basic Protection plan, each insurer would be interested not in the tendency of his customers to harm other people, but in their tendency to harm themselves. Consequently, it is conceivable that the insurers would charge higher premiums on cars whose occupants are more endangered.[11] It might cost two or three times as much to insure a Corvair or a VW as to insure a Cadillac. This presumably would be welcomed by Ralph Nader.

The converse effect is interesting if one applies it to collisions between passenger cars and large trucks. There will be no so-called "second collision" in the truck, which will roll relentlessly over an imported compact. Even the truck itself, well armored with a big bumper, is unlikely to suffer any damage. Consequently, the truck owner might get his Basic Protection insurance virtually free.

Of course most people don't want to drive semi-trailers around to cocktail parties, but maybe they could buy Chrysler Imperials. According to the good news recently released in Detroit, the 1968 Imperial will weigh 5,000 pounds without any driver or passengers. This sort of car should pay a very low premium under the Basic Protection plan. I can hardly believe that this will please Professor O'Connell who has scorned the spewing of offensive weapons on the highway.[12]

Realistically, I think that these possible effects of the Basic Protection plan, which are partly beneficial, will be inhibited by another feature of the

[10] *Id.* at 49.

[11] On the topic of the changes wrought by the Basic Protection plan in underwriting considerations, both as they relate to safety and rating of risks, *see* Wolfrum, *Review of Harwayne's Paper*, 53 Proceedings of the Casualty Actuarial Society 164, 172-78 (1966). *See also* Keeton & O'Connell, After Cars Crash—The Need for Legal and Insurance Reform ch. 12 (1967); Keeton & O'Connell, *Automobile Insurance Underwriting Through the Perspective of the Basic Protection Plan*, 68 Best's Ins. News, No. 1, p. 22 (Fire & Cas. Ed. 1967).

[12] J. O'Connell & A. Myers, Safety Last—An Indictment of the Auto Industry (1966); O'Connell, *Taming the Automobile*, 58 Nw. U.L. Rev. 299 (1963).

plan, which is compulsory insurance. When insurance is compulsory, a tremendous pressure develops to keep the rates within the reach of all drivers. Consequently, a free rating of risks will not take place. Anything which an insurer saves on preferred risks he will lose on bad risks which he cannot refuse, and we will all pay premiums which are high enough to cover the insurer's share of irresponsible operators.

## VII. CONCLUSION

In these few lines, I have been able to give you only a glimpse of some probable impacts of the Basic Protection plan. The total impacts will be varied and subtle, and some of them cannot be foreseen. What I have tried very earnestly to do is to offer some statistical facts and concepts which will help each of us to evaluate objectively and impersonally the significance of this historic proposal.

# REMARKS

## OF LOUIS G. DAVIDSON*

I SUPPOSE most of us who have practiced in the courts over the years would agree with Professors Keeton and O'Connell in some degree. But I'm also sure that we would not agree fully with the dimensions of the problem as they outline it.

For example, fraud or exaggeration has been part of the activity of the human animal as long as we have known anything about him. Lawyers think it stays within as reasonable and decent bounds in automobile negligence litigation as in any other area. Furthermore it will not vanish because a switch is made to some other plan.

Similarly we can have no assurance that the problem of delay, which we agree exists in metropolitan centers, will disappear if a switch is made to the Basic Protection plan. Under the plan, all persons hurt will be entitled to be paid, but payment will be subject to the question—and possibly dispute—as to whether the charges being made are reasonable,[1] as to whether the self-employed person has lost the amount of wages he claims up to $750 a month,[2] and as to whether the injury arose out of the ownership, maintenance, or use of an automobile in an accident or occurrence unwitnessed by anyone but the injured party himself.[3]

Certainly, the present system of reparations does not fully and adequately meet all the problems that exist. But by and large, as human systems go, it does a pretty good job. And a great deal has been done to try to improve it and make it a more efficient instrument. Taking for granted, however, that there are matters which should be improved, is the solution proposed in this Basic Protection plan a particularly effective one? I'm sure that its authors—most distinguished and learned scholars—should be willing, and will be willing in this academic atmosphere to examine their own proposal to see where merit rests and where it does not.

First of all, the plan has a deductible for loss below $100.[4] As a result, a motorist out for a ride with his wife and four children who is involved in a minor accident—with medical bills for each slightly under $100—may have to bear an out-of-pocket expense of close to $500. This amount of money

---

* LOUIS G. DAVIDSON, LL.B. 1932, De Paul University; Vice Chairman, Rules and Procedure Committee, Section of Insurance, Negligence and Compensation Law of the ABA; Chairman, Illinois Supreme Court Committee on Jury Instructions, 1966-; Attorney at Law, Chicago.

---

[1] KEETON & O'CONNELL, BASIC PROTECTION FOR THE TRAFFIC VICTIM: A BLUEPRINT FOR REFORMING AUTOMOBILE INSURANCE 280 (1965) [both hereinbefore and hereinafter this book is often cited as Basic Protection]. *See also* Keeton & O'Connell, *Basic Protection Automobile Insurance*, p. 56 *supra*.

[2] *Id.* at 58-59.

[3] *Id.* at 52-53.

[4] *Id.* at 56-57.

might be very important to that family, but they'll have no recovery. The deductible eliminates 20 per cent of the cases, according to one estimate.[5] That's one way to dispose of the problem—sweep it under the rug.

Nor do the plan's problems stop there. Basic Protection insurance pays in those cases with a *net* economic loss of $10,000 or less.[6] Thus, in order to keep rates down and make the plan saleable to the public, the Basic Protection plan will live off other insurance—whether it be Blue Cross or Blue Shield or social security or workmen's compensation. But other companies writing, say, accident and health insurance, may, after a while, balk at paying bills arising from traffic injuries. Why shouldn't they provide in their policies that such insurance will not apply when Basic Protection applies? I'm sure if you were legal counsel advising such health and accident companies functioning in a state where Basic Protection had been adopted, you would so advise your client (if such a step were permissible in that state). Why pay someone else's bills if you don't have to?

We might also ask what is the level at which the Basic Protection plan will eliminate tort litigation? As I read the plan, it will virtually wipe out all automobile tort litigation with very, very few exceptions. If a client comes to a lawyer with a claim ordinarily worth $20,000-$25,000, the lawyer knows that under the Basic Protection plan, the first $5,000 of damages for pain and suffering and the first $10,000 of damages for out-of-pocket loss will be deducted.[7] (Incidentally, why $5,000? Who arbitrarily selected that amount as a fair figure at which to say to a man or woman or child who has been hurt, "You cannot be paid for the real pain and suffering you have undergone"?) Thus the lawyer can fairly charge his client only on that portion above the deduction. Note, too, there will be costs of litigation, not to speak of the gamble involved in most trials. Won't the lawyer be tempted to say to the client, "I'm sorry that I have to tell you that although you're really entitled to more money even under the Basic Protection plan, you cannot afford to litigate this matter." I suggest, therefore, that the tort exemption under the Basic Protection plan does not merely wipe out the so-called small case, as the authors state; it virtually eliminates all other cases with few exceptions.

The plan seeks to work on two levels, and this is part of its problem. While the authors speak of eliminating fraud and exaggerated claims, the remedy is applied only to the so-called under-$10,000 case, but not to the case above $10,000.[8] Certainly the authors don't think that claimants who are seriously hurt are more virtuous or more honest. Perhaps they fear it would shock the conscience of the community to provide explicitly that such per-

---

[5] Marryott, *The Tort System and Automobile Claims: Evaluating the Keeton-O'Connell Proposal*, 52 A.B.A.J. 639, 640 (1966).

[6] Keeton & O'Connell, *Basic Protection Automobile Insurance*, pp. 54-56 *supra*.

[7] *Id*. at 50-51.

[8] *Id*.

sons should not be compensated for severe, crippling or paralyzing injuries.

I would be the first to agree with the proponents of the plan that too much money and too much time of able people is spent in processing the so-called small cases—the case where loss is under $2,000. But I believe that we can retain the rights of persons who have these claims in the proper environment of a court where justice can be done, if they reach litigation. We can process these cases with speedier trials, with six-man juries—five of the six jurors being able to bring in a verdict—with the judge conducting the voir dire, and with jury waivers. In other words, we can streamline the trial of these lawsuits. There are, for example, many ways limiting discovery. The Illinois Supreme Court recently adopted a rule that no discovery be permitted in a case involving less than $500 except by order of court.[9] I would be the first to urge that the limits be raised, because discovery can be one of the great costs to insurance companies in processing small cases.

There are other problems with the Basic Protection plan. There are problems if the automobile goes outside the enacting jurisdiction.[10] There are problems if an insured buys Basic Protection coverage and then doesn't buy coverage for a tort claim that may be filed against him;[11] note that even with Basic Protection insurance, an insured is exposed to a tort suit for the first $100 of loss[12] and for loss above the tort exemption in his own jurisdiction,[13] as well as to total tort liability outside his jurisdiction.[14] All of these are troublesome problems, I am sure, for the proponents of the plan, as well as for the rest of us.

I don't think that lawyers approach this or other proposals with the idea that they are necessarily going to oppose change. A lawyer's professional training and experience is such that the lawyer is generally inclined to examine problems objectively. Moreover, if we serve no useful function for society in the role we're performing, then we will atrophy. Society will find another way, and do without our services. So we *must* look at this problem objectively. And it is on an objective basis that I protest a solution which, in effect, takes away an arbitrary amount of damages for pain and suffering, and which makes it impossible, to recover damages for disfigurement.

I know that the plan as proposed is not inflexible; it is going to grow and change and be adapted. Perhaps it will reach a form acceptable to the public; but in its present state, some of its confiscatory provisions make it unacceptable. Once the public understands this, it will reject it. Perhaps this

[9] Ill. S. Ct. Rs. 281 and 287. (The new Illinois Supreme Court Rules, effective Jan. 1, 1967, may be found in Sullivan, Law Directory pt. 2, at 131.)

[10] *See* Keeton & O'Connell, *Basic Protection Automobile Insurance*, pp. 66-67 *supra*.

[11] *See id.* at 50-51.

[12] *Id*. at 51.

[13] *Id*. at 50-51.

[14] *Id*. at 67.

is unfortunate because, undeniably, there is a problem, and it needs attention and a solution. But we cannot accept a solution that—except for a miniscule number of cases—renders obsolete in the field of automobile litigation and claims, the whole body of law and thought developed by the courts and lawyers and insurance men for more than half a century. Literally millions of man hours have been devoted to structuring the present system, all of which will become meaningless, except, as I say, in the very small handful of cases left to the negligence system.

It has been estimated that under the Basic Protection plan 80 per cent of traffic accident victims in New York would get less than they now receive. Thus the plan will take benefits away from those who under our present system of law are entitled to compensation in order to compensate the driver who is at fault, the driver in the single-car accident, and the victim of the unavoidable accident. Note that although the plan will compensate the drunken driver, it retains some element of the fault reasoning, because it will not benefit the man who intentionally causes or suffers harm.[15] Is it equitable to take away from those whom society today deems fairly paid in order to compensate this other group?

Likewise, a person who would take out Basic Protection insurance does not thereby acquire public liability insurance. He only has another form of accident and health insurance. Thus the plan makes no provision for defense of actions which might be brought against the insured. If one were sued in an accident, he would have to employ attorneys and obtain his own defense—unless he bought other insurance to provide this protection.

If everyone who is hurt is to be compensated, why tie compensation into a motor vehicle plan? Why not extend compensation all across society? People may slip on a floor in their apartment and be badly hurt and need help. Why not take care of them too? On the other hand, if we do approach the problem this way, I don't hesitate to say that this can only lead to government insurance. It won't stop short of that.

Since 1946 Saskatchewan's automobile insurance system has covered everyone on a nonfault basis and is government operated.[16] Under Saskatchewan's plan, incidentally, no one receives less than he would have under the tort system. Rather, the amount of the nonfault insurance—payable to all—is deducted from any recovery payable to those who are entitled to recover under the tort criterion.[17] There has been much dispute among scholars and experts as to whether you could transpose the Saskatchewan plan to the United States with its more urban, motorized society.[18] But it is interesting

[15] *Id.* at 52-53.
[16] The Automobile Insurance Act, Saskatchewan Rev. Stat. c. 409 (1965), as amended March 15, 1967, 16 Eliz. 2, c. 89 (Saskatchewan).
[17] Saskatchewan Rev. Stat. c. 409, § 77(1) (1965).
[18] Basic Protection 146-48.

to note a system of nonfault automobile insurance, so long in operation, where nothing is taken from the public but rather everyone has at least what he had under the tort system, with some getting more.

During the years that I have worked in this field, I have not had the feeling that people are being unjustly enriched; I have had the feeling that people are usually well-entitled to every dollar they get; that no one wants an accident, no one wants to be hurt, and no one wants a claim. But if accident and injury should happen to him, at least he should have the opportunity of being taken care of under the present system.

Do not underestimate the flexibility of the present fault system. Recently, for example, in Illinois we have seen adoption by judicial decision of the comparative negligence doctrine to ameliorate any harshness or injustice accompanying the rule of contributory negligence.[19] I suggest that the proper solution is to be found in the present fault system by exploiting its flexibility and adapting it to meet the needs of our modern society.

[19] Maki v. Frelk, 85 Ill. App. 2d 439, 229 N.E.2d 284 (2d Dist. 1967).

# THE BASIC PROTECTION PLAN: REFORM OR REGRESSION?

*BY JAMES S. KEMPER, JR.**

THE KEMPER INSURANCE GROUP retained Professors Keeton and O'Connell in August 1966 as independent consultants to help us understand and evaluate their Basic Protection plan. Over a period of six months ending in March 1967, they conducted 12 workshops for us, involving more than 200 of our key management, professional, and technical personnel. During the following six months—in fact on a continuing basis culminating in our preparation for this conference—a special group drawn from the actuarial, statistical, claims, legal, marketing, and underwriting functions has been studying the implications of the plan. At the general management level, working with the data and the findings of this special study group, we have explored its political and social implications. Our studies have reached sufficient depth to enable us to arrive at some conclusions.

Because we have thus had the benefit of consultation with the authors themselves and the opportunity to mount our own studies upon the experience afforded by this unique client-consultant relationship, I intend to devote most of my remarks to the Basic Protection plan proposed by Professors Keeton and O'Connell. It should be understood, of course, that I speak only for the group of companies of which I am an officer, and that I do not speak for any other insurance company or any trade association.

By way of preface, however, I do want to comment on the posture of the automobile insurance industry as a whole in the matter of proposed improvements or reforms of the system. It has been said by some that we have not listened to responsible criticism and that the reaction of the insurance industry to the Basic Protection plan has been one of indifference or precipitous rejection—somewhat akin to the reaction of auto manufacturers to criticisms of vehicle safety.[1]

The Kemper companies have reacted with keen interest to the possibilities suggested by the Basic Protection plan. In fact, they have been exempted from the charge of indifference.[2] Thus, it seems fitting for me to challenge the assertion that the industry as a whole has failed to give Professors Keeton and O'Connell a proper hearing.

Of course, the charge is absurd.

* *JAMES SCOTT KEMPER, JR. B.A. 1935, Yale University; LL.B. 1938, Harvard University; President and Chairman of the Executive Committee of the Chicago-based Kemper Insurance Group—Lumbermens Mutual Casualty and American Motorists Insurance Company.*

[1] Moynihan, *Next: A New Auto Insurance Policy*, N.Y. Times, Aug. 27, 1967, § 6 (Magazine), at 26.
[2] *Id.* at 82.

In a well-publicized speech shortly after publication of the full text of the Basic Protection plan, Guy Mann of the Aetna group urged a joint study by the three principal trade associations of the entire system of compensating automobile accident victims.[3] Since publication of the plan the insurance industry has openly and genuinely welcomed this significant contribution to the effort we have been making for at least a decade to find and use ideas for improving the automobile insurance system. Certainly the plan's authors have no reason to feel rejected: it is no exaggeration to say they have been virtually lionized by the insurance industry during the past year and a half. Their plan has been the subject of more complimentary speeches by top insurance executives than any other topic relating to auto insurance in the past decade. They have been invited by companies, producers, and professional insurance associations to explain, discuss, and debate their proposal from one end of the country to the other. Of considerable significance is the fact that the three principal trade associations are conducting studies of the Basic Protection plan on a priority basis.

There is a too-easy assumption by some social critics that because an entire industry does not instantly embrace a proposal which will work vast changes in that industry, this connotes indifference or resistance to change. It can just as well, and in this case does, connote a prudent concern for the public interest.

## I.    The Basic Protection Plan

Everyone in this conference has read and studied the full text of the proposal: *Basic Protection for the Traffic Victim.*[4] You are also familiar, at least in a general way, with the many prior proposals made during the past 50 years for introducing some type of non-fault element into the bodily injury and property damage coverages.[5] The statutory expression of the Basic Protection plan is the definitive source for information about its provisions.[6] Here I will simply summarize its principal features.

The Basic Protection statute establishes, within certain limits, a compulsory[7] two-party[8] accident insurance system in place of liability insurance.[9] It abolishes the common law doctrine of tort liability where damages for pain and suffering are less than $5,000 and economic loss is less than $10,000, but preserves the tort liability system for pain and suffering and economic

---

[3] National Underwriter, Oct. 29, 1965, p. 2.

[4] Keeton & O'Connell, Basic Protection for the Traffic Victim: A Blueprint for Reforming Automobile Insurance (1965) [both hereinbefore and hereinafter cited as Basic Protection]. *See also* Keeton & O'Connell, *Basic Protection Automobile Insurance*, p. 40 *supra*.

[5] *See* Basic Protection ch. 4.

[6] *Id*. ch. 7.

[7] Keeton & O'Connell, *Basic Protection Automobile Insurance*, pp. 62-63 *supra*.

[8] *Id*. at 49-50.

[9] *Id*. at 49-51.

loss in higher amounts.[10] Provision is made for the purchase of optional supplementary coverages beyond Basic Protection limits,[11] and the establishment of an assigned claims plan for certain non-covered accidents.[12] This plan abolishes the right to trial by jury for Basic Protection benefits where the amount of money in controversy is less than $5,000,[13] and abolishes the collateral source rule by providing mandatory deductions for workmen's compensation, group and individual accident and health, wage continuation, Blue Cross, Blue Shield, Medicare, Medicaid, and Social Security benefits.[14] It establishes additional deductibles as well as a 15 per cent deduction to recognize the tax-free status of wage-loss awards.[15]

The authors have described the principal purposes and claimed advantages of the Basic Protection plan as follows: (1) It will substantially reduce the cost of bodily injury coverage, by lowering administrative and legal expenses charged to the system. (2) It will produce a more equitable distribution of loss payments among claimants. (3) It will speed up claim payments. (4) It will greatly reduce court congestion. (5) It will reduce fraud in accident claims.

Each one of these claimed advantages relates to an important problem: (1 )Auto insurance costs have been rising (although to a far less degree than many other products and services). (2) Some claimants are paid too much, some too little, and some not at all. (3) Some claim settlements, perhaps three per cent to five per cent of the total, are delayed because they are tried in court or require prolonged negotiation. (4) Some courts, notably in about a dozen large metropolitan areas, are woefully behind in their dockets. (5) There is indeed a great amount of fraud in accident claims.

It should be noted, however, that the authors of the plan do not claim that it will have any effect on other major automobile insurance issues, such as insolvencies, cancellations, market restrictions, and the mounting traffic accident toll. (I mention these subjects because some supporters of the Basic Protection plan have apparently misunderstood the plan and think it may be a panacea for all our problems.) In each of these areas, I think we have reason to take comfort in the strides which have been made under the present system:

> *Insolvencies* are rapidly being eliminated as a problem. The growing acceptance of mandatory uninsured motorist coverage with added insolvency protection, combined with strict regulatory legislation such as the recently enacted Illinois plan,[16] will eliminate even the small

10 *Id.*
11 *Id.* at 59-61.
12 *Id.* at 63-65.
13 *Id.* at 68.
14 *Id.* at 54-56.
15 *Id.* at 54, 56-58.
16 Senate Bill No. 183, 75th Gen. Assembly, June 28, 1967, which amends § 143a of

fraction of one per cent of premiums written by companies which failed.

*Cancellations*, which have never involved more than one per cent of all policies country-wide, have become even more limited under the industry-supported, model legislation which is rapidly spreading among the states.

*Market restrictions*, which are a direct function of inadequate rates, are being alleviated by the growing tendency of states to legislate open competition for the industry, by the rapid growth of special risk companies as marketing affiliates of financially sound and responsible underwriters, and by better public understanding of the existence and operation of assigned risk plans.

*Traffic safety legislation* passed by Congress, and implemented by vehicle and highway safety standards, gives real promise of a major improvement in the area which is endemic to the whole "automobile insurance problem"—the spiralling losses for which the system must pay.

In all of these problem areas we are making good progress—encouraging progress—within the framework of the present system of marketing and regulation.

## II. The Kemper Insurance Study

Against this background, I will report the essence of our own conclusions about the Basic Protection plan. It may be of interest that we took an informal poll of a representative cross section of those who participated in the Keeton-O'Connell workshops. Most of those polled included our younger management, professional, and technical people. Nearly 100 per cent felt that improvements were necessary; more than 60 per cent rejected the Basic Protection plan as the preferred method of making improvements; of the remaining 40 per cent a few favored the plan, but most felt that not all aspects of the plan were desirable and only some should be incorporated in any broad program for change. We have identified 12 major problems, weaknesses, or unresolved issues in connection with the plan.

### A.  Objections to Claimed Advantages

First, I will discuss those questions which apply to the five principal advantages for the plan claimed by its authors, to which I have already referred.

### 1.  Cost Reduction

Will the Basic Protection plan reduce the cost of bodily injury cover-

the Illinois Insurance Code. The amendment expands uninsured motorist coverage to include motor vehicles where the liability insurer is unable to make payments because of insolvency on or after accident date. Coverage is restricted to bodily injury or death resulting from accidents occurring before insolvency in limits in amounts of $10,000 per person, and $20,000 per accident. Ill. Rev. Stat. ch. 73, § 755a (1967).

ages? Mr. Harwayne, in his frequently cited actuarial study,[17] estimated cost savings ranging from a low of 11 per cent to a high of 24 per cent on those coverages if the plan were introduced in New York. This would mean a saving of only 5 per cent to 11 per cent on the total cost to the individual New York policyholder of the complete automobile insurance package including physical damage. The latest available average annual premium for this package of coverages in New York is $192.00, or $16.00 per month. On this basis, assuming the validity of all of the assumptions upon which the Harwayne study was predicated, as well as the accuracy of its conclusions, there is a projected saving ranging from a low of 80 cents to a high of $1.75 per month for the average individual New York State policyholder. The question must be asked: is the gamble on so modest a saving worth the other consequences of enacting the plan?

On the other hand, the chief actuary of the Massachusetts Department of Banking and Insurance, Mr. M. G. McDonald, estimated last month that if the plan were introduced in Massachusetts the cost of coverage required by statute for private passenger car owners would increase from 19 per cent to 35 per cent. Other actuarial studies have predicted a wide variety of results, nationally and in individual states. From the studies made by our own actuaries, we conclude that no estimate thus far presented is sufficiently reliable to form an adequate basis for decision.

### 2. *Distribution of Loss Payments*

Will the plan produce greater equity? Certainly it will eliminate those cases where, because of contributory negligence or the lack of a third-party tortfeasor, a claimant receives nothing; and this is a strong point in its favor. But those hardship cases so movingly described by the authors and others to induce resentment against the present system can be countered by equally moving recitals of hardship cases produced by the Basic Protection plan. Is it equitable to pay benefits to the drunken driver, the convicted felon fleeing from his crime, the drag racer and the multiple accident repeater, and deny full recovery to innocent victims such as housewives and children whose economic loss will be limited mainly or entirely to medical bills, and who will recover nothing for pain and suffering unless the damage exceeds $5,000?

The Basic Protection plan assumes that no one should be paid for $5,000 worth of pain and suffering, but that above that amount payment is socially

[17] Harwayne, *Insurance Cost of Automobile Basic Protection Plan in Relation to Automobile Bodily Injury Liability Costs,* 53 PROCEEDINGS OF THE CASUALTY ACTUARIAL SOCIETY 122 (1966). *See also* Keeton & O'Connell, *Basic Protection and the Costs of Traffic Accidents,* 38 N.Y.S.B.J. 255 (1966). For another actuarial report by Harwayne concerning the comparative costs of Basic Protection and tort liability insurance in a midwestern state—Michigan, *see* Harwayne, *Insurance Costs of Basic Protection Plan in Michigan,* p. 119 *infra.*

desirable. What equitable principles dictate this assumption? This is a social question of considerable importance, and it needs to be carefully weighed, not only by people such as those attending this conference, but by a well-informed public.

### 3. Speed of Claim Payments

Will this plan expedite claim payments? The assertion is made that the whole process will be far simpler than at present—that settling an auto accident claim will be "just like dealing with your own fire insurance company." There is little real basis for comparison. A fire insurance claim is for a definite, ascertained amount and it is settled in a lump sum. Claims under Basic Protection would involve significant variables, such as the existence of collateral source payments, claimant income levels, extent of rehabilitation and recovery, and the like. They are paid monthly, and can vary from month to month. Even explaining how the figures are computed to the average claimant would be a difficult task: examine, for example, section 1.9 of the proposed act,[18] dealing with the computation of loss, and the illustration of the mathematics involved.[19] In addition, the retention of tort liability in the more serious cases makes every case involving more than superficial injuries a potential lawsuit to be investigated by the liability carrier.

It is exceedingly difficult to picture a speeding-up of claim settlements in comparison with the prompt payment of the great majority of claims under the present system. Furthermore, the program of "Advance Payments and Rehabilitation"[20] is being offered by more and more insurance companies. Prompt payment of medical expenses and regular household expenses which will minimize immediate economic hardship promises to eliminate a large part of the claim payment problem at which the Basic Protection plan is focused.

### 4. Court Congestion

It is argued that, since up to 75 per cent of automobile injury claims will be embraced by the Basic Protection plan, court congestion will be drastically reduced. In fact, this is perhaps the weakest claim made for the plan. It is stoutly contradicted by many respected judges and law professors, including Chief Justice Tauro of the Massachusetts Superior Court, Professor Harry Kalven, Jr., of the University of Chicago Law School, and Professor Milton D. Green of Hastings College of Law. These critics point out, among other things, that it is doubtful if personal injury litigation is the principal

[18] Basic Protection § 1.9, at 305-06.

[19] *Id.* at 399-400.

[20] Under the so-called "advance payments" plan, a tort liability insurer will make payments in cases of clear, and in some cases probable, liability, to cover medical expenses and other out-of-pocket loss prior to the determination of liability, without requiring a release from the recipient. Such payments, however, are deducted against any final payment. *See* Wall St. J., Jan. 13, 1967, p. 1, col. 6.

or even a significant cause of court congestion. In fact, the Basic Protection plan is likely to increase the burden on civil judges.[21]

By preserving tort suits for the more serious claims, the plan would finance the bringing of an avalanche of such actions, since the claimant will have everything to gain and little to lose if he tries for the jackpot. Even more important, the statute implementing the plan makes administrative tribunals out of the courts. The administrative details to be policed by the courts are simply horrendous. It seems highly probable that congestion in those few metropolitan court systems that now have the problem will be unrelieved or increased, and that congestion will become a problem for that part of our judicial system which is now free from it.

### 5. Fraud

Will the Basic Protection plan lower the incidence of fraud? Automatic payment of claims without the need to prove the negligence of the other driver and one's own freedom from negligence will clearly eliminate the kind of subjective testimony which frequently deserves no other name but fraud. To more than balance this benefit, the definition of injury under the Basic Protection statute as "bodily harm, sickness or disease . . . arising out of the ownership, maintenance or use of motor vehicle as a vehicle"[22] is a broad invitation to fraudulent claims based upon the unwitnessed accident. It will be almost impossible to defeat a claim for any household injury, for example, if the claimant asserts he suffered it while getting in or out of his car, washing the car, or otherwise using or maintaining it. There is also a vast potential opportunity for fraud in the concealment of collateral source benefits which, if disclosed, would reduce the amount of recovery. We do not believe the Basic Protection plan will reduce fraud.

### B. Other Objections

Thus, as to each of the five principal advantages claimed by its authors for the Basic Protection plan, we conclude they have failed to sustain the burden of proof which society must require of those who seek drastic change in a major social and economic system. We also found other apparent defects.

### 1. Constitutionality

The authors of the plan admit that it is unconstitutional in all states where the constitutions prohibit any limitation upon the amount recoverable for injury.[23] It is probably unconstitutional in states like Illinois and Massachusetts whose constitutions guarantee a remedy certain for injuries or wrongs without an obligation to purchase it.[24] Beyond this, our attorneys

---

21 *See, e.g.*, Green, *Basic Protection and Court Congestion*, 52 A.B.A.J. 926 (1966).
22 Basic Protection § 1.4, at 303.
23 *Id.* at 504-05.
24 ILL. CONST. art. II, § 19; MASS. CONST. pt. 1, art. XI.

are of the opinion that the authors' analogy to workmen's compensation insurance[25] will not stand up, and that the Basic Protection plan will be struck down as a violation of the due process and equal protection clauses of the federal and state constitutions. A similar result has been suggested by other members of the bar.[26]

One consequence of the doubt in this area could be disastrous: if a state legislature passed the Basic Protection statute, the system might be instituted and operating before a ruling of the United States Supreme Court on its constitutionality; and the Basic Protection plan represents an irrevocable step. Trying to return to the tort liability system to meet constitutional requirements would be like trying to unscramble an egg.

### 2. Distribution of Costs

Under the Basic Protection plan, a large portion of the insurance cost is shifted from those people most likely to cause accidents to those persons likely to collect the most money as a result of accidents. There will be a major redistribution of premiums, with some socially dubious results.

Commercial trucking concerns, operating fleets of trucks over long distances with heavy use of roadways, will pay less than they now do because of the collateral source benefit of workmen's compensation insurance, while a school district, operating a fleet of buses over short distances with light roadway use, will pay a larger share. A college student with a small sports car will pay relatively less, while a middle-aged, middle-income family man with a sedan or station wagon and several children will pay relatively more than he now does. The plan will definitely create discrimination in costs against the farmer, the small entrepreneur such as a shopkeeper, and against a high proportion of those who dwell in villages, towns and small cities, since relatively few of these people will be entitled to rate credits because of workmen's compensation and group accident and health insurance benefits.

### 3. Rating

This plan will create a nightmare for actuaries. At a session of the Mutual Insurance Claims Conference last May, Professor O'Connell himself stated:

> "If I had a business as dependent as yours is on actuarial experience of the past, I would be reluctant to see the rules changed very radically because one of my assets—that is, the effect of the past on the future—is greatly undercut in terms of its validity. The industry has feared this, and I suppose the industry has also feared, rightly, that there isn't a logical correlation between what happens and what kind of rates you

---

[25] Basic Protection 485-87.

[26] *E.g.*, Knepper, *Alimony for Accident Victims?*, 15 DEFENSE L.J. 513, 536-38 (1966), *reprinted in* INSTITUTE OF CONTINUING LEGAL EDUCATION, PROTECTION FOR THE TRAFFIC VICTIM: THE KEETON-O'CONNELL PLAN AND ITS CRITICS 179, 206-09 (Mich. 1967).

get. It often becomes a jungle where cause and effect are very confused, as you know much more bitterly than I."

This is really an understatement. It is our opinion that the plan will require such a tremendous range in rates as to be incomprehensible to the public; the total number of "undesirable" risks going into assigned risk plans will probably be increased; and the reliance on honest disclosure of collateral source benefits will be so great as to introduce a permanent element of inequity into any rating system which may be devised.

### 4. *Abolition of the Fault System*

A main criticism of the fault system by Professors Keeton and O'Connell is that complex time and distance relationships prevent accurate testimony, and that parties and witnesses are subject to the temptations of perjury and invention.[27] They urge that juries cannot reach fair verdicts under such circumstances.[28] We feel that the authors' retention of fault for serious cases is irreconcilable with this point of view: it is the handling of the serious injury cases which has provoked the most trenchant criticism of the present system. Do witnesses and parties testify with greater honesty when the case is worth more than $10,000 in economic loss and $5,000 in pain and suffering? Are juries wiser and more even-handed when the case is a big one?

Moreover, most judges and trial lawyers believe that a jury will reach an equitable result in cases involving facts far more complex than those normally involved in an accident case.[29] And in support of this thought I can again quote Professor O'Connell, at the same Mutual Claims Conference:

"I think that Professor Kalven's studies of juries have been very heartening in terms of how seriously they take their duties. The facts would seem to indicate they are exceedingly sophisticated; they are increasingly aware that this is not a game of Santa Claus."

The question must be asked: why should we arbitrarily decide that juries may be trusted to fix liability accurately in the larger cases, but not in the smaller ones?

### 5. *Interstate Complications*

Ours is a nation on wheels. Millions of automobiles are driven each year from state to state, indeed from coast to coast, creating hundreds of thousands of interstate accident situations.

A description of some situations that will undoubtedly occur will serve to illustrate the problems that will arise. Assume Michigan has enacted the Basic Protection plan and Illinois has not:

[27] Basic Protection 15-22.
[28] *Id*. at 22-34.
[29] *E.g.*, BLUM & KALVEN, PUBLIC LAW PERSPECTIVES ON A PRIVATE LAW PROBLEM—AUTO COMPENSATION PLANS 9-12 (1965), *published earlier as an article*, 31 U. CHI. L. REV. 641, 647-49 (1964).

(a) If a reckless driver from Illinois runs into a tree in Michigan, he collects Basic Protection benefits from the Michigan assigned-claims fund which has been financed by money taken from Michigan's motorists.[30]

(b) If an Illinois driver collides in Michigan with a Michigan driver, both collect Basic Protection benefits,[31] but the Illinois driver may retain his right of action in Illinois if he can serve the Michigan driver.

(c) A Michigan driver who has an accident in Illinois with an Illinois driver collects Basic Protection benefits but has a tort action against the Illinois driver, who in turn has a tort action against him.[32]

The potential chaos presented by just these three of the many possible variations of interstate accident situations is not likely to be eliminated even if both Michigan and Illinois enact Basic Protection statutes; it is highly probable, judging from recent experience in Massachusetts, that no two states will enact exactly the same law.

*6. Competition*

The automobile insurance industry has been spared the progressive extinction of small and medium-sized companies which has overtaken most of our major industries. More than 800 companies compete actively for an estimated 92 to 95 per cent of the total market—the remainder of the market is that smaller segment which, because of loss predictability and loss experience, must be written at surcharged rates or placed in the assigned risk plan.

If the Basic Protection plan is widely enacted, most of the highly competitive and efficient small and medium-sized auto insurance writers will be doomed to extinction. None but the giants will be able to afford the rating uncertainties, administrative costs and retraining of personnel necessary to make the Basic Protection plan an operative reality. Even more ominous is the certainty that huge blocks of automobile insurance will move out of the hands of the smaller companies and their agents into mass merchandising and group programs—a market available almost exclusively to the giants in the industry. If it were demonstrated that the Basic Protection plan met a crying social and economic need, the price of destroying most of the producing units in this business might be justified; but no such demonstration has been made.

*7. Regulation and Pre-emption*

The authors have declared themselves on these points. As succinctly stated by Professor O'Connell at the Mutual Claims Conference last May:

"The question is: Can the present system of private automobile in-

---

[30] Keeton & O'Connell, *Basic Protection Automobile Insurance*, pp. 65-66 *supra*.
[31] *Id.*
[32] *Id.* at 66-67.

surance, supervised by the states, be preserved? And I want to say, unhesitatingly, that I am for state regulation of insurance, and I am for private insurance coverage."

I take him at his word, and I assure him that the surest road to federal regulation *and* federal automobile insurance is the Basic Protection plan.

This plan will present state regulators and the public with rates based upon a welter of actuarial assumptions necessarily made without benefit of relevant prior loss experience. Being denied the benefit of such experience (to which Professor O'Connell properly ascribes much value), even the best staffed and most conscientious insurance departments will find it impossible to avoid rates which are inadequate, excessive, or unfairly discriminatory. The danger of insolvencies due to rate inadequacies will increase, and may largely offset the corrective measures against insolvencies already taken by the industry and by legislatures in many states. And to such problems will be added the job of groping through the interstate chaos that will result from having a wide variety of Basic Protection plans in some states and a continuation of the present system in others.

The burdens certain to be laid upon state regulation by the Basic Protection plan will increase the pressure for federal regulation of the insurance industry. But federal regulators will be no better equipped to cope with the confusion and inherent inequities than will state regulators. At this point, in order to make federal regulation effective, the temptation to seek uniformity through a system of federal automobile insurance will become irresistible. Moreover, the Basic Protection plan, a compulsory accident insurance system which abolishes the collateral source rule and largely eliminates the need for determining fault, is primarily a system for dispensing benefits, and therefore a natural precursor to a complete takeover of this segment of the private sector by the federal government.

Two artificial alternatives have been stated by supporters of the Basic Protection plan: Basic Protection *or* federal insurance—take your choice. But these are not alternatives; it is a matter of cause and effect: Basic Protection leading irresistibly to federal insurance. I would expect the refreshing new breed of pragmatic liberals among social and political scientists, those who have expressed alarm at the extent to which large segments of the private sector are being absorbed by the public sector, to be in the forefront of those sounding the alarm about the Basic Protection plan.

### III.  THE MASSACHUSETTS EXPERIENCE

Before concluding with some suggestions as to what the insurance industry and others might do with regard to the Basic Protection plan, I must discuss the events of the past six weeks in Massachusetts, because they are instructive. The Basic Protection plan statute as conceived by Professors Keeton and O'Connell was introduced verbatim as House Bill 1844 last January. Nobody thought it had the slightest chance of being voted on this year.

Due to a confusing parliamentary situation, plus a vast amount of public dissatisfaction with the highest auto insurance rates in the nation, the bill passed the House by a substantial margin on August 15.

During the next few days a wave of enthusiasm for what was described as a "major reform" swept over the Commonwealth. The press and other information media unanimously commended their legislators for vision and courage. Then, as opposition began to form, the picture changed. It was reported in the press that most of the House members who voted for the bill had had no opportunity to become familiar with its provisions. Public support was characterized as follows by the majority leader of the Senate (who also predicted passage by the Senate): "People do not necessarily understand the Keeton-O'Connell plan. But they want a change, any change." At about the same time the Chairman of the Senate Ways and Means Committee, after a hearing at which Professors Keeton and O'Connell explained the plan, announced that the plan was "full of holes."

The public was then told that the Basic Protection plan involved a reduction of benefits, that payments from collateral sources would be deducted, that there were additional deductions. They learned that territorial rating might be upset, and that drunken drivers could collect more benefits than their innocent victims.

A slugging match between proponents and opponents developed in the newspapers and in radio debates. A prominent judge said the plan would *increase* court congestion, and another one said it would "cause fraud and deceit to reach new and unprecedented dimensions." The powerful Teamsters Union came out publicly in violent opposition to the plan, and the AFL-CIO, originally expected to support the bill, began to swing over to the other side. The Governor said he would probably veto the bill if it passed the Senate. The Insurance Commissioner issued a statement which picked the bill to pieces. Professor Calvin Brainard, Chairman of the Finance and Insurance Department of the University of Rhode Island, who had studied the plan under a grant by the same foundation that financed the work of Professors Keeton and O'Connell, issued a scathing denunciation of the plan.

One of the most regrettable aspects of the whole situation was the debate about possible cost savings. In a statement to the Joint Committee on Insurance of the Massachusetts Legislature on March 28, 1967, Professor Keeton had said the Harwayne study concluded that if New York adopted the Basic Protection plan, "*insurance premiums* would be reduced by 15 to 25 per cent or more." This statement was repeated over and over again by the press, leading the public (and, I suspect, many legislators) to believe that the claimed savings applied to all coverages, when in fact they applied to less than half the total auto insurance premium. Newspapers typically stated that its backers claimed "motorists would save 25 percent on their premiums due to substantially lower insurance rates." Then, after the Chief Actuary of the Insurance Department had presented his opinion that the Basic Protection plan would *increase* rather than reduce insurance premiums, an out-of-state "expert" was reported in the press as claiming that "rate decreases of 30 to 40 percent would be certainly conservative." Finally, Professor O'Connell came to Boston and declared that savings of *86 per cent* were possible!

The bill was defeated in the Senate by a 2½ to 1 majority. It was defeated even though its authors were reported in the press as agreeing to accept "any amendments that might strengthen our bill and close the so-called or alleged loopholes which have been mentioned lately." There will now be an opportunity for a careful and responsible study of the plan in Massachusetts. But all of us who are truly concerned with legislating improvements in the automobile insurance system can learn a lesson from this experience.

We are dealing with an economic and social problem of enormous complexity. It touches the tap roots of the common law system of jurisprudence upon which western civilization has been built. It involves the most sensitive and delicate balances between individual responsibility and the social needs of the community. The Basic Protection plan poses serious political, social, and economic questions which may not have been apparent to those of its supporters who have not had the opportunity for thorough analysis of the plan.

I do hope there will be no further attempts to enact the Basic Protection plan anywhere, until all of us—government officials, academicians, lawyers, insurance men, and the authors of this bold and innovative plan—have had a chance to study the issues and create a solution in the public interest together.

## IV. A COURSE FOR THE FUTURE

The Federal Department of Transportation will make a thorough study of all of the matters discussed here, including the Basic Protection plan and other proposals for fundamental change. Comparable studies have been ordered in New York by Governor Rockefeller, and in California and Michigan by legislative enactment. Each of the three principal trade associations—The American Insurance Association, The National Association of Independent Insurers, and the American Mutual Insurance Alliance—is conducting its own study, and plans are developing for a comprehensive research assignment to a qualified independent institution to be financed on an all-industry basis. A means must be found to coordinate these efforts so that, proceeding independently, they can lend mutual aid and support by sharing information and techniques.

In the meantime, we in the insurance industry have a public responsibility to accelerate our efforts to strengthen and improve the existing system of automobile insurance by every possible means. Three developments in particular will do much to meet the problems at which the Basic Protection plan is aimed: the rapid advance of the doctrine of comparative negligence, continued expansion of the advance payments program now being followed by nearly all large writers of auto insurance, and increased use of insurance-financed rehabiliation for accident victims.

Others must join with us in searching for a solution to the manifest dissatisfaction of large segments of the public with automobile insurance rates. One fact that cannot be denied is this: there are at least a million people driving cars today who have demonstrated by their records of criminal driving convictions that they cannot be trusted behind the wheel. There is a large but unknown number whose physical condition is such that they are a menace to themselves and their families, as well as the public, when they drive. These cases present a sensitive political and law enforcement problem, but we have reached the point where such people simply must be denied the privilege of driving. To take this small percentage of all the licensed drivers off the road would have more favorable impact on loss costs, and therefore on insurance rates, than any plan that has yet been proposed.

The people in my company believe the present system can be made to work, with modifications suitable to the rightful demand of our society for the fairest and most efficient system of compensating accident victims. We urge restraint, cooperation and, above all, a mutual concern for the public interest.

# REMARKS

## OF GUY E. MANN*

AMONG THE MULTITUDE of critics of our mores in America, there are those who find it fashionable to criticize insurance companies' approach to the problem of compensating those who are injured in automobile accidents.

Insurance is one of man's devices for providing an economic good. Like all human pursuits, it is operated by human beings, and subject to human frailties. However, much of the criticism of insurance today, and particularly of automobile insurance, seems to be aimed at the concept of insurance. Such criticism stems from a fundamental misconception of what automobile insurance is designed to accomplish.

It should be remembered that automobile insurance arose because of the recognition by the owners and drivers of the newly-invented machine that they needed protection from the possibility of financial loss imposed upon them by our system of tort negligence laws. Automobile liability insurance was designed to satisfy this need. It accommodated itself to the requirements of the legal system. Automobile liability insurance was not designed to protect the injured party. There were, and are, other forms of insurance which protect us against the financial losses of injury, disability and death. As long as we have our tort liability legal system, automobile liability insurance's basic function will be to protect the owner and operator from the liability imposed on him by law.

If we are unhappy—and many of us are—about the plight of the injured accident victim, and feel that he must be compensated regardless of his contribution to his condition, it is our legal system which must be modified to accomplish this objective. It is the legal system and the way that it is operated to which informed and thoughtful critics should direct their attention, not to the automobile insurance system which was developed to satisfy the requirements of our system of laws. The automobile insurance system can accommodate itself to whatever those laws may be, to the satisfaction of the public need.

Professors Keeton and O'Connell, being among the more discerning observers and students of the current scene, have recognized this basic truth. They have proposed a program that is imaginatively conceived and, with modification, may go far toward a solution of the problem.[1]

* GUY E. MANN. B.S. 1926, *University of Pennsylvania; Chairman (1966-1967), American Insurance Association; Senior Vice President and Director, Aetna Life & Casualty, Hartford, Connecticut.*

[1] Keeton & O'Connell, Basic Protection for the Traffic Victim: A Blueprint for Reforming Automobile Insurance (1965) [both hereinbefore and hereinafter this book is often cited as Basic Protection]. *See also* Keeton & O'Connell, *Basic Protection Automobile Insurance*, p. 40 *supra.*

# REMARKS

## OF ROBERT A. RENNIE*

WHILE I AM SPEAKING only as an individual insurance company official and not as a representative of an insurer or association of insurance companies, I would like to state that Nationwide Insurance has always approached any proposal for change, including the Basic Protection plan,[1] with an open mind. Over the years, Nationwide has developed many innovations in insurance services. Beginning almost a decade ago, Nationwide offered a family compensation coverage which gave third-party claimants the option of accepting payments regardless of fault under a schedule contained in the policy in lieu of resorting to their common law remedy.[2] Nationwide has also pioneered in providing advance payments and rehabilitation services for third-party claimants.[3] Other insurance companies have taken similar initiatives.

I recite this record only to demonstrate that we have no built-in resistance to change. On the contrary, we welcome and strive for constructive changes in the insurance business. This concern has motivated our own detailed investigation of the Basic Protection plan. We continue to hope that, with further research and refinement, a revised plan might offer an acceptable solution to some of the current auto insurance problems, both from the viewpoint of public welfare and the industry which provides insurance services.

Nationwide has not arrived at any final policy decision. It neither supports nor opposes the Basic Protection plan in its present form. There are many features of the plan which are attractive, and which, in our opinion, should be considered in any major reform of the present system. Conversely, it seems to me that there are aspects of the plan which create uncertainties, both in principle and in execution, and which could cause difficulties, both for the insuring public and for insurers. Some of these weaknesses are set forth in Mr. Kemper's paper, although in general I feel that he has sometimes overstated the shortcomings of the plan. I also believe that there are additional unresolved problems.

Mr. Kemper correctly points out that the cost estimates of the Basic Protection plan vary widely. But the problem is even more basic than the failure of actuaries to agree on their current cost estimates. Regardless of initial cost, the ultimate cost is equally uncertain and depends upon an un-

---

* ROBERT A. RENNIE. B.A. 1939, Connecticut Wesleyan University; M.A. 1942, Ph.D. 1947, Harvard University; Vice-President, Nationwide Insurance Companies, Columbus, Ohio.

---

[1] KEETON & O'CONNELL, BASIC PROTECTION FOR THE TRAFFIC VICTIM: A BLUEPRINT FOR REFORMING AUTOMOBILE INSURANCE (1965) [both hereinbefore and hereinafter this book is often cited as Basic Protection]. See also Keeton & O'Connell, Basic Protection Automobile Insurance, p. 40 supra.

[2] Rennie, An Experiment in Limited Absolute Liability, 29 J. Ins. 177 (1962).

[3] Henle, Liability Insurance and the Rehabilitation Movement, J. Rehabilitation, May-June (1965), at 12.

known factor: whether the benefits are paid to claimants under the Basic Protection plan or from other collateral sources.

The Basic Protection statute, you will recall, abolishes the collateral source rule by providing mandatory deductions from Basic Protection payments for workmen's compensation, group and individual accident and health insurance, wage continuation, Blue Cross, Blue Shield, Medicare, Medicaid, Social Security benefits, and so forth.[4] Professors Keeton and O'Connell implicitly assume that these other systems of health and disability insurance will be content to be primary, leaving the Basic Protection plan to pay only excess losses. They may be right; each insurance system might try to maintain and even strengthen its basic role in the whole pattern of insurance protection. On the other hand, there are those who anticipate that when the Basic Protection plan begins to pay benefits without regard to fault and in a fashion—closely adjusted to the amount of loss and the time of loss—that rivals collateral forms of protection, these other systems will coordinate benefits in a manner which will cast such losses upon the auto insurers.

Mr. Franklin Marryott outlined this difficulty clearly last year in his article in the *American Bar Association Journal.* "There is the possibility," he wrote, "that some of these collateral sources will take steps to make themselves inapplicable if basic protection benefits are available. . . . It is a certainty that an important and perplexing series of readjustments will occur in the process of settling who, among competitors for the role, will be the ultimate provider of benefits."[5] Not only from the standpoint of cost analysis, but also from the standpoint of basic national policy, the Basic Protection plan poses a fundamental problem of the distribution of losses among insuring institutions.

Mr. Kemper's question about the equity of disregarding pain and suffering valued at less than $5,000[6] raises another significant issue. I have not been able to discover any clear concept of what function the payment for pain and suffering is supposed to perform. Is it to pay legal fees, or excess losses over those covered by the damages for out-of-pocket losses—such as permanent injury or disfigurement? Is it in the nature of punitive damages against the tortfeasor? Is it really correlated to actual physical pain and suffering? Or is it some combination of these factors? It appears to me that the inherent legitimacy of the concept is at issue, and on that question turns the equity of including or excluding payments for pain and suffering at any level.

Mr. Kemper's doubts about how much the Basic Protection plan will speed up the payment of benefits are probably valid. However, it must be conceded that just as advance payments help injured claimants and improve the whole system by providing prompt benefits, so an increased borrowing from the accepted procedures in health and disability insurance will serve better to

---

[4] *See* Keeton & O'Connell, *Basic Protection Automobile Insurance,* pp. 54-56 *supra.*

[5] Marryott, *The Tort System and Automobile Claims: Evaluating the Keeton-O'Connell Proposal,* 52 A.B.A.J. 643 (1966).

[6] *See* Keeton & O'Connell, *supra* note 4, at 50-51.

render satisfaction and to deliver auto insurance benefits in a more timely fashion. I believe that this is possible under the Basic Protection plan. I believe also that monthly payments which are geared to economic losses as they occur may contribute to a lowering of total settlement costs by lowering expenses which can be attributable to the hardship of delayed payments.

An economist would be rash to get into a debate with distinguished legal counsel on the issue of court congestion. But I suspect that the effect of the Basic Protection plan on litigation will depend on the economics of litigation, that is, on whether the underlying loss which can be legally supported is sufficient to justify suit for an award which will be reduced by the limits under the plan. One must also consider Professor Conard's observation that any lessening of the periods required to reach trial may be offset by a rise in the number of cases seeking trial.[7]

As to the possibilities for producing fraud under the Basic Protection plan, the opportunities for fraud mentioned by Mr. Kemper are common to existing forms of health insurance. My colleagues in the health insurance business tell me they have found them to be manageable, if not negligible. Moreover, the Basic Protection plan would entirely remove a major area in which fraud can be practiced, namely that of the presence or absence of negligence.

Nor would I enter into a debate with authorities on the constitutionality of the proposal. I would only observe that there seems to have been a growing disposition on the part of the courts, at least since 1938, to take into account the reasonableness of the law being tested in the light of the social and economic conditions to which it is addressed. Our constitution is a living document.

One must agree with Mr. Kemper that the Basic Protection plan will result in a redistribution of costs, and that as far as rate-making is concerned, it will be a new ball game. This would come about more and more as the system took on the characteristics of health and disability insurance. It suggests the need for a greater community of experience and practice between the auto casualty actuaries and the health insurance actuaries. There is no doubt it would require a lot of reorientation for auto insurance practitioners.

I would agree with Mr. Kemper as to the anomaly of the Basic Protection plan in retaining tort trials for the more serious cases while effectively eliminating them for the less serious.[8] Keeton and O'Connell concede, I think, that it is the smaller cases which are now most adequately—if not over-adequately—compensated, while the serious problems of inadequate compensation are mainly confined to the larger cases. While political considerations are important, I do not feel that they can fully explain away this inverted treatment of the problem of assuring reasonable and adequate reparation for auto-

---

[7] A. CONARD, J. MORGAN, R. PRATT, C. VOLTZ & R. BOMBAUGH, AUTOMOBILE ACCIDENT COSTS AND PAYMENTS—STUDIES IN THE ECONOMICS OF INJURY REPARATION 4 (1964).

[8] *See* Keeton & O'Connell, *supra* note 4, at 50-51.

mobile injuries. Any revision of the Basic Protection plan might well begin at this point.

Without making a final judgment on the system, I suggest that there are times when economic and social institutions do require major changes and the test of private business is to adjust to those changes. Certainly, there are those who have no doubt that the social insurance institutions, through an extension of workmen's compensation principles, Medicare, and the disability provisions of the Social Security system, could take on the job of reparation for auto injuries. Indeed, there are those here at this Conference who think they should. But it is more likely that a pluralistic answer to the auto accident reparation problem is needed. Among the elements that should be considered in such an answer is Nationwide's original alternative compensation coverage, amended to provide for much higher benefit limits and a deductible equal to an expanded medical payments coverage. If enacted into law and integrated with the medical payments coverage, it could provide protection for the serious cases as well as for those covered by the Basic Protection plan. Furthermore, it would give *all* claimants the voluntary option of accepting payments to cover their out-of-pocket loss, regardless of fault, or of pursuing their rights under the law of negligence to reclaim damages for injury. Such an evolutionary plan would not require the abandonment of tort law in order to implement a compensation plan. As Messrs. Conard and Jacobs have pointed out, our society has already instituted several compensation plans related to automobile accidents, each of which functions relatively independently of each other and of the tort liability system itself. Currently, tort law provides only about one-half of the aggregate amount of compensation received by auto accident victims.[9]

Turning now to Mr. Kemper's point that differences in state laws will cause difficulties in the administration of the Basic Protection plan, it is obvious that troublesome incongruities will emerge, though I would scarcely describe them as resulting in chaos. The undue fear of such a situation may be one reason why at least one person in Washington (Dean Sharp) has suggested a federal solution. Doubtless, similar problems arose as workmen's compensation laws were enacted state by state. But surely we cannot oppose a system, if it is a better system, merely because it could cause interjurisdictional problems at the outset. To do so would be to stifle much social progress and to undermine essential new legislation far removed from the Basic Protection plan.

I must also take issue with Mr. Kemper's comments on the threat of federal regulation and federal preemption. In my view, the threat lies not in reform of state systems, but in the absence of state action. It is when the states fail to follow clearly identified lines for dealing with a social problem that the federal government moves in.

[9] Conard & Jacobs, *New Hope for Consensus in the Automobile Injury Impasse,* 52 A.B.A.J., 533, 534 (1966).

Nor do I share Mr. Kemper's concern about the effect on competition. There are over 1,000 insurance companies providing health insurance protection which are facing most of the uncertainties of which Mr. Kemper speaks. What mass merchandising will do to the automobile insurance business is a different story, but I think its history will not be closely tied to what happens to the Basic Protection plan.

Anyone who questions the Basic Protection plan should suggest a reasonable alternative. Mr. Kemper and the people in his company attempt to do so. They believe that the present system can be made to work, "with modifications suitable to the rightful demand of our society for the fairest and most efficient system of compensating accident victims." Achieving a reasonable consensus on what constitutes "suitable modifications" should be one of the goals of this Conference.

I could not agree with Mr. Kemper more than when he says that we are dealing with an economic and social problem of enormous complexity. I also join him in urging thorough-going research of the whole problem by all parties promising a contribution to its solution, with the objective of improving our system of reparation for automobile injuries in the public interest.

# INSURANCE COSTS OF BASIC PROTECTION PLAN IN MICHIGAN

BY FRANK HARWAYNE*

## I. SUMMARY

AUTOMOBILE INSURANCE COSTS paid by Michigan motorists would be reduced in the order of 25 per cent if that state adopted the new plan of Basic Protection automobile insurance.[1] Along with reducing premiums, the new plan would also mean payments to approximately half again as many people in Michigan as receive payment today under liability insurance.

Under one estimate, the following study focuses on the costs for automobile insurance paid by a one-car family in Pontiac, Michigan, for whom the base premium is close to the state-wide average premium, covered by one of the most popular insurance packages available today—one with $25,000 limits available to any one victim in an accident and $50,000 limits as totally available to all persons injured in the accident, plus uninsured motorist coverage and $2,000 of medical payments coverage. This family would pay 24 per cent less than the cost of such present automobile insurance for insurance protection under the Basic Protection plan, including both $10,000 of Basic Protection insurance, payable by one's own insurance company without reference to fault, and also including tort liability protection above that amount.

According to another estimate in this study, the cost of automobile insurance for Michigan motorists generally for Basic Protection insurance alone, covering in-state accidents, with limits of $10,000 per person and $100,000 per accident, would be 25 per cent less than present liability insurance costs with limits of $10,000 per person and $20,000 per accident, plus uninsured motorist coverage and $2,000 of medical payments coverage. These savings would amount to an aggregate of $48 millions annually at the insurance levels of 1966, when Michigan bodily injury liability insurance premiums amounted to $193.8 millions. If Basic Protection is enacted generally throughout the United States there will be no need to carry negligence liability insurance covering out-of-state accidents in the range of the Basic Protection negligence exemption since both in-state and out-of-state accidents would be paid by Basic Protection insurance instead of by negligence liability insurance. Until such action by other states, however, the additional cost of such out-of-state liability coverage would mean that Basic Protec-

* FRANK HARWAYNE. B.A. 1942, Brooklyn College; Fellow, Casualty Actuarial Society; Director, American Academy of Actuaries.

[1] KEETON & O'CONNELL, BASIC PROTECTION FOR THE TRAFFIC VICTIM: A BLUEPRINT FOR REFORMING AUTOMOBILE INSURANCE (1965) [hereinbefore and hereinafter this book is often cited as Basic Protection]. See also Keeton & O'Connell, Basic Protection Automobile Insurance, p. 40 supra.

tion savings compared to present liability insurance costs would be 19 per cent instead of 25 per cent. The premium savings of 24 per cent for the one-car family in Pontiac, Michigan, included out-of-state liability coverage; with such out-of-state coverage eliminated, such savings would equal 26 per cent instead of 24 per cent.

These estimates of savings are, generally speaking, conservative and tend to underestimate rather than overestimate the savings from the Basic Protection plan.

## II. Description of Study

### A. Objective

The purpose of this report is to evaluate the average Michigan policyholder's automobile insurance cost under the proposed Basic Protection system developed by Professors R. E. Keeton and Jeffrey O'Connell, compared with current automobile bodily injury costs. This report presents an evaluation of a large number of factors affecting costs. Though as to some of these factors the Basic Protection plan adds cost, the savings from other factors are more than enough to offset these additions, thus producing net savings.

An introductory explanation is needed with respect to the treatment in this report of one cost factor—loss adjustment costs. The authors of the Basic Protection plan designed it with the purpose, among others, of reducing the administrative costs of processing claims.[2] Data concerning total loss adjustment costs under other nonfault coverages (workmen's compensation, for example) can be cited to support this prediction of savings. Although there is no entirely satisfactory actuarial basis for proving or disproving this thesis as to administrative savings, it is possible to estimate the impact on premiums of various degrees of savings in administrative costs of settling claims. This study presents three sets of calculations for comparison. The principal calculations, presented in the main body of this paper, are based on the assumption of 50 per cent savings in allocated claim expense only (with no assumed savings in unallocated claim expense).[3] In the appendices two alternative calculations are presented, one assuming greater administrative savings and the other assuming lesser administrative savings. The former of the alternative calculations is based on an assumption of 75 per cent savings in allocated claim expense and 25 per cent savings in unallocated claim expense. The latter of the alternative calculations is based on an assumption of no savings in either allocated or unallocated claim expense.

---

[2] Basic Protection 296 n.79.

[3] Allocated claim expense is defined as claims expenses specifically allocated to individual claims, such as the expense of adjustors and lawyers to work on a given case. Allocated claim expense is to be distinguished from unallocated claim expense which includes overall maintenance of the claim department, claim files, etc. Both of these items are exclusive of other costs, such as production expenses (commissions and other acquisition costs), taxes, or insurers' expenses in policy writing, or record keeping, etc.

In all three sets of calculations (that presented in the main body of this paper and the two alternative sets of calculations in the appendices), the remaining allocated claim expense is distributed one-half each to the Basic Protection insurance and the first layer of tort liability insurance above the tort exemption available to the Basic Protection insured. This is done because a certain core of investigation and defense cost now chargeable to the first $10,000/$20,000 of tort liability insurance will still be incurred, under the Basic Protection plan, not by the Basic Protection insurer but rather by the tort liability insurer, even though it is not liable for paying any benefits within this layer of protection against tort liability because of protection afforded by the tort exemption.[4] In other words, claims will sometimes be made for amounts in excess of the tort exemption even though in the final analysis such claims will not be proven. Thus, tort liability insurers will have expenses defending these claims, even though they defeat them.

The Basic Protection proposal results in estimated possible policyholder cost equal to 75 per cent of present bodily injury premium costs and, conversely, savings of 25 per cent which would approximate $48 millions on Michigan's 1966 automobile bodily injury premiums of $193,752,139.[5] This estimate presupposes Basic Protection coverage with the standard deductible excluding reimbursement for the $100 of all net loss of all types or 10 per cent of work loss, whichever is greater.[6] (This deductible is hereinafter referred to as the standard deductible.) The estimate also excludes tort liability coverage for out-of-state accidents since Basic Protection coverage does not protect against liability for out-of-state accidents.[7] Thus, supplementary out-of-state tort liability protection will be wise—and perhaps necessary under financial responsibility laws—at least until other states adopt the Basic Protection plan. If a Basic Protection insured elects, as he is permitted to do, to remove the standard deductible and to cover himself for out-of-state tort liability,[8] the savings would be reduced to 10 per cent or approximately $19 million annually.

Under the lower alternative of cost heretofore described (which assumes a 75 per cent reduction in litigation expense for each claim and a 25 per cent reduction in unallocated claims expense), the Basic Protection plan results in an approximate estimated annual saving of 28 per cent or $54 millions (14 per cent or $27 millions with optional removal of the standard deductible and inclusion of out-of-state tort liability insurance coverage). Under the second alternative which assumes no reduction in administrative expense, the Basic Protection plan results in an estimated annual saving of 22 per cent or $43

[4] Keeton & O'Connell, *Basic Protection Automobile Insurance*, pp. 50-51 *supra*.
[5] INSURANCE BY STATE, PROPERTY LIABILITY, SURETY, AND MISCELLANEOUS LINES IN 1966, at 26 (Michigan) (Spectator, 1967 ed.).
[6] Keeton & O'Connell, *supra* note 4, at 56-58.
[7] *Id.* at 66-67.
[8] *Id.* at 59-61.

millions (6 per cent or $12 millions with optional removal of the standard deductible and inclusion of out-of-state tort liability insurance coverage).

The annual saving under Basic Protection *with* the standard deductible but supplemented with out-of-state tort liability insurance coverage is estimated to be 19 per cent or $37 millions; the lower alternative cost (the one assuming greater administrative savings) is estimated to save 24 per cent or $47 millions, while the higher alternative cost (the one assuming no administrative savings) is estimated to save 15 per cent or $29 millions annually.

### B.  Method

At the heart of the automobile liability insurance ratemaking process is the pure premium, *i.e.*, pure of—or free of—expenses not directly associated with the claim.[9]

In arithmetic terms the pure premium may be expressed as

$$\frac{\text{annual aggregate cost of claims}}{\text{annual number of cars insured.}}$$

Mathematically this can be restated as

$$\frac{\text{annual aggregate cost of claims}}{\text{annual number of claims incurred}} \quad \text{x} \quad \frac{\text{annual number of claims incurred}}{\text{annual number of cars insured}}$$

which is: annual average claim cost x annual average of claim frequency.

By appropriate adjustments the Michigan average claim cost[10] and average claim frequency[11] for automobile liability insurance pure premium have been converted into their corresponding Basic Protection average claim cost and average claim frequency; in turn, the latter have been synthesized into a Basic Protection pure premium, which is thereafter further synthesized to reflect varying assumptions concerning current expense overhead—as it will be influenced by the adoption of Basic Protection—in a total premium for the Basic Protection coverage.

It also follows that, given the various percentages of premium which are utilized in synthesizing actual automobile tort liability insurance premiums, each layer of expense may be stripped away from the premium to reveal the underlying pure premium, and this in turn may be further analyzed into its components.

### C.  Results

Insurance company records show that, during the period used as the basis for this study, individual claim costs under tort liability coverage lim-

---

[9] More technically, pure premium is defined as that "portion of the premium rate calculated to enable the insurer to pay losses . . . ." U.S. CHAMBER OF COMMERCE, DICTIONARY OF INSURANCE TERMS 50 (1949).

[10] Average claim cost is the amount obligated to be paid by an insurer on the average to dispose of a single claim.

[11] Average claim frequency is the number of claims per 100 insured cars incurred during a period of one year.

ited to $10,000 each and individual accidents limited to $20,000 each ($10,000/ $20,000) produced an average claim cost, exclusive of any expenses for defending or adjusting claims, of $803. This includes the effect of payments for pain and suffering. Also, as developed later, when claims are limited to $10,000 /$20,000 and the payments for pain and suffering are excluded, a liberal estimate of resulting average claim cost is only $697. While average claim costs are lower under insurance like Basic Protection which does not cover pain and suffering,[12] available data show there will be a gross increase in claim frequency of approximately 55 per cent because, unlike tort claims, claims under Basic Protection will be payable regardless of fault;[13] however, the effects of higher claims frequency will be offset by a deductible and by exclusion under Basic Protection of losses reimbursed from collateral sources.[14] The net measured effect of all these changes under Basic Protection is 81 per cent of present costs for $10,000/$20,000 tort liability limits, uninsured motorist, and $2,000 medical payments insurance coverage. This premium, at the level of 81 per cent of the premium one pays under the present system, would provide (1) Basic Protection benefits of $10,000/$100,000 limits (with a standard deductible of the first $100 or 10 per cent of wage loss,[15] and deductibles to take account of the income tax saving[16] and benefits received from collateral sources[17]), (2) an exemption from tort liability for injuries occurring in Michigan accidents to the extent of the first $5,000 per person for pain and suffering and the first $10,000 per person for out-of-pocket damages,[18] (3) automobile tort liability insurance protection of $10,000/ $20,000 limits against all persons involved in accidents resulting from the operation of the automobile outside the boundaries of Michigan, and (4) $10,000/$20,000 limits of uninsured motorist coverage for accidents occurring outside the boundaries of Michigan.

The derivation of the 81 per cent figure is shown in Table 1 (pp. 127-29 *infra*). Near the end of Table 1 (line 28), the inclusion of supplementary coverage, to eliminate the standard deductible feature for wage loss, increases the 81 per cent figure to 90 per cent. For further purposes of comparison, also shown immediately below in the text, is the cost estimate of the Basic Protection plan coverage (including supplementary coverage to eliminate the standard wage loss deductible) measured against a present automobile tort liability policy with $25,000/$50,000 limits, plus $10,000/$20,000 limits of tort coverage against uninsured motorists and $2,000 of medical payments insurance coverage. The $25,000/$50,000 unit is chosen because it is one of the most popular among policyholders. This $25,000/$50,000 tort coverage would con-

---

[12] Keeton & O'Connell, *supra* note 4, at 61.
[13] *Id*. at 52-53.
[14] *Id*. at 54-56.
[15] *Id*. at 56-58.
[16] *Id*. at 54.
[17] *Id*. at 54-56.
[18] *Id*. at 50-51, 66-67.

tinue out-of-state; however, inside Michigan, Basic Protection limits of $10,000/$100,000 (with a corresponding exemption from tort liability for the first $5,000 of pain and suffering and the first $10,000 of out-of-pocket loss)[19] would be afforded as well as supplementary tort liability protection up to $25,000/$50,000 limits. The figures are for a one-car family in Pontiac, whose base premium is close to the statewide average premium. Limits equivalent to $10,000/$50,000 limits of tort liability are already included in the Basic Protection plan's tort exemption of $5,000 + $10,000/unlimited (*i.e.* $5,000 for pain and suffering and $10,000 for all other damages per person, and with no per accident limit).[20] Therefore automobile tort liability insurance cost between $10,000/$50,000 and $25,000/$50,000 limits is included in this calculation of the cost of providing coverage comparable to $25,000/$50,000 limits of tort liability. The cost of the package as described with the standard wage loss deductible is 76 per cent of present automobile liability insurance costs; with the standard deductible eliminated it is 84 per cent of present automobile liability insurance cost, an amount less than the comparable 90 per cent figure of Table 1. It should also be noted that if other states adopted Basic Protection there would be no need to provide out-of-state third-party tort liability insurance protection for the first $10,000 per claim; consequently the cost would be reduced to 74 per cent for Pontiac policyholders in the illustration.

A pie chart* shows the relative proportions of cost under the tort liability system and under the Basic Protection system. Aside from the broader coverage indicated by the larger circle for the $10,000/$100,000 limits of the Basic Protection program, it will be seen that the inclusion of nonliability claims is more than offset by exclusion of the value of the first $5,000 cost of

| Coverage | October 1, 1967 Auto Liability Policy Premium |
|---|---|
| TORT LIABILITY FOR INJURY TO OTHERS $10,000/$20,000 Limits | $41.00 |
| INJURY BY UNINSURED MOTORIST LIABLE IN TORT $10,000/$20,000 Limits | 4.00 |
| Medical Payments Insurance $2,000 Limits | 10.00 |
| Total | $55.00 |
| Increased Tort Liability Coverage from $10,000/20,000 to $25,000/$50,000 | 8.00 |
| Total Cost | $63.00 |

[19] *See* note 25 *infra*.

[20] I term this $10,000/$50,000 rather than $15,000/$50,000 because there will be instances where the $5,000 exemption for pain and suffering will be exhausted but not all the $10,000 exemption for out-of-pocket loss will apply; *e.g.*, this would be true if pain and suffering damages were $12,000 and out-of-pocket loss were $5,000. Thus the exemption is not the equivalent of a flat $15,000 tort exemption.

* *See* p. 486 *infra*.

| Coverage | Basic Protection Policy Premium |
|---|---|
| Basic Protection | |
| $10,000/$100,000 Limits ($41[21]×100.3%[22]) | $41.12 |
| Additional Coverage | |
| Tort Liability for Pain and Suffering Between $5,000 and $10,000 Per Claim ($41[23]×4.3%[24]) | 1.76 |
| Supplementary Coverage | |
| $25,000/$50,000 Bodily Injury Liability Insurance Less a Deductible for Instate Injuries to the Extent of $10,000 Protection[25] Against Liability Afforded by the Tort Exemption of Basic Protection ($41[26]×9.0%[27]) | 3.69 |
| Total Cost (In-State Basis) | $46.57  74% |
| Total Cost (Incl. Out-of-State) 95% Intra-State + 6% Out-of-State[28] Total Cost Relative to Present Cost | $48.02  76% |
| Cost of Eliminating Deductible In-State ($41[29]×95%[30]×13.1%[31]) | $ 5.10  8% |

pain and suffering per claim, the income tax deductible, the exclusion of receipts from collateral sources, the optional standard deductible, and the elimination of the need for medical payments insurance. In fact, as the chart con-

[21] Forty-one dollars is the cost of $10,000/$20,000 bodily injury tort liability limits with no other coverage, the figure being taken from the rating manual for a one-car family in Pontiac, on Oct. 1, 1967, whose base premium is close to the statewide average.

[22] Basic Protection with $10,000/$100,000 limits will cost 0.3% more than bodily injury tort liability insurance with limits of $10,000/$20,000. Thus to arrive at the cost of Basic Protection, $41 is multiplied by 100.3%.

[23] *See* note 21 *supra.*

[24] It will cost $4.38 to cover the cost of pain and suffering payments between $5,000 and $10,000 per claim, as well as investigation and defense in third party tort liability actions. *See* Table 1, line 24; *see also* Appendix Table I, line 24.

[25] Under the standard Basic Protection coverage of $10,000, every motorist is assured of a corresponding exemption equivalent to $10,000 of coverage against tort liability to each person regardless of how many victims are injured in an accident. *See* note 20 and accompanying text. *See also* Keeton & O'Connell, *supra* note 4, at 50-51, 63-65; Basic Protection 452-54. Thus Basic Protection provides protection against tort liability of $10,000 per person/unlimited per accident.

[26] *See* note 21 *supra.*

[27] This cost is computed as follows: The cost of the per person element of $25,000/$50,000 coverage can be viewed as composed of two components—the cost of the first $10,000 per person and the cost of the second $15,000 per person. Basic Protection by providing, through its tort exemption, protection against tort liability up to $10,000 per person/unlimited per accident (*See* note 25 *supra*) includes any cost of the lesser coverage of $10,000/$50,000. The present cost increase in tort liability coverage from $10,000/$50,000 to $25,000/$50,000 is 9% of the $10,000/$20,000 liability premium according to provisions of the rate manuals.

[28] The assumption is that 95% of accidents occur in-state and 5% out-of-state. *See* notes 41-42 and accompanying text *infra. See also* Table 1, line 27 and Appendix Table I, line 27.

[29] *See* note 21 *supra.*

[30] *See* note 28 *supra.*

[31] It will cost 13.1% to remove the standard deductible. *See also* p. 130 *infra,* and Table 1, line 21, and *also* Appendix Table I, line 21.

firms, even if the insured were to purchase coverage for the otherwise excluded optional standard deductible, Basic Protection plus the deductible waiver would still be less costly than present day automobile bodily injury liability plus medical payments insurance coverage.

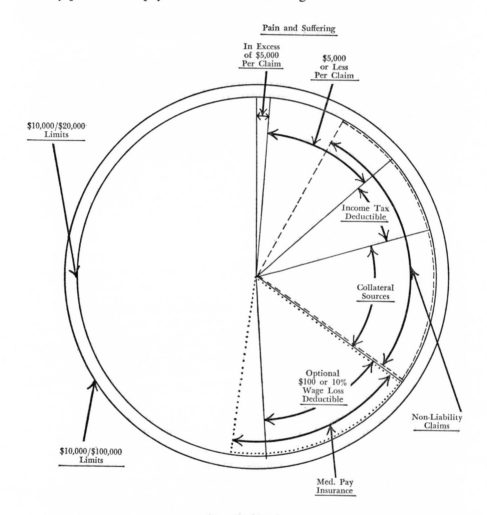

## D.   *Table 1*

Table 1* begins with the component elements of allocated claim expense and pure premium (including and excluding pain and suffering) which are derived in Table 2 (Table 1, line 1). These pure premiums are adjusted first to reflect 55 per cent more claims under a nonfault system (line 2). This 55 per cent figure represents the difference between the number of personal

* For all other tables except Table 2, *see* pp. 151-77 *infra*. Table 2 is at p. 133 *infra*.

injury claims being paid by automobile insurance today and the total number of personal injuries in traffic accidents as reported to police authorities. Not all of the 55 per cent greater number of claims will increase the premium per policy, however. In the first place, there is an offset to the extent of the

TABLE 1
MICHIGAN
BASIC PROTECTION PROGRAM

| | Allocated Claim Expense Per Car (a) | Pure Loss Pure Premiums With Pain and Suffering | |
| --- | --- | --- | --- |
| | | Included (b) | Excluded (c) |
| **A.** *Modified to $10,000/$20,000 Basis* | | | |
| 1. Liability Basis (from Table 2) | $2.41 | $24.19 | $20.98 |
| 2. Non-Liability Basis line 1 × 1.55 (from Table D-1, line C) | 3.74 | 37.49 | 32.52 |
| Reduction to Reflect Removal of | | | |
| 3. Uninsured Autos Under Compulsory Insurance line 2× .09 | — .34 | — 3.37 | — 2.93 |
| 4. Coverage by Self-Insurers line 2 × .05 | — .19 | — 1.87 | — 1.63 |
| 5. Coverage Under Workmen's Compensation line 2 × .03 | — .11 | — 1.12 | — .98 |
| 6. Line 2 After Foregoing Reductions lines 2+3+4+5 | $3.10 | $31.13 | $26.98 |
| 7. Estimated Saving in Allocated Claim Expense line 6(a) × 50% | —$1.55 | | |
| 8. Lines 6(a)+7(a) | $1.55 | $31.13 | $26.98 |
| 9. Line 8(a) in Basic Protection Insurance line 8(a) × 50% | $ .78 | | |
| 10. Line 8(a) in Liability Insurance above Tort Exemption lines 8(a)—9(a) | .77 | | |
| 11. Line 8(c) After Funds From Other Sources line 8(c) × 83.1% (from Table C-4, line 4) | | | $22.42 |
| 12. Line 11(c) After $100 or 10% Deductible line 11 x 85.0% (from Table D-3, line G) | | | 19.06 |
| 13. Line 12(c) After 15% Deduction of Net Income Loss line 12 × (100.0%—10.6%) (from Table C-4, line 6) | | | 17.04 |
| 14. Line 9(a) increased by 50% of line 6(a) to include half of claimants' attorneys' fees | $2.33 | | |

TABLE 1 *(continued)*
MICHIGAN
BASIC PROTECTION PROGRAM

| | Pure Prem. incl. Alloc. Claim |
|---|---|
| **A. *Modified to $10,000/$20,000 Basis*** | |
| 15.  All Pain and Suffering Excluded<br>lines 13(c) + 14(a) | $19.37 |
| **B. *Modified to $10,000/$100,000 Basis*** | |
| 16.  Cost of Coverage Between $10,000/$20,000 and<br>$10,000/$100,000<br>.15 × line 15 | 2.91 |
| 17.  Cost of Basic Protection<br>$10,000/$100,000 Basis<br>lines 15 + 16 | $22.28 |
| Insurer's Expenses | |
| 18.  General—Table 2, line 2.1, col. (e) increased<br>15% for $10,000/$100,000 limits, $2.90 × 115% | $ 3.34 |
| 19.  Unallocated Claim—Table 2, line 3, col. (e)<br>increased 15% for $10,000/$100,000 limits,<br>adjusted to reflect more claims in ratio of<br>lines 6(a) ÷ 1(a) and no saving, $2.69 ×<br>115% × lines (6(a) ÷ 1(a)) × 100% | $ 3.79 |
| 20.  Losses Including Loss Adjustment Expense and<br>General Expense,<br>lines 17 + 18 + 19 | $29.59 |
| 20a. Premium Chargeable, line 20 ÷ (100.0%—load-<br>ing for acquisition, tax, profit) or line 20 ÷<br>(100.0% − 28.0%) | $41.10 |
| **C. *Basic Protection with Deductible Eliminated—Intrastate Coverage*** | |
| 21.  Premium Elimination of Deductible in line 12<br>[lines (11-12 ÷ (100.0%—28.0%)] × 1.15 | $5.37 |
| 21a. Premium with Deductible Eliminated<br>lines (20a + 21) | $46.47 |

| | Premiums Per Car | |
|---|---|---|
| | Amount | Per Cent |
| **D. *Present Auto Liability Premiums*** | | |
| 22.  $10,000/$20,000 Liability Premium<br>Including Uninsured Motorist and<br>$2,000 Med. Pay. | $54.54 | 100% |
| 23.  Basic Protection, line 20a | $41.10 | 75% |
| **E. *Additional Coverage*** | | |
| 24.  Tort Liability for Pain and Suffering<br>Between $5,000 and $10,000 Per Claim<br>1.15 [line 10(a)+.10 × lines (1(b)—1(c))] ÷<br>(100.0%—28.0%) | 1.74 | |

TABLE 1 *(continued)*
MICHIGAN
BASIC PROTECTION PROGRAM

| | Premiums Per Car | |
|---|---|---|
| | Amount | Per Cent |
| **F.** *Basic Protection Plus Additional Coverage* | | |
| 25. lines 23 + 24 | $42.84 | 79% |
| 26. lines 24 + 21a (Removal of Deductible) Including Out-of-State Tort Liability Coverage | $48.21 | 88% |
| 27. With In-State Wage Deductible 95% × line 25 + 6%[1] × line 22 | $43.97 | 81% |
| 28. Without Wage Deductible 95% × line 26 + 6%[1] × line 22 | $49.07 | 90% |
| **G.** *Basic Protection Only* | | |
| 29. Basic Protection Only, line 20a | $41.10 | 75% |

[1] *See* notes 41 & 42 *supra* and accompanying text.

claims not now covered because the legally responsible persons are uninsured (9%) (line 3). These claims would be covered under Basic Protection,[32] but would not add to the premium cost per policy under Basic Protection. This is true because there would be a correspondingly higher number of persons paying Basic Protection premiums since it is a compulsory coverage.[33] Also there are other claims in this 55 per cent not now paid by automobile liability insurance that still would not increase Basic Protection premiums per policy. This applies to claims now paid not by automobile liability insurers but by political subdivisions and other self-insurers (5%) (line 4). These claims, if covered by Basic Protection, would not add to the premium cost per policy because, again, there would be a correspondingly higher number of persons or other legal entities (such as political subdivisions) paying Basic Protection premiums. Moreover, there is a still further offset (3%) because of benefits that will continue to be paid to traffic victims under workmen's compensation and will therefore not be due under Basic Protection (line 5).

Included in the calculation is an estimated 50 per cent savings in allocated claim expense (line 7(a)), with the balance distributed equally to Basic Protection and tort liability insurance above the tort exemption so that funds are available to the tort liability insurer for investigation and defense (lines 8(a)-10(a)).[34] (Alternative computations based on a 75 per cent savings in allocated claim cost and 25 per cent saving in unallocated claim cost are

[32] Keeton & O'Connell, *supra* note 4, at 63-65.
[33] *Id.* at 62-63.
[34] *See* p. 121 *supra*.

shown in Appendix Table II. Another alternative computation based on no saving in claim expense is shown in Appendix Table III.)

Additional offsets are the funds from collateral sources (16.9% reduction; *i.e.* the remaining cost will be 83.1%) (line 11), the standard deductible (15.0% reduction, with the remaining cost equalling 85.0%) (line 12) and the deduction for income tax saving (10.6% reduction with the remaining cost 89.4%) (line 13). The 50 per cent increase in allocated claim expense to provide for payment of half the claimants' attorneys' fees[35] (line 14(a)) is added to this (line 15). The cost increase to afford coverage between $10,000/$20,000 and $10,000/$100,000 is obtained by multiplying the $10,000/$20,000 pure premium, including allocated claim expense from the previous line, by a factor of .15, which factor is taken from the table of increased limits charges customarily applied in calculating the added cost of increasing limits from $10,000/$20,000 to $10,000/$100,000 (line 16); this latter increment plus the $10,000/$20,000 pure premium of line 15 gives the pure premium, including allocated claim cost of Basic Protection on a $10,000/$100,000 basis (line 17). The resulting total pure premium, including allocated claims expense, is then increased (line 20) to reflect the dollar cost of general administration and unallocated claim expenses of the insurer (lines 18-19). The present cost for general expenses is $2.90 on $10,000/$20,000 tort liability coverage including uninsured motorist coverage. See Table 2, line 2.1(e). To this is added 15 per cent to take account of the increased general expenses when limits are raised from $10,000/$20,000 to $10,000/$100,000. See Table 1, line 18. This figure is converted to an appropriate overall (as opposed to pure) premium charge by adding an amount to provide for acquisition, tax, and profit.[36] For the purpose of computing the overall premium charge for the supplementary coverage to eliminate the standard deductible, the amount heretofore eliminated (lines 11-12) is also increased to reflect acquisition costs, taxes, and profit, and the result is increased by .15 to convert to $10,000/$100,000 limits (line 21).

The Basic Protection insurance premium with the standard deductible eliminated is shown on line 21a. Line 22 shows the present $10,000/$20,000 tort liability insurance premium including uninsured motorist cost and $2,000 medical payments coverage. Lines 23 and 29 repeat, for comparative purposes, the Basic Protection cost with standard deductible which was first shown on line 20a. At line 24 the premium cost to the Basic Protection insured for additional tort liability coverage for pain and suffering above the $5,000 exemption[37] is derived from the pure premium difference between

---

[35] Keeton & O'Connell, *supra* note 4, at 68. *See also* p. 138 *infra*.

[36] Twenty per cent for acquisition costs, 3% for taxes, and 5% for profit. *See* p. 137 *infra*. It will be seen that when 28% of the amount at line 20a, Table 1, is subtracted from that amount, the remainder will be the amount for losses, loss adjustment, and general expenses shown at Table 1, line 20.

[37] Under Basic Protection's tort exemption, an insured is exempt only for the first $5,000 for pain and suffering. Keeton & O'Connell, *supra* note 4, at 50-51.

lines 1(b) (which includes payment for pain and suffering) and 1(c) (which excludes payment for pain and suffering) in the following manner: since the present automobile liability insurance manuals indicate a charge of approximately .10 for coverage between $5,000/$10,000 and $5,000/$20,000, .10 has been applied to the pure premium difference between lines 1(b) and 1(c). To this has been added part of allocated claim expense[38] and the total has been adjusted by the 1.15 manual factor to convert from a $10,000/$20,000 basis to $10,000/ $100,000;[39] finally, the pure premium has been converted to a premium basis by loading for acquisition cost, tax, and profit (28% of the premium)[40] (line 24). The sum of Basic Protection cost and tort liability for pain and suffering between $5,000 and $10,000 per claim is 79 per cent of present automobile liability insurance (plus uninsured motorist and $2,000 medical payments) premiums (line 25); with the standard deductible removed, it is 88 per cent (line 26). Basic Protection plus additional tort liability for out-of-state coverage plus pain and suffering between $5,000 and $10,000 per claim costs 81 per cent of present costs (line 27); with the standard deductible removed the cost is 90 per cent (line 28). In calculating the out-of-state costs, since the percentage of out-of-state accidents is taken to be 5 per cent, the cost of liability insurance for such accidents is therefore 5 per cent of the liability premium alone. However, to take account of the fact that there are also Basic Protection payments for these out-of-state accidents,[41] the premium base to which the 5 per cent is applied in lines 27 and 28 includes not only liability insurance but also uninsured motorist and medical payments coverage. In addition, since Basic Protection coverage pays benefits even beyond these latter two coverages for out-of-state accidents (covering wage loss on a nonfault basis, for example), the 5 per cent figure has been increased by 1 per cent, thus reaching 6 per cent, to take account of these further payments. [42]

Finally, Basic Protection alone would cost 75 per cent of present costs (line 29) if other states adopted first party insurance programs similar to Basic Protection.

It should be noted again at this point that Table 1, being based, generally speaking, on conservative estimates, tends to overstate rather than understate cost estimates of the Basic Protection plan.[43]

[38] Concerning this distribution of allocated claim expense, *see* p. 129 *supra* and Table 1, line 10(a).

[39] Concerning this factor of 1.15, *see* p. 130 *supra*.

[40] Concerning this loading factor, *see* note 36 *supra* and accompanying text.

[41] Keeton & O'Connell, *supra* note 4, at 66-67.

[42] In addition to Table 1, lines 27 and 28, *see* note 28 *supra* and accompanying text.

[43] Concerning such conservative estimates and values, see, for example, (1) material related to the use of workmen's compensation data which does not reflect any per accident limit, at p. 134 *infra*; (2) material relating to the number of serious cases at note 77 *infra* and accompanying text; (3) material relating to offsets for other medical coverage, especially Medicare and Medicaid, at note 87 *infra* and accompanying text; (4) material relating to the number of females over age 15 assumed to be engaged in housekeeping,

## E.   *Appendix Tables I, II, III*

Appendix Table I is a restatement of Table 1, expressed solely in percentages rather than in dollars and cents; uninsured motorists premium is included at 9 per cent of $10,000/$20,000 bodily injury liability premiums (line 1a) and medical payments premium is included in current premiums at 24 per cent. Appendix Table II reflects an assumed saving in claim expense at 75 per cent of allocated claim cost (line 7) and 25 per cent of unallocated claim cost (line 19).[44] Under this assumption the estimated cost of Basic Protection alone is 72 per cent (line 29) compared with the 75 per cent figure of Table 1 and Appendix Table I. Appendix Table III assumes no saving in claim expense[45] and the resulting comparable cost estimate for Basic Protection alone is 78 per cent (line 29). In each case, removal of the optional standard deductible exclusion and inclusion of tort liability coverage out-of-state plus pain and suffering benefits between $5,000 and $10,000 per claim increases the above figures by 14 to 16 percentage points of cost (lines 28-29 Appendix Tables II and III).

## F.   *Table 2*

Table 2 shows the premium structure generally used by insurers affiliated with the National Bureau of Casualty Underwriters. Allocated claims expense is taken at 9 per cent of losses including allocated claims expense. The $10,000/$20,000 auto bodily injury liability pure loss pure premium of $22.16 at line 5(c) is based on data reported to the Mutual Insurance Rating Bureau and the National Bureau of Casualty Underwriters and is the product of an $803 average claim cost and a 2.76 per cent claim frequency; all other figures of column (c) are derived from the percentages used in ratemaking and are in conformity with the premium structure.[46] The $3.75 per car premium for uninsured motorist coverage (line 1(d)) assumes that one out of three families owns a second car; the elements of the $3.75 are developed from the component percentages of the premium rate structure.[47] The cost of $2,000 medical payments coverage (line 1(f)) is taken at 24 per cent of the $10,000/$20,000 automobile bodily injury liability premium, and is a good approximation of actual charges; here too each component element is in accord with the premium rate structure.[48] At the lower part of Table 2, the

---

as opposed to wage earning (note 3, Table A), who are also assumed to be entitled to receive 50% of wage loss (*see, e.g.,* Table C-3, Part III); (5) the estimate that the amount being paid for pain and suffering under the present tort liability system is the difference between $803 (average claim costs) and $697 (average claim cost with pain and suffering excluded) (*see* p. 145 *infra*), compared to Richard Wolfrum's estimate that the amount being paid for pain and suffering under the present system amounts to 2½ times out-of-pocket loss. Wolfrum, *Remarks,* p. 183 *infra*.

[44] *See* p. 120 *supra*.

[45] *Id.*

[46] The percentages are found in the table appearing at p. 137 *infra*.

[47] *Id.*

[48] *Id.*

TABLE 2
MICHIGAN
AVERAGE COMPONENT ELEMENTS
OF AUTOMOBILE BODILY INJURY INSURANCE

| Item (a) | $10,000/$20,000 Liability | | | | $2,000 Med. Pay. (f) | Grand Total (g) |
|---|---|---|---|---|---|---|
| | Rate Structure (b) | Bodily Injury (c) | Uninsured Motorist (d) | Total (e) | | |
| 1. Premium | 100.0% | $40.96 | $3.75 | $44.71 | $9.83 | $54.54 |
| 2. Expenses Except Claim (Incl. Profit or Contingencies) | 34.5 | 14.13 | 1.29 | 15.42 | 3.39 | 18.81 |
| 2.1 General Expense | 6.5 | 2.66 | .24 | 2.90 | .64 | 3.54 |
| 2.2 Other Expenses Except Claim (Incl. Profit or Contingencies) | 28.0 | 11.47 | 1.05 | 12.52 | 2.75 | 15.27 |
| 3. Unallocated Claim | 6.0 | 2.46 | .23 | 2.69 | .59 | 3.28 |
| 4. Allocated Claim | 5.4 | 2.21 | .20 | 2.41 | .53 | 2.94 |
| 5. Pure Loss | 54.1 | 22.16 | 2.03 | 24.19 | 5.32 | 29.51 |

$10,000/$20,000 LIABILITY
PURE LOSS PURE PREMIUMS

| Item | | Explanation |
|---|---|---|
| **Pain and Suffering Included** | | |
| 6. Average Claim Cost | $803 | Based on Experience Reported to the Mutual Insurance Rating Bureau (MIRB) and the National Bureau of Casualty Underwriters (NBCU). |
| 7. Pure Premiums | $ 24.19 | Based on Experience Reported to MIRB and NBCU, modified to include uninsured Motorist Coverage. |
| 8. Average Claim Frequency | 3.01% | $24.15 ÷ $803 |
| **Pain and Suffering Excluded** | | |
| 9. Average Claim Cost | $697 | See Table C-4 |
| 10. Average Claim Frequency | 3.01% | Taken from line 8. |
| 11. Pure Premium | $ 20.98 | lines 9 x 10. |

average claim frequency, including uninsured motorist coverage and including pain and suffering (line 8), is derived by dividing the total pure loss (pure premium) (line 5(e)) by the $803 average claim cost. This latter frequency is applied to the average claim cost derived from motor vehicle, workmen's compensation and labor force data to produce the pure premium with pain and suffering excluded (lines 8-11).[49] In passing, it should be noted that the use of the workmen's compensation data makes for a conservative calculation of Basic Protection cost in that the average claim costs based on workmen's compensation data, while limited to $10,000 per case, do not reflect any limitation per accident. In other words, since it does not include a per accident limit, use of the workmen's compensation data overstates the cost of a system like Basic Protection which includes a per accident limit. Some idea of the magnitude of the difference in cost caused by a per accident limit can be gained from the fact that, under the present tort liability system, insurers reflect the increase in coverage from $10,000/$20,000 to $10,000/$100,000 by a premium charge amounting to 15 per cent of the premium for $10,000/$20,000 coverage.

### III.   General Background

A previous study of Basic Protection costs in New York State considered the impact of the proposed Basic Protection plan on the cost of automobile bodily injury liability insurance in that state.[50] Only minor consideration was given in that study to the effect of other sources of insurance available to a majority of New York state residents.[51] In this study, attempts have been made to reflect to a greater degree the continuing broad scale availability of collateral insurance under various forms of accident protection, including that most recently made available through Medicare.

Persons who are ineligible under Title XVIII of the 1965 amendments to the Social Security Act (Medicare)[52] may nevertheless receive medical care under Title XIX of the 1965 amendments to the Social Security Act (Medicaid)[53] if they meet certain means tests. Although possible cost offsets against Basic Protection arising from this situation may be substantial, it is not too clear that the federal government is amenable to a state-defined means test which would permit Title XIX to include a substantial part of our population. Therefore, possible offsets on account of Title XIX have not been reflected in these computations.

The problem considered in the body of this study is one of estimating

---

[49] *See* note 77 *infra* and accompanying text.

[50] Harwayne, *Insurance Cost of Automobile Basic Protection Plan in Relation to Automobile Bodily Injury Liability Costs*, 53 Proceedings of the Casualty Actuarial Society 122 (1966). *See also* Keeton & O'Connell, *Basic Protection and the Costs of Traffic Accidents*, 38 N.Y.S.B.J. 255 (1966).

[51] Harwayne, *supra* note 50, at 130.

[52] 42 U.S.C.A. § 1395 (Supp. 1966).

[53] 42 U.S.C.A. § 1396 (Supp. 1966).

costs for Basic Protection insurance as it would be expected to affect the state of Michigan in comparison with present day automobile bodily injury liability insurance costs. Since the problem is a unique one, standard techniques and methods have not always been suitable to the task. Wherever practicable, however, techniques, methods, and statistical data used have been grounded in developments which are recognized and accepted in insurance circles.

Throughout this study, efforts have been concentrated on measuring the effect of the Basic Protection plan on costs for the state as a whole. Undoubtedly, some shift would occur in the distribution of insurance cost compared with that incurred under the present liability system. The relatively higher cost between city and rural areas under the present liability system would probably remain because of the higher income levels prevailing in the cities. On the other hand, the dramatically higher automobile liability insurance premiums currently paid by young drivers probably would be reduced under the proposed Basic Protection plan on account of their relatively lower earnings; frequency involvement would be an offset to this to some extent, however. Any consideration of reallocation of costs among communities or automobile classifications has been postponed while primary attention is given to the measurement of statewide costs.

The cost of the Basic Protection plan was first considered from the standpoint of present day liability or tort costs in the aggregate; on this there could be superimposed necessary adjustments and modifications determined from sample surveys. Such surveys, however, were not utilized in this study. In the light of the wealth of material which may be extracted from somewhat more complete and publicly available data reported by insurers, motor vehicle authorities and others, it is apparent to me that such material covers many more automobile incidents for a given period of time than does a sample survey of several hundred cases. Thus, it has been concluded that more relevant information may be gathered from reported insurance data and motor vehicle records as well as census data than could be obtained through interview techniques which might be derived from a small fraction of the total automobile accidents.[54]

In a sense, insurance data may be viewed as the end product of a study in depth of the economic consequences of the injury to the individual and his actual damages. The claims evaluator has and does exercise material control over the situation and is actually able to supply paramedical knowledge, credit report information, etc., to the specific claim. In workmen's compensation cases the application of such knowledge and information is even more precise. In sample studies, on the other hand, controls can not normally be as good: The sample design must be free of bias; the interviewer, except for

---

[54] In addition to the material immediately following, *see* p. 139 *infra*.

some elements which are included to promote internal consistency, must rely mainly on the veracity of the interviewee, who does not have a specific reason to cooperate and may, in fact, feel a need to do otherwise. Nonresponse may be a large problem and special techniques may be necessary to overcome this. The Conard study reported in *Automobile Accident Costs and Payments*[55] screened 2,872 persons reported injured or killed in Michigan automobile accidents during 1958. Questionnaires were not completed for 818 of these and 63 per cent of these individuals were never located. Questionnaires were completed by telephone for 767 and by mail for 1,287. Follow-ups on apparently serious cases produced completed interview results in 407 questionnaires; some of these involved pending litigation and they were replaced by equivalent closed court cases.[56] Both the design and results appear reasonable; however, it should be noted that the serious cases are split almost 50 per cent male and 50 per cent female,[57] which does not appear consistent with overall accident data reported by the State Police.[58] Also, approximately 48 per cent of those involved in nonserious injuries reported no medical or hospital expense and no days lost from work because of the accident.[59] This is at variance with the report of the nationwide United States National Health Survey that 92.7 per cent of the persons injured in moving motor vehicle accidents are medically attended.[60] The Conard data[61] does not appear to be entirely consistent with the fact that insured personal injury claims equal approximately 74 per cent of the number of persons reported killed or injured in State Police data.[62] In spite of these qualifications the discrepancy between Conard's findings and this study is not too great; the Conard study indicates a gross personal injury present value loss per case of approximately $1,135 (as adjusted by the author of this report)[63] and $745[64] more on the basis of periodic cash payments in the future instead of present lump-sum values. If one adjusted Conard's $1,135 figure based on the late 1950's[65] for inflationary increases in earnings and medical costs, it would

[55] A. CONARD, J. MORGAN, R. PRATT, C. VOLTZ & R. BOMBAUGH, AUTOMOBILE ACCIDENT COSTS AND PAYMENTS—STUDIES IN THE ECONOMICS OF INJURY REPARATION (1964) [both hereinbefore and hereinafter this book is often cited as CONARD, *et al.*].

[56] For a description of the survey methods used in the study by Conard and his colleagues, *see* CONARD, *et al.* ch. 9.

[57] This computation is based on my work with the worksheets formulated by Conard and his colleagues from their questionnaires. Harwayne, *Comparison of Data Used in Estimating Michigan Basic Protection Costs With Michigan Data Used in the Conard Study* (undated and unpublished manuscript available from the author).

[58] See Table A.

[59] Harwayne, *supra* note 7, Table 6, at p. 17.

[60] *See* note 76 *infra* and accompanying text.

[61] Out of 407 serious cases, 217 involved liability settlements. Harwayne, *supra* note 57, Table 7, at p. 18.

[62] Table D-1 (81,832 ÷ 110,030).

[63] Harwayne, *supra* note 57, at 7.

[64] *Id.* at 18.

[65] CONARD, *et al.* 323-24.

bring the present value costs closer to the average of $1,794 based on 1966 conditions developed in the following pages.[66]

The information developed in this study has been converted to a unit cost basis, *i.e.*, the premium a hypothetical individual consumer would pay, in order to permit comparisons to be made with current insurance costs to the individual. It is believed that this method provides a more practicable basis for comparing premium determination under a fault system with that under the proposed Basic Protection system.

Consideration was given to various elements of the insurance premium. However, there appears to be no basis for assuming that the marketing system of insurance under the proposed Basic Protection plan need be different from the current marketing system. Accordingly, calculations have thus been developed on the basis that there would be no differences in marketing method. If the Basic Protection system were to be accompanied by marketing changes, such changes would have to be separately reflected.

In carrying forward the estimates of unit costs under the present liability system and the Basic Protection plan, attention has been directed to changes only in losses and loss adjustment expenses to the exclusion of other costs such as production expenses (commissions and other acquisition), taxes or insurers' general expenses (policy writing, record keeping, etc). Nevertheless, for completeness, it is well to note these elements as part of the overall premium structure generally used by the leading stock and mutual insurance ratemaking groups. The expense and profit or contingency provisions, which are periodically revised to reflect actual expenses, are approximately as follows:

| Component Elements of the Insurance Premium | | |
|---|---:|---:|
| Premium | | 100.0% |
| Production Expense | 20.0% | |
| Tax | 3.0% | |
| General Expense | 6.5% | |
| Profit or Contingency | 5.0% | |
| Sub-Total | | 34.5% |
| Balance for Loss and Loss Adjustment | | 65.5% |

Of the 65.5 per cent for loss and loss adjustment expenses, approximately 6.0 per cent of premium is expended for unallocated claims expense, *i.e.* maintenance of the claim department, claim files, etc. In addition, as developed in this study, it is estimated that allocated claims expense, *i.e.*, claims expense specifically allocated to individual claims, absorbs approximately 5.4 per cent[67] of the stock and mutual insurance company premium in Michigan, so

---

[66] *See* Table C-4, Part I.
[67] Nine per cent of (65.5% − 6.0%). *See* Table D-2.

that total claims adjustment expense amounts to 11.4 per cent of premium; on the 1966 premium volume this amounts to $22.1 million.

The elements of loss and loss adjustment are summarized below as percentages of premiums:

| Loss and Loss Adjustment Expense | Per Cent of Premium |
|---|---|
| Loss and Loss Adjustment Expense | 65.5 |
| Unallocated Claim Expense | 6.0 |
| Loss and Allocated Claim Expense | 59.5 |
| Allocated Claim Expense | 5.4 |
| Pure Loss (No Claim Expense) | 54.1 |

Measured against pure loss payments, allocated claims expense is equal to approximately 10 per cent on the average. It is assumed that the insurers' allocated claims expense amounting to 10 per cent of recovery under the liability system will correspond approximately to the cost of the current system's expenditures on claimants' attorneys. While this may appear low at first for claimants' attorneys, it is not unreasonable to the extent that insurers incur allocated claims expense in almost every case, whereas plaintiffs attorneys' fees are paid only in those fewer cases where plaintiffs' attorneys are retained and are successful. Thus, even though percentages paid in those cases they handle are higher, it is not unreasonable to reflect the averages of attorneys' fees on *all* cases with and without plaintiffs' representation at 10 per cent. Also, parity of costs tends to be maintained between insurers and claimants in that both compete for legal services. In other words, if one side were getting a great deal more than the other, almost all lawyers would be trying to work for the higher-paying side, which is not the case.

### A.  Statistics Background

In Michigan, all insurers report their automobile bodily injury liability insurance statistics to either the Mutual Insurance Rating Bureau, the National Association of Independent Insurers, the National Bureau of Casualty Underwriters, or the National Independent Statistical Service. The best available automobile personal injury cost data are contained in such records of the insurers. For purposes of this study, it is fortunate that the statistical requirements necessary to comply with insurance rate regulation have resulted in disclosure of much detailed insurance information regarding private passenger automobile experience separate from vehicles used for commercial and other purposes. In addition to this, frequency of claims in relation to number of vehicles insured, average claim costs and pure premiums or loss costs per car can be computed from the data which is publicly available in reasonable detail.

It should be understood, as noted above, that insurance information, if used with care, is superior to a limited sample survey such as may be obtained by canvass. The sheer volume of insurance claims in relation to all injuries almost makes this self-evident. For example, I have analyzed insurance claims reported as a result of accidents occurring in 1962. For that year, insurers reported 71,318 claims on $78,886,599 of Michigan bodily injury automobile liability insurance premiums; this is 904 claims per million dollars of premiums in relation to the $90,522,000 for automobile bodily injury liability insurance premiums from all sources in the state.[68] (The difference in the dollar figures for total premiums is due to the fact that not all insurance premiums are shown in the detailed statistical calls issued by licensed statistical organizations to insurers in the form necessary; in some instances automobile bodily injury liability insurance premiums have been combined with other coverages; also, in part, Michigan experience on some minor classifications is reported together with that for other states.) Persons killed or injured in automobile accidents as reported to the Michigan State Police numbered 110,030 in 1962.[69] Reflecting the fact that approximately 15 per cent of the persons involved in motor vehicle accidents (mainly minor injuries) may not report such incidents to the State Police, it is clear that the number of persons injured or killed is no more than 55 per cent[70] more than the number of persons reported as having automobile bodily injury liability insurance claims. Even taking into account that the above insurance data does not reflect approximately 9 per cent of the costs arising from uninsured motorists,[71] 5 per cent from self-insurers, and 3 per cent from workmen's compensation claims, it is apparent from a comparison of insurance and State Police data that claims reported to insurers cover the majority of situations which involve injuries or fatalities.

Much valuable information is available from workmen's compensation

---

[68] *See* Table D-1.

[69] *Id.*

[70] *Id.*

[71] At first blush, it might be thought that uninsured motorist claims are already reflected in insurance data through uninsured motorist coverage. In fact, however, the above figures are based on the year 1962, when relatively little uninsured motorists coverage was either (1) bought, or (2) utilized after it had been bought. Thus, losses caused by uninsured motorists were not reflected to any substantial extent in the statistical data.

Secondly, the question arises as to why the figure 9% is used. The Michigan police data, it is true, indicates that only 7% of motorists report that they are uninsured. Letter to the author from the Director of Driver Services, Mich. Dep't of State, May 3, 1966. On the other hand, 9% *is* the present relationship of the uninsured motorist premium to the average automobile liability insurance premium. Beyond that, the uninsured motorist premium only covers accidents between insureds and uninsureds. In addition, there will be accidents between uninsureds. But these additional accidents will be paid for under Basic Protection since everyone will have insurance under Basic Protection's compulsory feature; thus, these accidents will not be an additional cost to the new Basic Protection system. This, in turn, means that even the 9% figure covering only accidents involving an insured and an uninsured may be conservative.

insurance data reported to the National Council on Compensation Insurance, a statistical organization, and from ratemaking data reported by the Michigan Workmen's Compensation Rating Bureau, a ratemaking organization which acts on behalf of insurers. Workmen's compensation claims in certain classifications, such as truckmen, outside salesmen, delivery men and bus and taxicab company employees, are mostly generated from automobile accidents. This is indicated by the records of the Workmen's Compensation Board in New York State and would also apply in Michigan. Moreover, the average claim costs in these classifications by type of injury are applicable, with some adjustment,[72] to automobile accidents generally not necessarily involving workmen's compensation. The economic loss which results directly from injuries in automobile accidents is accurately determined by applying these costs to the distribution of injuries reported to the State Police.

Although the primary emphasis in this study is on data disclosed through insurance records rather than from noninsurance sources, much information has also been included from other sources and given proper weight in measuring cost factors. The noninsurance information considered was taken from sources such as the records of the Michigan State Police, the United States Bureau of the Census, the United States Deparment of Health, Education and Welfare, Public Health Service, the National Safety Council, the National Industrial Conference Board, and the Health Insurance Institute.

The Michigan State Police provide extremely valuable detailed information regarding injuries and fatalities according to description of the accident situation, age, sex and other characteristics. In measuring economic (as opposed to intangible or psychic) loss for this study, it has been necessary to translate information published by age and sex to census format so that the information from all sources can be properly combined to measure economic loss.[73]

## B.   United States Department of Health, Education & Welfare National Health Survey

There is a general belief that motor vehicle accidents tend to be more severe than other accidents. This is borne out by the following:

"The 2,890,000 persons injured per year in moving motor vehicle accidents represent a rate of 1.6 persons injured per 100 population. Moving motor vehicle accidents resulted in 49.1 days of restricted activity and 14.6 days of bed disability per 100 population, and 25.3 days lost from work per 100 currently employed population. . . . [T]he number of persons injured in moving motor vehicle accidents is a small percentage of the number of persons injured in all accidents. However, the days of disability resulting from moving motor vehicle accidents are a much

[72] *See* notes to Table B.
[73] *See* Tables A & B.

higher proportion of the total disability days for all accidents. This would indicate that moving vehicle accidents involving injury occur less frequently than other types of accidents, but the injuries incurred tend to be more severe. The severity of motor vehicle injuries is substantiated by the fact that in 1960 about two of every five persons killed in accidents were killed in moving motor vehicle accidents"[74]

It should be noted that the United States Department of Health, Education and Welfare reports that 24 per cent of all injuries from all causes caused the individual to spend at least one day in bed; included with these disabling injuries were 5 per cent of the total which necessitated hospitalization.[75] Also, of the persons injured in moving motor vehicle accidents, 93 per cent were medically attended, 71 per cent suffered activity-restricting injuries, 42 per cent suffered bed-disabling injuries and 23 per cent suffered hospitalizing injuries.[76] Serious injuries for the selected automobile classifications used in this study are reported as approximately only 1.5 per cent of all injury categories; but figures for serious injuries from the adjusted State Police figures are also applied in this study. These latter reflect that serious injuries amount to 7.8 per cent of all injuries. It is these adjusted State Police figures which are in fact relied on in this study for the *number* of cases, including the number and distribution of serious injuries. As to *costs* per case, data from the selected workmen's compensation classifications have been applied to the distribution of cases according to severity of injury based on the adjusted State Police figures.[77]

## C.  *Health Insurance Institute*

The Health Insurance Institute provides a wealth of information on medical care, morbidity, and income maintenance in the United States. Detailed information is also provided on the extent of coverage available under health insurance.[78] The number of people protected for hospital, surgical, and regular medical expense coverages such as are afforded by Blue Cross, Blue Shield and other medical insurance plans is reported for every state; for example, approximately 6,838,000 persons in the state of Michigan were protected for hospital expense, 6,595,000 were protected for surgical expenses and 5,625,000 were protected for regular medical expenses, as of December

---

[74] U.S. Dep't of Health, Education & Welfare, National Health Survey, Series B, No. 42, *Health Statistics: Persons Injured in Motor Vehicle Accidents: Associated Disability* 6 (Feb. 1963).

[75] U.S. Dep't of Health, Education & Welfare, Public Health Service, Series 10, No. 8, *Types of Injuries: Incidence and Associated Disability, U.S. July 1957-June 1961*, at 3 (April 1964).

[76] *Supra* note 74, at 7.

[77] Notes to Table B. *See also* Tables C-3, Parts I-V and C-4, Parts I-III.

[78] The figures which follow in the text exclude any payments made on the policies issued for automobile insurance either under the liability or medical payments coverage; nor do they include costs incurred under workmen's compensation insurance.

31, 1964.[79] These numbers of persons compare with the estimated total population in Michigan of approximately 8,098,000 persons for 1964.[80] This signifies that approximately 80 per cent of the total Michigan population is covered for at least some hospital, surgical, and regular medical expense.[81]

In 1964, for the United States as a whole, approximately 48 million persons were covered by loss of income protection. Approximately 36 million were covered by insurance policies, 4 million of whom had more than one policy. In addition, approximately 11 million of these were protected through formal sick leave plans and 1 million were protected through other plans, such as union administered plans and employee mutual benefit associations.[82] Generally, the sick leave plans provide high percentages of salary income while other plans, including insurance, tend to be payable at somewhat lower percentages. These have been recognized in this study at average income percentages of 70 per cent and 35 per cent respectively, or 43 per cent of income for covered persons in the labor force. The 48 million covered persons are comparable to the United States currently employed population of approximately 70 million for the fiscal year July 1964-June 1965,[83] or 68 per cent of the labor force. The average income protection of 43 per cent applied to 68 per cent of the labor force affords approximately 29 per cent of lost income to the total labor force. This has been recognized in the section of the study which considers persons injured in automobile accidents according to labor force characteristics appearing in Table C-3, Parts I-IV.

### D.  *Social Security, Medicare, and Aid to the Medically Indigent*

The Basic Protection plan provides for deductions on account of payments made from outside sources.[84] The Social Security System is an important source of Basic Protection cost defrayment, particularly on account of Medicare, from which substantial offsets may be expected. In brief, Medicare provides that normally the individual pays the first $40 of medical cost plus 20 per cent of the remainder.[85] In cases of extended illnesses, the cost per individual will often be higher since the hospital benefits can be exhausted. In connection with automobile accidents, I have assumed that Medicare would afford no reduction in the Basic Protection costs associated with

[79] HEALTH INSURANCE INSTITUTE, SOURCE BOOK OF INSURANCE HEALTH DATA 1965, at 26 (1966).

[80] U.S. DEP'T OF COMMERCE, STATISTICAL ABSTRACT OF THE UNITED STATES 1965, Table 7 (1966).

[81] *See* notes to Table C-3, Parts I-IV.

[82] *Supra* note 79, at 22.

[83] U.S. DEP'T OF HEALTH, EDUCATION & WELFARE, PUBLIC HEALTH SURVEY, Series 10, No. 25, *Current Estimates From the Health Interview Survey U.S. July 1964-June 1965,* Table 18, at 20 (1965).

[84] Keeton & O'Connell, *Basic Protection Automobile Insurance,* pp. 54-56 *supra.*

[85] Parts A & B of the system have not been separately considered as most persons purchase Part B in addition to Part A.

death claims, since the death case will normally exceed $10,000 in overall loss. With respect to serious claims, I have estimated that the eligible individual would bear 25 per cent of the medical cost while 75 per cent would be paid by the federal government, and would therefore be an offset under the Basic Protection plan. With respect to claims other than death or serious claims, I have assumed the individual would bear the cost of the first $40 plus 20 per cent of the remaining average medical cost; for these claims, the offset under the Basic Protection plan is estimated at 80 per cent of the average medical cost after first deducting $40 from the average medical cost in nonserious and medical only cases (cases with medical loss alone).[86]

It is estimated that benefits afforded through Blue Cross, Blue Shield, and similar medical plans would be 90 per cent of the comparable Medicare amounts per case for all except medical only cases. Offsets for medical only cases have been taken at $3 per eligible case, the same amount as developed for Medicare cases. Offsets for loss of income under the Social Security System have not been included since the proportion of persons age 65 and over who are in the labor force is relatively small. Even though aid to the medically indigent under Title XIX[87] in Michigan could result in very extensive offsets under the Basic Protection plan, we cannot tell what effect will be produced; therefore, the figures are developed without offset for Title XIX and on this account must be viewed as conservative estimates of actual costs.

### E. *Michigan Cost Elements of Automobile Accidents*

Additional sources and descriptions of information bearing on personal injuries which result from automobile accidents are given later in this report.

The largest single body of homogeneous insurance information available is that pertaining to private passenger type automobiles classified according to elaborate statistical plans and regularly reported to insurance supervisory authorities. Such private passenger data comprise seven-eighths or more of all automobile bodily injury liability insurance experience. The records reported by two so-called statistical agents—the Mutual Insurance Rating Bureau and the National Bureau of Casualty Underwriters—whose members

---

[86] Such offset understates the actual offsets since the average cost is heavily weighted by relatively large claims.

[87] Aid to the medically injured under Title XIX affords very substantial medical benefits to persons not covered by Medicare (Title XVIII), based on income criteria which are established by the individual states, subject to approval by the federal government. The recent situation in New York State gives some indication of how far-reaching the program can be. "Under the New York plan, the average family of four with one wage-earner (the example usually used in public assistance programs) can qualify for full coverage under Medicaid as long as his net income does not exceed $6,000 a year." N.Y. Times, Dec. 12, 1967, col. 2. Moreover, it is possible for persons to be eligible for aid as medically indigent even though they are property owners or owners of non-liquid assets.

and subscribers write a significant[88] element of the total amount of automobile bodily injury liability insurance have been used as representative of present cost levels. The Michigan private passenger automobile bodily injury liability insurance experience of these companies was used to determine the comparative cost estimates set forth in Table 1.

### F.  Michigan State Police Statistics on Traffic Accidents

### 1.  Table A

The Michigan State Police publish data[89] regarding reported deaths and personal injuries resulting from automobile accidents. However, the information as published was not entirely suitable for use in summary form. Through the excellent cooperation of the State Police, I was given access to the detailed worksheets. This permitted me to develop my own summaries consistent with labor force characteristics and other data necessary to make a determination of costs under the proposed Basic Protection plan. The information which is summarized in Table A shows persons injured in automobile accidents covering the year 1965. Other significant characteristics such as age and sex are also recorded. For the current study, individual characteristics which bear on economic loss were identified and combined with specific economic and other cost factors in Table A. Also part of Table A are the United States Census reports of percentages of persons in the labor force in Michigan according to age and sex.[90] These percentages have been applied to persons injured in automobile accidents according to pertinent age and sex characteristics. Injured persons in Michigan automobile accidents are then distributed to reflect the numbers of such injured persons both in and outside of the labor force.

### 2.  Table B

The results of Table A are used in Table B to separate the persons injured and their labor force characteristics into three categories of injury reported to the State Police, namely: A—injuries that include bleeding wounds, distorted member or any condition that required victim to be carried from the scene. B—other visible injuries. C—no visible injury but complaint of pain. Also added in Table B are adjustments for unreported cases at 10 per cent for nonserious injuries and 20 per cent for medical only cases.[91]

---

[88] Approximately 20% to 25% of all automobile liability insurance business is written by these bureau companies and most other companies adjust their rates according to the rates made by the two bureaus.

[89] MICHIGAN STATE POLICE, MICHIGAN TRAFFIC ACCIDENT FACTS (published annually).

[90] U.S. DEP'T OF COMMERCE, BUREAU OF THE CENSUS, UNITED STATES CENSUS OF POPULATION 1960, Michigan, General Social and Economic Characteristics, Table 54, Status by Age and Sex.

[91] The resulting average increases for all cases is approximately 14%. Serious cases then make up 7.8% of all injury cases whereas workmen's compensation cases show serious cases to be 1.1% to 1.5% of all injury cases; the adjustments tend to be conservative for computing Basic Protection costs and result in high estimates of average claim costs. *See* p. 141 *supra*.

Thirty per cent of the *A* type traffic cases are taken to correspond to serious workmen's compensation cases; 70 per cent of the *A* type and all *B* type traffic cases are taken to correspond to the nonserious workmen's compensation cases; all *C* type traffic cases are taken to correspond to the medical only workmen's compensation cases. All traffic death cases are taken to correspond to the workmen's compensation death cases. The resulting figures of Table B are utilized in Table C-3, Parts I-V and Table C-4, Parts I-III to obtain average economic loss before and after collateral source benefits are paid.

## G.   *Extension of Statistical Data*

Before going into detail concerning the workmen's compensation data, several aspects pertinent to applying such data to available automobile information might be noted as perhaps especially illustrative of the variables that affect the cost of Basic Protection.

The cost elements derived from automobile bodily injury liability insurance data include the cost effects of paying for pain and suffering; the workmen's compensation data are based on only economic loss. Thus, the average claim cost (individual claims limited to $10,000) based on automobile insurance is $803 for the year ending June 30, 1964 (Table 2) compared with $697 on cost levels of September 1, 1965 derived from workmen's compensation data (Table 2 and Table C-4, Part II). The computed workmen's compensation net average claim costs tend to be overstated because the effect of limiting claims to $10,000 has been conservatively calculated.[92]

Medical cost, which is paid on an unlimited per claim basis under workmen's compensation, is approximately 29 per cent of combined income loss and medical cost ($204 as a percentage of $697; Table C-4, Part II). The high cost of death and major permanent cases which number only approximately 2.6 per cent[93] of the cases make up approximately 37 per cent[94] of the total cost limited to $10,000 per claim.

At the $10,000 limit per claim level, the average value of economic loss after offsets for other insurance appears to be approximately 83.1 per cent[95] of economic loss. Or to put it conversely, collateral sources cover 16.9 per cent of the first $10,000 of out-of-pocket losses for automobile accidents.

In connection with its ratemaking activities, the Michigan Workmen's Compensation Rating Bureau provides data on all workmen's compensation insurance classifications of risk.[96]

---

[92] Concerning this conservative calculation, *see* p. 147 *infra* and Table C-3, Part III.
[93] Derived from Table C-4, Part II.
[94] *Id.*
[95] *See* Table C-4.
[96] This data is Michigan workmen's compensation classification experience compiled from reports submitted from workmen's compensation insurance carriers to the National Council on Compensation Insurance, a statistical and advisory organization.

### 1. *Table C-1, Part I*

Table C-1, Part I sets forth the basic experience data reported to that Bureau on policies effective July 1, 1962 through June 30, 1963 (all except the relatively few three-year policies expire from July 1, 1963 through June 30, 1964) and adjusted to reflect additional benefits mandated by law effective September 1, 1965. The experience of the classifications which mainly cover automobile exposures, namely, outside salesmen, chauffeurs, drivers, truckmen, parcel delivery, and bus or taxicab company employees, is shown separately; for comparative purposes, the experience of all classes of workers is also shown. Work loss and medical costs, as well as the number of claims, are shown by category of injury, *i.e.*, death, permanent total, major permanent partial, minor permanent partial, temporary, and noncompensable medical (cases not serious enough to be compensated under workmen's compensation due to the waiting period before payment is due).

### 2. *Table C-1, Part II*

Table C-1, Part II carries forward the Table C-1, Part I data and reallocates the number of claims and dollar amounts in recognition of waiting periods before payment is due under the Workmen's Compensation Law.[97] The reallocation procedures are based upon and are consistent with the tables used in standard workmen's compensation law amendment adjustment procedures.[98]

### 3. *Table C-2*

Table C-2 sets forth the calculated average wage loss and medical loss; it is based on the data shown in Table C-1, Part II. This cost information is carried forward into Table C-3, Parts I through V.

### 4. *Table C-3, Part I*

Table C-3, Part I shows the cost of permanent total claims (1 per cent of the number of serious claims). Unlimited cost of injury to employed persons is shown as well as costs limited to $10,000 and costs to all persons (including housekeepers), with each case limited to $10,000. The offset effects of Medicare, Blue Cross and similar plans of insurance are also shown. In every instance, these offsets have been included as a reduction of medical cost which has been counterbalanced by an equal amount of increase in the cost of work loss so that only the unlimited cost per case is affected. In other words, the work loss in a case of permanent total disability is so large that

---

[97] MICH. STAT. ANN. § 17.153 (Supp. 1965).

[98] The information necessary for the adjustment will be found in the 1965 workmen's compensation rate revision filed by the Michigan Workmen's Compensation Rating Bureau with the state insurance supervisory authority; the underlying tables used in the rate revision will be found in the 1952 PROCEEDINGS OF THE NATIONAL ASSOCIATION OF INSURANCE COMMISSIONERS.

it will eat up the $10,000 limit, regardless of how much the medical losses are taken care of by collateral medical insurance.

### 5. *Table C-3, Part II*

Table C-3, Part II deals with cases of major permanent partial injury (17 per cent of the number of serious claims). The technique for developing average costs per case is identical to that used in Table C-3, Part I, including the manner in which offsets are applied.

### 6. *Table C-3, Part III*

Table C-3, Part III develops the cost of cases of minor permanent partial injury (82% of all serious injuries). The technique used in developing these figures is similar to that of the two preceding tables; however, the unlimited average cost per case is $9,568 and thus, unlike the prior two tables, would be seriously affected when each case is limited to a maximum cost of $10,000. In other words, if every case in a given category is clearly worth more than $10,000 (as is true with cases of permanent total disability or major permanent partial injury), the $10,000 limit applies to limit benefits in every case. Conversely, if every case in a given category is clearly under $10,000 (as is the case with relatively trivial injuries), the limit never applies to cut off benefits. The trouble for costing purposes comes when many cases in a category are under while many are also over the $10,000 limit, with the average being close to the limit. In that situation, measuring the effect of the limit is difficult because one finds it hard to know how many claims will fall above or below.

Observations of skewed distributions (for example, a distribution with a preponderance of small claims) of automobile liability claims by size indicate that if the amount of each claim is cut off at the *average* cost of all claims, then *more* than half of the total cost would be eliminated. In other words, the relatively few large claims constitute a very large proportion of the total cost. But, for employed persons, the minor permanent partial cost per case, shown in Table C-3, Part III converted to a basis limited to $10,000, has been conservatively taken at only 50 per cent of the unlimited cost. In recognition of the fact that medical costs for particular types of cases tend to have a narrow distribution centering around the average, no reduction in the medical cost has been reflected, and the 50 per cent reduction from the unlimited average claim costs has been taken entirely on the work loss portion. With respect to offsets for Medicare, Blue Cross, Blue Shield and similar plans, these have been computed as a reduction in average medical costs, of which half an equal amount has been included as a counter-offset or increase in the average work loss of injury to all persons (including housekeepers) with each case limited to $10,000. To illustrate, it is assumed that the typical case will be affected in the following way: If an injured person had $9,000 of wage loss and $1,500 of medical loss, with $1,000 of collateral sources in medical insurance, he would be paid $9,500 in Basic Protection benefits ($9,000 for wage loss and $500 for medical loss). In other words, the $1,000 collateral source has reduced the Basic Protection payment by only $500. It might be noted that the offset effect of income has been applied entirely to reduce the limited wage loss amount of all cases (including housekeepers), with no assumption that the offset of collateral income loss protection will affect reimbursement for medical loss (contrary to the assumption concerning the effect of collateral medical payments on wage loss benefits under Basic Protection).[99] This was done because—having been conservative in taking the minor permanent partial cost per case on a limited basis as only 50 per cent of the unlimited cost despite the fact that if the amount of each claim is cut off at the *average* cost of all claims, more than half of the total cost will be eliminated—it was not felt that additonal conservatism was required concerning the offset effect of collateral income loss protection.

### 7.    *Table C-3, Part IV*

Table C-3, Part IV considers the effect of claims of nonserious injury. The unlimited average claim cost of $694 for employed persons is assumed to be unaffected when each case is limited to $10,000. In other words, here—unlike where the average cost per case is $9,568 (as in cases of minor permanent partial injuries, Table C-3, Part III)—the average cost is so low that the $10,000 limit will not cut off payment. The average claim cost is reduced to $485 when all persons (including housekeepers whose work losses are taken to be less) are included. The offset effects of Medicare, Blue Cross, Blue Shield and similar programs are applied to the average medical costs. Also, the offset effect of loss of income is applied to reduce the cost of work loss per case.[100] In other words, with relatively small losses, the collateral sources to the extent paid *do* reduce to the same extent the payment under Basic Protection, unlike the situation in cases of permanent total injury (Table C-3, Part I), major permanent partial injury (Table C-3, Part II), and minor permanent partial injury (Table C-3, Part III).

### 8.    *Table C-3, Part V*

Table C-3, Part V shows the average cost per cases where medical loss, but no work loss, is involved. The unlimited average claim cost of $31 is expected to be unaffected by limiting the cost of each case to $10,000. A minor offset is estimated to be available on account of Blue Cross, Blue Shield and similar programs.

---

[99] *See also* pp. 146-47 *supra* for a discussion of applying collateral medical loss protection to wage loss and vice versa.
[100] *Id.*

9. *Table C-4*

Table C-4 compares overall average claim costs in Michigan automobile accidents with costs as reflected by limitations of coverage and deductibles. It summarizes the average claim cost for all automobile accidents on various bases, including an unlimited cost basis. The weighted averages for claim costs are developed in Table C-4, Parts I-III, where the average claim cost for each type of injury has been taken from Table C-3, Parts I-IV and weighted by the number of persons injured in Michigan automobile accidents in 1965. The average claim cost for all persons (including housekeepers) with each case limited to $10,000 is taken as an index of 100.0 per cent. The percentage effects and cumulative effects of funds from other collateral sources, deductibles and nonrecoverable income loss (roughly 15 per cent equal to income tax deduction)[101] are shown as percentage factors. These have been carried forward into Table 1 to calculate an estimate of the cost of the proposed Basic Protection plan. The standard deductible effect of 15.0 per cent (Table 1, line 12) has been taken from Table D-3. The reduction of cost on account of nonreimbursable net income loss has been derived from the work loss part of the average claim cost for all persons (including housekeepers), with each case limited to $10,000, which appears in Table C-4, Part II.

*H.  Automobile Bodily Injury Liability Insurance*

1. *Table D-1*

Insurers report their experience in a variety of ways. Annual statewide aggregate results are shown in the annual statement filed by every insurer each year. Reports to statistical agents[102] are also made in great detail according to classifications of vehicles, amount of excess loss, etc. For the year 1962 premiums from both sources are shown in Table D-1. In addition, the number of bodily injury liability claims reported to statistical agents (such as the National Bureau of Casualty Underwriters) is shown and converted to the number of claims per million dollars of premiums for that year. This latter figure has been applied to more inclusive annual statement figures for the state.[103] The resulting figure is compared with State Police records of the number of persons reported killed or injured in 1962. To include minor accidents which are not reported,[104] the number was increased by 15 per cent,

---

[101] Keeton & O'Connell, *supra* note 84, at 54.

[102] Summaries are reported to insurance departments. Consolidations of data are also reported by the statistical agents to member and subscriber insurers.

[103] Some insurance data is not reported for each state in the insurance statistics by classification (of, for example, private passenger, commercial, or public automobiles). However, all *premiums* are reported for each state, including Michigan. Consequently, the number of Michigan claims which are not included in insurance statistics by classification can be obtained in proportion to the total premiums. *See* Table D-1.

[104] *See* MICHIGAN STATE POLICE, 1964 MICHIGAN TRAFFIC ACCIDENT FACTS 5-6: "The

paralleling studies in Canada[105] and New York.[106] On this basis, there are 55 per cent more persons killed and injured in Michigan than are reported in automobile bodily injury liability insurance statistics.

It is pertinent here to reflect that the insurer counts only those claims where it has put up an amount in reserve on account of an accident or where it has made a payment on the claim. Initially, the count of claims will reflect the insurer's practices and evaluation of an incident described by its insured and not by the accident victim; thus there may be confusion between property damage and personal injury and uncertainty as to whether personal injury occurred, even though an insurer records a claim. This confusion of facts, together with unsuccessful liability claims under the present system, is reflected in the subsequent reports of statistics filed by insurers. For example, the Mutual Insurance Rating Bureau discounts the first report of claims to the Mutual Insurance Rating Bureau and the National Bureau of Casualty Underwriters by 4.7 per cent to compensate for this situation and, in effect, converts the first reports of claims to a later report basis for the same incidents. Summaries from the usual classification records reported to the statistical agents are contained in Table D-1.

## 2.  *Table D-2*

Experience by classifications of types of vehicles in detail includes allocated claim expense—that is, the insurer's loss adjustment expense which is allocable to the specific claim. The information of Table D-2 shows how claim expense on a countrywide basis is divided into claim expense allocable to the particular claim and unallocated claim expense (*i.e.*, maintenance of files, records, etc.). The total loss adjustment expense of the members of the two leading statistical organizations has been used to determine the 1964 allocated claims expense and is expressed in terms of losses and allocated claims expense as they are reported in the detailed statistical plan used by the statistical agents. In both instances, for Mutual Insurance Rating Bureau and for National Bureau companies, allocated claims expense averages to approximately 9 per cent of losses plus allocated claims expense.

## 3.  *Table D-3 and Table D-4*

The Mutual Insurance Rating Bureau and the National Bureau of Casualty Underwriters function as both statistical and rate-making organizations.

data . . . include accurate comparable information on the number of traffic deaths but not on injury and property damage accidents since many of the latter are never reported."

[105] Wittick, *Estimating the Cost of Accident Insurance as a Part of Automobile Liability Insurance*, 51 PROCEEDINGS OF THE CASUALTY ACTUARIAL SOCIETY 105, 115 (1964), which uses a 15% increase on all nonfatal cases.

[106] Harwayne, *Insurance Cost of Automobile Basic Protection Plan in Relation to Automobile Bodily Injury Liability Costs*, 53 PROCEEDINGS OF THE CASUALTY ACTUARIAL SOCIETY 122, 132 (1966).

For purposes of computing the amount of losses eliminated by various sizes of deductible insurance cost, these organizations call for and collect data by size of claim. Such countrywide information, excluding New York State experience for the year 1962, is shown in summary form in Table D-3. Under a program to pay 90 per cent of the amount of claims subject to a deductible of the first hundred dollars of loss, the cost would be 85.0 per cent of the cost without a deductible feature. A minor variation due to the fact that only work loss is subject to the standard deductible for losses in excess of $100[107] need not be included in the foregoing factor.

### APPENDIX TABLE I
MICHIGAN
BASIC PROTECTION PROGRAM
($10,000/$20,000 B.I. LIABILITY PREMIUM = 100%; UNINSURED MOTORIST PREMIUM—9%;
MEDICAL PAYMENTS PREMIUM = 24%)

| | Allocated Claim Expense Per Car (a) | Pure Loss Pure Premiums With Pain and Suffering | |
| --- | --- | --- | --- |
| | | Included (b) | Excluded (c) |
| A. *Modified to $10,000/$20,000 Basis* | | | |
| 1. Liability Basis | 5.4% | 54.1% | 47.1% |
| 1a. Including Uninsured Motorist, line 1 × 1.09 | 5.9 | 59.0 | 51.3 |
| 2. Non-Liability Basis line 1 × 1.55 | 9.1 | 91.5 | 79.5 |
| Reduction to Reflect Removal of | | | |
| 3. Uninsured Autos Under Compulsory Insurance line 2 × .09 | — .8 | — 8.2 | — 7.2 |
| 4. Coverage by Self-Insurers line 2 × .05 | — .5 | — 4.6 | — 4.0 |
| 5. Coverage Under Workmen's Compensation line 2 × .03 | — .3 | — 2.7 | — 2.4 |
| 6. Line 2 After Foregoing Reductions lines 2+3+4+5 | 7.5% | 76.0% | 65.9% |
| 7. Estimated Saving in Allocated Claim Expense line 6(a)×50% | —3.7 | | |
| 8. Lines 6(a)+7(a) | 3.8% | 76.0% | 65.9% |
| 9. Line 8(a) in Basic Protection Insurance line 8(a)×50% | 1.9% | | |
| 10. Line 8(a) in Liability Insurance above Tort Exemption line 8(a)—9(a) | 1.9% | | |
| 11. Line 8(c) After Funds From Other Sources line 8(c) × 83.1% | | | 54.8% |

[107] Keeton & O'Connell, *supra* note 84, at 56-58.

APPENDIX TABLE I *(continued)*
MICHIGAN
BASIC PROTECTION PROGRAM

| | Allocated Claim Expense Per Car (a) | Pure Loss Pure Premiums With Pain and Suffering | |
|---|---|---|---|
| | | Included (b) | Excluded (c) |
| 12. Line 11(c) After $100 or 10% Deductible line 11 × 85.0% | | | 46.6 |
| 13. Line 12(c) After 15% Deduction of Net Income Loss line 12 × (100.0%—10.6%) | | | 41.7 |
| 14. Line 9(a) increased by 50% of line 6(a) to include half of claimant's attorney's fees | 5.7% | | |

| | Pure Prem. incl. Alloc. Claim |
|---|---|
| A. *Modified to $10,000/ $20,000 Basis* | |
| 15. All Pain and Suffering Excluded lines 13(c) + 14(a) | 47.4% |
| B. *Modified to $10,000/$100,000 Basis* | |
| 16. Cost of Coverage Between $10,000/$20,000 and $10,000/$100,000 .15 × line 15 | 7.1% |
| 17. Cost of Basic Protection $10,000/$100,000 Basis lines 15 + 16 | 54.5% |
| Insurer's Expenses | |
| 18. General—Table 2, line 2.1, col. (b) increased 15% for $10,000/$100,000 limits, and 9% for uinsured motorist coverage, 6.5%×115%× 109% | 8.2% |
| 19. Unallocated Claim—Table 2, line 3, col. (b) increased 9% for uninsured motorist coverage and increased 15% for $10,000/$100,000 limits, adjusted to reflect more claims in ratio of lines 6(a) ÷ 1a(a) and no saving, 6.0% × 109% × 115% × lines (6(a) ÷ 1a(a)) × 100% | 9.5% |
| 20. Losses Including Loss Adjustment Expense and General Expense lines 17 + 18 + 19 | 72.2% |
| 20a. Premium Chargeable, line 20 ÷ (100.0% — loading for acquisition, tax, profit) or line 20 ÷ (100.0% — 28.0%) | 100.3% |
| C. *Basic Protection with Deductible Eliminated—Intrastate Coverage* | |
| 21. Premium Elimination of Deductible in line 12 [lines (11-12) ÷ (100.0% — 28.0%)] × 1.15 | 13.1% |
| 21a. Premium with Deductible Eliminated lines (20a + 21) | **113.4%** |

APPENDIX TABLE I *(continued)*
MICHIGAN
BASIC PROTECTION PROGRAM

| | Premiums Per Car | |
|---|---|---|
| | Index Number | Per Cent |
| **D.** *Present Auto Liability Premiums* | | |
| 22. $10,000/$20,000 Liability Premium Including Uninsured Motorist and $2,000 Med. Pay. | 133. | 100% |
| 23. Basic Protection, line 20a | 100.3 | 75% |
| **E.** *Additional Coverage* | | |
| 24. Tort Liability for Pain and Suffering Between $5,000 and $10,000 Per Claim 1.15 [line 10(a) + .10 × lines (1a(b) — 1a(c))] ÷ (100.0% — 28.0%) | 4.3 | |
| **F.** *Basic Protection Plus Additional Coverage* | | |
| 25. lines 23 + 24 | 104.6 | 79% |
| 26. lines 24 + 21a (Removal of Deductible) Including Out-of-State Tort Liability Coverage | 117.7 | 88% |
| 27. With In-State Wage Deductible 95% × line 25 + 6%[1] × line 22 | 107.4 | 81% |
| 28. Without Wage Deductible 95% × line 26 + 6%[1] × line 22 | 119.8 | 90% |
| **G.** *Basic Protection Only* | | |
| 29. Basic Protection Only, line 20a | 100.3 | 75% |

[1] *See* notes 41 & 42 *supra* and accompanying text.

APPENDIX TABLE II
MICHIGAN
BASIC PROTECTION PROGRAM
($10,000/$20,000 B.I. LIABILITY PREMIUM = 100%; UNINSURED MOTORIST PREMIUM—9%;
MEDICAL PAYMENTS PREMIUM = 24%)

| | Allocated Claim Expense Per Car (a) | Pure Loss Pure Premiums With Pain and Suffering | |
|---|---|---|---|
| | | Included (b) | Excluded (c) |
| **A.** *Modified to $10,000/$20,000 Basis* | | | |
| 1. Liability Basis | 5.4% | 54.1% | 47.1% |
| 1a. Including Uninsured Motorist, line 1 × 1.09 | 5.9 | 59.0 | 51.3 |
| 2. Non-Liability Basis line 1 × 1.55 | 9.1 | 91.5 | 79.5 |
| Reduction to Reflect Removal of | | | |
| 3. Uninsured Autos Under Compulsory Insurance line 2 × .09 | — .8 | — 8.2 | — 7.2 |

APPENDIX TABLE II *(continued)*
MICHIGAN
BASIC PROTECTION PROGRAM

| | Allocated Claim Expense Per Car (a) | Pure Loss Pure Premiums With Pain and Suffering | |
|---|---|---|---|
| | | Included (b) | Excluded (c) |
| 4.  Coverage by Self-Insurers line 2 × .05 | — .5 | — 4.6 | — 4.0 |
| 5.  Coverage Under Workmen's Compensation line 2 × .03 | — .3 | — 2.7 | — 2.4 |
| 6.  Line 2 After Foregoing Reductions lines 2 + 3 + 4 + 5 | 7.5% | 76.0% | 65.9% |
| 7.  Estimated Saving in Allocated Claim Expense line 6(a) × 75% | — 5.6 | | |
| 8.  Lines 6(a) + 7(a) | 1.9% | 76.0% | 65.9% |
| 9.  Line 8(a) in Basic Protection Insurance line 8(a) × 50% | 1.0% | | |
| 10.  Line 8(a) in Liability Insurance above Tort Exemption line 8(a) — 9(a) | .9% | | |
| 11.  Line 8(c) After Funds From Other Sources line 8(c) × 83.1% | | | 54.8% |
| 12.  Line 11(c) After $100 or 10% Deductible line 11 × 85.0% | | | 46.6 |
| 13.  Line 12(c) After 15% Deduction of Net Income Loss line 12 × (100.0% — 10.6%) | | | 41.7 |
| 14.  Line 9(a) increased by 50% of line 6(a) to include half of claimant's attorney's fees | 4.8% | | |

| | Pure Prem. incl. Alloc. Claim |
|---|---|
| *A.  Modified to $10,000/$20,000 Basis* | |
| 15.  All Pain and Suffering Excluded lines 13(c) + 14(a) | 46.5% |
| *B.  Modified to $10,000/$100,000 Basis* | |
| 16.  Cost of Coverage Between $10,000/$20,000 and $10,000/$100,000 .15 × line 15 | 7.0% |
| 17.  Cost of Basic Protection $10,000/$100,000 Basis lines 15 + 16 | 53.5% |

APPENDIX TABLE II *(continued)*
MICHIGAN
BASIC PROTECTION PROGRAM

| | |
|---|---|
| Insurer's Expenses | |
| 18. General—Table 2, line 2.1, col. (b) increased 15% for $10,000/$100,000 limits, and 9% for uninsured motorist coverage, 6.5% × 115% × 109% | 8.2% |
| 19. Unallocated Claim—Table 2, line 3, col. (b) increased 9% for uninsured motorist coverage, and increased 15% for $10,000/$100,000 limits, adjusted to reflect more claims in ratio of lines 6(a) ÷ 1a(a) and 25% saving, 6.0% × 109% × 115% × lines (6(a) ÷ 1a(a)) × 75% | 7.1% |
| 20. Losses Including Loss Adjustment Expense and General Expense lines 17 + 18 + 19 | 68.8% |
| 20a. Premium Chargeable line 20 ÷ (100.0% − loading for acquisition, tax, profit) or line 20 ÷ (100.0% − 28.0%) | 95.6% |

C. *Basic Protection with Deductible Eliminated—Intrastate Coverage*

| | |
|---|---|
| 21. Premium Elimination of Deductible in line 12 [lines (11-12) ÷ (100.0% − 28.0%)] 1.15 | 13.1% |
| 21a. Premium with Deductible Eliminated lines (20a + 21) | 108.7% |

| | Premiums Per Car | |
|---|---|---|
| | Index Number | Per Cent |
| D. *Present Auto Liability Premiums* | | |
| 22. $10,000/$20,000 Liability Premium Including Uninsured Motorist and $2,000 Med. Pay. | 133. | 100% |
| 23. Basic Protection, line 20a | 95.6 | 72% |
| E. *Additional Coverage* | | |
| 24. Tort Liability for Pain and Suffering Between $5,000 and $10,000 Per Claim 1.15 [line 10(a) + .10 × lines (1a(b) − 1a(c))] ÷ (100.0%−28.0%) | 2.8 | |
| F. *Basic Protection Plus Additional Coverage* | | |
| 25. lines 23 + 24 | 98.4 | 74% |
| 26. lines 24 + 21a (Removal of Deductible) | 111.5 | 84% |
| Including Out-of-State Tort Liability Coverage | | |
| 27. With In-State Wage Deductible 95% × line 25 + 6%[1] × line 22 | 101.5 | 76% |
| 28. Without Wage Deductible 95% × line 26 + 6%[1] × line 22 | 113.9 | 86% |
| G. *Basic Protection Only* | | |
| 29. Basic Protection Only, line 20a | 95.6 | 72% |

[1] *See* notes 41 & 42 *supra* and accompanying text.

APPENDIX TABLE III

MICHIGAN

BASIC PROTECTION PROGRAM

($10,000/$20,000 B.I. LIABILITY PREMIUM = 100%; UNINSURED MOTORIST PREMIUM—9%;
MEDICAL PAYMENTS PREMIUM = 24%)

| | Allocated Claim Expense Per Car (a) | Pure Loss Pure Premiums With Pain and Suffering | |
| --- | --- | --- | --- |
| | | Included (b) | Excluded (c) |
| *A.  Modified to $10,000/$20,000 Basis* | | | |
| 1.  Liability Basis | 5.4% | 54.1% | 47.1% |
| 1a. Including Uninsured Motorists, line 1 × 1.09 | 5.9 | 59.0 | 51.3 |
| 2.  Non-Liability Basis line 1 × 1.55 | 9.1 | 91.5 | 79.5 |
| Reduction to Reflect Removal of | | | |
| 3.  Uninsured Autos Under Compulsory Insurance line 2 × .09 | — .8 | — 8.2 | — 7.2 |
| 4.  Coverage by Self-Insurers line 2 × .05 | — .5 | — 4.6 | — 4.0 |
| 5.  Coverage Under Workmen's Compensation line 2 × .03 | — .3 | — 2.7 | — 2.4 |
| 6.  Line 2 After Foregoing Reductions lines 2 + 3 + 4 + 5 | 7.5% | 76.0% | 65.9% |
| 7.  Estimated Saving in Allocated Claim Expense line 6(a) × 0% | | | |
| 8.  Lines 6(a) + 7(a) | 7.5% | 76.0% | 65.9% |
| 9.  Line 8(a) in Basic Protection Insurance line 8(a) × 50% | 3.8% | | |
| 10. Line 8(a) in Liability Insurance above Tort Exemption line 8(a) − 9(a) | 3.7% | | |
| 11. Line 8(c) After Funds From Other Sources line 8(c) × 83.1% | | | 54.8% |
| 12. Line 11(c) After $100 or 10% Deductible line 11 × 85.0% | | | 46.6 |
| 13. Line 12(c) After 15% Deduction of Net Income Loss line 12 × (100.0% − 10.6%) | | | 41.7 |
| 14. Line 9(a) increased by 50% of line 6(a) to include half of claimant's attorney's fees | 7.6% | | |

APPENDIX TABLE III *(continued)*
MICHIGAN
BASIC PROTECTION PROGRAM

|  | Pure Prem. incl. Alloc. Claim |
|---|---|
| **A.** *Modified to $10,000/ $20,000 Basis* | |
| 15. All Pain and Suffering Excluded | |
| lines 13(c) + 14(a) | 49.3% |
| **B.** *Modified to $10,000/$100,000 Basis* | |
| 16. Cost of Coverage Between $10,000/$20,000 and $10,000/$100,000 | |
| .15 × line 15 | 7.4% |
| 17. Cost of Basic Protection $10,000/$100,000 Basis | |
| lines 15 + 16 | 56.7% |
| Insurer's Expenses | |
| 18. General—Table 2, line 2.1, col. (b) increased 15% for $10,000/$100,000 limits, and 9% for uninsured motorist coverage, 6.5% × 115% × 109% | 8.2% |
| 19. Unallocated Claim—Table 2, line 3, col. (b) increased 9% for uninsured motorist coverage and increased 15% for $10,000/$100,000 limits, adjusted to reflect more claims in ratio of lines 6(a) ÷ 1a(a) and no saving, 6.0% × 109% × 115% × lines (6(a) ÷ 1a(a)) × 100% | 9.5% |
| 20. Losses Including Loss Adjustment Expense and General Expense, | |
| lines 17 + 18 + 19 | 74.4% |
| 20a. Premium Chargeable line 20 ÷ (100.0% — loading for acquisition, tax, profit) or line 20 ÷ (100.0% — 28.0%) | 103.3% |
| **C.** *Basic Protection with Deductible Eliminated—Intrastate Coverage* | |
| 21. Premium Elimination of Deductible in line 12 | |
| [lines (11-12) ÷ (100.0% — 28.0%)] × 1.15 | 13.1% |
| 21a. Premium with Deductible Eliminated | |
| lines (20a + 21) | 116.4% |

|  | Premiums Per Car | |
|---|---|---|
|  | Index Number | Per Cent |
| **D.** *Present Auto Liability Premiums* | | |
| 22. $10,000/$20,000 Liability Premium Including Uninsured Motorist and $2,000 Med. Pay. | 133. | 100% |
| 23. Basic Protection, line 20a | 103.3 | 78% |

APPENDIX TABLE III *(continued)*
MICHIGAN
BASIC PROTECTION PROGRAM

| | Premiums Per Car | |
| --- | --- | --- |
| | Index Number | Per Cent |
| E. *Additional Coverage* | | |
|   24.  Tort Liability for Pain and Suffering Between $5,000 and $10,000 Per Claim 1.15 [line 10(a) + .10 × lines (1a(b) − 1a(c))] ÷ (100.0% − 28.0%) | 7.2 | |
| F. *Basic Protection Plus Additional Coverage* | | |
|   25.  lines 23 + 24 | 110.5 | 83% |
|   26.  lines 24 + 21a (Removal of Deductible) Including Out-of-State Tort Liability Coverage | 123.5 | 93% |
|   27.  With In-State Wage Deductible 95% × line 25 + 6%[1] × line 22 | 113.0 | 85% |
|   28.  Without Wage Deductible 95% × line 26 + 6%[1] × line 22 | 125.4 | 94% |
| G. *Basic Protection Only* | | |
|   29.  Basic Protection Only, line 20a | 103.3 | 78% |

[1] *See* notes 41 & 42 *supra* and accompanying text.

TABLE A

MICHIGAN

ALL PERSONS INJURED IN MOTOR VEHICLE ACCIDENTS
REPORTED IN 1965, BY AGE AND SEX
ADJUSTED TO REFLECT LABOR FORCE CHARACTERISTICS

| Age | Males Injured | | | |
| --- | --- | --- | --- | --- |
| | Total Number | % in Labor Force | Number In Labor Force | Number Not In Labor Force |
| Under 15 | 11,092 | | | |
| 15–24 | 32,369 | 56.3% | 18,224 | 14,145 |
| 25–34 | 14,657 | 95.4 | 13,983 | 674 |
| 35–44 | 12,249 | 96.2 | 11,784 | 465 |
| 45–64 | 14,654 | 90.7 | 13,291 | 1,363 |
| 15–64 | 73,929 | | 57,282 | 16,647 |
| 65 & Older | 3,784 | 26.2 | 991 | 2,793 |

| Age | Females Injured | | | |
| --- | --- | --- | --- | --- |
| | Total Number | % in Labor Force | Number In Labor Force | Number Not In Labor Force |
| Under 15 | 8,949 | | | |
| 15–24 | 20,892 | 33.3% | 6,957 | 13,935 |
| 25–34 | 9,441 | 31.7 | 2,993 | 6,448 |
| 35–44 | 9,831 | 39.3 | 3,864 | 5,967 |
| 45–64 | 12,934 | 38.6 | 4,993 | 7,941 |

TABLE A (*continued*)

| | | | | Housekeeping | Not Housekeeping |
|---|---|---|---|---|---|
| 15-64 | 53,098 | | 18,807 | 32,577 | 1,714 |
| 65 & older | 3,453 | 9.2 | 318 | 2,978 | 157 |

Notes: 1. Total number injured by age and sex is based on 1965 reports to the State Police.
2. Per cent in labor force is based on United States Census of Michigan Population 1960—Table 54, Labor Force Status by Age and Sex.
3. Female Housekeeping taken at 95% of Number Not in Labor Force. Not Female Housekeeping taken at 5% of Number Not in Labor Force.

TABLE B

MICHIGAN

NUMBER OF PERSONS INJURED IN 1965 AUTOMOBILE ACCIDENTS
BY CATEGORY OF SERIOUS, NON-SERIOUS, AND MEDICAL

| Age, Sex and Labor Force Characteristics | All Categories (Excluding Unreported) | By Category (Including Unreported) | | |
|---|---|---|---|---|
| | | Serious | Non-Serious | Medical |
| *Age 15-16* | | | | |
| Number in Labor Force: | | | | |
| Male | 57,282 | 5,134 | 28,639 | 31,758 |
| Female | 18,807 | 1,686 | 9,403 | 10,427 |
| Number Not in Labor Force: | | | | |
| Male | 16,647 | 1,492 | 8,323 | 9,230 |
| Female—not housekeeping (at 5% of total) | 1,714 | 154 | 857 | 950 |
| Female—housekeeping (at 95% of total) | 32,577 | 2,920 | 16,288 | 18,061 |
| *Age 65 and older* | | | | |
| Number in Labor Force: | | | | |
| Male | 991 | 89 | 495 | 550 |
| Female | 318 | 29 | 159 | 176 |
| Number Not in Labor Force: | | | | |
| Male | 2,793 | 250 | 1,396 | 1,549 |
| Female—not housekeeping (at 5% of total) | 157 | 14 | 79 | 97 |
| Female—housekeeping (at 95% of total) | 2,978 | 267 | 1,489 | 1,651 |
| *Under Age 15* | | | | |
| Male & Female | 20,041 | 1,796 | 10,020 | 11,111 |
| Total Stated Ages | 154,305 | | | |
| Total—including Unreported | 176,529 | 13,831 | 77,148 | 85,550 |

See Notes to Table B (immediately following) for description of allocation to categories and inclusion of unreported cases. Totals for each category were obtained from Table A and have been distributed in proportion to amounts shown in first column.

### Notes to TABLE B
#### MICHIGAN

Note: 1. 155,256 injury cases were reported according to category of (A) bleeding wounds, distorted member or any condition that required victim to be carried from the scene; (B) other visible injuries; and (C) no visible injury but complaint of pain. Definitions of type differ somewhat for motor vehicle and workmen's compensation accidents; 30% of motor vehicle accidents identified under (A) above are taken as a high estimate comparable to serious accidents in the workmen's compensation sense, that is, permanent total, major permanent partial or minor permanent partial. (C) type accidents above are considered to correspond to the medical only type of accident under workmen's compensation. All others correspond to workmen's compensation non-serious accidents.

2. Non-serious injury cases have been increased 10% and medical cases have been increased 20% to include cases unreported to the State Police.

3. Death cases are included as reported to the State Police.

| Under State Police Definition | Cases | Under W.C. Definition | With Unreported Cases Excluded | With Unreported Cases Included |
|---|---|---|---|---|
| Death | 2,129 | Death | 2,129 | 2,129 |
| A | 46,102 | (Serious (30%)) | 13,831 | 13,831 |
|  |  | (Non-Serious (70%)) | 32,271 | 35,498 |
| B | 37,864 | Non-Serious | 37,864 | 41,650 |
| C | 71,292 | Medical | 71,292 | 85,550 |
| Total | 157,387 | Total | 157,387 | 178,658 |

The following is derived from Table C-1, Part II:

|  | Selected Auto Classes | | All Classes | |
|---|---|---|---|---|
|  | No. | Per cent | No. | Per Cent |
| Permanent Total) Major Permanent) Minor Permanent) | 141 | 1.5 | 2,933 | 1.1 |
| All cases excl. death | 9,241 | 100.0 | 250,698 | 100.0 |

This compares with figures for serious injuries developed from motor vehicle data:

| | | |
|---|---|---|
| Serious cases | 13,831 | 7.8% |
| All cases excluding death | 176,529 | 100.0% |

## TABLE C-1 (Part I)

MICHIGAN

EXPERIENCE ON POLICIES EFFECTIVE JULY 1, 1962–JUNE 30, 1963—WORKMEN'S
COMPENSATION–ACTUAL BASIS

Outside Salesmen, Chauffeurs, Drivers
Truckmen, Parcel Delivery, Bus or
Taxicab Company Employees

| Category | No. Of Claims | Work Loss Benefit | Medical | No. Of Claims | Work Loss Benefit | Medical |
|---|---|---|---|---|---|---|
| | | | | | All Classifications | |
| Death | 39 | $ 894,613 | $ 21,415 | 259 | $ 5,908,207 | $ 141,010 |
| Permanent Total | 2 | 36,083 | 18,129 | 30 | 813,533 | 302,183 |
| Major Permanent | 24 | 307,288 | 76,912 | 615 | 8,173,113 | 1,616,602 |
| Minor Permanent | 115 | 560,967 | 127,009 | 2,288 | 8,286,585 | 2,087,751 |
| Temporary | 1,528 | 1,179,477 | 574,050 | 24,089 | 17,769,020 | 8,052,633 |
| Non-Compensable) Medical ) | 7,527 | | 232,680 | 223,676 | | 5,608,441 |
| TOTAL | 9,280 | $2,978,428 | $1,050,195 | 250,957 | $40,950,458 | $17,808,620 |

Note: Reported figures were adjusted to reflect changes in the Michigan Workmen's Compensation Law as of September 1, 1965.

## TABLE C-1 (Part II)

### MICHIGAN

WORK LOSS AND MEDICAL COSTS—SELECTED AUTOMOBILE CLASSIFICATIONS AND ALL CLASSIFICATIONS FROM WORKMEN'S COMPENSATION WITH ADJUSTMENT FOR WAITING PERIOD

| Category | Outside Salesmen, Chauffeurs, Drivers Truckmen, Parcel Delivery, Bus or Taxicab Company Employees | | | All Classifications | | |
|---|---|---|---|---|---|---|
| | No. Of Claims | Work Loss Benefit | Medical | No. Of Claims | Work Loss Benefit | Medical |
| Death | 39 | $1,634,458 | $ 21,415 | 259 | $10,794,294 | $ 141,010 |
| Permanent Total | 2 | 63,181 | 18,129 | 30 | 1,424,496 | 302,183 |
| Major Permanent | 24 | 533,452 | 76,912 | 615 | 14,409,198 | 1,616,602 |
| Minor Permanent | 115 | 973,327 | 127,009 | 2,288 | 14,352,365 | 2,087,751 |
| Temporary | 4,523 | 2,474,708 | 666,895 | 71,303 | 37,281,892 | 9,232,983 |
| Non-Compensable Medical ) | 4,577 | | 139,835 | 176,462 | | 4,428,091 |
| TOTAL | 9,280 | $5,679,126 | $1,050,195 | 250,957 | $78,262,245 | $17,808,620 |

Note: 1. The number of temporary cases for all classifications includes those lasting 7 days or less taken at 196% of reported temporary cases. *See* note 98 *supra* and accompanying text. These cases were transferred from the non-compensable category at average non-compensable medical cost to the temporary category.

2. Work loss benefit figures on September 1, 1965 benefit levels were adjusted to full indemnity basis by regular limit factor procedures used by the rating organization. In addition, temporary indemnity cost was increased 21% for elimination of 7 day waiting period.

3. Medical costs reflect 1965 levels.

TABLE C-2

MICHIGAN

AVERAGE WORK LOSS AND MEDICAL COSTS
SELECTED AUTOMOBILE CLASSIFICATIONS
AND ALL CLASSIFICATIONS

| Outside Salesmen, Chauffeurs, Drivers Truckmen, Parcel Delivery, Bus or Taxicab Company Employees | | | All Classifications | |
|---|---|---|---|---|
| Category | Work | Medical | Work | Medical |
| Death | $41,909 | $ 549 | $41,677 | $ 544 |
| Permanent Total | 31,591 | 9,065 | 47,483 | 10,073 |
| Major Permanent | 22,227 | 3,205 | 23,430 | 2,629 |
| Minor Permanent | 8,464 | 1,104 | 6,273 | 912 |
| Temporary | 547 | 147 | 523 | 129 |
| Non-Compensable (Medical) | | 31 | | 25 |
| Average | 612 | 113 | 312 | 71 |

*Note:* Based on figures from Table C-1, Parts I and II.

## TABLE C-3 (Part I)

### MICHIGAN

SERIOUS INJURIES IN AUTOMOBILE ACCIDENTS IN 1965 (PERMANENT TOTAL=1% OF ALL SERIOUS INJURIES)—DOLLAR COSTS WITH OFF-SETS FOR FUNDS FROM OTHER SOURCES AND WITH AVERAGE COSTS PER PERMANENT TOTAL CASE

| Group | No. of Serious Cases | Permanent Total Work Loss & Medical* Cost per Case (Max. $10,000) | Amount | Amount* Deducted a/c Medicare | Blue Cross etc. | Loss of Income |
|---|---|---|---|---|---|---|
| *Age 15-64* | | | | | | |
| At 100% of wages | 6,820 | $10,000 | $ 68,200,000 | | | |
| At  50% of wages | 2,920 | 10,000 | 29,200,000 | | | |
| At   0% of wages | 1,646 | 10,000 | 16,460,000 | | | |
| Sub-Total | 11,386 | $10,000 | $113,860,000 | | | |
| *Age 65 and Older* | | | | | | |
| At 100% of wages | 118 | 10,000 | 1,180,000 | | | |
| At  50% of wages | 267 | 10,000 | 2,670,000 | | | |
| At   0% of wages | 264 | 10,000 | 2,640,000 | | | |
| Sub-Total | 649 | $10,000 | $ 6,490,000 | $4,412,551 | | |
| *Under Age 15* | | | | | | |
| At 0% wages | 1,796 | $10,000 | $ 17,960,000 | | | |
| Grand Total Serious | 13,831 | $10,000 | $138,310,000 | $4,412,551 | | |
| 80% of Grand Total | 11,065 | | | | $67,706,735 | |

* Costs of all serious cases at permanent total cost per case. Permanent total amounts are 1% of amounts shown.

## Notes to TABLE C-3 (Part I)

*Note*: Medicare applicable to age 65 and older taken at 75% of average of medical cost of $9,065 or $6,799. Blue Cross, etc., taken at 90% of medicare amount or $6,119 and applied to 80% of grand total serious cases.

Recapitulation—Permanent Total Disability Cost Per Case

| | Work Loss | Medical | Total |
|---|---|---|---|
| Employed Persons: | | | |
| Unlimited | $31,591 | $9,065 | $40,656 |
| Limited to $10,000 | $ 935 | $9,065 | $10,000 |
| | | | |
| All Persons (incl. Housekeepers): | | | |
| (a) Limited to $10,000 | $ 935 | $9,065 | $10,000 |
| (b) Medicare Offset† | + 319 | − 319 | — |
| (c) Blue Cross, etc. Offset† | +4,895 | −4,895 | — |
| (d) (a) + (b) + (c) | $ 6,149 | $3,851 | $10,000 |
| (e) Loss of Income Offset | | | |
| (f) Net Cost Before Deductible (d) + (e) | $ 6,149 | $3,851 | $10,000 |

† The dollar amount of reduction in medical cost is estimated to be offset by a comparable increase in work loss cost up to $10,000 limit.

## TABLE C-3 (Part II)
### MICHIGAN

SERIOUS INJURIES IN AUTOMOBILE ACCIDENTS IN 1965 (MAJOR PERMANENT PARTIAL=17% OF ALL SERIOUS INJURIES)—DOLLAR COSTS WITH OFF-SETS FOR FUNDS FROM OTHER SOURCES AND WITH AVERAGE COSTS PER MAJOR PERMANENT PARTIAL CASE

| Group | No. of Serious Cases | Major Permanent Partial Work Loss & Medical* | | Amount* Deducted a/c | | |
| --- | --- | --- | --- | --- | --- | --- |
| | | Cost per Case (Max. $10,000) | Amount | Medicare | Blue Cross etc. | Loss of Income |
| *Age 15-64* | | | | | | |
| At 100% of wages | 6,820 | $10,000 | $ 68,200,00 | | | |
| At  50% of wages | 2,920 | 10,000 | 29,200,000 | | | |
| At   0% of wages | 1,464 | 10,000 | 16,460,000 | | | |
| Sub–Total | 11,386 | $10,000 | $113,860,000 | | | |
| *Age 65 and Older* | | | | | | |
| At 100% of wages | 118 | $10,000 | $ 1,180,000 | | | |
| At  50% of wages | 267 | 10,000 | 2,670,000 | | | |
| At   0% of wages | 264 | 10,000 | 2,640,000 | | | |
| Sub–Total | 649 | $10,000 | $ 6,490,000 | $1,560,196 | | |
| *Under Age 15* | | | | | | |
| At 0% of wages | 1,796 | $10,000 | $ 17,960,000 | | | |
| Grand Total Serious | 13,831 | $10,000 | $138,310,000 | $1,560,196 | | |
| 80% of Grand Total | 11,065 | | | | $23,944,660 | |

* Costs of all serious cases at major permanent partial cost per case. Major permanent partial costs are 17% of amounts shown.

## Notes to TABLE C-3 (Part II)

*Note:* Medicare applicable to age 65 and older taken at 75% of average medical cost of $3,205 or $2,404. Blue Cross, etc. taken at 90% of medicare amount or $2,164 and applied to 80% of grand total serious cases.

Recapitulation—Major Permanent Partial Cost Per Case

|  | Work Loss | Medical | Total |
|---|---|---|---|
| Employed: |  |  |  |
| Unlimited | $22,227 | $3,205 | $25,432 |
| Limited to $10,000 | $ 6,795 | $3,205 | $10,000 |
| All Persons (incl. Housekeepers): |  |  |  |
| (a) Limited to $10,000 | $ 6,795 | $3,205 | $10,000 |
| (b) Medicare Offset† | + 113 | − 113 | — |
| (c) Blue Cross, etc. Offset† | +1,732 | −1,732 | — |
| (d) (a)+(b)+(c) | $ 8,640 | $1,360 | $10,000 |
| (e) Loss of Income Offset |  |  |  |
| (f) Net Cost Before Deductible (d) + (e) | $ 8,640 | $1,360 | $10,000 |

† The dollar amount of reduction in medical cost is estimated to be offset by a comparable increase in work loss cost up to $10,000 limit.

TABLE C-3 (Part III)

MICHIGAN

SERIOUS INJURIES IN AUTOMOBILE ACCIDENTS IN 1965
(MINOR PERMANENT PARTIAL = 82% OF ALL SERIOUS INJURIES)—
DOLLAR COSTS WITH OFF-SETS FOR FUNDS FROM OTHER SOURCES
AND WITH AVERAGE COSTS PER MINOR PERMANENT PARTIAL CASE

| Group | No. of Serious Cases | Minor Permanent Partial Work Loss & Medical* | | Medicare | Amount* Deducted a/c | |
| --- | --- | --- | --- | --- | --- | --- |
| | | Cost per Case (Max. $10,000) | Amount | | Blue Cross etc. | Loss of Income |
| *Age 15-64* | | | | | | |
| At 100% of wages | 6,820 | $4,784 | $32,626,880 | | | $7,276,940 |
| At 50% of wages | 2,920 | 2,944 | 8,596,480 | | | |
| At 0% of wages | 1,646 | 1,104 | 1,817,184 | | | |
| Sub-Total | 11,386 | | $43,040,544 | | | |
| *Age 65 and Older* | | | | | | |
| At 100% of wages | 118 | $4,784 | $ 564,512 | | | 125,906 |
| At 50% of wages | 267 | 2,944 | 786,048 | | | |
| At 0% of wages | 264 | 1,104 | 291,456 | | | |
| Sub-Total | 649 | | $ 1,642,016 | $537,372 | | |
| *Under Age 15* | | | | | | |
| At 0% of wages | 1,796 | $1,104 | $ 1,982,784 | | | |
| Grand Total Serious | 13,831 | $3,374 | $46,665,344 | $537,372 | | $7,402,846 |
| 80% of Grand Total | 11,065 | | | | $8,243,425 | |

* Costs of all serious cases at minor permanent partial cost per case, with employed persons' total cost limited to $10,000 per case taken at 50% of unlimited cost per case and indemnity cost limited to $10,000 per case obtained by deducting full unlimited medical amount from total cost per case, as shown below. Minor permanent partial amounts are 82% of total amounts shown.

## Notes to TABLE C-3 (Part III)

*Note:* Medicare applicable to age 65 and older taken at 90% of average medical cost of $1,104 or $828. Blue Cross, etc., taken at 75% of medicare amount or $745 and applied to 80% of grand total serious cases. Loss of income taken at 29% of work loss limited to $10,000, i.e. 29% of $3,680 or $1,067 applied to employed persons.

Recapitulation—Minor Permanent Partial Cost Per Case

|  | Work Loss | Medical | Total |
|---|---|---|---|
| Employed Persons: |  |  |  |
| Unlimited | $8,464 | $1,104 | $9,568 |
| Limited to $10,000 | $3,680 | $1,104 | $4,784 |
| All Persons (incl. Housekeepers): |  |  |  |
| (a) Limited to $10,000 | $2,270 | $1,104 | $3,374 |
| (b) Medicare Offset† | + 20 | − 39 | − 19 |
| (c) Blue Cross, etc. Offset† | + 298 | − 596 | − 298 |
| (d) (a) + (b) + (c) | $2,588 | $ 469 | $3,057 |
| (e) Loss of Income Offset | − 535 |  | − 535 |
| (f) Net Cost Before Deductible (d) + (e) | $2,053 | $ 469 | $2,522 |

† Half of the dollar amount of reduction in medical cost is estimated to be offset by an increase in work loss cost up to $10,000 limit.

## TABLE C-3 (Part IV)

### Michigan

#### Non-Serious Injuries in Automobile Accidents in 1965—
#### Dollar Costs with Off-Sets for Funds from Other Sources
#### and with Average Costs per Non-Serious Case

| Group | No. of Non-Serious Cases | Non-Serious Work Loss and Medical | | Deduction a/c | | Loss of Income |
|---|---|---|---|---|---|---|
| | | Cost Per Case (Max. $10,000) | Amount | Medicare | Blue Cross etc. | |
| *Age 15-64* | | | | | | |
| At 100% of wages | 38,042 | $694 | $26,401,148 | | | $6,048,678 |
| At  50% of wages | 16,288 | 421 | 6,857,248 | | | |
| At   0% of wages | 9,180 | 147 | 1,349,460 | | | |
| Sub-Total | 63,510 | | $34,607,856 | | | |
| *Age 65 and Older* | | | | | | |
| At 100% of wages | 654 | $694 | $   453,876 | | | 103,986 |
| At  50% of wages | 1,489 | 421 | 626,869 | | | |
| At   0% of wages | 1,475 | 147 | 216,825 | | | |
| Sub-Total | 3,618 | | $ 1,297,570 | $311,148 | | |
| *Under Age 15* | | | | | | |
| At 0% of wages | 10,020 | $147 | $ 1,472,940 | | | |
| Grand Total | 77,148 | $485 | $37,378,366 | $311,148 | | $6,152,644 |
| 80% of Grand Total | 61,718 | | | | $4,752,286 | |

## Notes to TABLE C-3 (Part IV)

*Note:* Medicare applicable to age 65 and older taken at 80% of (average medical cost less $40) or $86. Blue Cross, etc., taken at 90% of medicare amount or $77 and applied to 80% of total cases. Loss of income taken at 29% of work loss limited to $10,000, i.e., 29% of $547 or $159 applied to employed persons.

| | Recapitulation—Cost per Case | | |
|---|---|---|---|
| | Work Loss | Medical | Total |
| Employed: | | | |
| Unlimited | $547 | $147 | $694 |
| Limited to $10,000 | $547 | $147 | $694 |
| | | | |
| All Persons (incl. Housekeepers): | | | |
| (a) Limited to $10,000 | $338 | $147 | $485 |
| (b) Medicare Offset | | − 4 | − 4 |
| (c) Blue Cross, etc. Offset | | −62 | −62 |
| (d) (a) + (b) + (c) | $338 | $ 81 | $419 |
| (e) Loss of Income Offset | −80 | | −80 |
| (f) Net Cost Before Deductible (d) + (e) | $258 | $ 81 | $339 |

TABLE C-3 (Part V)

MICHIGAN

MEDICAL INJURIES IN AUTOMOBILE ACCIDENTS IN 1965—
DOLLAR COSTS WITH OFF-SETS FOR FUNDS FROM OTHER SOURCES
AND WITH AVERAGE COSTS PER MEDICAL ONLY CASE

| Group | No. of Medical Only Cases | Cost per Case (Max. 10,000) | Amount | Deduction a/c Medicare | Blue Cross etc. |
|---|---|---|---|---|---|
| 65 and over | 4,013 | $31 | $ 124,403 | $12,039[1] | |
| under 65 | 81,537 | 31 | 2,527,647 | | |
| Grand Total | 85,550 | $31 | $2,652,050 | $12,039 | |
| 80% of Grand Total | 68,440 | | | | $205,320[2] |

[1] Medicare applicable to age 65 and older taken at 10% of average medical cost of $31 or $3.

[2] Blue Cross, etc., taken at medicare amount of $3 and applied to 80% of total cases.

| Recapitulation—Cost Per Case | Medical | Total |
|---|---|---|
| Employed Persons: | | |
| Unlimited | $31 | $31 |
| Limited to $10,000 | $31 | $31 |
| All Persons (incl. Housekeepers): | | |
| (a) Limited to $10,000 | $31 | $31 |
| (b) Medicare Offset | —3 | —3 |
| (c) Blue Cross, etc. Offset | —2 | —2 |
| (d) (a) + (b) + (c) | $29 | $29 |
| (e) Loss of Income Offset | | |
| (f) Net Cost Before Deductible (d) + (e) | $29 | $29 |

[3] No offset because of $40 deductible under Medicare. *See* notes 85-86 *supra* and accompanying text.

TABLE C-4

MICHIGAN

COMPARISON OF AVERAGE CLAIM COSTS IN AUTOMOBILE ACCIDENTS—
EFFECT OF LIMITATIONS AND DEDUCTIBLES

| | Average Claim Cost | Effect of Limitation or Deductible | Cumulative Index |
|---|---|---|---|
| Employed Persons: | | | |
| 1. Unlimited | $1,794 | | |
| 2. Limited to $10,000 | 877 | | |
| All Persons (incl. Housekeepers) Limited to $10,000: | | | |
| 3. Before Funds From Other Sources | 697 | | 100.0% |
| 4. After Funds From Other Sources and Before Deductible | 579 | —16.9% | 83.1 |
| 5. Less: 15.0% Deductible Credit | | —15.0 | 70.6 |
| 6. Less: 15.0% of Net Income Loss Applied to Work Loss (15.0% x $493) ( $697) | | —10.6 | 63.1 |

*Note:* Dollar amounts carried forward from Table C-4, Parts I-III. Deductible of 15.0% taken from Table D-3. Concerning the equation against which 15.0% for tax equalization is applied, *see* Table C-4, Part II.

TABLE C-4 (Part I)

MICHIGAN

AVERAGE CLAIM COSTS BY TYPE OF INJURY IN AUTOMOBILE ACCIDENTS IN 1965—
EMPLOYED PERSONS, UNLIMITED BASIS

| Type of Injury | No. of Persons Injured | Average Claim Cost | | |
|---|---|---|---|---|
| | | Work Loss | Medical | Total |
| Permanent: | | | | |
| Total (1% of Serious) | 138 | $31,591 | $9,065 | $40,656 |
| Major Partial (17% of serious) | 2,351 | 22,227 | 3,205 | 25,432 |
| Minor Partial (82% of serious) | 11,342 | 8,464 | 1,104 | 9,568 |
| Serious | 13,831 | $11,034 | $1,541 | $12,575 |
| Non-Serious | 77,148 | 547 | 147 | 694 |
| Medical | 85,550 | | 31 | 31 |
| Sub-Total | 176,529 | $ 1,104 | $ 200 | $ 1,304 |
| Death | 2,129 | 41,909 | 549 | 42,458 |
| GRAND TOTAL | 178,658 | $ 1,590 | $ 204 | $ 1,794 |

TABLE C-4 (Part II)

MICHIGAN

AVERAGE CLAIM COSTS BY TYPE OF INJURY IN AUTOMOBILE ACCIDENTS IN 1965—EMPLOYED PERSONS LIMITED TO $10,000 AND ALL PERSONS (INCL. HOUSEKEEPERS) LIMITED TO $10,000 *Before* OFFSETS FOR FUNDS FROM OTHER SOURCES

| Type of Injury | No. of Persons Injured | Average Claim Cost Limited to $10,000 | | | | | |
|---|---|---|---|---|---|---|---|
| | | Employed Persons | | | All Persons (incl. Housekeepers) | | |
| | | Work Loss | Medical | Total | Work Loss | Medical | Total |
| Permanent: | | | | | | | |
| Total (1% of serious) | 138 | $ 935 | $9,065 | $10,000 | $ 935 | $9,065 | $10,000 |
| Major Partial (17% of serious) | 2,351 | 6,795 | 3,205 | 10,000 | 6,795 | 3,206 | 10,000 |
| Minor Partial (82% of serious) | 11,342 | 3,680 | 1,104 | 4,784 | 2,270 | 1,104 | 3,374 |
| Serious | 13,831 | $4,182 | $1,541 | $ 5,723 | $3,026 | $1,541 | $ 4,566 |
| Non-Serious | 77,148 | 547 | 147 | 694 | 338 | 147 | 485 |
| Medical | 85,550 | | 31 | 31 | | 31 | 31 |
| Sub-Total | 176,529 | $ 567 | $ 200 | $ 767 | $ 385 | $ 200 | $ 585 |
| Death | 2,129 | 9,451 | 549 | 10,000 | 9,451 | 549 | 10,000 |
| GRAND TOTAL | 178,658 | $ 673 | $ 204 | $ 877 | $ 493 | $ 204 | $ 697 |

*Note:* Average claim costs carried forward from Table C-3, Parts I-V. Medical costs in death cases carried forward from Table C-2.

TABLE C-4 (Part III)

MICHIGAN

AVERAGE CLAIM COSTS BY TYPE OF INJURY IN AUTOMOBILE ACCIDENTS IN 1965—ALL PERSONS (INCL. HOUSEKEEPERS) LIMITED TO $10,000 *After* OFFSETS FOR FUNDS FROM OTHER SOURCES

| Type of Injury | No. Of Persons Injured | Average Claim Cost Limited to $10,000 | | | | | |
|---|---|---|---|---|---|---|---|
| | | Including Medical Offsets | | | Including Medical Offsets and Loss of Income | | |
| | | Work Loss | Medical | Total | Work Loss | Medical | Total |
| Permanent: | | | | | | | |
| Total (1% of serious) | 138 | $6,149 | $3,851 | $10,000 | $6,149 | $3,851 | $10,000 |
| Major Partial (17% of serious) | 2,351 | 8,640 | 1,360 | 10,000 | 8,640 | 1,360 | 10,000 |
| Minor Partial (82% of serious) | 11,342 | 2,588 | 469 | 3,057 | 2,053 | 469 | 2,522 |
| Serious | 13,831 | $3,652 | $ 654 | $ 4,306 | $3,214 | $ 654 | $ 3,868 |
| Non-Serious | 77,148 | 338 | 81 | 419 | 258 | 81 | 339 |
| Medical | 85,550 | | 29 | 29 | | 29 | 29 |
| Sub-Total | 176,529 | $ 434 | $ 101 | $ 535 | $ 365 | $ 101 | $ 465 |
| Death | 2,129 | 9,451 | 549 | 10,000 | 9,451 | 549 | 10,000 |
| GRAND TOTAL | 178,658 | $ 541 | $ 106 | $ 647 | $ 473 | $ 106 | $ 579 |

*Note:* Average claim costs carried forward from Table C-3 Parts I-V. Medical costs in death cases carried forward from Table C-2.

TABLE D-1

MICHIGAN

1962 AUTOMOBILE BODILY INJURY LIABILITY INSURANCE DATA FOR
ALL INSURERS COMBINED

| Item | Premiums | No. of Claims |
|---|---|---|
| A. Insurance Data | | |
| (1) Private Passenger Non-Fleets | $59,603,423 | 56,602 |
| (2) All Others | 19,283,176 | 14,716 |
| (3) Total[1] | $78,886,599 | 71,318 |
| (4) Number of claims per $1,000,000 of premiums | | |
| (5) 1962 Premiums Reported in Annual Statements[2] | $90.522 | |
| (6) Number of claims for all insurers combined (5) × (4) | | 82,832 |
| B. Comparative Reports Elsewhere— State Police | | |
| (a) Number reported killed or injured 1962 | | 110,030 |
| (b) Increase for non-reporting at 15% of number injured | | 16,221 |
| (c) Total injured and killed | | 126,251 |
| C. Total injured and killed as ratio to claims under A | | 1.54 |
| Rounded | | 1.55 |

[1] Available in detailed statistical reports. Does not include some miscellaneous and public automobile classifications insured by mutual insurers.

[2] INSURANCE BY STATES, OF FIRE, MARINE, CASUALTY AND MISCELLANEOUS LINES 1962, at 16 (Mich.) (SPECTATOR, 1963 ed.).

TABLE D-2

MICHIGAN

ALLOCATED CLAIM EXPENSE FROM A COMPARISON OF INSURANCE EXPENSE EXHIBIT RESULTS
FOR CALENDAR YEAR 1964 AUTO BODILY INJURY LIABILITY INSURANCE

Experience of Member Companies:

| Claim Expense | Countrywide Ratios as % of Earned Premium | |
|---|---|---|
| | MIRB | NBCU |
| A. Allocated | 5.8% | 5.6% |
| B. Unallocated | 9.3 | 6.8 |
| C. Total Loss Adjustment | 15.1% | 12.4% |
| D. A as % of C | 38% | 45% |

Allocated Claim Expense as a Ratio to Losses and Allocated Claim Expense

| Item | Countrywide Ratios as % of Earned Premium | |
|---|---|---|
| | Mutual | Stock |
| E. Loss Adjustment | 16.3% | 13.2% |
| F. Allocated Claim D × E | 6.2 | 5.9 |
| G. Losses | 64.2 | 62.1 |
| H. Losses and Allocated Claim | 70.4% | 68.0% |
| I. F as % of H | 9% | 9% |
| J. Average of Stock and Mutual Insurers' Allocated Claim Expense as a Per Cent of Losses Including Allocated Claim Expense | 9% | |

TABLE D-3
MICHIGAN
INDICATED COST OF THE STANDARD DEDUCTIBLE OF $100 OR 10% PER CLAIM
(WHICHEVER IS LARGER) COUNTRYWIDE EXCLUDING NEW YORK STATE

| Item | Private Passenger | | All Cars | |
|---|---|---|---|---|
| | No. of Claims | Amount | No. of Claims | Amount |
| A. Less than $100 | 128,282 | $ 4,625,404 | 155,375 | $ 5,574,842 |
| B. $100 and less than $1,000 | 171,418 | 65,259,504 | 212,889 | 81,225,373 |
| C. $1,000-$10.000 | 78,629 | 228,567,003 | 99,314 | 293,161,283 |
| D. TOTAL | 378,329 | $298,451,911 | 467,578 | $379,961,498 |

Losses Eliminated by $100 or 10% Deductible Per Claim:

| | | | | |
|---|---|---|---|---|
| From A ($100) | | 4,625,404 | | 5,574,842 |
| From B ($100) | | 17,141,800 | | 21,288,900 |
| From C (10%) | | 22,856,700 | | 29,316,128 |
| E. Total Losses Eliminated | | $ 44,623,904 | | $ 56,179,870 |
| F. E as % of D | | 15.0% | | 14.8% |
| G. Charge with Deductible 100.0%-F | | 85.0% | | 85.2% |

TABLE D-4
MICHIGAN
1962 PRIVATE PASSENGER AUTO BODILY INJURY LIABILITY LOSSES BY SIZE OF CLAIM
(LIMITED TO $10,000 PER CLAIM) COUNTRYWIDE EXCLUDING NEW YORK STATE

| Size of Claim Group | Amount of Losses of Group Size | No. of Claims in Excess of Group Size |
|---|---|---|
| Less than $ 25 | $ 657,893 | 329,643 |
| Less than 50 | 1,841,604 | 292,732 |
| Less than 100 | 4,625,404 | 250,047 |
| Less than 250 | 14,535,169 | 185,065 |
| Less than 500 | 31,894,563 | 134,753 |
| Less than 1,000 | 69,884,908 | 78,629 |
| Less than 2,000 | 121,114,895 | 41,031 |
| Less than 3,000 | 158,650,793 | 25,199 |
| Less than 4,000 | 187,034,789 | 16,782 |
| Less than 5,000 | 208,060,041 | 11,974 |
| Less than 10,000 | 266,411,911 | 3,204 |
| First 10,000 | 298,451,911 | |

# REMARKS

*OF RICHARD J. WOLFRUM*†

## I. Introduction

DURING MY CAREER of some 20 years in the insurance business and especially during the last two years, several different types of changes in the insurance industry's present method of handling automobile injury claims have been proposed. Past experience demonstrates that most of these proposed changes have very little chance of being implemented unless they receive large-scale public support. It does not appear that generalized legal and philosophical objections to the present method can produce this support since an ordinary member of the public will probably not understand them. One cannot be expected to support any change unless he can be shown that he, personally, will benefit in some way. A demonstration that he will receive a reduction in the cost of the insurance premium that he pays is a benefit he understands. This has been shown to be true in a dramatic fashion during recent political developments in Massachusetts.

However, these same political developments showed that if one suddenly finds out that to obtain this reduction in cost he may lose some benefit that he is now getting from the present system, even at a higher cost, his enthusiasm for the change will probably become more restrained. If enough members of the public, possibly only a vocal minority, believe that the benefits they may lose by the change outweigh the benefits they will gain, the proposed change, in my opinion, is doomed to failure.

## II. Make-Up of Insurance Premium Dollar

In public announcements that mention some evaluation or cost of many of these proposed changes, I believe too much emphasis has been placed upon the amount of estimated overall reduction in insurance premium, and too little emphasis placed upon the sources of these reductions. In fairness, the public should be told that in order to obtain a reduction in insurance premiums, some element or elements that make up the present cost of the insurance dollar must be reduced or eliminated. They also should be adequately informed how the reduction or elimination of one or more of these elements will affect them, not only in terms of premium costs, but in terms of services or benefits they will no longer receive under any proposed change.

Let us examine the elements that make up an insurance dollar and in particular the normal breakdown of the premium dollar for a nonparticipat-

* *RICHARD F. WOLFRUM, B.A. 1941, Harvard College; Vice President 1961–1962, Casualty Actuarial Society; Actuary, Liberty Mutual Insurance Company, Boston.*

† *The editors report with regret the sudden death of Mr. Wolfrum a few weeks after delivering this paper.*

ing stock company charging the so-called "bureau" or "standard" rates. These companies generally operate through an independent agency or brokerage merchandising system. Companies using a different merchandising system, such as mutuals, direct writers, or "captive agency" companies, will generally have lower expense provisions which are reflected in lower rates or dividends paid to policyholders. If we examine the breakdown, we will see that the insurance dollar is composed essentially of three major parts: (Taken from the National Bureau of Casualty Underwriters Mutual Insurance Rating Bureau. See Appendix I for more detailed description of each element.)

1.  The loss portion, or that part which is used to carry out the provisions of the policy contract—to investigate, defend, settle and pay judgments on claims that are brought as the result of an accident covered under the policy.

2.  The company expense portion, or that part which is used principally to cover the various expenses that an insurance company must incur in selling, underwriting, rating, and writing of the insurance contract itself.

3.  The profit and contingency portion, or that part which is supposed to be left over to provide for future safety and growth of the company by additions to surplus or for dividends to stockholders and policyholders. (During recent years this portion has been used frequently as an additional source for the first two portions which did not prove adequate.)

### III.  Sources of Premium Reductions

Many legislators, members of the press, and members of the public seem to think that a reduction in insurance costs somehow can be produced by the waving of a magic wand. Unfortunately this is not true. In order to obtain a reduction in the insurance premium cost for an individual policyholder, a change has to occur in one or more or these elements. Generally speaking, a reduction can come from one or more of the following seven sources:

1.  Reduce the number of automobile accidents on the highway, *i.e.*, prevent accidents from happening through accident prevention programs or other safety measures—better highway engineering, better traffic enforcement, driver education and re-examination, car inspection, and removing unsafe drivers and cars from the roads.

2.  Reduce the number of automobile accidents covered under the insurance policy, *i.e.*, restrict the coverage—require certain conditions under which the accidents have to happen or put in exclusions that eliminate claims of certain types or sizes.

3. Reduce the number of persons who can successfully bring claims against the policy as a result of the accident—tighten up on the negligence requirements so that in order to collect, a claimant must be fault-free, or almost fault-free, and eliminate the fake claimants through more restrictive but more costly claim control procedures.

4. Reduce the benefits that the insurance company is required to pay out to the claimants under the system—do not pay any or pay only certain layers of some types of losses, require offsets for benefits paid by other coverages, and so forth.

5. Reduce some expense that the insurance company is now incurring, *i.e.*, eliminate the function causing the expense, or enable the company in some way to pay less for this function—reduce agent's commissions, claim expenses, or eliminate some policyholder service.

6. Eliminate some or all of the profit and contingency portion that the companies believe necessary for their safety and growth.

7. Reduce the cost of one individual by shifting part or all of his cost to some other individual—establish more refined classification systems or accident record systems that reduce some rates but are offset by increases in other rates.

## IV.  Sources of Various Proposed Changes

Most of the proposed changes discussed in this symposium have their principal source of reductions from the first four ways mentioned, although some will also, to a degree, involve the other three. Many efforts within the insurance industry have been and are presently being made to reduce costs, principally by working in the areas of sources (1), (5), and (7). Considerable efforts outside the industry are being currently directed towards source (6). I will limit myself for the most part to (a) the first four sources and to (b) an analysis of how one of the suggested changes, the Basic Protection plan,[1] proposes to obtain its cost reductions.

## V.  Sources of Cost Reductions for Basic Protection Coverage

### A.  *Source (1)—Reduction in Total Number of Accidents*

There is nothing in the Basic Protection plan that appears to be directed towards reducing accidents or their severity. In fact, by eliminating the requirement that there has to be an absence of negligence or fault in order to collect benefits for economic—or out-of-pocket as opposed to psychic—loss, the coverage may have an effect of increasing the number of accidents, since the accident-prone driver has little to lose or to deter him from continuing

---

[1] Keeton & O'Connell, Basic Protection for the Traffic Victim: A Blueprint for Reforming Automobile Insurance (1965) [both hereinbefore and hereinafter this book is often cited as Basic Protection]. *See also* Keeton & O'Connell, *Basic Protection Automobile Insurance*, p. 40 *supra*.

his reckless driving habits. However, let's estimate no change in claims or cost from this source.

### B. *Source (2)—Reduction in Accidents Covered Under Policy*

There are two major changes proposed under the Basic Protection plan that affect the number of bodily injury accidents covered. They have contra-acting effects since one adds accidents covered while the other eliminates certain accidents.

First, since it removes the requirement of negligence on the part of a third party in determining whether benefits will be paid,[2] this change will allow benefits to be paid to certain classes of persons injured in automobile accidents who are not now covered under third-party liability contracts. The most obvious group includes drivers who are injured as a result of a one-car accident. These injured drivers constitute about seven or eight per cent of all injuries,[3] according to an analysis of New York and California accident data by their respective motor vehicle departments. I have not included passengers in the car in such accidents since they are covered under present contracts. Except in the few states requiring gross negligence on the part of the driver, an analysis of our claim files indicates that in more than 95 per cent of the cases, these passengers are able to settle a claim against the driver's insurance carrier.

Let us estimate that 8 per cent of the total number of claims result from the increased coverage for these types of accidents. Because these types of accidents generally involve more severe injuries, I would estimate that the loss cost for these accidents would be about 10 per cent of the total.

However, the plan also provides for a sizeable restriction in accidents covered by excluding any injuries for which the net economic loss is less than $100.[4] In other words, if there is a net wage loss, medical and hospital bills of $100 or less (after deducting all other offsets which I will mention later), there is no coverage under the policy. A tort action must be started to collect this loss and these losses are shifted to another policy. The amount of reduction from this source will, of course, vary by state depending upon the distribution of injuries by severity of injury. Accurate statistical data is presently not available, but analyses of automobile bodily injury settlements by size of settlement can be used to provide a good estimate. I have done such analyses[5] and estimate that this will exclude from coverage a very large number of small injuries—about 40 per cent of the total. Since they are the very small injuries, this exclusion will reduce the cost only about four per cent.

[2] Keeton & O'Connell, *Basic Protection Automobile Insurance*, pp. 49-50, 52-53 *supra*.

[3] *See* Appendix 2.

[4] Keeton & O'Connell, *supra* note 2, at 56-58.

[5] *See* Appendix 3.

## C.  *Source (3)—Reduction in Claimants Who Can Successfully Bring Claims*

The Basic Protection plan eliminates absence of fault as a criterion to collect benefits in automobile accidents[6] so there are no reductions from this source. Rather there are some sizeable increases. One group becoming newly eligible to collect benefits are drivers who are involved in accidents which involve clear negligence on their part, for example, hitting a legally parked car or another car in the rear. A study of our claims indicates that in some of these cases both drivers bring claims but the clearly negligent driver almost never collects. An analysis of New York motor vehicle accident reports reveals that this group of clearly negligent drivers represents about five per cent of total automobile injuries and that the addition of this group will represent about the same percentage increase for both claims and losses.[7] (Here again I have excluded passengers in the car since they normally are successful in collecting benefits under the present system.)

The largest group of claimants who will be newly eligible to receive benefits are those claimants who are injured in questionable multi-car type accidents but who receive no settlement under the present liability contracts. (It should be pointed out, however, that many of these potential claimants receive benefits under the medical payments coverage of a liability policy.) I have made an analysis of the claim files of accidents reported to the company by our policyholders that could possibly involve a bodily injury claim by another party. We found that we closed, on the average, about 30 per cent of these files without making a payment under the liability coverage of the policy. (This percentage varies by state.) This represents a large number of potential claims but our analysis showed further that: (1) About two-thirds of these so-called CWP's (closed without payment) involved an accident reported by our policyholder for which no claim was made by another party. Most of these were minor cases. (2) About one-half of the remaining files (five per cent of CWP's) were relatively minor cases but we did receive a claim therefrom. On the basis of our investigation we denied liability on the part of our policyholder and did not hear further from the claimant. (3) The remaining five per cent were cases with a normal distribution of severity which were actively pursued by a claimant or his lawyer, but we successfully argued that the claimant was negligent and settled for no payment or obtained a favorable outcome in a suit.

The additional benefits to be paid on these cases under a no-fault system of claims administration is very difficult to evaluate because of the many imponderables presented which are not susceptible to actuarial analysis. While the large majority of these claims settled for no payment are minor ones, with little out-of-pocket loss, the elimination of fault would generate many practical claim handling problems that may substantially increase costs.

[6] Keeton & O'Connell, *supra* note 2, at 52-53.
[7] *See* Appendix 4.

Here are just a few: (1) There will be increased difficulty in handling a claim on a first-party basis with your own policyholder[8] under a coverage which provides many benefits based upon subjective standards. This is particularly true if non-wage earners are claimants. (2) Malingering by claimants to build up wage loss is likely to be more troublesome. (3) The presentation of unreasonable medical and hospital fees must be investigated. (4) There will probably be an increase in small claims from non-wage earners for disability or loss of services. These items are not easily evaluated. (5) There will be pressure on insurers to make payments over and above economic loss merely to conclude settlement.

Looking at these additional cases from a purely economic loss basis and assuming that there would be no increase in claims or benefits paid due to the "imponderables" mentioned, I would personally estimate this 30 per cent of multi-car claims presently closed without payment represents an increase of only about 10 per cent in benefits that would be paid out under the Basic Protection plan.

### D. Source (4)—Reduction in Benefits to Claimants

As we have seen, the overall effect of Basic Protection coverage on the first three sources is to bring about an increase in benefits paid and not a decrease. This is mainly due to the elimination of the third-party claims method and the fault principle. However, when we come to source (4), this coverage makes very substantial and drastic reductions in benefits compared to the benefits that claimants receive under the present negligence system. These reductions in benefits more than offset all of the increases in losses due to the other changes.

### 1. Limitation on Recovery for Pain and Suffering

No benefits are paid for the first $5,000 of pain and suffering.[9] If damage for such elements amounts to more than $5,000, the excess over $5,000 is collectible in a tort action under the defendant's liability insurance coverage.[10]

I have been able to find very little statistical data available on just what proportion of present settlements of various types of tort liability cases are for "pain and suffering." I have talked to many people from claims departments in various companies and there appears to be a consensus that, on the average, tort liability settlements are 2½ times "specials." As I understand their terminology, "specials" are wage loss, medical and hospital costs. If this consensus is true, this means that these "specials," or the economic loss, represent only 40 per cent of the settlements under the present system and the Basic Protection coverage cuts benefits to claimants by 60 per cent.

[8] *See* Keeton & O'Connell, *supra* note 2, at 49-50.
[9] *Id.* at 50-51.
[10] *Id.*

Proponents of the Basic Protection plan argue that this is not true since a large portion of this 60 per cent is paid out as claimants' attorneys' fees. Several studies have been made by people outside the insurance industry as to the percentage of a trial court judgment that goes to the claimants' attorneys, but this provides very little information as to the amount of money that is paid claimants' attorneys in those cases where the settlement is negotiated between the attorney and the insurance company. If we can believe the estimates of many people in the legal profession who advocate changes in the present claims systems, claimants' attorneys take as much as 50 per cent of some settlements.[11]

Before we accept that these large percentages of loss payments do not reach the injured victim, I believe some attempt should be made to obtain reasonably accurate data on attorney fees in an objective way. Surely the claimants' attorneys have a stake in the present tort system. Therefore, they should provide complete statistical data in this area, at least so that they themselves can recognize the scope of the problem and defend their role in the current method of handling automobile injuries. If they do not, their silence will give credence to the large percentages which are bandied about by their critics.

However, as far as the reduction in insurance payments is concerned, it doesn't make any difference where this 60 per cent goes. The reduction in benefits paid out from this one area alone must be in the vicinity of 50 per cent if the consensus of the claims people is accurate.

## 2. *Elimination of Collateral Source Rule*

The next revolutionary reduction in benefits paid is caused by the abrogation of the collateral source rule, thereby eliminating payment of any benefits for wage loss, and hospital and medical bills which are payable to the claimant from other sources.[12] The principal other sources of benefits include: (1) Individual or employer-provided wage continuation and health plans; (2) Workmen's Compensation benefits; (3) Medicare; (4) Social Security benefits; (5) Medicaid; (6) Governmental disability or health benefits; (7) Military and Veterans benefits; and (8) Union Welfare plans. A long list of other miscellaneous sources which provide some benefits in case of an automobile injury could also be considered.

The Health Insurance Institute estimates that during 1965, 156 million people or 81 per cent of the civilian population in the United States had some form of private health insurance.[13] The breakdown is as follows:

---

[11] *See* A. Conard, J. Morgan, R. Pratt, C. Voltz & R. Bombaugh, Automobile Accident Costs and Payments—Studies in the Economics of Injury Reparation 190-91 (1964).

[12] Keeton & O'Connell, *supra* note 2, at 54-56.

[13] Health Insurance Institute, 1966 Source Book of Health Insurance Data ch. 2, at 10-12.

Hospital expense ............................................................ 81%
Surgical expense ............................................................. 75%
Regular medical expense ............................................... 58%
Major medical expense ................................................... 26%
Loss of income protection ............................................. 26%

However this only considers statistical data for the first source listed above (individual or employer-provided health and wage continuation plans), and only formal plans provided by insurance companies or Blue Cross and Blue Shield. It does not include any informal arrangements made by employers.

Let us consider practical operating problems: (1) How will the Basic Protection carrier obtain accurate information of the existence of these other sources? (2) Would coverage for any benefits paid out under the Basic Protection plan be eliminated by these other sources? Assuming these other sources will be available as offsets, I would give a conservative estimate of at least an average 25 per cent reduction in benefits paid to the claimants. Many claimants, however, will suffer a 100 per cent reduction in benefits.

### 3. Deductible

After the wage, hospital and medical losses are reduced by benefits available from other sources,[14] the plan provides for a deductible of $100 or 10 per cent of wage loss, whichever is greater.[15] Using statistical data on insurance liability claims settlements by size, and making certain assumptions with respect to what portions of the settlements are for pain and suffering, wage loss, and medical and hospital bills, this reduction amounts to about eight per cent.[16]

### 4. Additional Deductible for Tax Impact

In addition to the standard deductible, a further deductible of 15 per cent of wage loss is made under the plan to recognize the fact that a disabled wage earner has a sizeable income tax saving during his period of disability.[17] Using the same liability settlement data as we used before, this will result in a reduction of about 12 per cent.[18]

### VI. SUMMARY OF THE EFFECTS OF PROPOSED CHANGES

Let me recapitulate and sum up the various possible increases and decreases that I have estimated from these first four sources, based upon my assumptions.

[14] Keeton & O'Connell, *supra* note 2, at 54-56.
[15] *Id.* at 56-58.
[16] *See* Appendix 3.
[17] Keeton & O'Connell, *supra* note 2, at 54.
[18] *See* Appendix 3.

BASIC PROTECTION PLAN

EFFECT OF PROPOSED CHANGES ON LOSS PORTION OF AUTOMOBILE BODILY INJURY LIABILITY
PREMIUM DOLLAR

|  | % of total claims | % of total benefits |
|---|---|---|
| **ADDITIONS:** | | |
| One-car accidents ............................................. | 8% | 10% |
| Multiple car accidents | | |
| Clearly negligent drivers ............................. | 5% | 5% |
| Claims made but now closed without payments ...................................................... | 30% | 10% |
| INCREASE OVER PRESENT LIABILITY SYSTEM .... | 63% | 30% |
| **REDUCTIONS:** | | |
| Claims with less than $100 of economic loss ..................................................... | 40% | 4% |
| Pain & suffering benefits .............................. | — | 50% |
| Collateral sources of economic loss .......... | — | 25% |
| Deductible of $100 or 10% of wage loss | — | 8% |
| Income tax deductible of 15% of wage loss | — | 12% |
| DECREASE FROM PRESENT LIABILITY SYSTEM .. | 40% | 70% |
| TOTAL CHANGE FROM PRESENT LIABILITY SYSTEM ................................................................ | 2% decrease | 60% decrease |

Since these are not additive percentages but some apply after another prior change is made, the totals do not add to the sum of each column.

The Basic Protection plan, then, provides a very restricted coverage compared to the benefits provided by the standard 10/20 bodily injury liability coverage purchased today by the large majority of the public.

I would like to emphasize that these are only my estimates of the possible increases in injuries covered and benefits provided, based upon my personal assumptions and my knowledge and evaluation of present claim settlements and procedures. The percentages shown are not actuarially precise and not intended to be. The purpose of this evaluation is to put the changes proposed by this revolutionary and complex Basic Protection plan in their proper perspective and to compare the relative importance of each one of them. In my opinion, detailed statistical data, not presently available, should be made available and analyzed more precisely in order to check the basic assumptions, and more importantly, to evaluate the effect of these changes on individual car owners or homogeneous groups of car owners.

## VII. OTHER COVERAGES STILL REQUIRED

It should be realized that under the Basic Protection plan any responsible person would still need to buy liability insurance to cover the excess of $5,000 for pain and suffering. He may also wish to buy liability insurance to cover the first $100 of net loss, for which he also remains liable.[19] He will also continue to buy property damage liability and physical damage insur-

---

[19] Keeton & O'Connell, *supra* note 2, at 50-51.

ance (of the Collision or Comprehensive type). The premiums for these last two coverages amount to more than 50 per cent of the present insurance bills.[20] If he wishes to provide partial protection for himself and his family beyond that provided by Basic Protection, he will need to buy for each member of his family a form of disability insurance. If he wants to be paid actual damages for his pain and inconvenience, as such, he will need a new form of coverage,[21] not yet written by anyone, to provide for such coverage.

## VIII. Effect of Reduction on Expenses

Space limitations prevent any discussion of the probable effect that the Basic Protection plan would have on company claim investigations and legal expenses or on the other two elements of the insurance liability premium dollar: (1) company operation expenses, and (2) profit and contingency provisions. I will only say that I believe the Basic Protection plan, with its sizeable and drastic reduction in the loss portion of the premium dollar, will necessitate entirely new concepts of how to arrange the pricing structure to collect the required amount of money to take care of company services, operating functions, and safety margins items which traditionally have been collected as a function of the benefits paid out under the policies. Unless new, far-reaching, and revolutionary methods of merchandising, administering, and servicing the proposed insurance system under the Basic Protection plan can be instituted, there is no possible way, in my view, that a continuation of the current percentage mark-ups will provide enough money to service, underwrite and produce this policy, bill and collect the premium, and service the claims presented.

It is also important to realize that this will have an effect on the well over half a million people now involved in the present system of handling the automobile liability insurance system, not only the employees within the companies but others outside the companies who service the business such as agents, brokers, salesmen, independent adjusters, lawyers, judges, and court officials. And it should also be borne in mind that the automobile injury liability market amounted to $4\frac{1}{2}$ billion dollars in 1966. Therefore, any such changes deserve careful consideration before they are actually adopted.

## IX. Distributing the Overall Cost

I have not described in detail the vast and far-reaching changes that would be required to distribute equitably the overall cost of the benefits provided by the Basic Protection plan among the insurance buying public under the two-party (or related insurer) insurance system that the authors

[20] According to insurance data released by *The Spectator* for 1965 regarding countrywide automobile premiums, bodily injury premiums amounted to $4,107 million, while property damage premiums and physical damage premiums amounted to $1,646 million and $3,022 million, respectively.

[21] *See* Keeton & O'Connell, *supra* note 2, at 61.

propose to follow, replacing long established third-party (or unrelated insurer) procedures that make up the core of the liability system today.[22] Rates for many individuals will have greater reductions than the estimated overall average reduction, while rates for others will increase or have a substantially lower decrease because of the shifting of overall costs from one individual to another. Underwriting rules, classification systems, and rates based upon individual accident records all will require a new set of underlying principles. Discussions of these changes have been published elsewhere,[23] but there are two interesting aspects in this area that have not been covered adequately.

First, there is shifting of most of the cost of the accidents caused by commercial and long haul trucks to private passenger car owners. These accidents generally have higher than average claim costs and most of these losses fall on the commercial firms under the third-party negligence system. Under the proposed two-party claims system, each insurer will pay the economic loss of his own policyholder. Since most commercial firms carry Workmen's Compensation for their drivers, their net economic loss will be negligible except in the rare instances when their truck or tractor hits a pedestrian. Consequently, the major cost of the injuries in these accidents would be shifted to the private passenger car owners.

Another aspect of the plan not fully revealed is the shifting of the burden of the cost of bodily injuries caused by nonresidents of a state to the residents of the state in which the plan is effective. This is because a nonresident of the state has immunity to tort claims up to Basic Protection limits if he causes an accident in the state, and, in addition, under the assigned case plan system will receive reimbursement for his economic loss under Basic Protection. Also, if a resident of the state is injured outside the state by a resident of this outside state, he can receive Basic Protection benefits. He may still pursue his tort remedies by bringing an action against the resident of the outside state, but since settlement or judgment would require a reimbursement of the Basic Protection payments and since he has been compensated for economic loss, it is likely that he will not go to the trouble of bringing action against the resident of the outside state.[24] Therefore, the cost of many out-of-state accidents will also be borne by residents of the state.

## X. Conclusion

The total possible reductions are substantial to the point of being shocking, but they raise the question whether it is reasonable to believe that a

22 *Id.* at 49-50.

23 Wolfrum, *Discussion of Harwayne's Paper*, 53 Proceedings of the Casualty Actuarial Society 164, 173-75 (1966). *See also* Keeton & O'Connell, After Cars Crash —The Need for Legal and Insurance Reform ch. 12 (1967); Keeton & O'Connell, *Automobile Insurance Underwriting Through the Perspective of the Basic Protection Plan*, 68 Best's Ins. News, No. 1, p. 22 (Fire & Cas. Ed. 1967).

24 Concerning out-of-state accidents and victims, *see* Keeton & O'Connell, *supra* note 2, at 65-67.

going system can stand such a drastic and revolutionary readjustment and whether these benefit reductions would last over the long pull. Here are just a few practical questions that need answering:

1.  If each of these changes under the Basic Protection coverage were proposed separately as an amendment to the present system, which ones would be acceptable from a public or political standpoint?
2.  How long will injured claimants, either alone or through attorneys who represent them, sit still and accept silently such a substantial reduction in benefits compared to what have been considered for many years as equitable and justifiable benefits awarded by juries of their peers, particularly when their injuries are caused by no fault on their part?
3.  Will members of the public stand for a system in which they pay the bill for reimbursing persons injured due to their own grossly negligent conduct?
4.  Will private passenger car owners agree to cover the cost of their injuries caused by the commercial and long haul trucks?
5.  Will residents of a state accept a plan that pays for injuries caused by residents of another state, including the injuries to these non-residents?
6.  What period of preparation would be necessary for the entire insurance system to develop entirely new operating procedures and control systems to handle the myriad changes proposed in the Basic Protection plan?

Raising questions such as these should not be considered as being opposed to progress or as being against some of the changes in the present system proposed in the Basic Protection plan. In this regard, I resent and am getting weary of the attitude of people outside the industry who propose changes in our systems, ask our advice, and then either ignore some of the questions we raise or use them to present a picture of the industry as being a status-quo or do-nothing group. I am proud of the fact that I chose the insurance business as a career; I am proud of the company I work for, the people in my company working with me, and most of the people in the industry that I have dealt with. They are dedicated, hard-working people who are attempting to serve the public at a reasonable cost and in the manner they believe the public wants. Most responsible and thinking people in the insurance industry are aware of several shortcomings of the present automobile liability system and are continually spending a great deal of their time trying to come up with solutions and changes to cure these shortcomings. They welcome any help they can get from any source.

Many proposed changes from outside the industry, particularly from academic circles, have great merit. But, somehow or other, many of these people misinterpret questions raised by the industry and feel that they should ignore advice from the industry itself. They forget that the people within the industry will have the responsibility of actually putting the changes into effect and administering them—with all the accompanying practical operating problems and political problems. Obviously, not all of our advice will be followed, but, surely, somewhere or somehow a better working arrangement can be evolved to blend the theoretical with the practical and come up with proposed changes that will be in the public interest. This conference is one example of a start in this direction. More steps along these lines would be beneficial to all of us.

## APPENDIX 1

### More Detailed Breakdown of Private Passenger Premium Dollar

I. *Company Expense Portion—29.5¢*

   1. *Production Cost Allowance—20¢*

      (a) Commission to agents or broker or salaries to salesmen, including expense of office space, etc.

      (b) Sales training and supervision of sales activities including such activities by field man.

      (c) Writing of policy contracts.

      (d) Billing, receiving, and paying of premiums and commissions.

      (e) Advertising and publicity for sales purposes.

   2. *Company Operating Expenses—6.5¢*

      (a) Inspection and accident prevention expenses, including surveys and underwriting reports.

      (b) Dues, assessments, and fees for membership in boards, bureaus, and associations.

      (c) Underwriting department and statistical department expenses.

      (d) Corporate expenses such as corporate legal, financial, actuarial, and field audit.

   3. *Taxes, Licenses, and Fees—3¢*

      (a) State premium taxes.

      (b) Insurance department licenses and fees.

      (c) Payroll taxes (including old age benefit and unemployment insurance taxes).

      (d) All other (excluding federal income tax).

II. *Loss Portion—Provisions of Policy Contract—65.5¢*

   1. *Claim Investigation Expenses—6¢*

      (a) Claim department expenses—investigation, recording and settlement of claims, including the supervision of such activities.

      (b) Expenses of outside claim adjusters, excluding attorneys' fees for claims in suit.

2. *Company Claim Legal Expense—6¢*
    (a) Attorneys' fees for claims in suit, including salaries and traveling expenses for company attorneys engaged in the suit.
    (b) Court or other specific items of legal expense such as:
        (1) Expert medical or other testimony.
        (2) Witnesses and summonses.
        (3) Medical examinations to determine extent of company's liability.
        (4) Copies of documents.

3. *Losses Paid to Claimants—53.5¢*
    The losses paid provide for one or more of the claimant's losses or expenses due to his injury.
    (a) Loss of wages.
    (b) Hospital and medical expenses.
    (c) Pain and suffering.
    (d) Survivors' loss.
    (e) Funeral expenses.
    (f) Loss of consortium or services to family.
    (g) Disfigurement.
    (h) Loss of potential wage increases (due to permanent partial or total disability).
    (i) Claimant's attorney fees.

III. *Profit and Contingencies Portion—5¢*
    (a) To take care of unforeseen or unexpected inadequacies in the provisions contemplated in I and II.
    (b) To provide funds which will protect the company's assets and insure policyholders and claimants the company will carry out its contractual obligations.
    (c) To provide funds for future premium growth of the company.

## APPENDIX II

### ESTIMATE OF THE PERCENTAGE OF TOTAL INJURIES WHICH ARE INJURIES TO DRIVERS FROM ONE-CAR ACCIDENTS

I. Estimate based on NEW YORK STATE DEPARTMENT OF MOTOR VEHICLES, 1964 ACCIDENT FACTS, Table 4 (1965 ed.).

| Type of One-Car Accidents | Number of Drivers Killed or Injured | |
|---|---|---|
| Collision with: | | |
|   (a) Fixed object | 13,872 | |
|   (b) Other object | 108 | |
|   (c) Animal | 175 | |
| Overturned on road | 1,359 | |
| Ran off road | 3,681 | |
| Other non-collision | 279 | |
| One-car driver injuries | 19,474(a) | |
| Total killed or injured | 297,770(b) | Ratio (a) to (b): 6.5% |

II. Estimate based on DEPARTMENT OF THE CALIFORNIA HIGHWAY PATROL, 1964 TRAFFIC ACCIDENT STATISTICS, at 68.

| Type of One-Car Accidents | Number of Drivers Killed or Injured | |
|---|---|---|
| Collision with: | | |
| (a) Fixed object .............. | 4,209 | |
| (b) Animal ................... | 318 | |
| Overturned on road .............. | 2,308 | |
| Ran off road .................... | 17,439 | |
| Other non-collision .............. | 894 | |
| One-car driver injuries ........... | 25,168(a) | |
| Total killed or injured ........... | 220,138(b) | Ratio (a) to (b): 11% |

III. SINCE NEW YORK GIVES ACTUAL DISTRIBUTION BY TYPE OF VICTIM WHILE CALIFORNIA DATA GIVES TYPE OF VICTIM IN TOTAL ONLY, NEW YORK DATA MUST BE GIVEN MORE CREDIBILITY. A JUDGMENT PERCENTAGE OF 8% WAS USED.

## DISTRIBUTION I

### Distribution of Injured by Type of Accident and Type of Victim

Statistical Report of Motor Vehicle Accidents

Table 4–1964 Accident Facts

State of New York–Department of Motor Vehicles

| Type of Accident | Total Killed or Injured | Type of Persons Killed or Injured | | | |
|---|---|---|---|---|---|
| | | Driver | Passenger | Pedestrian | Other |
| **A. *Pedestrian Type—*** | | | | | |
| 1. Pedestrian | 27413 | 203 | 275 | 26932 | 3 |
| 2. Bicycle | 5515 | 29 | 33 | 1 | 5452 |
| 3. Subtotal | 32928 | 232 | 308 | 26933 | 5455 |
| % by Type of Victim | 100% | 0.7% | 0.9% | 81.8% | 16.6% |
| **B. *Collision with Another Vehicle*** | | | | | |
| 4. Other Auto | 228379 | 123906 | 104415 | XXX | 58 |
| 5. Train & Streetcar | 173 | 110 | 52 | 3 | 8 |
| 6. Subtotal | 228552 | 124016 | 104467 | 3 | 66 |
| % by Type of Victim | 100% | 54.3% | 45.7% | — | |
| **C. *Collision with Objects*** | | | | | |
| 7. Animal | 353 | 175 | 150 | 1 | 27 |
| 8. Fixed & Other Object | 24363 | 13980 | 10264 | 73 | 46 |
| 9. Subtotal | 24716 | 14155 | 10414 | 74 | 73 |
| % of Type of Victim | 100% | 57.3% | 42.1% | 0.3% | 0.3% |
| **D. *Non-Collision*** | | | | | |
| 10. Overturn on Road | 2491 | 1359 | 1126 | 5 | 1 |
| 11. Ran off Road | 6594 | 3681 | 2910 | 2 | 1 |
| 12. Other Non-Collision | 2489 | 279 | 2157 | 15 | 38 |
| 13. Subtotal | 11574 | 5319 | 6193 | 22 | 40 |
| % by Type of Victim | 100% | 46.0% | 53.5% | 0.2% | 0.3% |
| **E. *Grand Total*** | 297770 | 143722 | 121382 | 27032 | 5634 |
| % by Type of Victim | 100% | 48.2% | 40.8% | 9.1% | 1.9% |

## DISTRIBUTION II

### DISTRIBUTION OF ACCIDENTS BY TYPE OF ACCIDENT & TYPE OF VICTIM

California—1964 Traffic Accident Statistics—Page 68
Department of the California Highway Patrol

| Type of Accident | Total Killed or Injured | Type of Persons Killed or Injured* | | | |
|---|---|---|---|---|---|
| | | Driver | Passenger | Pedestrian | Other |
| **A. Pedestrian Type** | | | | | |
| 1. Pedestrian | 14859 | 109 | 115 | 11030 | 3605 |
| 2. Bicycle | 5053 | 37 | 38 | 3752 | 1226 |
| 3. Subtotal | 19912 | 146 | 153 | 14782 | 4831 |
| **B. Collision with Another Vehicle** | | | | | |
| 4. Other Auto | 151924 | 89688 | 62236 | XX | XX |
| 5. Train & Streetcar | 790 | 467 | 323 | XX | XX |
| 6. Subtotal | 152714 | 90155 | 62559 | XX | XX |
| **C. Collision with Objects** | | | | | |
| 7. Animal | 514 | 318 | 193 | 1 | 2 |
| 8. Fixed Object | 6295 | 3891 | 2357 | 18 | 29 |
| 9. Subtotal | 6809 | 4209 | 2550 | 19 | 31 |
| **D. Non-Collision** | | | | | |
| 10. Overturn on Road | 4551 | 2308 | 2213 | 9 | 21 |
| 11. Ran off Road | 34388 | 17439 | 16723 | 66 | 160 |
| 12. Other Non-Collision | 1764 | 894 | 858 | 4 | 8 |
| 13. Subtotal | 40703 | 20641 | 19794 | 79 | 189 |
| **E. Grand Total**** | 220138 | 115151 | 85056 | 14880 | 5051 |

* Distributed by type of victim within each group of type of accident on the basis of the % distribution of New York data for such group.

** Distribution by type of victim adjusted to the totals given on page 68.

# APPENDIX III

## AUTOMOBILE BODILY INJURY LIABILITY SETTLEMENTS—
### No. OF CLAIMS AND AMOUNT OF LOSS BY SIZE OF CLAIM
### Private Passenger Cars

| Size of Settled Claim (1) | Average Size of Economic Loss* Total (2) | Wage Loss (3) | Policy Year 1965 Massachusetts No. of Claims (4) | Amount (5) | Calendar Year 1962 New York State No. of Claims (6) | Amount (7) | Calendar Year 1962 Other States No. of Claims (8) | Amount (9) |
|---|---|---|---|---|---|---|---|---|
| (a) Under $250 | Under $100 | Under $50 | 32,207 | 3,398,955 | 47,819 | 4,663,115 | 193,264 | 14,536,169 |
| (b) 250-4,999+ | 100-1,999 | 50-999 | 80,308 | 70,028,040 | 80,700 | 107,596,111 | 185,065 | 283,915,742 |
| (c) 5,000-25,000++ | 2,000 & over | 1,000 & Over | XX | 21,293,829 | XX | 13,471,107 | XX | 35,814,229 |
| (d) TOTAL | | | 112,515 | 94,720,824 | 128,519 | 125,730,333 | 378,329 | 334,266,140 |

**A. Elimination of Claims with Economic Loss of $100 or less**

| | | | | | | | | |
|---|---|---|---|---|---|---|---|---|
| (e) as a % of (d) | | | 29% | 3.6% | 37% | 3.7% | 51% | 4.3% |

**B. Percentage Reduction Due to Deductible of 10% of Wage Loss or $100 Whichever Is Greater**

| | | | | | | | | |
|---|---|---|---|---|---|---|---|---|
| (f) (b) No. of Claims x $100 | | | 80,308 | 8,030,800 | 80,700 | 8,070,000 | 185,065 | 18,506,500 |
| (g) (c) Amount x .020* | | | XX | 425,877 | XX | 269,422 | XX | 716,285 |
| (h) (f) + (g) | | | 80,308 | 8,456,677 | 80,700 | 8,339,422 | 185,065 | 19,222,785 |
| (i) Indicated Reduction — (h) ÷ .40* [(b) + (c)] | | | XX | 23% | XX | 17% | XX | 15% |
| (j) 50% of Indicated Reduction** | | | XX | 11.5% | XX | 8.5% | XX | 7.5% |

**C. Percentage Reduction For 15% Income Tax Offset**

The percentage reduction for this further 15% income tax offset depends on the percentage of the total economic loss that is wage loss and payable under the Basic Protection coverage after all offsets for collateral sources of benefits are first made. For example, if the wage loss represents 50% of this economic loss payable under Basic Protection, the percentage reduction for the 15% income tax offset would be 7.5%. Because a much greater proportion of the population is covered under collateral sources for medical and hospital benefits than is covered for wage continuation benefits, I have estimated that wage loss represents about 80% of the residual economic loss payable under the Basic Protection coverage. Consequently, the percentage reduction for this further 15% income tax offset would amount to 12% based upon this assumption (80% of 15% = 12%).

+ The number of claims include claims of $5,000 and over, but the dollar amounts include only the first $5,000 of each claim.
++ The number of claims for this group is included in the $250—$4,999 group, but the dollar amount in excess of $5,000 of each claim up to $25,000 is shown in the amount columns.
* It is assumed that 40% of the settled cost represents economic loss and 50% of such economic loss is wage loss.
** To be conservative and to recognize the limitations of the data analyzed, only 50% of indicated reduction is used. These percentages average about 8%.

## APPENDIX IV

### Basic Protection Coverage

Estimate of % Multi-Car Accidents Which Involve Clearly Negligent Drivers

(1)  Collision Type Accidents Which Would Include Clearly Negligent Drivers. Source: New York State Department of Motor Vehicles, 1964 Accident Facts, Table 4 (1965 ed.)

| Type of Accident | Number of Accidents |
|---|---|
| Head on | 5,336 |
| Rear end | 73,304 |
| Backed into | 2,633 |
| TOTAL (1) | 81,273 |

(2)  Estimated Drivers Involved in These Accidents—2 x (1): 160,000
(3)  Ratio of Drivers Killed and Injured to Total Drivers in Collision of Two Motor Vehicles.
    1.  Total collision of two motor vehicles—141,353
    2.  Estimated number of drivers—282,000
    3.  Total Drivers killed or injured in such collisions—123,906
    4.  % of drivers killed or injured—42%
(4)  Estimated Number of Drivers Killed or Injured in Accidents Listed in (1)— (2) x 42%: 62,700
(5)  Estimated % of Drivers Killed or Injured Who Would Be Found To Be Clearly Negligent—25%*
(6)  Estimated Number of Clearly Negligent Drivers—25% x 67,200: 16,800
(7)  Estimated % of Clearly Negligent Drivers as a % of Total Killed or Injured. Total Killed or Injured—297,770; 16,800÷297,770=5.7%

* This percentage is based upon an analysis of a small sample of claims involving types of collisions categorized in (1). While under pure chance conditions it would be expected that about one-half of the drivers killed or injured would be clearly negligent in such collisions, in the classification "Rear-ended" (the largest category of collision accident in Table 4) the driver who "rear-ended" the other car brought a successful claim and a payment was made in about 50% of the cases under the present system. The driver in the other car who was injured received benefits under the present system almost 100% of the time. Consequently, it is estimated only 25% of the drivers were denied payment due to a finding of "clear negligence" on their part.

# REMARKS

*OF ROBERT A. BAILEY**

THE COST OF A NEW PROPOSAL is always one of the important considerations for deciding whether to adopt it. The Basic Protection plan[1] is one in which the cost is difficult to evaluate because the proposal is complicated and it involves radical changes from the past.

It is hazardous to be the first to make an estimate. It is much easier and safer to review someone else's estimate. I don't envy Mr. Harwayne's task; I find mine as a reviewer much easier. After studying Mr. Harwayne's paper, it is clear that he has put a tremendous amount of work and probably more than a year of time into his analysis. I can make no pretense that in the month I have had his paper, I have been able to check all his work.

My review will cover only three points: (1) Mr. Harwayne's estimate is an estimate and like all estimates is subject to random error; (2) considerations that would tend to make the cost higher than Mr. Harwayne's estimate; and (3) considerations that would tend to make the cost lower.

## I. The Range of Error in Estimates

Mr. Harwayne has estimated that the Basic Protection plan, including tort liability protection for pain and suffering up to $10,000 per claim,[2] will cost 21 per cent less than the present cost for bodily injury liability, uninsured motorists, and medical payments insurance.[3] He has also made two alternate estimates, a high one and a low one, of 17 per cent[4] and 26 per cent.[5]

What are the chances that the actual cost might be between his high and low estimates? Even if he has done a perfect job and taken everything into consideration, the chances would still be rather small that the actual cost would fall within such a narrow range. When ratemakers make rates today for automobile bodily injury liability insurance, under the present law and with past experience to go on, they don't claim to be able to make rates that will be accurate within a range of 9 per cent—the difference between Harwayne's low estimate of 17 per cent and his high estimate of 26 per cent.

* *ROBERT A. BAILEY. M.S. 1953, University of Iowa; Director, Insurance and Actuarial Section, Property and Liability Division, Insurance Bureau, State of Michigan.*

---

[1] Keeton & O'Connell, Basic Protection for the Traffic Victim: A Blueprint for Reforming Automobile Insurance (1965) [hereinbefore and hereinafter this book is often cited as Basic Protection]. *See also* Keeton & O'Connell, *Basic Protection Automobile Insurance*, p. 40 *supra.*

[2] Concerning this particular protection and its component parts, *see* Harwayne, *Insurance Costs of Basic Protection Plan in Michigan, supra* notes 20, 24, 27 and accompanying text.

[3] *Id.* at Table I, line 25.

[4] *Id.* at Appendix Table III, line 25.

[5] *Id.* at Appendix Table II, line 25.

The definition of "100 per cent credible" for automobile bodily injury liability insurance is a statistical probability that the actual result will fall within a range of 10 per cent, 90 per cent of the time. And judging from the size of some rate increases, it is obvious that forecasting the cost of automobile bodily liability insurance is difficult even with data that is "100 per cent credible."

Mr. Harwayne's high and low estimates reflect the possible variation in the estimated cost of claim expense. But that is only one of the subsidiary estimates that go together to make up his total estimate. I counted about 40 other estimates or assumptions that he made in the 59 pages of his study. Surely it is not possible that all the other 40 estimates will prove to be precisely correct. If one subsidiary estimate could produce a variation of 9 per cent in the final estimate, what might the cumulative effect of 40 subsidiary estimates be?

## II.    Possibility of Higher Costs

In evaluating the cost of the Basic Protection plan it is important to know how many additional claims will be paid if the question of fault is removed from the liability system. Mr. Harwayne originally estimated the increase to be 40 per cent. The Conard study, to which he refers, indicates a much larger increase—an increase of about 200 per cent.[6] The Temple University study of 1955 New Jersey automobile accidents would indicate an increase of about 100 per cent.[7]

In view of Mr. Harwayne's low estimate, I checked his supporting data. He compared the number of injuries reported to the state police with the number of bodily injury claims reported to the liability insurers. The difference was 40 per cent. But he had used some incorrect data.

The data he originally used to obtain the total insurance data was as follows:

| Statistical Agent | Premium | No. of Claims | No. of Claims per $1,000,000 of Premiums |
|---|---|---|---|
| NBCU[8] | $20,739,305 | 14,118 | 681 |
| MIRB[9] | 4,557,459 | 3,944 | 865 |
| NAII[10] | 25,603,157 | 25,300 | 988 |
| NISS[11] | 24,197,257 | 31,407 | 1298 |
| Total | $75,097,178 | 74,769 | 996 |

[6] A. Conard, J. Morgan, R. Pratt, C. Voltz & R. Bombaugh, Automobile Accident Costs and Payments—Studies in the Economics of Injury Reparation 139, 149 (1964) [hereinbefore and hereinafter often cited as Conard, *et al.*].

[7] Adams, *A Comparative Analysis of Costs of Insuring Against Losses Due to Automobile Accidents—Various Hypotheses—New Jersey, 1955*, at 3 Temple Univ. Econ. & Bus. Bull., March 1960.

[8] National Bureau of Casualty Underwriters.

[9] Mutual Insurance Rating Bureau

[10] National Association of Independent Insurers.

[11] National Independent Statistical Service

I obtained the following data from the reports filed with the Michigan Insurance Department. This does not include any package policy data for which separate bodily injury data was unavailable.

| Statistical Agent | Premium | No. of Claims | No. of Claims per $1,000,000 of Premiums |
|---|---|---|---|
| NBCU | $18,960,569 | 12,428 | 655 |
| MIRB | 4,709,438 | 3,863 | 820 |
| NAII | 25,790,725 | 17,055 | 661 |
| NISS | 29,381,794 | 31,409 | 1069 |
| Total | $78,842,526 | 64,755 | 821 |

Using this corrected data in Mr. Harwayne's Table D-1 would produce fewer insured claims. Comparing the resulting insured claims with the number of injuries reported to the state police would indicate an increase in claims under the Basic Protection plan of 70 per cent rather than 40 per cent. Later Mr. Harwayne partially corrected his estimated increase in claims from 40 per cent to 55 per cent after I told him about the error in this data. But his overall estimate of the cost of the Basic Protection plan was virtually unaffected because he simultaneously revised several other estimates by offsetting amounts. This illustrates the flexibility of the 40 or more estimates and assumptions that are the foundation of his overall estimate.

With Mr. Harwayne, using a comparison of insurance and noninsurance data, estimating 55 per cent and Conard and others, using noninsurance data, estimating an increase of 100 per cent to 200 per cent in cost due to removing the question of fault, it would be helpful to get another estimate from purely insurance data. Such an estimate can be obtained from a comparison of the medical payments experience under the family auto policy and the special auto policy. The family auto policy (FAP) provides full medical payments to the insured, his family, and his guest passengers regardless of fault. The special auto policy (SAP) provides similar coverage except that payments are only for the excess over tort liability recoveries, other medical insurance, individual and group accident and health insurance, and disability benefits and similar laws.

A comparison of the medical payments experience under FAP and SAP appears on page 297 of the *1966 Proceedings of the Casualty Actuarial Society*. The SAP medical payments data reveals a saving from FAP of 48 per cent beyond what is attributable to selective underwriting. The 48 per cent is the saving from collateral sources and recoveries under tort liability. If all the saving is attributed to tort liability recoveries, the cost of the full medical payments coverage would be 108 per cent greater than the portion attributed to the liability recoveries. If two-thirds of the saving in SAP is attributed to the liability recoveries, the cost of the full medical payments coverage would be 213 per cent greater than the liability portion. This is close to the 200 per cent increase indicated by the Conard study. Accordingly, I must conclude that Mr. Harwayne's estimate of a 55 per cent increase is probably too low.

Another of Mr. Harwayne's 40 or more estimates is a 9 per cent reduction in cost as a result of making insurance compulsory and thereby eliminating the cost of uninsured motorists coverage. However the claims for uninsured motorists are already included in his data for Table D-1; since they are used to reduce the estimate in Table D-1, I question whether an additional reduction should be made for them in Table 1, line 3. There appears to be duplication.

### III.   Possibility of Lower Costs

The present automobile liability system is the least efficient of the present insurance methods of distributing benefits to claimants for bodily injuries. If Mr. Harwayne's forecasts are correct, the Basic Protection plan will be even less efficient. For every dollar paid to the claimant, the overhead expenses of the insurer are as follows:

|  | Claim Adjustment Expense | Other Expenses, Taxes, Profit | Total Overhead |
|---|---|---|---|
| Basic Protection (per Harwayne) | 38% | 77% | 115% |
| Auto Bodily Injury Liability | 23% | 37% | 60% |
| Workmen's Compensation | 14% | 44% | 58% |
| Group Accident and Health | 2% | 12% | 14% |
| Social Security |  |  | 2% |

It is hard to understand the basis for such high expense estimates since the Basic Protection plan is supposed to be more efficient than our present slow and cumbersome liability system.

Another estimate that I believe questionable is Mr. Harwayne's estimate that the elimination of pain and suffering will reduce costs only 13 per cent. Claims adjusters report that settlements often run more than twice the medical bills and lost wages, which would seem to indicate a saving of 50 per cent or more if pain and suffering were eliminated.

### IV.   Summary and Alternatives

I have discussed four of Mr. Harwayne's 40 or more estimates and have shown that each of them is subject to wide variations, even as much as 100 per cent. I have not had time to study all 40 estimates but I am sure that similar uncertainty and variation apply to many others. Accordingly I do not have much confidence that the overall cost will be less than present costs, or that the cost will be between Mr. Harwayne's high and low estimates. More data and more study are needed.

The Basic Protection proposal has performed a valuable service in publicizing the nature of the problems in our present system and in offering a possible solution to these problems. We certainly need a system that is more efficient, more prompt, and more equitable than the present one.

A number of other systems have also been proposed—and some even adopted—which involve varying levels of benefits and costs and varying degrees of change in the tort liability system: the Saskatchewan Plan,[12] the Ontario Plan,[13] Morris and Paul's Plan,[14] the various systems used in Europe,[15] and others.

Another possibility, rather simple in concept, would be an exemption from liability for all automobile injuries except those caused by gross negligence. Michigan and some other states already have such an exemption for guest passengers. In effect, this would turn automobile bodily injury liability insurance into accident and health insurance. Each person would insure his own losses to whatever extent he desires. The group approach, which is available in accident and health insurance, is a very efficient system as shown above. Costs would be easier to estimate because of existing statistical data. And in many cases the costs would be borne partly by employers, making the cost to employees very low.

Further study should be made on the costs of these various proposals. But cost alone should not be the deciding factor. What we really need is more for our money—a more efficient, more prompt, and more equitable system which fits our modern mobile way of life.

I attach some remarks written especially for this symposium by Michigan Insurance Commissioner David J. Dykhouse:

"A reasonable observer of the current scene must conclude that the present tort system of distributing loss from auto accidents is inefficient and unfair, especially in the ordinary negligence area. The answer does not lie in appointing more judges, conserving judicial energy more effectively, or speeding up some of the claims procedures. Such solutions simply allow the basic inefficiency and unfairness to happen more rapidly.

"The answer lies in getting down to fundamentals and questioning the continued social utility of metaphysical fault concepts in the distribution of concrete losses to real people, who, in the ordinary situation, happen to have had an auto accident. If the fault system has any utility it is as a cautionary device and should operate only against those who drive as if they did not care what they did to other people.

"So much for fundamentals. What about Basic Protection? Professors Keeton and O'Connell deserve great credit for their concern with reforming a clumsy system and carrying that concern to the point of suggesting concrete solutions.

[12] SASKATCHEWAN REV. STAT. c. 409 (1965).

[13] Ontario Legislative Assembly Select Committee on Automobile Insurance, Final Report (March 1963). For a summary of the report, *see* Basic Protection 152-59.

[14] Morris & Paul, *The Financial Impact of Automobile Accidents*, 110 U. PA. L. REV. 913 (1962).

[15] For a description of various European systems, *see* CONARD, *et al.* chs. 11-14; Basic Protection 189-219.

"We should not be misled, however, into believing that with the adoption of their proposal the millenium will arrive. While I share their concern, I cannot buy the specifics of their proposals unless and until a great deal more is done to test them, and alternatives are fully considered. The plan is not, in my judgment, a solution which, at this juncture, I could recommend to the Michigan Legislature for adoption. Much more study of this whole problem is required. I will mention just three items out of many:

"(1) *The $100 to $10,000 range of the plan.* The Conard study demonstrates conclusively that the greatest unfairness in the present system comes at the lower and upper ranges of loss—the lower being overcompensated and the upper being undercompensated.[16] Yet Basic Protection preserves the present system in these two areas.[17]

"(2) *Complexity.* The jurisdictional amount concept for tort plus the extreme complexity of the benefit schedules will, in my judgment, produce more, not less, litigation.

"(3) *Cost.* This plan is currently being oversold on its cost savings potential. No credible evidence has been produced to indicate that total insurance costs will decline under this system. For example, shifting part of the auto losses to Accident & Health coverages does not necessarily produce lower total insurance costs. The savings may be illusory. There are, on the other hand, some very good projections that total insurance costs will increase, if the plan is adopted. Mr. Bailey has undoubtedly discussed this with you."

[16] CONARD, *et al.* 6, 196, 197, 250-52.
[17] Keeton & O'Connell, *supra* note 1, at 50-51.

# REJOINDER TO MR. BAILEY

BY FRANK HARWAYNE

MR. BAILEY SENT ME his review only a few days before this conference. I really didn't have time to go over it in detail. I must say this—assumptions in costing a new system can't be avoided; the real question is not whether you make an assumption, but whether the assumption you make is reasonable. I think I have been reasonable.

With reference to the special automobile policy (SAP) data, it is Bailey's straw man based on suppositions and assumptions and not on any substantial volume of Michigan experience; it has the cloak of respectability because of the discussion in the *Proceedings of the Casualty Actuarial Society*.[1] As to Mr. Bailey's objection that my figure of 55 per cent more claims (as a result of paying claims on a nonfault basis) is low, if one combines Michigan liability frequencies with medical payments coverage frequencies, they add up to 1.67 times the liability frequencies. But, as a matter of fact, there is substantial duplication in this 1.67 figure since the same person is often collecting from both medical payments coverage and liability insurance. Thus, in light of the figure 1.67 being too high, the figure of 1.55 may very well not be too low. In using these limited SAP data, then, there is this problem of duplication of the claim frequencies which Mr. Bailey has failed to recognize.[2]

As to expense overhead, Professor Conard showed that the present expense overhead in automobile liability is 127 per cent[3] of all liability payments, and if you take Mr. Wolfrum's breakdown of the premium dollar, you can very well come up with a similar figure, both contradicting Mr. Bailey's 60 per cent figure. Aside from the incorrectness of Mr. Bailey's figures, his expense comparison concept is not entirely fair to the Basic Protection system which he matches against systems which have been honed by competition and experience. My cost estimates recognize that insurers probably would not willingly reduce some of their own expenses at the outset of a new and less costly system. Mr. Wolfrum referred to that. Ultimately, however, experience and competition could reduce expenses as has happened in workmen's compensation and group accident and health insurance;

[1] Lange, *Implications of Sampling for Package Policy Ratemaking*, 53 PROCEEDINGS OF THE CASUALTY ACTUARIAL SOCIETY 285, 297 (1966).

[2] A subsequent reading of Mr. Bailey's reference (note 1 *supra*) reaffirms my conclusion that the article contains a limited amount of data, unidentified as to state (probably not Michigan), and irrelevant to my 1.55 figure. The data it does contain are used to produce a ratemaking system for SAP policies which will be consistent with FAP policies; Mr. Bailey's exposition thus perpetuates certain assumptions at the source cited in note 1 *supra*, which assumptions, in turn, are built into Mr. Bailey's speculation on the 48% "savings." In 1967, the actual failure to realize the assumed "savings" of SAP policies has belied the raw assumptions to such an extent that a number of states have begun to challenge the end results.

[3] CONARD, *et al.* 59.

the marketplace will determine this, and I'm sure insurers in the long run will cut their costs when they can.

Regarding Mr. Bailey's remarks about my treatment of uninsured motorist coverage, I just recommend that he read my report a little more carefully.[4]

---

[4] Table D-1 of my study includes a limited number of uinsured motorist claims for 1962, when uninsured motorist coverage was not purchased so extensively, nor was the coverage utilized to any great extent. *See id.* at note 71 *supra* and accompanying text. Table 2 includes the present day cost of buying uninsured motorist coverage liability insurance protection. Table 1 removes the cost on a nonliability basis.

# LAWYERS VIEW PROPOSED CHANGES

BY JACOB D. FUCHSBERG*

## I. INTRODUCTION

DEATH AND DESTRUCTION on our highways is but a minor part of the widespread injury in our mechanically dynamic society. In fact, only 15 per cent of our accidents involve autos. Nevertheless, auto accidents are the most visible, the most talked-about, and, therefore, the most politically opportunistic. That is because the carnage produced by cars takes place on the highways in public, unlike accidents in the home or factory. And, though the drama is created by the injuries, ironically, the type of plans with which this conference has been asked to concern itself would not induce safety one bit.

I welcome the opportunity to speak from the vantage point of the lawyer, who, after all, knows first hand from daily experience how our present system works and how it affects the individual citizen who is supposed to be its ultimate beneficiary and upon whom the effect of any changes would fall. I find important indorsement of the objectivity of my views in the fact that they are shared by both plaintiffs' and defendants' lawyers. It appears to me that the very partisanship of the adversary system provides some assurance of reliability in those areas where agreement is reached by lawyers approaching these questions from opposite sides.

## II. HYSTERIA AND STATISTICS

I have suggested that the auto accident rate generates political opportunism. The suggestion was deliberate in order to create an antidote against the rush to do something for politics' sake and to avoid the scare and bugaboo of the threat that the government will take everything over unless there is a hasty consent to some revolutionary plan of change.

Our present system is far from perfect, but I suggest that panic is not warranted and that one of the first things we ought to dispel is the misinformation which generates the panic and provides a fertile ground for suggestions of panaceas that would hurt rather than help. For instance, in early September, a *New York Times* article announced that Governor Nelson Rockefeller was about to appoint a commission of inquiry for the auto accident field in the pivotal State of New York.[1] According to the article, there was no mere implication that this was a problem area; the issue was expressly prejudged. One bit of information in the article was that liability premiums

---

* JACOB D. FUCHSBERG. BA. 1933, LL.B. 1935, New York University; Past President, the American Trial Lawyers Association; Attorney-at-Law, New York City.

---

[1] N.Y. Times, Sept. 11, 1967, at 41, col. 5.

are supposed to have gone up 91 per cent since 1950. I am sure the average reader said "wow!" and mumbled to himself about the stupendous increase.

## A.    *Are Insurance Costs Too High?*

I am not defending or condemning insurance-pricing practices or their efficiency, nor proclaiming that they should be higher or lower, nor exploring such questions as whether investment income should be utilized in rate-making. But I do know that compared to other things, insurance costs have not risen dramatically during this 17-year period and that the "high and excessive price" theme is based upon myth.

The reference to the year 1950 makes it sound like it was yesterday. If the year of reference was 1949 it would have sounded much longer ago, in the shade of World War II. In addition, if the comparative costs of the ingredients which make up claims in this field are placed side-by-side, a different picture emerges.

There are four direct ingredients of "claims costs." One of them, pain and suffering, is not capable of exact mathematical measurement. But the other three—medical costs, loss of earnings, and auto replacement and repair costs—are susceptible of comparative cost evaluation. I checked the Bureau of Labor Statistics and found the following cost increases:

|  | Annual Average 1950 | December 1966 |
|---|---|---|
| Medical care | 73.4 | 131.9 |
| Personal care | 78.9 | 113.7[1] |
| Transportation | 68.4 | 126.5[2] |
| Hospital costs |  |  |
|    Semiprivate rooms | 59.3 | 163.5 |
|    Private rooms | 61.2 | 165.5[3] |
| Average Hourly Earnings of Prod. |  |  |
|    Workers, Manufacturing | $ 1.44 | $  2.71 |
| Average Weekly Earnings of Prod. |  |  |
|    Workers, Manufacturing | $58.32 | $111.92[4] |

[1] U.S. Bureau of Labor Statistics, Dep't of Labor, Bull. No. 1555, Handbook of Labor Statistics 1967, Table 105, at 200.
[2] *Id*. Table 106, at 201.
[3] *Id*. Table 110, at 214.
[4] U.S. Bureau of the Census, Statistical Abstract of the United States 1967, Table 334, at 237 (88th ed. 1967).

As we all know, 1967 has brought further substantial increases. In the perspective of these figures, insurance rates have done no more than keep up with the pace of inflation in the categories of products and services fundamental to the automobile insurance claim. Aside from these specific items, the value of the 1949 dollar is now only 69.5 cents.[2]

The same sort of thing is true with some of the arguments we hear bandied about to describe the so-called costliness of "delivering a dollar of

[2] N.Y. Post, Sept. 27, 1967, p. 2.

benefits to the claimant." Professor Moynihan's recent article in the *New York Times Magazine*[3] contained diagrams illustrating Keeton and O'Connell's contention that it "costs" $2.20 or so in premiums to deliver a dollar of insurance benefits. That does sound like someone is profiteering along the way. But no one makes any comparisons with the increased prices which other industries and businesses have charged to deliver services or products in our free enterprise society. The three professors urge that private insurance be retained, so they must agree that the private enterprise system is worth the price. In fact, an actuarial report on Professors Keeton and O'Connell's plan assumes that the present private insurance industry would continue to operate the new system—and on its present basic system of expense charges.[4]

What are the cost figures? Insurance rates now generally include five per cent for "allocated expense" for individual files. (This includes fees to defend cases.) "Unallocated expense" (general claims handling) absorbs another six per cent. A standard 35 per cent is allocated for "loading," including 20 per cent agents' commissions, 5 per cent for taxes and 5 per cent for profit. The grand total is 46 per cent.

Under the so-called Basic Protection plan,[5] I estimate that the only alteration would be a slight drop in the attorneys' fees element of "allocated expense," reducing it to approximately three per cent (if we assume that the prediction of less resulting litigation is accurate—a premise that has been seriously challenged).[6] However, I also estimate that there will be an increase of approximately 7.2 per cent in the "unallocated" column because of the greater number of Basic Protection claims that are inevitable from paying without reference to fault. The other items would remain the same so that the grand total under the Basic Protection plan would still be about 46 per cent.

Put another way, out of the $2.20 that is being collected to give the victim each dollar of benefits, the largest part of the differential, at least $102.10 (46 per cent), stays with insurance companies. If this is reasonable, because it is what things must fairly cost and, therefore, must also be included in the cost of the Basic Protection plan, why make the dramatic comparison of $2.20 in cost to $1.00 in benefits? The fact is that the Basic Protection plan can be painted the very same way.

In this connection, acting under legislative mandate, Mr. Justice Joseph

[3] Moynihan, *Next: A New Auto Insurance Policy*, N.Y. Times, Aug. 27, 1967, § 6 (Magazine), at 26.

[4] *See* Keeton & O'Connell, *Basic Protection and the Costs of Traffic Accidents*, 38 N.Y.S.B.J. 255, 257 (1966).

[5] KEETON & O'CONNELL, BASIC PROTECTION FOR THE TRAFFIC VICTIM: A BLUEPRINT FOR REFORMING AUTOMOBILE INSURANCE (1965) [both hereinbefore and hereinafter this book is often cited as Basic Protection]. *See also* Keeton & O'Connell, *Basic Protection Automobile Insurance*, p. 40 *supra*.

[6] *E.g.*, Green, *Basic Protection and Court Congestion*, 52 A.B.A.J. 926 (1966).

M. Callahan of the Appellate Division of the City of New York investigated New York's workmen's compensation system, often mistakenly idealized as a model. He found that 45 per cent of each compensation premium did not go to the claimant.

## B. *Attorneys' Fees*

While we are discussing costs, a word ought to be said about the fees of claimants' attorneys. Figures obtained from governmental sources and insurance actuaries indicate that claimants' attorneys' fees presently average about 11 per cent of the premium dollar. This figure takes into account the cases that are settled without lawyers (who are, of course, in the background establishing the standards that govern such direct dispositions), and then includes an average contingent fee of one-third (though in larger cases, in practice, fees are often less), at the same time realistically weighting the figures on the assumption that the cases in which lawyers appear are larger in size than those without counsel.

Further, according to figures furnished to a legislative insurance committee by John M. Dillon, vice-president of Glens Falls Insurance Company, the total percentage of total premiums going to pay claimants' attorneys may be only slightly less than nine per cent.

It is hard to believe that a figure of 9 to 11 per cent for counsel fees should give rise to any criticism. In fact, it emphasizes why the average lawyer's earnings, according to the Internal Revenue Service, run below many of the other major professions.

The actuarial study of Basic Protection conducted at the request of Professors Keeton and O'Connell assumes attorneys' fees will be the same per case as they are today—and that there will be more cases—in spite of their prediction that less attorneys' services would be required under their plan.[7] I submit that unless they predict comparable use of attorneys and comparable attorneys' fees, they would be unrealistic—ignoring everything happening in our country today. One of the most important developments in the law in this decade has been the extension of the obligation to make sure that every American citizen, regardless of economic or educational handicaps—whether produced by deep-rooted social problems, or, as with some accident victims, by the acute stress of an injury or death—is provided with a spokesman as available and as skilled as one obtainable by people not so handicapped. This has been basic to the renaissance that we have been witnessing in the criminal law. It is behind the expansion of the Office of Equal Opportunity (OEO) legal services program which this year saw government lawyers appearing in some 300,000 civil cases—and that's just a start.

Note that negligence cases were not handled by OEO lawyers or as-

[7] *See* Keeton & O'Connell, *supra* note 4.

signed counsel, primarily because the contingent fee makes that unnecessary. But to base any plan on the premise that lawyers would become less necessary is to ignore the course of the law and the history of our legal institutions. Need I remind you that workmen's compensation also started with the idea that payments would be automatic and that the need for lawyers would be minimal and exceptional. Originally even laymen were allowed to appear for claimants. Now, as we all know, widespread representation of compensation claimants by lawyers is the common practice.

### C. Court Delay

Another type of statistical criticism that needs modulation is the so-called calendar-congestion problem. This has great public appeal and certainly has been played up. Concededly, there are long delays in many localities—Chicago is as notorious as any in this regard. There are things that ought to be done to alleviate this situation. But it is not necessary under our present system that there be such delay as to unconscionably inconvenience the claimant. And, on the other hand, some delay exists under any system. By way of example, at times there has been considerable delay in Pennsylvania and other states under workmen's compensation. Indeed, the *New Testament's* "Corinthians," as well as a study of Roman history in the days of the Emperor Claudius, or our own American court congestion in the nineteenth century, provide ready examples that court congestion is an ancient problem, antedating the automobile.

Likewise, conditions are not nearly as bad as they are painted. When a client comes to me and, having read the newspaper, asks whether it is true that his case will not be reached for three years, I can say to him that that is not likely to happen. Instead, the chances are we will settle his case within the first year, and, if not, it is likely to be settled somewhere along the line long before the terminal point on the court calendar assembly line. If it is not settled, and delay would constitute a great hardship to the particular client because he is crippled or disabled or threatened with becoming a public charge, or is in danger of not surviving, or even has to face a drastic uprooting in his usual way of life, he can get a preference and an immediate trial. If his case is the one in a hundred that goes to the end of the line, it is likely that it is one of the kind that will not suffer inordinately by the delay.

### III.   Is Change Worth the Price?
#### A.   *Price Must Be Judged by What You Can Get for It*

It is in the light of these illusory figures and the uncertainty which must cloud the cost projections of any plan never yet tried that I find myself especially critical of the emphasis on cost in the promotion of the Basic Protection plan. Even if it really would cost less, in premiums, it is only because it takes away many rights that people now have. Who says our citizenry wants to, or should, give them up? No one has carried the burden of proof on such speculation.

The insurance industry, like any other business, must operate at a profit to survive. It is a matter of simple arithmetic that everything else being equal it can only charge less if it gives less (unless it is overcharging to begin with, but that is not what has been urged.) If the object is to reduce rates, then I submit that the *cheapest insurance is no insurance at all.* No benefits, *ergo*, no premiums.

## B.    *Inadequacies of Basic Protection Type Plans*

We should not be impressed with claims of bargain rates (of questionable certainty in any event) purchased at the price of eliminating the right to recover for pain, suffering, and disfigurement by millions of our people; purchased at the price of removing the value of collateral benefits which our most provident citizens have prudently purchased to aid them in emergencies (or have accepted in lieu of wage increases); and purchased at the price of failing to protect them from a large part of their wage loss or the cost of the defense of many claims which might be brought against them. These are among the many "contributions" that would be required of injured people and insureds in order to produce a so-called bargain. The proposed changes put the burden on reliable and respectable people; they mostly benefit the drunken and reckless driver. Under the Basic Protection plan, the preferred risk would be the teenage hot-rodder, jobless, and given to driving a sports car, while the nonpreferred risk would be the family man who earns at least $750 a month. That is mainly because, absent the fault criteria, rates would not be proportionate to careful driving by the premium-payer, but would depend on how valuable an adjunct of society he is. And by conventional standards, the most responsible and careful people are usually also the ones with larger earnings and families in jeopardy.

As Keeton and O'Connell have conceded, their plan is really an expansion of our present medical payments type of insurance—a kind of excess insurance, requiring additional and supplemental coverage for adequate protection. So we are back where we started, minus many rights and plus much dislocation.

## C.    *Can We Afford Justice?*

We do not live in an impoverished society, but in one that has been labeled not only affluent, but the wealthiest the world has ever known. In the light of that wealth—whether exaggerated or not, no matter what its limits and whether distributed equitably or not—it seems to me we can afford one thing (along with tobacco, cosmetics, whiskey, fast cars, exploration of the stratosphere): a non-niggardly system of justice. I believe that what the American people want and what we should have is not a cheap premium for little insurance, but full coverage at the best price obtainable. In other words, what we should be urging and what the American public should be getting is quality, not just a bargain. The question is: are we to be affluent in everything but justice?

And, if we provide such quality, it will necessarily remedy the main criticisms of our present system.

## IV. Chief Problems Today

What are these criticisms? That many victims of accidents are not now compensated either adequately or at all. That payment is too often delayed (though modern-day collateral sources have substantially softened this cause for criticism). And one criticism that I, as a lawyer, would like to put in the forefront: the hypocrisy and pretense in some of our legal formalisms that serve to demean justice.

The impact of fraud is greatly exaggerated. The fact is that fraud is so rare that it does not even constitute a measurable statistic. J. F. Miazza of the General Adjustment Bureau, a leading insurance source, estimated a few years back that only 3 out every 50,000 claims are fraudulent—truly an infinitesimal number.

### A. Some Suggestions

Few of the following suggestions are new, but they are put together with the strong feeling that we can afford them, as we can mass air travel systems, mass housing programs, mass highways, the stratoplane, and other things that only limited imagination has prevented us from reaching out for in the past. They can be adopted gradually, one at a time, or in a combination of some or all. We may test the workability of each one without having to undermine and abandon what we already have. In any event, I believe they deserve our careful, forward-looking consideration.

### 1. Compulsory Insurance

Liability insurance should be compulsory. The New York, North Carolina, and Massachusetts experience teaches us that it does not lead to public ownership of the insurance business, and, as in New York, need not appreciably affect rates.

### 2. Unlimited Coverage

Coverage should be unlimited. This is not a revolutionary idea. It prevails in England and other places. As we all know, premiums for such insurance need not be very high, for the simple reason well known to statisticians and demonstrated by Professor Alfred Conard of the University of Michigan Law School and his colleagues, that there are relatively few large claims.[8] The risk of financial irresponsibility, in part or whole, will

---

[8] *See* A. Conard, J. Morgan, R. Pratt, C. Voltz & R. Bombaugh, Automobile Accident Costs and Payments—Studies in the Economics of Injury Reparation chs. 6-7 (1964).

then disappear and where it counts most dramatically—to the severely injured. If an agricultural society, with its limited risks, in Saskatchewan, Canada, can afford minimum liability limits of $35,000 how do we measure up with our $5,000, $10,000, or even $15,000 limits?

### 3.  Comparative Negligence

Comparative negligence should take the place of contributory negligence. Few now dispute that the rule of contributory negligence is unconscionable, antisocial, and survives only because it is usually given little more than lip service. There would be more respect for law if it were more forthright, as by a frank use of comparative negligence. It would also assure that fewer claimants with at least some merit to their claims would end up uncompensated.

### 4.  Universal Medical and Disability Payments

The compulsory liability policy might have a compulsory medical payments feature, which could be eliminated at the option of the policyholder only by his filing and maintaining proof of equivalent collateral arrangements through other sources. Thus a policyholder could maintain and pay for more than one coverage if he so desires, but could avoid that expense and utilize his other sources alone if he preferred. This would, of course, lessen the social impact of such delays as still exist and would disturb costs little since collateral sources, we have been told, already exist in some 80 per cent of the cases[9] and pay almost 50 per cent of what is paid to traffic victims.[10] The same principle could be applied to disability payments.

### 5.  Direct Suit Against Carriers

We ought to consider permitting direct suit against insurers. With compulsory insurance—even with widespread if not compulsory insurance—carrying on the fiction that we are actually looking to the auto owner and driver does not serve a practical purpose. Further, it will make for more intellectual honesty at trials, instead of the ill-concealed game being played today by everyone, including jurors. And, once defendants learn how to handle it, it can even be a weapon to keep unworthy plaintiffs from mulcting this "joint, quasi-public, insurance fund."

### 6.  Insure People, Not Cars

Liability insurance might be sold to cover individual people instead of car-owners. This would permit more equitable ratings, better experience records, better incentives for safety, and lower cost. This could also be the basis for sounder driving licensing and revocation procedures, which would eliminate the occasion for most cancellation abuses.

---

[9] *See* Harwayne, *Insurance Costs of Basic Protection Plan in Michigan*, p. 142 *supra*.
[10] *See* Conard, *et al.*, *supra* note 8, at 62-64.

## 7.  *Other Suggestions*

Massive safety campaigns ought to be our first order of business.

We should expand advance payment and rehabilitation programs,[11] such as have been started in the last year or two by a number of insurers.

An insolvency insurance fund should be created or uninsured motorist coverage extended to cover defalcations by fly-by-night companies. Nothing but good has come of the comparable Federal Deposit Insurance Corporation in banking.

Guest laws and governmental, charitable, and intra-family immunities should be abolished, along with the removal of death action limits where they still exist.

We must work for an adequate court system, instead of starved courts. We are limping along with inadequate judicial budgets. It is like trying to operate our automobiles of 1967 on the roads and with the mechanics of 1927.

There should be tough traffic law enforcement against both the individual and the car involved, thus putting family pressure on the careless driver.

### B.  *Our Suggestions Constitute a Full Protection Plan*

If compulsory liability coverage, unlimited coverage, compulsory medical and disability payments coverage and comparative negligence—these four items alone—were adopted, there would be no one injured who would not receive some money towards his expenses. Financial irresponsibility (for big and small cases both) would be a thing of the past; and meritorious claims would be fully compensated.

This would all be within the framework of our present insurance structure, utilizing the experience of our people, the financial structure and resources of our existing companies and our familiar and painstakingly-developed court structures, and all at little, if any, increase in costs.

It would eliminate the basis for the major criticisms which now rightfully arise. It would abort panaceas like the Basic Protection plan, which take root in soil created by our failure to remove the causes for such criticisms.

If we embrace these, we would be advocating—*positively and not negatively*—a Full Protection plan which spells out an ideal goal. In contrast, such proposals as the socially-disrupting and mis-described "Basic" Protection plan ("Basic" appears to mean "little" or "minimal" when its specific provisions are spelled out) would appear to be what in truth, they are—not progressive but retrogressive. Under a Full Protection plan, we would have provided a good program through which, with the support of our legislatures, we could meet the needs of our people.

[11] For a definition of "advance payment," *see* Kemper, p. 104 n.20 *supra.*

## V.  ADD TO—NOT SUBTRACT FROM—RIGHTS

Insurance companies are in the business of selling the insurance the public wants—not how little, but how much. We are long past the days of a "poorhouse" philosophy. There was a time when we took care of our needy aged by relegating them to a place out-of-sight with just enough to keep them alive. That was also the day of the $5,000 verdict for a leg, if you got a verdict at all. Only yesterday, too, manufacturers hid behind rules of privity.

That is no longer what this country is about. We are not looking to subtract from the rights of people but to add to them. And, if our private insurance system does not provide it, if justice is rationed as under the Basic Protection plan, then governmental bureaucracy will take over, because people today will not long be neglected. There is something fundamentally wrong with a proposal that would severely disturb the claimants in the up-to-$10,000 class, whom Professor Conard has told us are now the most fairly treated group.[12] We would thus create a whole new class of dissatisfied people while, at the same time, completely neglecting those whose cases are in a range over these limits, whom Professor Conard correctly tells us are the ones most unjustly treated.[13]

The basic question, which Keeton and O'Connell's "Basic" Protection plan would ignore is whether an honest plaintiff, whom no one can deny was harmed, is to bear his harms himself? Or should the erring wrongdoer do so?

It took a long and frustrating time to bring the right to recover for pain and suffering to its present state. Non-economic losses like pain and suffering may be of great value. Our society is sensitive enough to social justice to appreciate that. It has long passed the day when only property interests are entitled to judicial protection. The rights of personality now stand on at least an equal level.

[12] Conard, *Remarks*, pp. 80-82 *supra*.
[13] *Id*.

# REMARKS

## OF EDWARD C. GERMAN*

I WOULD LIKE to begin by telling you some of the features concerning automobile claims that I favor, instead of telling you what I'm against. I can enumerate five. First, the adversary system must be preserved. Second, a civil jury trial must be available to all litigants. Third, all tort liability must be based on determination of fault. Fourth—and as a corollary to the third point—any compensation plan which denies fault as the basis of payment must not be allowed to substitute for any part of the present system. Fifth, all of us must strive to improve the present system of reparation, and to adapt it in the public interest through evolution and not revolution.

Every litigant is entitled to a fair trial. He is entitled to have his case presented by an attorney in accordance with the rules handed down to us by our Anglo-Saxon ancestors in the common law, which, I think all of us agree, are grounded in common sense. Without this right of redress, every individual citizen would be relegated to second-class citizenship.

The purpose of the law through the courts and the adversary system is to achieve the nearest possible approximation to truth. This end can only be gained by means of a contest of attorneys committed to their clients and committed to present the best possible evidence for the consideration of 12 persons who form a jury, and who, in turn, reach a decision through argument and counterargument. Such a process cannot and must not be replaced by a system of compensation which automatically rewards all injured persons regardless of fault, replacing the attorney and jury with governmental bureaucracy. I agree with those who assert that the Basic Protection plan heads us down the road clearly and definitely toward governmental bureaucracy. Such a compensation plan would not serve truth; it would be costly to the American people; and it would contradict the principles of justice under which this country has flourished.

The criticisms of our present system by the professors really do an injustice to those of us who make our livelihood in and have dedicated our lives to the arena of the courtroom. The function of gentlemen such as Jacob Fuchsberg, Edward Kuhn, a former President of the American Bar Association and an eminent trial lawyer, myself, and many others taking part in this program is to elicit the truth from the parties involved and from the witnesses who are called to the courtroom. If we don't do this job, the whole system fails. It fails not only in the field of automobile compensation, it fails generally; it fails especially when the rights—and the lives—of those accused of crime are involved. If we trial lawyers cannot elicit the truth in a courtroom in an automobile accident case, then we are subject to equal

---

*EDWARD C. GERMAN. LL.B. 1950, Temple University; President (1966-1967), Federation of Insurance Counsel; Partner in the firm of LaBrum and Doak, Philadelphia.

condemnation in any other type suit. And in that event, the whole adversary common law system should be scrapped.

Let me approach another subject which I realize is somewhat delicate. But I think perhaps it's about time we lay all our cards on the table, and I hope that this is accepted in the right light. Ever since I have been engaged in discussions of the Basic Protection plan,[1] including several times throughout the course of this conference, it's been said that the only men who can tell us what's wrong with our present system and the only men who can tell us how to improve our system are the professors in the ivory towers of academia. And why is this so? It has been said that lawyers and insurance executives have an economic interest in preserving the present system. Charts are shown indicating how much of the insurance executive's salary and the lawyer's fee comes out of premiums paid under the present system. Because of that, supposedly, they cannot look at this subject objectively, since all they are trying to do is preserve their own economic status. Therefore, only the college professors, who are not on the charts, can tell us what to do.

I agree that the college professors are not on the little charts. But I do not agree that the college professors have no economic interest. The college professors have a great economic interest at stake. I am not critical of them; they should be paid for their time and work. Indeed, Professors Keeton and O'Connell were paid for their work on this plan by two foundation grants. I don't know what the grants were, but have reason to believe they were sizable grants. In addition, Professors Keeton and O'Connell have income from books on the plan; they were paid by Mr. Kemper as consultants to the Kemper Companies, and if the plan is adopted, they will be paid more by many others for their consulting time. I want to make clear that I do not condemn them for this. On the contrary, as I said, they are entitled to be paid. However, I do resent the fact that only insurance executives and lawyers are not considered to be impartial spokesmen because of their economic interest. Rather, let's lay all our cards on the table and admit that we all have an economic interest at stake.

In this connection, I might also say in all candor that if the Keeton-O'Connell plan were adopted, my economic interest would skyrocket. I agree with Professor Green and others that the Keeton and O'Connell plan would stimulate litigation, rather than curtail it.[2]

Turning to another aspect of this subject, most people—including almost everyone attending this conference—are covered by some sort of insurance paying both medical expenses and loss of income, in the event of illness or accident. For such people, the Basic Protection plan would mean that

---

[1] KEETON & O'CONNELL, BASIC PROTECTION FOR THE TRAFFIC VICTIM: A BLUEPRINT FOR REFORMING AUTOMOBILE INSURANCE (1965) [both hereinbefore and hereinafter this book is often cited as Basic Protection]. *See also* Keeton & O'Connell, *Basic Protection Automobile Insurance*, p. 40 *supra*.

[2] Green, *Basic Protection and Court Congestion*, 52 A.B.A.J. 926 (1966).

they are being required, regardless of the amount of health and accident insurance they might have, to carry what is in effect an additional health and accident policy. Practically every health and accident policy has a limitation in the amount of benefits for medical losses, but as to wage loss, practically every policy pays not with, say, a $10,000 limit, but for the rest of your life. Some people are going to cancel such health and accident policies in light of the $10,000 Basic Protection compulsory policy,[3] on the assumption that if they are involved in an accident they won't need the accident and health policy. On the other hand, if they retain the accident and health policy—since Basic Protection insurance pays only to the extent that other insurance doesn't pay[4]—they will be paid nothing from their Basic Protection insurance after an accident. Professors Keeton and O'Connell have enumerated waste as one of the five weaknesses of the present system.[5] Are we eliminating waste by making almost each and every one of us attending this conference buy an insurance policy that pays him absolutely nothing? That is what is called replacing waste with waste—assuming there is waste today, which I don't necessarily agree is the case.

Another example of the Basic Protection plan's inadequacy is its $100 deductible.[6] Look at what happens to the $50 or $100 deductible today under collision insurance. Talk about perpetrating fraud! A man walks into a garage and the first thing he says to the man making up the estimate is, "Now be sure you cover the $50 deductible, so I don't have to pay it out of my pocket."

As still another example of the plan's deficiencies, Professors Keeton and O'Connell have said that the big case is the one where the victim is most inadequately compensated. But if that is so, why are cases over $10,000 still left under our present system?

These are only a few examples of the plan's deficiencies and inconsistencies. They have been more than adequately covered by Mr. Kemper and others, and I will not belabor the point.

I think Professor Kimball is right when he says that we know what the present system costs because we can see what the premiums are, but that we don't know what any other system is going to cost.[7] If we're going to cut costs, somehow or other we have to cut corners. An actuary has estimated that the cost of administering the Basic Protection plan is not going

[3] Keeton & O'Connell, *Basic Protection Automobile Insurance*, pp. 58-59, 62-63 *supra*.

[4] *Id*. at 54-56.

[5] *Id*. at 42-43.

[6] *Id*. at 56-58.

[7] Oral remarks of Professor Spencer Kimball, University of Michigan Law School, at the conference "Changes for Automobile Claims?," University of Illinois College of Law, Urbana, Ill., Oct. 2, 1967. For the manuscript of Kimball's remarks, which does not include the cited comment, *see* Kimball, *Automobile Accident Compensation Systems: Objectives and Perspectives*, p. 10 *supra*.

to be less.[8] As a result, if we are going to effect a savings, then we must cut the payments to the injured people. It's very difficult for me to conceive of the American people accepting a system where they'll be paid on a schedule of benefits if they're involved in an automobile accident, but, on the other hand, if they are hurt in a fall, they can go into court and receive payment for their pain and suffering.

When I was a young fellow, I played sandlot baseball. The oldest fellow on the team during the course of one game hurt his knee, and I felt sorry for him, because I knew he had a wife and three children. I walked up to him and I said, "What are you going to do now that you won't be able to work?" "Well," he replied, "don't worry about it. I drive a bread truck, and to-morrow when I go to work, I'll take my truck out. But soon after I'll call in and say, 'Look, my knee went out of place as I was stepping off the breadwagon.' Then I'll collect workmen's compensation." How, indeed, are you going to have a different reparation system for different types of ac-cidents without inviting people who are injured in automobile accidents, for example, to claim that they were injured at work or to claim that they fell down on someone's pavement?

We hear from time to time that the reforms which are suggested are the result of public clamor. I have never witnessed this public clamor, although I am in constant contact with the public in my everyday life. In this connec-tion, I'd like to quote Edward Kuhn, a past President of the American Bar Association:

> "The clamor for a system of liability without fault does not come from the general public but from the hallowed halls of the theoreticians and the sequestered chambers of harried judges whose work load causes them to favor a change. The public is not clamoring for an abrogation of individual responsibility and is not willing to treat the innocent and guilty completely alike. It is not willing to reward the careless, the profligate and the incompetent at the expense of the industrious and the responsible. There is no demand by the public to forego the right to have their fault and damage assessed by a jury. The public has a strong philosophical attachment to the concept of guilt."[9]

I couldn't agree more.

Our juries still make (or withhold) awards on the basis of fault, despite recent attempts to undermine the fault system. Let me illustrate: The Ameri-can Law Institute's *Restatements* were originally supposed to be statements of the law as it exists in a majority of the states. But the professors have taken over the *Restatement of Torts*. It is no longer a statement of the law as it exists, but a statement of the law as the professors think it should exist.

---

[8] *See* Keeton & O'Connell, *Basic Protection and the Costs of Traffic Accidents,* 38 N.Y.S.B.J. 255, 257 (1966).

[9] Kuhn, *In Defense of the Tort System,* 56 Ill. B.J. 106, 110 (1967).

One of the primary examples of this is section 402A of the *Restatement of Torts, Second*, which changes the rule in products liability cases in a manner inconsistent with the law in the majority of the states. This section says that in order to hold a manufacturer, vendor, or seller of a product liable, the plaintiff need only prove that a defect existed. In other words, a seller, for example, is still liable, even though a reasonable inspection would not have disclosed the existence of a defect. But I have been on products liability programs with Jacob Fuchsberg, when he was lecturing to plaintiffs' attorneys, and I have heard him tell them, "Gentlemen, juries are not willing to buy this law in spite of the judge's charge. Juries still want to hold people responsible for something that they did wrong, and, conversely, they don't want to make a man pay damages when he didn't do anything wrong. Thus, if you can prove fault, don't rely on the law that fault is not required or you may cost your client his case."

As a matter of fact, Dean Prosser has said that even under section 402A of the *Restatement*, results of jury trials are not different in more than one out of a hundred cases from what they were prior to its inception. If the people are clamoring to scrap the fault concept, why, when they sit on juries, have they rejected section 402A of the *Restatement of Torts*? Why do they adhere to the fault concept even after a judge tells them they need not find fault? I suggest to you that people are not ready to scrap fault; they are still living with their basic concepts, which include liability based on fault.

This next area of consideration may get me into trouble with some of my brethren at the bar. If there will be any saving under the Basic Protection plan, it is because of the elimination of duplication of benefits from collateral sources.[10] I want to make it clear that I am not in favor of abolishing the collateral source rule. On the other hand, I suggest there should be some modifications in the rule. For example, if a victim had life insurance, certainly the tortfeasor should not have the opportunity of taking advantage of such coverage. On the other hand, assume a widow remarries, and has as much income at the time of trial as if her husband had lived. I recently tried a case of the death of a 21-year-old male which resulted in a $375,000 verdict (the verdict was not against my client—so I can tell you about it), where the widow had remarried twice by the time of trial. She was probably better off financially, even though her first husband had been a very brilliant young man. Defense counsel, however, were not even allowed to call her by name. Why shouldn't the jury have heard the facts? If they wanted to give no weight to such facts, that could be their prerogative. But shouldn't the American people—as jurors—decide what weight to give to such matters? Similarly, if an employer pays a victim his salary, as a gift, shouldn't we let the American people decide what weight they want to give this? If a victim

---

[10] Keeton & O'Connell, *Basic Protection Automobile Insurance*, pp. 54-56 *supra*.

has received workmen's compensation, shouldn't we let the jury hear that the man received such payment?

An interesting experiment on this subject of collateral sources was run at a recent meeting of the National Association of Independent Insurers. The same factual situation was presented to three different simulated jury panels. Before two jury panels the damages were argued, excluding any reference to collateral sources. But before the third panel references to the claimant's eligibility for retirement benefits (excluding life insurance) were permitted. The results were rather dramatic: The first panel came in with a verdict for over $200,000, the second with a verdict of over $100,000, but the third—which had only heard about the collateral source without being bound to consider it—came in with a verdict of around $50,000. Shouldn't we let the jury hear all of the facts?

I also think the references to court congestion under the present system are exaggerated. It has been demonstrated that congestion, where it exists, can be cleared up. Certainly Los Angeles and Dade County are living proof of that fact: The delay in Los Angeles is now 4.9 months and the delay in Dade County, Florida, is now 5.4 months, whereas both areas previously had delays of several years. A very interesting letter from the Chief Judge of the Superior Court of Massachusetts was published recently. Note his estimate of how the judges spent their time in Suffolk County (Boston) in 1966:

| | |
|---|---|
| Civil matters | 35% |
| Equity cases | 18% |
| Criminal sessions | 32% |
| Assignment and conciliation | 7% |
| Equity motions | 8% |

Of the 35 per cent represented by days spent in civil matters, motor vehicle tort cases consumed only 13 per cent of total judicial time, with the remainder of time on civil matters—22 per cent—spent on other civil cases.[11]

The Defense Research Institute recently ran a survey on court delay. It found that, as to state courts, in 17 cities in 8 states there was a delay upwards of two years. This should be corrected, and I hope it will be corrected. Thirty-eight cities in 25 states had delays between one and two years. This should be, and can be, improved. But 53 cities in 32 states had no delays, the time period to reach trial being less than one year. Federal courts are in even better condition than state courts.[12] Thus, the matter of delays has been exaggerated out of all proportion. In Philadelphia we are trying to cope with the problem. We have compulsory arbitration in all cases under $2,000, and in nine years 59,000 cases have been disposed of by

---

[11] Letter from Hon. G. Joseph Tauro to Gov. John A. Volpe of Massachusetts, Aug. 29, 1967, reprinted in *Automobile Torts Not Cause of Court Congestion*, 8 For the Defense . . 57 (1967).

[12] *Court Congestion—A Localized Urban Problem*, 8 For the Defense . . 49 (1967).

panels each made up of three lawyers sitting as arbitrators. Nor does this infringe upon the rights of trial by jury, since every litigant has the right to ask for a new trial *de novo* before a jury. This system has worked very satisfactorily.

Let me close with a quote from a speech made by the Honorable John F. Bolton, Jr., the Director of Insurance for the State of Illinois. Commenting on the Basic Protection bill before the Illinois Legislature, he said:

> "I am told that the insurance industry which I regulate has viewed the presentation of this bill with mixed emotions and has the plan under examination in an attempt to project its implications. I should imagine that the reactions of the trial bar would be somewhat less mixed.
>
> "As for myself, I sometimes suspect that I am something of an old fashioned lawyer. Compensation in automobile torts without regard to fault may—*perhaps*—be the wave of the future. But I am sufficiently old fashioned to suggest that proponents of the idea have to shoulder a heavy burden of proof in asking the [Illinois General] Assembly to scrap a tort system which has served society so well under the common law and our adversary system.
>
> . . . .
>
> "You don't have to be a classical scholar to reflect on the validity of the statement of the ancient Greek that *'men having often abandoned what was visible for the sake of what was uncertain, have not got what they expected and have lost what they had.'* "[13]

[13] Address by Hon. John F. Bolton, Jr., Director of Insurance, State of Illinois, before the Illinois Trial Lawyers Association, Chicago, May 8, 1967. (Emphasis in transcribed copy of the speech.)

# LEGISLATORS LOOK AT PROPOSED CHANGES

*BY MICHAEL S. DUKAKIS\**

WE HAVE WITNESSED a marked emphasis on legislation at the national level over the past three decades. This is not surprising, for as American society becomes increasingly national and increasingly less provincial, solutions to these national problems necessarily must come from Congress and not from 50 state legislatures.

The problem of insurance, and more specifically the compensation of the victims of automobile accidents, however, is a problem which for the most part remains primarily the concern of state legislatures and state chief executives. In part, this is because the strenuous efforts of the insurance industry to keep the federal government out of the field have been successful. But even more important is the fact that the legal framework under which we compensate the victims of automobile accidents has traditionally been a part of the common law; and common law in the United States is state law.

For this reason, what is happening in state capitals and legislative chambers is of vital importance to the future of auto insurance in this country. True, recent events suggest that the entire problem may receive a thorough Congressional airing. Even so, I think it likely that the major battlefield for auto insurance reform in the foreseeable future will be in the state legislatures, and not in Congress.

If this is so, then an analysis of precisely what goes on in state legislatures and what is likely to happen in and around those chambers is absolutely essential to an understanding of the prospects for change in both the legal framework and the system of insurance which will govern the compensation of the injured victims of motor vehicle accidents. Such an analysis is the purpose of this paper. For we can talk at this and other conferences long into the night about the need for change in our liability system and we can define and redefine what must be done to reform our auto insurance laws. Unless however the state legislative process is capable, as a practical matter, of effecting important and needed changes in this area, then we are either wasting our time or had better direct our attention exclusively to the prospect of a national system of compensation for the victims of motor vehicle accidents.

Let me say at the outset that I undertake this analysis as something of a legislative outsider in the insurance field. By this I mean that I am not, and never have been, a member of a committee handling insurance legislation during my five years in the Massachusetts Legislature. As such, I have not been exposed directly or indirectly to repeated testimony at hearings or the

*\* MICHAEL S. DUKAKIS. B.A. 1955, Swarthmore College; LL.B. 1960, Harvard University; Member, Massachusetts House of Representatives; Associate in the firm of Hill & Barlow, Boston.*

more subtle blandishments which insurance companies and others may direct at members of a legislative committee on insurance.

On the other hand, I am a legislator in that state which appears to be ripest for change in its auto insurance laws. One cannot represent a constituency in Massachusetts as an elected official and not be deeply concerned about the problem of auto insurance. Moreover, my sponsorship of the Basic Protection plan[1] in this session of the Massachusetts Legislature plunged me into the middle of a legislative maelstrom which must rank as one of the most violent in the Bay State. It took me into legislative hearings, before our regulatory agency, into the governor's office, before television cameras and the public press, and out on the hustings to such an extent that I have been more thoroughly immersed in this issue than in any other since I entered the Massachusetts House of Representatives in 1963.[2]

What follows is not an effort to lobby for Basic Protection or any other form of insurance or liability system. Rather, I shall attempt to analyze the legislative maze which attends the passage of any significant changes in this field and to assess the prospects, if any, for a reasonably rapid and meaningful legislative response to a problem which cries out for change in virtually every state in the Union.

## I. The Need for Reform

The need for reform has never been greater. Auto ownership in the United States is practically universal. The toll of the automobile on streets and highways continues day after day. Insurance cost spirals in almost every state. And the problem is further complicated by widespread denial of coverage, company failures and insolvencies, and a system of compensation which raises increasing doubts in the minds of many about its fairness and, indeed, its reason for being.

All of these problems are present in my home state—perhaps to a greater degree than in any other. Over 40 years ago Massachusetts adopted a system of compulsory motor vehicle insurance with required personal injury coverages of $5,000-$10,000.[3] It has the highest claim frequency in the country despite a highway safety record which is fairly good and considerably better than many other states. Massachusetts' courts are crammed with auto tort litigation. Delays in obtaining trials in its busiest trial courts are now approaching 40 months in spite of valiant efforts to employ a system of auditors for the initial hearing of auto tort actions and mandatory trial of smaller

---

[1] Keeton & O'Connell, Basic Protection for the Traffic Victim: A Blueprint for Reforming Automobile Insurance (1965) [both hereinbefore and hereinafter this book is often cited as Basic Protection]. *See also* Keeton & O'Connell, *Basic Protection Automobile Insurance,* p. 40 *supra.*

[2] The Basic Protection bill passed the Massachusetts House in Aug. 1967. It failed in the Senate in September, and failed to get a majority when an effort was made to pass it a second time in the House.

[3] Mass. Ann. Laws ch. 90, §§ 34A-L (1967).

motor vehicle claims in lower level, nonjury courts before a trial by jury is allowed.

Not surprisingly, public dissatisfaction with this state of affairs is massive. Although the high claim frequency rate suggests that Massachusetts motorists themselves are not averse to filing claims for personal injury at the bump of a fender, there is a vast amount of public cynicism about the entire compensation process, including widespread feeling that the process is shot through with exaggeration and outright fraud, and that lawyers, doctors and insurance companies are wedded to the status quo because they are all doing quite well with it and at it.

My impression is that all of the attitudes one can find in Massachusetts are common to most other states. Certainly, recent announcements of investigations of the problem by the Federal Department of Transportation and the House Judiciary Committee suggest that it is not Massachusetts alone which faces a crisis in dealing with the compensation of the victim of motor vehicle accidents.

## II. The Regulatory Agency

State departments of insurance, or their equivalents, typically have the broadest kind of regulatory power in the auto insurance field. While state statutes may vary considerably in the manner by which auto insurance rates are set, or approved, or disapproved, the potential power of a state insurance commissioner over the field is enormous. In part, this is because state legislatures cannot possibly be expected to spell out the details of any state auto insurance system. To an even greater extent, perhaps, this enormous potential power stems from the fact that the statutes under which insurance commissioners operate are necessarily broad and include within them vague and poorly defined standards for insurance regulation.

In Massachusetts, for example, where the insurance commissioner is required to fix a rate for auto insurance within the Commonwealth each year, the statutory language contains words like "excessive," "inadequate, "and "unfairly discriminatory."[4] Such standards permit an insurance commissioner to exercise wide authority over rates, coverages, and accounting practices. His decisions, unless challenged successfully in the courts, are final, and insurance companies know that the courts will generally defer to the administrative agency charged with the regulatory responsibility unless that agency is acting arbitrarily or capriciously.

State insurance departments could be of great assistance to legislatures in the continuing debate over auto insurance reform. These departments often have large staffs, including actuaries, who continually review insurance company figures and performance. This staff capability far exceeds anything the legislature can possibly muster. The regulatory agency is, or can be, there-

---

[4] Mass. Ann. Laws ch. 175A, § 5 (a) (4) (1959).

fore, a key factor in legislative efforts to make far-reaching and fundamental changes in existing liability insurance systems.

Regrettably, however, it is a rare insurance department which leads the fight for innovation and reform. Like other regulatory agencies at the state level, insurance departments have tended to become constituent agencies. Contact with the insurance industry is close and continuous. Insurance commissioners are invited to industry banquets and testimonials as a matter of course. In Massachusetts a few years ago a testimonial to the incumbent insurance commissioner planned by the industry was hastily cancelled as a result of the public uproar it produced. I suspect that similar testimonials are being held in other states, but perhaps not with the same public outcry.

Moreover, the ability of the state insurance agency to match the assembled accounting and actuarial knowledge of the industry may be limited. While the size and expertise of the agency's staff far exceeds that directly available to the legislature, it is rarely endowed with the kind or number of personnel required for the job of confronting the vast resources of the industry. For example, in Massachusetts only one or two key people are doing the critical job of evaluating rates and coverages filed with the commissioner each year.

Then, too, the fact that an insurance commissioner must be responsive to the governor who appoints him often creates problems. In Massachusetts the insurance commissioner was outspokenly opposed to a change in the present compulsory system until last year. At that time the governor embraced the financial responsibility system as the answer to Massachusetts' needs, and within a matter of hours the insurance commissioner had become a passionate advocate of financial responsibility and an outspoken opponent of the existing Massachusetts system. To say that the switch created a credibility gap in the minds of most Massachusetts legislators is to put it mildly.

These generalizations cannot and should not be applied to insurance departments everywhere. On occasion one reads of a state insurance commissioner who meets current industry accounting practices head-on or recommends bold, imaginative changes to the legislature. But such commissioners are exceptions to the general rule, and for the most part, state insurance departments will not, I venture to say, be leading the fight for reform in state capitals across the nation.

This is not to say that state insurance departments cannot be helpful to legislatures—they can be, particularly in providing the kind of statistical and actuarial data which is so difficult for the average state legislator to find on his own or through the legislature's usually meager staff resources. But as champions of fundamental auto insurance reform—as agencies willing to stand up and fight for sweeping change against the special interest opposition which such a fight will inevitably produce—that, I fear, will rarely if ever be the role of the state insurance department.

## III. The Legislature

The failure of state insurance departments to provide forceful leadership in the debate over change means that in the absence of a governor who commits himself strongly to reform, state legislators will have to attack the problem of change via the legislative process, with all the obstacles and frustrations that normally entails.

Take the committee system, for example. Most state legislatures have a single standing committee in each branch or a joint committee, as we do in Massachusetts, which handles insurance legislation almost exclusively or as one of its major subject areas. These committees rarely have any staff at all. This means that they are compelled to rely on the insurance department in the executive branch for information they need or on lobbyists who either represent the industry or other special interests affected by proposed changes.

Like their counterpart in the executive branch, they tend to become constituent committees—and for the same reasons. Insurance legislation is complicated. It is rarely understood by the average legislator who is not a committee member or, at least, deeply immersed in some particular field of insurance legislation. Insurance bills dealing with complex matters like the regulation of insurance company investments and the relative competitive positions of stock and mutual companies, go flying through our legislature and are rarely challenged. Such legislation may be good, or it may be bad. The point is that the average legislator hasn't the slightest idea what it is all about, and his colleague who sits on the insurance committee may not be much better informed about the complexities of a particular insurance bill.

The usual membership of insurance committees invariably strengthens the process by which the committee gravitates toward the industry about which it is supposed to be legislating. New legislators request, and are most frequently assigned to, committees which are considering legislation in which they have a deep interest and some competence. Quite obviously, this means that legislators in the insurance business request and are assigned to insurance committees in much the same way that lawyers request and are assigned to judiciary or legal affairs committees.

Thus the relationship between the interests with which the committee is trying to deal and its members is already close before the first hearing is held and the first bill reported out. If that alone is not enough, committee members are wooed assiduously by the industry through industry banquets, constant contact with company lobbyists, and intimate gatherings at the best restaurants in town to discuss pending legislation—all paid for, of course, by the companies. Such activities naturally tend to soften up committee members and make them less eager to do battle on a broad front with existing industry or institutional arrangements.

The same process tends to be effective with the legislative leadership as well. I recall, for example, a conversation with one of my legislator colleagues in a position of leadership last June—a legislator, incidentally, for whom I have great respect. I was complaining to him rather bitterly that five and a half months had already passed in the current session and the insurance committee had still not reported out a bill of any kind; angry mutterings were beginning to be heard in the press and from the public at large. He quickly assured me that things were moving rapidly, that the stock companies had finally come up with a plan, and that the committee would probably be reporting out a bill within a matter of weeks—presumably embodying the stock company plan. I couldn't help responding that I didn't know why the Massachusetts Legislature had to wait around for five and a half months until one segment of the insurance industry decided what was good for the people of Massachusetts.

I think the point is clear. Long immersion in the legislative mill tends to condition veteran legislators to thinking in terms of conflicting special interests inside the state capital rather than the broad public interest outside it. This is particularly true where the subject under consideration is so complex that the average legislator is not equipped to deal with it effectively on its merits.

### IV. The Insurance Industry

The average legislator, then, is at a serious disadvantage in the fight for auto insurance reform, even if he wants to do something about it. He often finds himself confronted with a system which is difficult to crack, a state insurance department which is either unwilling or unable to give him any guidance or leadership, and a legislative committee on insurance which is very close to the industry.

Interestingly enough, however, my own experience in sponsoring the Basic Protection plan in the Massachusetts Legislature suggests that the influence of the industry or its lobby has been exaggerated. The industry has not done well this year in Massachusetts. The Massachusetts House approved the Basic Protection plan over its objections. Even the committee bill itself, which for the first time recommended a new competitive rating section in the Massachusetts law, was reported out of committee over the strong objection of industry spokesmen.

The reasons for this are many. To begin with, the industry itself is badly split on the question of auto insurance reform. At least four or five segments of the industry were present at hearings before the insurance committee of the Massachusetts Legislature last spring—each recommending something different. The industry has no clear idea of what it really wants in this area. It is deeply troubled by the threat of federal regulation, and yet it finds itself unable to come up with a proposal which can deal as fundamentally with the ills of the present as, in my opinion, Basic Protection does.

In Massachusetts this year this "heavyweight lobby" became a paper tiger. No real effort was made to influence legislators. None of the usual techniques—particularly the mass letter-writing campaign from insurance company employees which defeated tax increases for insurance companies in Massachusetts two years ago—were employed. When the Basic Protection bill passed the House in late August, insurance company lobbyists and leaders were stunned, and they admitted it. When it failed in the Senate recently, their attitude was one of relief, not the pride of a successful contender.

## V. The Bar

The infirmities of the insurance lobby in Massachusetts did not afflict those members of the bar who see in Basic Protection, or in some other form of sweeping change, a real threat to the present system of liability insurance and to the position of the attorney in that system. The opposition of some members of the bar to the Basic Protection bill in Massachusetts was tough, aggressive, and after the passage of the bill by the lower house, somewhat hysterical. This opposition took the form of thorough and hard-hitting testimony before legislative committees, mailings to all attorneys throughout the state, appearances on television and radio panel and "talk" shows, and a continuous stream of news releases from the desk of a full-time public relations man employed by one of the professional lawyers' associations fighting the bill.

Moreover, the opposition of lawyers is often more effective than that of insurance companies. There are attorneys in every city or town in Massachusetts. Many are well known and respected, and they are generally familiar with the political process. They are a formidable force for a legislature to contend with.

Lawyers have their champions—also lawyers—inside the legislative chamber. These legislators are usually well informed and they can be extremely adept at picking apart the language of a complex bill. They can often baffle a nonlawyer legislator with plausible arguments about constitutionality and due process. We have one prominent lawyer-legislator in Massachusetts who has repeatedly questioned the constitutionality of the Basic Protection bill on the grounds that it compels people to insure themselves. Apparently, he has never heard of Social Security or Medicare. But such arguments, particularly if delivered with an aura of legal authority, can raise doubts in the minds of the legislator who is not an attorney.

Nevertheless, in the eyes of some legislators, and of the public generally, lawyers who oppose fundamental changes such as Basic Protection are at a serious disadvantage. This is true, I fear, because of widespread public cynicism both in and out of state legislatures about the role of the lawyer in the present auto tort and insurance system. Rightly or wrongly, the public feels that lawyers are doing well by the status quo and that their opposition to change is motivated primarily by a fear of what will happen to their fees. This view may be unfair to the vast majority of lawyers, but the fact is that it exists to a very wide degree in my own state and, I suspect, in others, and it seriously hampers lawyers' efforts to block reform in state legislatures.

Moreover, the proponents of reform can marshal substantial lawyer support. In Massachusetts, for example, an ad hoc organization known as the Lawyers' Committee for Basic Protection Insurance was organized within five days after House passage of the bill. Almost two hundred and fifty Boston area attorneys issued a statement at a formal press conference supporting the bill. They furnished members of the state senate with information on the bill and prepared legal memoranda which refute charges that the bill is unconstitutional, or that it will encourage more fraud, or that it will produce more, not fewer, disputes between claimants and insurance companies.

Nevertheless, I think it fair to say that the majority of lawyers in Massachusetts strongly oppose the Basic Protection bill and will continue to do so. Its failure to pass the senate was the direct result of the organized and intensive efforts of members of the bar.

## VI. The Press

While legislators and legislatures are faced with conflicting pressures and interests in dealing with changes in our auto claims systems, experience in Massachusetts suggests that one of the strongest allies the proponents for reform will have in any state legislature is the press—including radio and television journalists as well as the more traditional newspaper scribe. Coverage of the "great debate" this year has been exhaustive and, on the whole, intelligently handled. The state's television channels have repeatedly provided large amounts of public service time for panel discussions and debates. The same has been true of radio coverage, particularly the radio talk show which has become extremely popular in Massachusetts within the past two or three years and which permits listeners to talk by telephone with the commentator and his guest.

Editorial coverage and, in many cases, forthright editorial support have also been impressive. Boston's two leading daily newspapers endorsed the Basic Protection plan very early in the legislative session, and they were followed by important regional dailies in various parts of the state. Moreover, the press has been invaluable in serving as a gadfly during the session—constantly prodding and pushing for legislative action in this area.

All of this coverage and interest on the part of the press, incidentally, has been completely spontaneous. There has been no organized effort to produce it. The proponents of the Basic Protection plan, for example, have carried the fight without office space or staff or public relations counsel of any kind.

## VII. The Individual Legislator

Faced with the competing claims of the professional lobbyists, totally lacking in staff of any kind, unguided by any agency or leader in the executive branch, and beset with the frenzied opposition of so many members of the bar, the individual and independent legislator has an extremely difficult task in trying to decide where he should stand on the problem of changing our auto claims system. He cannot cope very effectively with the barrage of material thrown at him by the insurance industry and the bar. If he is not himself an attorney or in the insurance business, he may find himself without even the most basic understanding of how the existing system works. And he is not alone; his colleagues may be just as confused as he is. Unless there are at least a few of them whom he respects and in whom he can place his confidence on crucial votes and at crucial times, he may prefer to stick with the status quo rather than adopt some untested scheme.

Furthermore, the legislator cannot make an idle decision on the matter. Law professors and lawyers can argue theory interminably. Politicians need votes. If a legislator does cast his vote for reform and later discovers to his dismay that he supported something worse than the present system, his constituents may retire him at the next election.

For the legislator and his constituents, the *cost* of any sweeping new change is of fundamental importance. Auto insurance in the United States today is a bread-and-butter issue. If there is one aspect of the present system which has produced massive public discontent, it is the spiralling cost of adequate coverage. For this reason, any serious suggestion for basic change in the present system of handling automobile injury claims *must guarantee some significant reduction in cost to the average motorist if it is to be sold to a state legislator*. That is why the Basic Protection plan appealed to a very substantial majority of the members of the Massachusetts lower house. That is also why recommendations from those segments of the bar which oppose Basic Protection and propose such things as increased minimum limits, mandatory property damage, fraudulent claims units, and more judges,[5] are doomed to failure. None of these proposals do anything about the problem of cost. All of them, in fact, guarantee that the average motorist's cost of insuring his car will be increased or that his taxes will go up to pay for the extra judges or for the fraudulent claims unit.

## VIII. Conclusion

Legislatures are peculiar places and at times one wonders whether they are capable of dealing with complex and important issues like the one under discussion. Nevertheless, no one has come up with anything better, and unless the Congress itself steps into the breach, it will be the 50 state legislatures which will become the battleground for meaningful reform of our auto claims systems.

Our experience in Massachusetts indicates that the prospects of reform in those legislatures are dim unless one of the following occurs: (1) forceful leadership from the state's chief executive backed by effective staff work from the state insurance department; (2) support and direction by the top

---

[5] *See* Fuchsberg, *Lawyers View Proposed Changes*, pp. 211-14 *supra*.

legislative leaders buttressed by first rate legislative staff assistance; or (3) such massive public dissatisfaction with existing systems of compensation that a combination of independent action within the legislature and strong spontaneous support from the public and the press can carry the day.

Of these three, I think the first is the most promising approach. Governors can to a very great extent ignore the lobbies and build strong support by so doing. They can have great influence over the press. They have public relations resources which are rarely available to members of the legislature. They have strong staff support in their own insurance departments, generally under a commissioner appointed by and responsive to the governor. They have an influence on legislatures which far exceeds that which any individual legislator or even a group of interested legislators can wield.

In short, I suggest that those interested in fundamental reform in the auto insurance field educate the legislators thoroughly and then train their guns on the chief executives of the various states. For the fight for reform will be far easier, I am convinced, if it is led by a strong and firmly committed chief executive than if it is set adrift in the uncertain currents of the legislative process.

# REMARKS

*OF ROBERT MORETTI**

I'M SURE THAT MANY would expect California to lead in the Basic Protection[1] revolution. After all, we are known as a wild and wacky state, given to mercurial changes in mood and mind. However, there has been little movement in California toward a radical change in compensating auto accident victims. There is no doubt that automobile insurance has become one of the problem children for casualty insurers. Nobody loves automobile insurers, not even their own insureds. But, automobile insurance is not the problem in California that Representative Dukakis would make it seem in Massachusetts. Property taxes stand alone as the major issue in the state of California. We have others, such as the University of California and welfare costs. Even fire insurance is a greater problem in California than automobile insurance. But it is one of significance to us.

Generally the complaints that reach legislators concerning automobile insurance are about the same as those pointed out by the critics of the present system in urging reform: First is the high cost of adequate coverage. The premium levels, although not as high in California as in some other states, represent a significant percentage of family income, particularly in California, where a two or three-car family is the rule, rather than the exception. Even when one can obtain coverage through the normal or standard market, the increasing cost of such coverage is of concern to the public, and thus to the legislator. Those who find themselves in the substandard market or in the assigned risk plan have an even greater economic burden to carry for what is, in some cases, very inadequate coverage.

Second is the availability of coverage in the normal or standard market. For those drivers who have had two or three traffic citations in a year or who have had one or two accidents in a year, whether or not they are at fault, the penalty is either substantially higher premiums or if they are unlucky, complete cancellation of insurance. Many persons find themselves branded as poor risks, whom no other insurer will voluntarily accept. Although there are relatively few cases of arbitrary cancellation, the reasons given for cancellation in many cases are simply unsatisfactory to the general public. This potential gap in the continuity of coverage presents serious economic problems to the insured and serious social problems to the legislator.

* *ROBERT MORETTI. Ph.B. 1958, Notre Dame University; Member of the California Assembly, 42d District; Chairman, Assembly Finance and Insurance Committee.*

[1] KEETON & O'CONNELL, BASIC PROTECTION FOR THE TRAFFIC VICTIM: A BLUEPRINT FOR REFORMING AUTOMOBILE INSURANCE (1965) [hereinbefore and hereinafter this book is often cited as Basic Protection]. *See also* Keeton & O'Connell, *Basic Protection Automobile Insurance*, p. 40 *supra*.

Third is the collection and settlement problem. An accident forces the insured into post-accident situations with which he is not able to cope. He needs his car fixed, and he needs some doctor bills paid. The insurer, either his own or the third party's, may be willing to enter into a quick settlement, but the insured may have legitimate worries about his physical condition for the future. Although he may not wish to resort to litigation, his relations with the insurer become a game of fierce competition and complicated bargaining, creating more and more frustrations for the claimant.

Fourth, and finally, there is the labyrinth of litigation in which, for 30 to 40 per cent of the potential award, an attorney will take you by the hand and lead you against the insurer. Some claimants will get more than they should, some will get less, some will get nothing. Unfortunately, there is often a less than perfect distribution based upon the merits of a particular case.

Certainly any reform of the compensation system must aim to solve these difficulties, irritants, and inequities. Attempts made up to now by the states with file and use laws[2] and uninsured motorist coverage, and by insurers in experimental advance payment plans,[3] while certainly aiding in the overall problem, simply have not been the answer. Whether the Basic Protection plan as developed by Professors Keeton and O'Connell is such an answer remains to be seen. I have some serious doubts, or at least some serious questions.

First, I am concerned that the payment of out-of-pocket loss up to $10,000 without regard to fault[4] will have the effect of financing many tort suits in excess of that amount. While this doubt may seem to reflect adversely upon the motives of plaintiffs or the plaintiffs' bar, it is not beyond the realm of possibility that a greater number of suits in excess of this limiting amount might be filed.[5] One aim of the Basic Protection plan is to reduce litigation, but we may find an unjustified increase in relatively large suits.

Under the current system, as I mentioned earlier, a great deal of time and inconvenience is involved in dealing with the insurer of the party at fault about damages and settlements. Is it not also possible that under the Basic Protection plan this same time, inconvenience, and frustration will now be transferred to one's own insurer as the parties argue over the amount of wage loss suffered? Questions of disability and inability to work will have to be settled. Presently under workmen's compensation where temporary disability is paid based on wage loss, there are, at least in California, literally thousands of disputes a year over the issue of the injured workman's ability to return to work, with each side hunting out claimants' or defendants'

---

[2] *See, e.g.,* CAL. INS. CODE § 779.9 (West's Cal. Legislative Service, No. 6, 1967).
[3] *See* Kemper, *The Basic Protection Plan: Reform or Regression?* p. 104 n.20 *supra* and accompanying text.
[4] Keeton & O'Connell, *Basic Protection Automobile Insurance,* pp. 52-53 *supra.*
[5] *See id.* at 50-51.

doctors to testify in their behalf. An added problem may be determining wage loss. Is this taken to be actual wage loss based upon wages earned at the time of the accident or should we not include or consider the plaintiff's reduced ability to compete in the open labor market?

While none of these concerns is sufficient alone to defeat consideration of the Basic Protection plan, they do require serious scrutiny before legislative action is taken. And I am sure that no politician relishes the thought of exposing himself to the wrath of insurance companies, the state bar, or trial lawyers without a firm conviction that his proposal is a significant improvement over the present system.

If I may make some comments about Representative Dukakis' paper, I think that the California Legislature stands pretty much alone in its situation in this country. We have worked very hard for the last eight years or so to develop an independent, equal, imaginative, and creative arm of government. We have taken steps to insure the achievement of equality between the executive and legislative branches of government. One of the ways we have made progress is through the development of a very strong and independent legislative research capability. I am chairman of the Finance and Insurance Committee. (We handle a great deal more legislation than that relating to insurance, including all related to the financial institutions in our state and all related to social insurance programs—workmen's compensation, unemployment insurance, disability insurance, etc.) I simply do not have time, in a legislature where some 5,000 to 7,000 pieces of legislation a year are introduced, to become an expert or develop expertise in very many areas. I simply am not an expert in the area of automobile insurance, but the consultant and the coordinator to our committee are experts. Because our committees have available this staff operation, in addition to other research capability developed by our own House, we do not have to depend upon the executive branch of government to tell us the truth or to give us correct information. We find out on our own.

Also, "the third house," as the lobbyists in California are called, does not have the power that lobbyists wield in many other states. The Speaker of California's Assembly is famous for his statement concerning lobbyists: "If you can't drink their booze, eat their food, take their contributions, and vote against them, you don't belong here." On many occasions we take great delight in doing precisely that. We would never have a situation such as Representative Dukakis describes in Massachusetts where a bill would be held up in committee for five and a half months waiting for the lobbyists. We simply don't allow it.

A legislator's party, too, simply does not have the power in California that it has in other states. If my county chairman in Los Angeles calls me and says he wants me to vote a particular way on a particular bill, I feel perfectly free, without blinking, to dismiss his advice. This isn't commonplace elsewhere, particularly on the Eastern Seaboard.

Our constituencies are also considerably different and tremendously larger than other states. Each member of the California Assembly represents an average of 230,000 people. This is higher, by about 90,000, on the average, than in New York State which is the next highest in size of constituencies—and *much* larger than many states.

In addition to our efforts to develop an independent branch of government, the California Legislature has been anxious to confer with our sister state legislatures. As one of the two representatives from California, I attended a conference last year conducted by the Eagleton Institute of Politics at Rutgers University. We met there with legislators from each of the 18 largest states in this country to discuss our mutual problems. We hope, along with our sister states, to redevelop the role of the state legislature and to regain some of the power and influence it once had. We hope some day to develop strong counterparts to the federal government, and to some degree, a decentralization of government in this country.

But, regardless of all that—and on this problem of auto insurance in particular—the insurance industry itself has an obligation and a responsibility to set its own house in order. Certainly up to now the industry has not come up with a sufficient answer to this problem. I much prefer that an industry find answers on its own, rather than have the government step in and dictate a mode of operations. But an industry unwilling to solve its problems, unwilling to face up to the complaints of the people, leaves legislators no alternative but to act. This often means acting in a direction which may be against the best interests of that particular industry, at least as the industry views it. If the insurance industry solves this problem, the industry will find it far more beneficial than if legislators do so.

# REMARKS

## OF ANTHONY SCARIANO*

I AM NOT AN ADHERENT of the anti-intellectual tradition which, according to Professor Richard Hofstadter,[1] moves through American history like a leitmotif. Since I don't share that anti-intellectual bias, I became the sponsor of the Basic Protection bill in Illinois.[2] But that bill did not have very smooth sailing, to put it mildly.

First of all, it was rather difficult to obtain sponsorship from other legislators. I was able to obtain only one other lawyer as a sponsor—the representative from the district which includes the University of Illinois. But to my utter dismay, lawyers in the so-called liberal bloc with which I am associated in the Illinois General Assembly stayed away in droves. This was rather unusual because in legislative matters of important social concern, these gentlemen are usually with me. I heard statements from them such as: "What are you trying to do, repeal my livelihood?" Indeed this was a recurring phrase from lawyers generally.

The Basic Protection bill was introduced with about five or six sponsors. This demonstrates the hold that the insurance industry has on the Illinois General Assembly. I wish I were as successful in both the legislature and my law practice as the insurance industry is with respect to insurance legislation in the Illinois General Assembly. Indeed, I am still trying to figure out how the industry let the bill removing limits of payment under the Wrongful Death Act[3] get by them. Perhaps the industry was too concerned with impending legislative investigations of insurance to focus on the Wrongful Death amendment; perhaps the industry dissipated all its energies blocking such investigations. Thus, if it served no other purpose, the threat of investigation at least served to gain passage of the removal of limits under the Wrongful Death Act. The investigations themselves never came to pass!

The insurance industry professed neutrality on the Basic Protection bill. If their position was one of "neutrality," I have an absorbing curiosity as to what opposition means. Since I have been in the legislature for over 10 years, I have seen what the industry has done to compulsory insurance bills, to unsatisfied judgments fund bills, and to comparative negligence bills. It now appears that if we are to get comparative negligence in Illinois, we are

---

* ANTHONY SCARIANO. B.A. 1942, George Washington University; J.D. 1948, Georgetown University; Member, Illinois House of Representatives; Partner in the firm of Scariano & Gubbins, Chicago Heights.

---

[1] R. HOFSTADTER, ANTI-INTELLECTUALISM IN AMERICAN LIFE (1963).

[2] KEETON & O'CONNELL, BASIC PROTECTION FOR THE TRAFFIC VICTIM: A BLUEPRINT FOR REFORMING AUTOMOBILE INSURANCE (1965) [hereinbefore and hereinafter this book is often cited as Basic Protection]. *See also* Keeton & O'Connell, *Basic Protection Automobile Insurance*, p. 40 *supra*.

[3] ILL. REV. STAT. ch. 70, § 2 (1967).

going to get it through judicial fiat—through judicial legislation, if you please.[4] We have been trying for a long time to get such a bill through the Illinois Legislature. We have also been trying for ages to make the guest statute just exactly that—truly a "guest" statute whereby a guest is treated as a guest. Somebody really ought to do a doctoral dissertation on the removal of the Wrongful Death Act limit so we may learn something about how to get other progressive legislation passed, whether it be the Basic Protection bill or something similar to it.

It's heartening to hear from Representative Dukakis that the press was very helpful, in fact militant, about automobile insurance reform in Massachusetts. I suppose the press in Illinois, like many people, had great difficulty in comprehending what the Basic Protection bill and similar measures are all about, not to speak of understanding the present system. But intertwined with the difficulty in understanding may have been subtle pressures on the press from the insurance industry—and indeed the Insurance Department itself. It is most interesting that when we tried recently to get an investigation of the industry and the Insurance Department in Illinois, we got little help from the press. We had more than two dozen casualty companies writing insurance in the automobile field go bankrupt in Illinois in the past five or six years—more than any other state in the Union. A rather disgraceful—indeed a criminal—situation. But at every effort to set up a commission to investigate what went wrong with the particular companies and how such situations could be avoided, both the industry and the Department put up a solid front of opposition. Both of them said, "Let us clean our dirty linen in private; we don't want to do it in public. What affects the insurance business is a private matter." This is what is wrong with the insurance industry and the Insurance Department—the industry is viewed by both as the private bailiwick of the people involved in it. Nobody pays any real heed to the general public which is footing the bills to the extent of over $2 billion a year in premiums in the State of Illinois alone. Thus, the Illinois Insurance Department wasn't any help at all with respect to the Basic Protection bill. Indeed, as pointed out in another paper,[5] the Director of the Insurance Department came out against the Basic Protection bill.

Actually my complaint is not about the Insurance Department alone. One can complain similarly of every regulatory agency in state and federal government, whether it be, for example, a Commerce Commission or a Power Commission: the regulated have become the regulators, as Professor Moynihan has pointed out.[6]

Representative Dukakis mentions a dinner in Massachusetts which was scheduled to be held for the Commissioner of Insurance and sponsored by

4 Maki v. Frelk, 85 Ill. App. 2d 439, 229 N.E.2d 284 (2d Dist. 1967).
5 German, *Remarks*, p. 221 *supra*.
6 Moynihan, *Changes for Automobile Claims?*, pp. 7-8 *supra*.

the insurance industry. He mentions a great public outcry that finally caused its cancellation. In Illinois, we not only went ahead with our dinner, sponsored by the industry for the Director of Insurance, but all the ranking political leaders from both parties were there with generous and uncritical coverage by the press!

The voice of the consumer no longer exists in the State of Illinois. The one great voice of the consumer used to be the labor unions, but the labor movement has become completely ossified, conservative, reactionary—indeed downright radical rightist in many cases. Labor has joined the legislature in presenting to the public the finest collection of twelfth century minds extant.

Turning from the insurance industy, the first group to be heard from on the Basic Protection bill was the judiciary. We learned that the judiciary in Illinois were opposed to the Basic Protection bill, not because of any intrinsic defect, but, as it was related to us, because so many of the trial judges in the state might have nothing to do if the bill passed! This information came to us indirectly, but it was nonetheless authentic. It is significant, is it not, that not one member of the judiciary is represented at this conference? (I understand, however, that at least one judge did advise and consult with respect to the conference.) My own guess is that if Illinois is any criterion, most judges would have nothing to do with a conference such as this. This is disheartening.

But the real hostility to such reform certainly doesn't stem from the bench but from the bar. For example, word came from one of the political leaders in my own district who is an attorney but is not directly involved in automobile accident litigation. He doesn't very often express disagreement with what I do in the legislature, but he was rather vehemently against this particular measure.

After the hearing before the Committee on Insurance of the House on the Basic Protection bill, which heard a most forceful and splendid presentation by Professor O'Connell, many of my friends on the committee came to me and said, "That was a great presentation. I'm convinced, but we're not ready for it: it's 10, 20, or 100 years ahead of our time." "You know I'm for it, I'd like to vote for it, but you know I have my commitments." I know what commitments mean in the Illinois Legislature.

Interestingly enough, except for the Secretary of State, who appeared through a representative in opposition to the bill in the House committee hearing, the opponents were heard at another meeting. Somehow there was no real integration of opponents and proponents at one meeting. No vote was ever taken. We weren't even given the courtesy of a vote in the House Committee on Insurance. Through one stall, one tactic, one dilatory device after another, we were finally put off until the last day of committee hearings. The committee chairman apologized. He said, "I couldn't get to it; there simply wasn't time." This despite the fact that I kept going back time after time to get a vote. I said, "I'm not really saying that anyone should necessarily vote for the Basic Protection bill or against it, but I think that under the tradition that exists in American deliberative bodies, we're entitled to the formality of a vote." We are still waiting for it. Unfortunately, however, the legislature adjourned a long time ago.

The best indication that the Basic Protection plan is a good plan is that you find both those who represent the defense and those who represent plaintiffs against it. Just as whenever labor appears with management on the same side against any bill in the legislature I know it is a good bill, whenever the representatives of the defense and the plaintiffs get together against a bill, I know it must be a good bill.

It also must be noted that there have been no really concrete alternatives to the Basic Protection plan offered. I am not necessarily committed to the Basic Protection plan. Rather, I think it or something similar must come about one of these days, because the public, as Representative Dukakis says, simply isn't going to stand for the present system. Something, then, is going to be done. And the undeniable fact is that there are no significant proposals available *other* than the Basic Protection plan.

# VIEWS AND OVERVIEWS

*BY GUIDO CALABRESI\**

DURING THE HEIGHT OF THE DEBATE ON FEDERAL SAFETY
STANDARDS for automobiles, the *New York Times* ran editorials dealing
with the problem. The *Times* took the position that it was outrageous for
auto manufacturers to contend that the cost of safety devices be considered
in deciding which ones should be required. Where human lives are at stake,
thundered *The Times* rather fatuously, no cost is too great. Of course, those
who argued that "costs" were relevant were really saying that virtually any
cost was too great and so the *Times* was probably on the side of the angels,
but this did not make the position taken in the editorials any less absurd.

Accidents and accident prevention are, to a substantial extent, questions
of costs. On the one hand, we have the question of how much accidents cost
us; on the other, the equally significant question of how much it costs
us, either in money spent or in pleasurable activities foregone, to avoid these
accidents. We need not have grade crossing accidents—we could abolish
grade crossings. But that would cost money. We need not have fatal car
accidents—we could banish all cars, or limit them to 20 m.p.h. But that would
also, presumably, cost us more than we are willing to pay in pleasures and
profits foregone. Short of such drastic measures, we could ban teen-age
drivers, or aged drivers, or require certain safety devices. The choice is
always basically the same—a choice between the cost of accidents and the
cost of limiting ouselves or some of us to less desirable (because more expensive or less pleasant) but safer activities.

The crucial question for any society is not whether it will make a decision to have some accidents and some accident-prone activities—all societies
choose to have some accidents—but how it goes about deciding how many it
will have. What I have elsewhere called a "decision for accidents"[1]—a decision as to the level of accidents deemed desirable in the light of what it costs
us to avoid such accidents—has to be made. The question is, simply, how does
our society propose to make that decision?

There are two methods which can be used in making this decision. In
theory, a society could use only one; in fact, all societies use each to some
degree. The first, and the easiest to understand, because we have seen it at
work in the recent auto debate, is the "collective" method. We can decide
politically that no one below a certain age will drive, or that autos must have
certain safety devices. When we do this we decide collectively, in effect,
that the costs of these requirements—the higher prices they imply or the

---

*\* GUIDO CALABRESI. B.S. 1953, Yale University; B.A. 1955, Oxford
University (England); LL.B. 1958, Yale University; M.A. 1959, Oxford
University (England); Professor of Law, Yale University.*

---

[1] Calabresi, *The Decision for Accidents: An Approach to Nonfault Allocation of
Cost*, 78 HARV. L. REV. 713 (1965).

pleasures they cause some to forego—are smaller than the cost of the accidents they presumably avoid. Conversely, a failure to ban or limit an activity beyond a certain point would imply, if the collective method of deciding accident levels were the only one available, that further reduction of accident costs is not worth the costs necessary to bring it about. Normally we stop short of collective proscription of a whole activity (perhaps the ban on fireworks is an exception), but in our society many, if not most, activities are limited by some collectively-decided rules aimed at making them safer.

The second method is harder to explain and I shall not attempt it fully right now. Shortly stated, it consists of letting market decisions determine the levels of accident costs and of accident-avoidance devices and limitations which will prevail. By this method, the decision for or against accidents is made in much the same way in which an essentially free enterprise society decides how many shoes, as against sandals, are to be produced. For reasons which need not concern us here, I have called the collective approach "specific deterrence of accidents," and the market approach "general deterrence of accidents."[2] The rest of this paper will be concerned with the limitations of each of these methods and their relationship to the fault system.

The recent debate on auto safety should have made us keenly aware of the limitations which inhere in the collective approach. On the one hand, we have had the auto makers declare that "safety doesn't sell," that people don't want to pay more for safer cars. On the other hand, the argument has been made with equal plausibility that if people could be made to pay the accident costs of driving an "unsafe" car when they buy it, they would buy safer cars. This general debate has been repeated with more and more specificity when each safety requirement is considered. Are seat belts worth their costs? How about certain types of brakes and steering equipment? Are cars designed with padding and with the "death seat" facing backwards worth their costs? Consider 16 to 18-year-old drivers; is allowing them to drive worth its costs? What of 18 to 21-year-olds, or people over 70? These questions highlight one problem with the collective method: it doesn't tell us how to decide the question of what limitations are worth their cost. We know that people over 70 and people under 21 would be very upset if they were barred from driving, and perhaps we can even figure out how many accidents they cause. But we really don't know, and can't determine collectively, whether the cost to them of being barred from driving is greater than the accident costs avoided by barring them.

An even more fundamental problem is that we cannot make intelligent collective decisions about everything. And yet almost any decision to do something in a certain way, at a certain time, involves choices between safer and less safe alternatives. We may gear ourselves up to resolving some of the most dramatic cases by collective action (though we might ponder how long it has

[2] *Id.*

taken us to consider auto safety as being dramatic enough to warrant collective action—and with what dubious and scanty results). But the less dramatic situations which require the great bulk of our decisions—those for or against a safer yet seemingly more expensive material, or those for or against a safer but less pleasurable activity or way of doing an activity—cannot successfully be the subject of collective decisions. Somewhere, somehow, we must use the market device—for if we don't, we are unwittingly, and probably unjustifiably, deciding collectively that (except for those few situations which we do regulate collectively) it would cost more to avoid accident costs than to have them. I don't mean to suggest by this that market decisions can solve the whole problem for us; far from it. But even this bare summary of the limits of collective or specific deterrence should be enough to suggest that we need market devices to control levels of accidents, and that collective decisions may work best when they are *modifications*—made for good and sufficient collective reasons—of a pre-existing market determination as to the level of accidents. In other words, if we have a market method to determine the level of accident costs and accident avoidance devices we want, we can always modify that decision by collectively determined regulations and still not be deciding collectively *for* the unsafe way wherever we don't ban, limit, or regulate activities to accomplish accident prevention.

All this discussion might seem superfluous. But it clearly is not, since there has been a powerful tendency in recent automobile accident discussion toward trying to do the whole job of reducing accident costs through collective decisions. This approach begins by citing the faults of the fault system (faults which, by the way, I more than admit) and specifically the faults of fault as a method of spreading accident costs. It concentrates on the enormous "secondary" costs of accidents under the fault system—failure of rehabilitation, social and economic dislocations, delay in compensation, and so on—and seeks to avoid these in the cheapest way possible. The solution which appears to be cheapest is some sort of social insurance. The trouble with this solution is that if social insurance paid out of general taxes minimizes these secondary costs of accidents, it only does so at a substantial cost: the destruction of the limited amount of market deterrence which the fault system gives us. Once auto accident costs are removed from both injurer and victim, and paid out of general taxes through a social insurance fund, no financial, that is, market, incentive to build safer cars and to limit driving by accident prone age groups remains.

If teenagers (and others for that matter) did not have to pay fantastic insurance premiums for driving, how many more cars and inevitably how many more accidents would we have? These insurance premiums represent an attenuated—since based on fault—market pressure against a dangerous activity, "driving"; and an even greater pressure against an even more dangerous subcategory of that activity, teen-age driving. If social insurance removed this pressure, the market deterrent—weak as it may seem to be—

would be gone and there would be no market control on the level of accidents caused by teen-age or other driving. Inevitably the primary costs of accidents, their number and severity, would increase and pressure would build up for "rules," "regulations," "restrictions"; in short, for a series of collective decisions to limit these primary accident costs. Removal of market pressure toward safety would bring in its wake collective pressure toward safety, and the debates of recent months would be multiplied a thousandfold as we sought politically to decide, to the smallest detail, what safety devices and regulations were "worth their costs" and "mandatory" and which were not and, therefore, totally optional.

Unfortunately, the faults of the fault system in dealing with the secondary costs of accidents are substantial enough so that if no adequate substitute other than social insurance is found, this nightmare of collective rules may well become real. Indeed, fault does a sufficiently bad job even of market deterrence so that quite apart from secondary accident costs, we may find ourselves forced either to abandon fault for a system which achieves better market deterrence, or to supplement it with a plethora of collectively determined rules. This weakness of the fault system may well serve to explain the recent auto safety debate (what financial incentive did the fault system create for placing seat belts in cars?) and may also serve to explain attitudes like those demonstrated in a recent broadcast by Bob Considine (sponsored by an insurance company) which told of nothing but the federal regulation of driving we could look forward to. The program cheerily forecast physical and mental examinations, losses of licenses right and left and so on, all by fiat of the federal government and all on the unspoken assumption that the great collective would somehow decide that these devices were the ones which were worth their costs in accident avoidance, while others were not. Before we accept such a world as inevitable, we should consider the possibility of achieving more through market pressure. In doing that, however, we should also be aware of the limitations in using market deterrence.

In theory, market deterrence operates very simply. If we can determine the costs of accidents and allocate them to the activities which cause them, the prices of activities will reflect their accident costs, and people in deciding whether or not to engage in particular activities will be influenced by the accident costs each activity involves. They will be influenced without having to think about it, for the accident costs will simply be a part of the price which will affect whether they buy one product or engage in one activity rather than another. If insurance charged for teen-age drivers accurately reflected the accident costs such driving causes—regardless of fault—and if teenagers have to carry insurance, the price of a car to a teenager will be the price of the jalopy plus the price of the premiums. At that price, some may still decide to drive (the price is worth it to them) but others will walk, and use the money saved in other ways. The effect will be that individuals, through the market, will have limited teen-age driving because of its accident costs. Similarly, if manufacturers of cars without seat belts were charged the accident costs which resulted from the absence of belts, no federal law would be needed requiring seat belts. A beltless car would save the cost of the belt, but bear the accident costs which resulted; a car with a belt would save on accident costs but bear the cost of putting in a belt. The decision as to whether belts were worth it would be made by buyers of cars in the light of the price of each kind of car. The question of whether safety sells would be given a market answer rather than the purely conjectural one to which we have been accustomed.

Of course, things aren't actually so easy. In the first place, it is very hard to say what the costs of accidents are. And a "perfect" market system would require "perfect" cost determinations. Actually, knowledge of what accident costs are is just as necessary for accurate collective (non-market) determination of what activities are worth their costs. But we don't think of this much in the collective context because we are accustomed to allowing collective decisions to be rather fuzzy ones. Still, so long as our determinations of accident costs are inexact, we cannot expect the market to do a perfect job for us.

Secondly, and perhaps more important, market decisions for or against accidents—such as the decisions as to how many and which teenagers will drive, and the decisions as to whether we will have seat belts or not—are inevitably affected by the distribution of income in our society. The rich man gets more of a say in the market than the poor man. By and large, we tolerate this when income distribution affects only the availability of goods and services (though we modify income distribution by progressive taxation), but we are not so willing to tolerate it when life and death are at stake. The current debate on the draft and our unwillingness to raise an army of volunteers by offering sufficiently high wages to attract enlistments indicates just this. We might allow this in peace time, but not when lives are at stake. Market decisions on accidents fall somewhere between these two extremes. We are not likely to allow a 10-year-old millionaire to drive simply because he can pay for the accidents he causes, but we may well let people decide whether they want one or two cars on the basis of their wealth (so long as they pay extra premiums for the extra car) even though we know that more cars mean more accidents. The fact that market decisions are based on unequal votes depending on wealth explains why we may wish to modify the market decision by collective regulations; regulations determined through the political process where supposedly all votes count equally. The fact of income inequality does not mean, however, that the market is not a very good first stage on which to base that relatively limited number of collective decisions which a society can intelligently make.[3]

---

[3] Such collective revisions can go either way. We may decide collectively that drunks may not drive regardless of ability to pay for accidents; on the other hand, we may decide to subsidize driving by the aged or the handicapped despite the fact that they can't pay for the accidents they cause.

Thirdly, the market method can be more expensive than it is worth. It costs money to allocate accident costs to the activities which cause them. And the more precise the allocation, the more it costs. As a result, the market method may be more effective in determining the level of relatively broad activities (driving by age groups, driving by people who live at various distances from work, and so on) than in controlling the smaller subcategories of these activities (driving at night, driving through a yellow light, etc.). These subcategories or subactivities, which we often call "acts," are perhaps better controlled through collective regulation than through any attempt to let the market regulate for us. Collective regulations are limited in that we can not rule collectively as to every act or activity, but there are some acts and even some activities whose proper level can be determined and controlled more efficiently by collective means than through the market. The reasons for this are analogous to those which keep insurance companies from differentiating risks beyond a certain point—it simply costs too much to do it in comparison with the accident costs avoided by doing it.

The final, and perhaps most difficult, problem with the market method of determining the appropriate level of accident costs is that for the market to work properly we must be able to decide which activities are responsible for which costs, and to do this perfectly is as impossible as it is to decide perfectly how much any accident costs. But just as the determination of the cost of accidents is as necessary to intelligent collective decisions as it is to market decisions, so the decision as to who is responsible for the cost is unavoidable under either collective or market approaches. In fact it is easier to decide what activities ought to bear accident costs when the aim of such decisions is to enable the market to operate effectively to reduce accident costs than it is to decide what activities are responsible for accident costs for the purpose of deciding what activities ought to be regulated collectively and to what degree. The problem of allocating accident costs to achieve optimal market deterrence is too complex to examine thoroughly here. Some indications of how the question can be handled, however, are possible.

Whenever the choice of cost bearers is between activities which bargain with each other with respect to the price of a product or service involved in an accident, it will, in theory, make no difference which of the activities bears the accident cost. In theory, it doesn't matter if car owners or car manufacturers are charged with car accident costs. The manufacturers will charge more for cars if they bear the costs; the owners will demand lower prices if they bear the costs. If both sides estimate the costs the same way, the same total price for the product and its accident costs will result. And combinations of activities and ways of doing them which minimize the sum of accident costs and costs of avoiding accidents will become established regardless of who is liable.

In practice, the results can be quite different. It is on the basis of this difference that we can decide which of two (or more) activities is the better cost bearer. First, those in charge of one of the activities may be better aware of the risk of accident costs: to an individual the chance of being injured or of injuring is an unknown; to an auto manufacturer it is a known statistic. Secondly, one activity may be able to insure more cheaply than the other. Thirdly, placing the cost on one activity may be more likely to result in efficient allocation of the cost to subcategories of activities than placing the cost on the other.[4] Finally, placing the cost on one activity rather than another may result, for political or practical reasons, in removing it from both, thus destroying market deterrence altogether. If liability is placed on drivers, but they insure inadequately and as a result fail to pay damages, or if the government steps in and pays the damages out of a generalized social insurance fund, neither the drivers nor the manufacturers will include these damages in future prices. What economists call externalization will have occurred and the price of the product will not reflect its accident costs.

While these criteria for determining the better cost bearer in a bargaining situation may seem very sketchy and indefinite as given here, they probably suffice in most situations to tell us which of several "bargaining" activities is the best cost bearer in terms of getting the optimal market deterrence. Occasionally they will indicate that it makes no difference, and that is, of course, all right too; it simply means that as good a job of market deterrence will be achieved regardless of who is liable.

The problem of cost allocations to achieve optimal market deterrence is harder when the choice of cost bearers is between independent parties or activities, parties who are not in a bargaining relationship with each other—for example, pedestrians and drivers, or pedestrians and car makers. Here, at first glance, it would seem as if the choice is crucial and a mistake in allocation would prevent the market from working tolerably at all. Suppose pedestrian-auto accident costs are allocated to car manufacturers or to owners and it turned out that the cheapest way of limiting such accident costs (by this I mean the lowest sum of accident costs and costs of avoiding accidents) is for pedestrians to wear flashing lights at night rather than for anyone to

---

[4] Different allocations may result in different subcategories of activities being efficiently reached, and then the choice can be quite hard. For instance, if auto manufacturers bore accident costs, differentiation in price according to accident records of different makes of car, and of cars with and without various safety features like seat belts, would be relatively easy. Instead, differentiation by age of driver, and by drivers' previous accident records, which are relatively easy if drivers are made liable, would be hard. Thus one allocation—to auto manufacturers—makes reaching the subcategories of brand of car and of cars with safety features easier, but another allocation—to drivers—makes reaching other subcategories, such as age and experience of drivers, easier. The question then is which subcategories is it most important to reach. In theory, either allocation could result in all subcategories being reached, but in practice this will not be so. Car manufacturers could, in theory, sell at different prices to different age drivers, but in practice this would be too expensive to work out and to police. Conversely, drivers, if they were made liable, could, in theory, demand different prices from cars according to the safety features, but again in practice this cannot come about to any adequate degree.

improve cars or their drivers. At first glance, it would seem as if a market pressure which might result in car or driver improvement had been exerted instead of pressure being exerted toward the more desirable change in how pedestrians behaved.

Recent economic writings associated with Professor Ronald Coase, of Chicago, indicate that the issue is not so cut and dried.[5] Coase has pointed out that, if there were no costs involved in establishing a bargain between car makers and pedestrians, car makers in my example would pay pedestrians to wear flashing lights because this would be cheaper than either paying for accident costs or changing how cars are made. In effect, Coase's analysis points out that, in theory, any "independent" situation can be transformed into a bargaining situation. Of course, as he is the first to realize, establishing such bargains may be expensive business—so that we cannot be indifferent to what activity bears accident costs. But all this means is that one further practical consideration must be considered in deciding who is the best cost bearer in such "independent" cases.

Most of the factors considered in the bargaining situation remain relevant in the non-bargaining situation. First, who can gauge the risk more precisely? Second, is the cost, if put on pedestrians, more likely to be removed, that is, externalized, from both car makers and pedestrians, than if it were put on car makers or drivers?[6] Third, is the cost, if put on car makers or car drivers, more or less likely to affect subcategories of activities than if put on pedestrians? The question is: placing the cost on which of the independent activities results in the greatest degree of what economists would call internalization; that is: what cost allocation can efficiently affect the greatest number of subcatagories of activities involved in the accident so that we maximize the chance of market pressure being placed on those subcategories which, if modified, can reduce accident costs most cheaply?

The fact that the activities involved are independent (that is, not in a bargaining relationship with each other) adds one factor to the search for the best bearer of accident costs. Suppose we have guessed wrong and allocated the costs to the wrong activity? Which mistaken allocation can be cured most cheaply by parties entering into transactions with each other in the market? If we place costs of auto-pedestrian accidents on pedestrians and the cheapest way of avoiding these is to change how cars are made, it would cost too much for pedestrians to gather together in the market to pay car

---

[5] *See, e.g.,* Coase, *The Problem of Social Cost,* 3 J. Law & Econ. 1 (1960).

[6] This could happen either because politically we believed the spreading of costs which would come about if pedestrians were left with the burden was inadequate and therefore decided to pay the cost out of general taxes, or because the only way pedestrians could efficiently spread the burden would be by buying a general accident policy against all accidents and not solely against car-pedestrian accidents. This, in turn, would result in failure of the cost of these accidents to affect pedestrian behavior, because the cost as borne by pedestrians would have been transformed into a general cost of living and would no longer be a cost of pedestrianism.

makers to change how cars are made.[7] It would be much cheaper for car makers to pay pedestrians to wear flashing lights, if car makers had wrongly been held liable and flashing lights, instead of differently made cars, avoided the cost most cheaply. In other words, unless we are collectively quite sure as to which of two or more independent parties can most cheaply avoid accident costs—can make the best choice between accident costs and the costs of avoiding them—we should put the burden on the party which can cure a mistake most cheaply if one has been made, and thus help the market to operate as effectively as possible.[8]

All this sounds very difficult, and, of course, it isn't easy. But it may be of some comfort to remember that when we collectively decide to ban or limit an activity to diminish accident costs, we are making exactly the same guess as to who can avoid what accident costs. The only difference is that we are giving ourselves less of a chance to let any mistake be corrected than if we make the choice according to the market methods I have been describing. In other words, the choice, though hard, cannot be avoided, regardless of what method of determining the level of accident costs we decide to use.

One further comment on choosing who is responsible for what accident costs is needed. I have been talking as if the choice were an all or nothing one—as if all the costs had to go on drivers or on pedestrians—and that isn't true at all. The best market pressure may well be achieved by splitting costs —or more likely, by splitting costs not merely quantitatively but also qualitatively. Thus car makers or drivers may be the best suited to choose between paying pedestrian-auto accident costs involving property damage, medical care and lost wages costs, and spending money to avoid them. Pedestrians, on the other hand, may be the cheapest cost avoiders of such highly individualized items as pain and suffering, or of unusual injuries like the special value of a hand to a great violinist. It may well be that the cheapest way to avoid most auto accident costs is to change cars or drivers, but that the cheapest way to avoid pain and suffering injuries to a hypersensitive person is for that person to stay home in bed and let someone else do her shopping!

I am not, of course, suggesting that these divisions of costs are the most desirable. I am, at this stage, only outlining very roughly the things we should be looking for in deciding what system can maximize market deterrence and, therefore, minimize the need for collectively decided rules and

---

[7] This is, in part, because some pedestrians would fail to pay their share, for the same reasons which cause some people to fail to get vaccinated: "There is no danger of disease as everyone else is vaccinated, so why should I bother." Since the cost of excluding these pedestrians from the benefits of more safely made cars is prohibitive, it almost always happens that the bargain—even though clearly advantageous—can't come about in the market.

[8] It should not be necessary to point out that I am not in this analysis advocating car manufacturer liability as against, say, driver liability; I am only illustrating how liability by one party rather than another can result in more, or in less, desirable market effects.

regulations. I am doing this in order to point out how far from the goal of maximizing market deterrence the fault system is. For it is only when we realize this that we can appreciate the fact that the fault system is the single most significant source of pressure moving us towards collectively determined rules and regulations on the one hand, and generalized social insurance to cover accident costs on the other. With that in mind, let us look at fault for a moment.

The first thing that strikes everyone about fault is that it is an extremely expensive system. From the standpoint of market deterrence, another system which did as well or nearly as well, but was cheaper to administer, would be clearly superior. Much of the expense of fault derives from the fact that most cases must be decided on a case-by-case basis, and hence by a jury—it is virtually impossible to establish who is at fault by general rules. It can be shown that if the aim is to find the cheapest accident cost avoider—that is, to allocate costs in order to maximize market deterrence—instead of to find the faulty party, there is little advantage in making decisions on such an individualized basis. Scheduled damages, if kept up to date, and rules of thumb as to division of costs between activities involved in an accident, do as good or better a job of market deterrence as case-by-case decisions.

The second most obvious thing about fault is that it spreads the costs of accidents inadequately. As a result, it is a very unstable system, constantly under pressure from those who would substitute for it a system which compensated better—which did a better job of minimizing economic and social dislocations and other such secondary costs of accidents. In theory, a "perfect" system of market deterrence would also be a poor spreader. (With perfect foreknowledge there would be no insurance and each person would bear exactly the costs of the accidents he would cause.) In fact, however, it can be shown that the insurance categories which would arise from a system which sought to maximize market deterrence efficiently would give us much more spreading of losses than we have under fault—enough spreading, indeed, so that most current demands for adequate and speedy compensation would be met. All this is very important in evaluating fault as a system of market deterrence, because one of the faults of fault as a system of market deterrence is that it is so poor a system of compensation that it bids fair to be replaced by the worst possible general system of market deterrence, namely generalized social insurance.[9]

The third problem with fault as a system of market deterrence is that in deciding who ought to bear accident losses, it considers many factors (by and large, moral factors) which are irrelevant to market deterrence and which are expensive to deal with. Conversely, fault does not take into ac-

---

[9] I say "general system" since there are undoubtedly situations where any system of market deterrence is not worth its costs, and in such areas social insurance is as good a system as any.

count those criteria which I have roughly summarized before (such as which cost bearer can correct an error in the market most cheaply) which are crucial to market deterrence. From this point of view, it is worth noting that fault fails to divide costs where neither side is "at fault," and yet from the standpoint of market deterrence, a division in these cases may well be essential.[10]

For all these reasons, and others, fault is not at all a good system of market deterrence. This fact can be summarized as follows: Fault uses the market in an expensive and unstable way to reduce fault-caused accidents, while from the standpoint of market deterrence, we want to use the market in an efficient and stable way to reduce accident costs, whether they are fault-caused or not.

The foregoing discussion, of course, cannot serve to condemn fault altogether. If fault were a good device for achieving collective non-market deterrence of accidents, or if fault served other ends which we can loosely call justice, it might well be worth its costs and its weaknesses as a market deterrent. In fact, however, it can be shown that where moral elements are strong and collective deterrence rules and regulations are desired and desirable, far more effective and efficient methods than a fault system, which allows insurance, are available. Uninsurable tort fines are possible examples. Similarly, it has been suggested that though the so-called justice elements of fault may make sense when the choice of ultimate loss bearer is limited to the parties immediately involved in the accident, they make no sense in the real world, where loss bearing can be spread or re-allocated among a much greater universe of possible loss bearers. Indeed, as Professor Conard's massive study indicates, in the world as it is, the "justice" of fault is much more a belief of some "experts" than an accurate reflection of what people at large feel—at least if other methods of punishing wrongdoers are available.[11]

These last considerations, of course, deserve far more space than can be given to them here—and they are not really directly relevant to the main theme of this article. That theme is simply this: Our society is inevitably faced with the need to decide how many accident costs and how many costs of avoiding accidents we want. This decision can be made mainly collectively, or mainly individualistically through market choices. If we, as a society, are generally committed to a free market, we should try to retain, expand, and make more efficient the market part of that decision. Fault, because it is expensive, because it is inadequate as a market system, and because it is such a poor spreader of accident costs that it is politically unstable, not only has resulted in more collective rules and regulations than might be needed, but seems likely to be ultimately replaced by other systems (like

[10] Consider, for instance, the effect of allocating nonfault work accidents to employers under workmen's compensation.

[11] A. Conard, J. Morgan, R. Pratt, C. Voltz & R. Bombaugh, Automobile Accident Costs and Payments—Studies in the Economics of Injury Reparation 106 (1964).

social insurance paid for out of general taxes) which will inevitably call forth even more collective rules and regulations. Under the circumstances, it may well be that it is "conservative" in the best and proper sense of the word to abandon fault and replace it with any of several systems which would give better, and more efficient market deterrence, together with sufficient spreading of losses as to be politically stable.

# REMARKS

## OF H. J. MAIDENBERG*

AT THIS CONFERENCE, I have listened to people from one of the most important industries in the country—the automobile insurance industry. This is an industry that, if we can believe some other speakers, is headed for a collision of sorts of its own. A question stays in my mind: Is the insurance industry going to get behind a particular change—whether it be what Professors Keeton and O'Connell want[1]—or will the attitude "let things stay as they are" prevail? That is a question I haven't really heard answered, except from Moynihan who touched on it. He said that the insurance industry is going to face federal regulation if it doesn't do something.[2] I'd also like to hear the answer to that.

Let me illustrate how the insurance industry can ignore questions—and the public. I have covered three industries in my time, the money market, the commodities trade, and now, with my left hand, the insurance business. I have had three different experiences with the three different groups.

You can always talk to the money men, even the President of the First National City Bank or The Bank of America. It is very refreshing, even though most of what they tell you is immediately classified as off the record. But they will talk with you.

I started on the commodity beat eight days before the so-called salad oil scandal. For many years if a reporter tried to speak to a commodities trader in New York, he was looked upon as somebody who was going to write an exposé or who had blundered into the wrong exchange. The difference in the industry's attitude after November 19, 1963—the day of the scandal—was fantastic. All of a sudden the industry was no longer a secret and was trying to tell its story to every financial reporter in New York City.

To me, the insurance industry is probably the most mysterious of all. If you talk to the average insurance executive, he'll tell you that the industry spends a tremendous amount of money educating the public. "We tell them not to smoke in bed. We tell them that they shouldn't drink before they drive, etc." But for a reporter to reach anybody on any policy-making level in the insurance industry is almost impossible. Consequently, when a reporter does write an article, his sources are an occasional actuary who has been let out for the day, a mutual fund company trying to raid some insurance company after having done a little investigation about it, or a banker who is trying to collect some bills from the company. The reporter can't

---

* H. J. MAIDENBERG. Consumer columnist for the New York Times.

---

[1] KEETON & O'CONNELL, BASIC PROTECTION FOR THE TRAFFIC VICTIM: A BLUEPRINT FOR REFORMING AUTOMOBILE INSURANCE (1965) [both hereinbefore and hereinafter this book is often cited as Basic Protection]. See also Keeton & O'Connell, Basic Protection Automobile Insurance, p. 40 supra.

[2] Moynihan, Changes for Automobile Claims?, p. 1 supra.

get to a company itself—which is very strange, because the companies will validly prove that they spend a fantastic amount of money in communications. Following any kind of story about insurance, the industry hits the roof. Executives insist that what you wrote is impossible and that whoever told you about it is a crook. If you quote another insurance company as a source, your irate complainant will reply, "Well, that's why they're 138th down on the list and we're 137th."

No one on the statistical force at the *New York Times* can make heads or tails out of any insurance company statement of earnings. I have always marvelled at how this battery of people can go through the reports of company after company in almost any industry plucking out the pertinent facts. But no one can do that with an insurance company report. The reserves, for example, seem to go up one year and down another. They seem to be the most fluid item in an insurance company.

Consequently, being one of a small group of people who has been thrust into the world of insurance, I am in a perpetual state of confusion. And that can be a very dangerous thing to the industry.

Moreover, people generally are just as confused as I am about insurance. If they were exposed to all the papers of this conference, they would be angry. Thy would feel that somehow they are being 'had.' They would feel that something is wrong and that very little is being done about it. Once they reach that point, they are an absolute goldmine for any political adventurer with political solutions. My confident bet is that there is going to be a political solution to the problems of insurance—which will be very unfortunate. But no industry has asked for it so repeatedly as has the insurance industry.

# REMARKS†

## OF DEAN SHARP*

I FIND IT REALLY DIFFICULT to quarrel with Professor Calabresi's thesis that the public interest would better be served by allowing individual choice in the free market to determine levels of accident costs and accident prevention devices. I would quarrel a little, though, with Mr. Maidenberg's statement that top insurance executives are unapproachable. Like many reporters and magazine writers on the Washington scene, I have found them to be rather approachable—some rather unknowledgeable, but at least approachable.

After being exposed to the candid papers of Michael Dukakis[1] and Anthony Scariano,[2] it's highly questionable whether changes at the state level could furnish us with a solution to the ills of auto insurance and the resultant ills in our legal system. (The remarks of Robert Moretti could, of course, lead to a different conclusion.[3]) Although the insurance industry, its lawyers, the plaintiffs' bar, many state legislators, and the insurance commissioners cannot be entirely blamed for the terribly inefficient and costly negligence system for adjusting auto accident claims, they certainly can be faulted for not taking a more constructive role in attempting to seek out changes which would bring about a more efficient, just, and less costly system. But perhaps this is asking too much. Spokesmen for the insurance industry and the legal fraternity seem able only to point out weaknesses in the Basic Protection plan[4] or other proposals, and to dismiss them on the grounds that the proponents have failed to sustain the burden of proving that they offer a valid solution or even a better solution. But the point is few, if any, meaningful alternatives have been offered by these same spokesmen.

Actually, any burden involved in all this rests not so much on the proponents of reform; rather the burden of proving that the present system for redistributing auto accident losses is the most efficient, just, and least expensive system rests by and large with the insurance industry and the bar.

† These thoughts do not necessarily reflect those of any particular member of the Senate Antitrust and Monopoly Subcommittee, or of its Chairman, Senator Philip Hart of Michigan.

* DEAN SHARP. B.S. 1953, University of Pennsylvania; LL.B. 1957, Boston University; LL.M. (Taxation) 1958, New York University; Assistant Counsel, United States Senate Antitrust and Monopoly Subcommittee.

---

[1] Dukakis, *Legislators Look at Proposed Changes*, p. 222 *supra*.

[2] Scariano, *Remarks*, p. 236 *supra*.

[3] Moretti, *Remarks*, p. 232 *supra*.

[4] KEETON & O'CONNELL, BASIC PROTECTION FOR THE TRAFFIC VICTIM: A BLUEPRINT FOR REFORMING AUTOMOBILE INSURANCE (1965) [hereinbefore and hereinafter this book is often cited as Basic Protection]. *See also* Keeton & O'Connell, *Basic Protection Automobile Insurance*, p. 40 *supra*.

In the alternative, they should bear the burden of coming forth with acceptable solutions. If *this* burden is not met—as many of the papers in this symposium state—a plan of government auto insurance may be the verdict of the public, who after all constitute the jury in this matter.

Other than the inefficiency of the present auto liability system, what are the public's complaints—real or imaginary—concerning auto insurance and its regulation? In short what are the symptoms?

The first symptom is that over the past six and a half years 80 casualty insurers writing auto insurance have failed. Projections based on the dollar amount of gross unevaluated claims for 33 of 58 companies insolvent at the time the projections were made showed that some 300,000 policyholders and accident victims were seeking an estimated $600 million out of net collectable assets of $25 million.[5] Not long ago, the Pennsylvania Insurance Commissioner said that his department would start enforcing collection of over $43 million in back assessments from 295,000 Pennsylvania policyholders of defunct mutual insurers most of whom were writing high-risk auto business. Late in August, the Maryland Insurance Commissioner was ordered by a local court in Maryland to collect some $4 million in assessments from 35,000 policyholders of two defunct Maryland high-risk auto insurers.

I might add that many of the policyholders being assessed are those in society who can least afford it. The Senate Anti-Trust Subcommittee has received letters outlining almost unbelievable hardships caused by these assessments.

Another troublesome area to the public and to the industry is that of cancellations, non-renewals, rejections, and black-out practices of many casualty companies in both automobile and fire lines. The industry and some state insurance departments dismiss the problem as *de minimis* since it affects only 3 per cent. But I must ask, 3 per cent of what? Total policies outstanding in any given period as, say, in the Wisconsin[6] and the Virginia[7] studies? But what is the percentage of policies cancelled or not renewed related to policies against which claims have been filed or paid?

The social problem here is that in seeking out only the better drivers and preferred risks, companies are perpetuating and regenerating racial and class discrimination against those in society who can least afford it. Exacerbating the situation, as was revealed in the aftermath of the Watts riot, is the fact that industry is increasingly moving out to the suburban areas

[5] Address by Dean Sharp Before the American Risk and Insurance Association's Meeting of 1967, in Chicago, Aug. 28, 1967. *See also* CONG. REC. 978 (daily ed. Jan. 26, 1967) (remarks of Senator Dodd).

[6] R. Haase, Automobile Insurance Cancellation Practices (undated, mimeographed report to Wisconsin Legislative Council).

[7] COMMONWEALTH OF VIRGINIA, REPORT OF ACTUARIES, *Case No. 17680—Investigation Into Private Passenger Automobile Liability Insurance Rate Making Procedures, Cancellation Provisions and Renewal Practices* (Woodward & Fondiller, Inc. 1966).

where low-cost, mass transportation is nonexistant. Unreasonably high auto insurance premiums, then, make driving prohibitive when it is absolutely essential for employment.

What are some of the other grievances? Rate boosts approved without public hearings rank high. Another grievance is failure to include investment income in computing rates, although the insurance commissioners in Kentucky[8] and Maryland[9] recently held investment income must be included.

Other complaints include the relatively unknown financial structure of the fire and casualty industry (including unrealistic profit formulas that can conceal actual underwriting results and understate profits), exaggerating the need for rate increases, interlocking financial arrangements, unreasonable management contracts, and holding company arrangements. On this last, it's hoped that the current New York Blue Ribbon study will shed some light on the holding company movement in the fire and casualty industry—a movement which the industry says is necessary because of stringent regulation which prevents it from investing accumulated assets and putting its money to use. The question comes to mind, what business are casualty insurance companies in—the insurance or financial investment business?

There are other complaints about the operating practices of the industry, for example, in the use of credit organizations to investigate policyholders. In this connection, of particular interest is a recent Senate hearing concerning the unavailability of fire insurance in low-income, depressed areas.[10] Placed into that hearing record were examples of credit organization reports used by insurers—inquiring into matters racial and religious. For example, in insuring a church, specific inquiries are made as to its denomination—whether Baptist, Episcopalian, Methodist, etc., and whether the congregation is Negro, White, Oriental, etc.[11]

These are some of the grievances that are being publicly aired across the country. They are not peculiar to one state. Nor are they all imagined; perhaps they are magnified in certain places, but the symptoms and the problems are real. The next step should be to conduct a study at the federal level,

[8] In the Matter of National Bureau of Casualty Underwriters Proposed Automobile Liability Rate and Rule Revisions for Private Passenger Automobiles (Ky. Dep't of Ins., Feb. 6, 1967). *See* Birkinsha, *Investment Income and Underwriting Profit: "And Never the Twain Shall Meet?,"* 8 B.C. IND. & COM. L. REV. 713, 715 n.14 (1967). *See also* Wall St. J., Feb. 23, 1967, p. 7, cols. 1-2. On the general subject of unrest over automobile liability insurance rate increases and controversy over rating procedures, *see* Wall St. J. Feb. 13, 1967, p. 1, col. 6.

[9] In the Matter of National Bureau of Casualty Underwriters' Proposed Revision of Automobile Liability Insurance Rates for Private Passenger Cars and Miscellaneous Classes for the State of Maryland (Maryland Ins. Dep't, Jan. 7, 1967). *See* Birkinsha, *supra* note 8, at 718 n.34.

[10] *Hearing on S.J. Res. 102 Before the Committee on Commerce of the Senate*, 90th Cong., 1st Sess. (1967).

[11] *See also* Wall St. J., Oct. 10, 1967, p. 32, cols. 1-4.

including full-scale hearings, to identify the facts and the problems and finally to propose solutions.

Whether the grievances of the auto insurance-buying public with respect to the insurance industry and the negligence lawyers are real or imaginary is not a job for public relations experts. This is no time to be pre-occupied with the wrapping, with the tinsel. We must get at the heart of the matter. Despite the fact that more negative than positive views have been advanced from the bar and the insurance industry, this conference is a start.

# THE WORKSHOP SESSIONS: SUMMARY REPORT*

## I. INTRODUCTION

THE CONFERENCE on which this symposium is based concluded with "Workshop Sessions" involving the speakers and conference attendants. There were twenty-one sessions, each with approximately 10 participants meeting for about an hour and a half. Although over 90 percent of the participants were from the automobile insurance industry, an attempt was made to include a lawyer in each group. Also participating in the sessions were legislators and other government officials, academicians and representatives of consumer groups. The workshops were thus structured so as to carry out the purpose of the conference: to bring together people with varying points of view and interests to discuss the problems of automobile insurance and claims.

At each workshop session a member of the *University of Illinois Law Forum* was present to act as an informal recorder.[1] This summary was distilled from the detailed written reports of these recorders. In oder to encourage open and spontaneous discussion the participants were assured that there would be no specific attribution of remarks.

It should be emphasized that the workshop sessions represented informal exchanges. Official viewpoints were not being advanced. Thus it would be unfair for the reader to draw from this report any conclusions regarding formal "insurance industry" or "consumer" positions. Rather, what follows is an attempt to capture the sense and substance of much of the exchanges that took place in casual and rather haphazardly assembled workshop sessions made up of a wide variety of individuals, many of whom—but by no means all—happened to be insurance personnel.

## II. WHAT IS THE PUBLIC THINKING?

Almost every session considered, as a threshold question, the attitudes of the consumer. Personnel from the insurance industry seemed to feel that public opinion will determine their future; if the public is or becomes dissatisfied, either the industry must react or legislative intervention is inevitable. Consequently, a great amount of time was devoted to the consumer.

---

* Prepared by The Board of Student Editors of the *University of Illinois Law Forum*. Those members principally involved in the preparation of this report were Richard W. Sweat and Gerry Van Wittkamper.

[1] The members participating were: Barry D. Bayer, Dennis L. Bekemeyer, Paul M. Brayman, Charles Briggle, Raymond Buschmann, Darlene M. Cathcart, Ronald L. Drumheller, Blair P. Friederich, Thomas E. Gardner, Stephen E. Goodman, David R. Grimes, Donald M. Hartshorn, Douglas A. Ingold, Richard M. Joy, Russell S. Koss, William F. Lemke III, Lynne E. McNown, John J. Moore, William A. Schroeder, Glen K. Seidenfeld, Jr., Joseph P. Skowronski, Jr., Ronald W. Szwajkowski, Stephen F. Von Till, Robert E. Wangard, and James A. Wilderotter.

The first question to receive attention was: "What has caused the recent criticism of the present insurance system?" A few participants felt that, despite claims to the contrary, the general public is not criticizing the present system. The suggestion was made that some legislators and law professors have led the press, the public and the insurance industry to believe that the general public is much more dissatisfied than it really is. Most did agree, however, that many responsible people *are* concerned about several aspects of automobile insurance and claims. "Blame" for this recent public concern was often placed at the doorstep of government officials and intellectuals ("These 'guys' are whipping the people into a frenzy!") who have convinced the American public that every driver is entitled, as a matter of right, to complete insurance protection and that therefore, everyone who can obtain a license to drive should be able to procure insurance. The public has also been persuaded that the insurance industry should perform a "social" function beyond mere protection of those who pay premiums. Although some maintained that the public's view of the role of insurance had not changed, while others protested the validity of the public's attitude, the majority of the industry participants accepted as a fact the new public attitude.

The next question often raised was: "What does the public want from insurance?" Most participants tended to feel, in line with the foregoing, that the public simultaneously wants personal protection from economic disaster at the lowest possible cost and full compensation for all injured persons. To a certain extent these public demands appeared mutually exclusive to the participants. To compensate everyone fully would require protecting them against the high risk drivers who presently may be unable to obtain insurance. If insurance were made available to such drivers, the result would be higher premiums for all drivers because all the increase in cost could not be passed on to high risk drivers. Thus the participants bemoaned the desire for more services and benefits without commensurate increase in cost. The following exchange between four insurance participants is pertinent:

"We are in business to . . . make money. [We make money] . . . selecting risks. If we are forced to take risks we don't want, the taxpayers will have to pay for it."

"We have [to take risks we don't want] . . . or we'll get a state-owned insurance company."

"[This may not be] . . . a job the public wants—namely to insure the habitual violator. . . . We've talked to political, ward and union meetings, telling the automobile insurance story. They don't want us to insure habitual drunks. They want to be insured against them—to get them off the road."

"Does this include themselves?"

The majority of those who discussed the desires of the consumer admitted that they did not know specifically what the public wants from its automobile insurance system. Moreover they felt that it will be difficult to find out what the public wants, since most people do not understand their own policies and coverage. According to one participant, it would be very optimistic to suggest that the public could comprehend the practical and philosophical implications of any new insurance scheme, such as the Basic Protection plan.[2]

Several participants stated that both the public and the insurance industry suffered from their ignorance of each other. Although the consensus was that independent surveys would shed a great deal of light on current problems, there was some reluctance to place too much hope on the results of a public opinion poll as the ultimate solution to the "information gap" facing the insurance industry. One participant felt that no one could conduct a valid survey concerning the fault system as a concept. The underlying problems and the fundamental issues involved in the present fault system are inherently not the types of issues that are resolved by using current survey techniques. As one insurance executive put it, "the public doesn't know what a tort is." Several, however, suggested that the survey should be framed in terms of costs versus benefits. A more specific suggestion, for example, was to ask the public whether they would give up $X$ dollars in benefits for, say, a 10 per cent decrease in their own premiums.

There was a general realization by the industry participants that a very real controversy surrounding the present system exists, and that there *is* dissatisfaction in the legislatures and in the public's mind with the current scheme of insurance. As one insurance company vice president rhetorically asked (to a chorus of agreement) "Would you say that 'the present system is a patient with a terminal malignancy'?"

Industry participants realized that the industry does not have a satisfactory perception of what its consumers, or potential consumers, want. There was general agreement with the proposition that the industry should conduct studies, that the needs and desires of the consumers must be determined, and that the industry *should* take immediate action. There were several who suggested that the industry undertake a unified program of consumer research. An all-industry conference was proposed, but the implementation of such a plan was not discussed.

### III.    Problems with the Present Insurance System

A significant percentage of the time spent in workshop sessions was devoted to the alleged problems of the present system. Those problems most frequently discussed are set out below:

### A.    Cost of Coverage

There was a general consensus that the cost of coverage was the chief source of discontent on the part of the public. As one participant said: "If

---

[2] Keeton & O'Connell, Basic Protection for the Traffic Victim: A Blueprint for Reforming Automobile Insurance (1965) [hereinbefore cited as Basic Protection]. *See also* Keeton & O'Connell, *Basic Protection Automobile Insurance,* p. 40 *supra.*

the costs are reduced, the whole problem will fade away." This importance of reducing premiums was further exemplified by the general belief that "[a]ny solution to the present insurance problem that does not result in a reduction of cost is doomed." Some countered with the question "[W]hy shouldn't insurance cost go up; everything else has?", and there seemed to be widespread feeling among insurance participants that from a practical point of view the present rates are by no means too high. Moreover it was felt that cost reduction would be difficult on an across-the-board basis unless other changes were made in areas beyond the control of the insurance industry. For example, several participants felt that much of the cost coverage is due to the present legal system and the costs of litigation. Others pointed to the failure of the government to reduce the number of accidents through effective driver regulation and proper safety standards in designing and producing cars. Many industry participants maintained that the amount a given individual pays for insurance is determined on the basis of actuarial experience tables, and that the industry has no control over the number and severity of accidents for which it must pay. Their conclusion was that a general reduction of rates is not possible as long as losses remain at their current level.

As suggested above, however, there was general agreement that all the problems the industry faces must be analyzed in terms of the cost of any solution. The threshold test of any suggested solution—whether comprehensive or partial—was: "Does it reduce the cost of insurance coverage?" One industry participant framed the issue in terms of costs to benefits efficiency, contending that the industry must find a way to pay out 75 cents for every dollar it takes in as premiums.

## B. Legal Services—The Contingent Fee

One attitude shared by many in the insurance industry was dissatisfaction with the contingent fee: "A real problem is the cost of legal services. Too much of the insurance dollar is spent on legal expenses." According to many participants the evil of the contingent fee system is that it tends to raise costs because plaintiffs' attorneys always seek to obtain the highest recovery possible, regardless of the expense to the client. Moreover, it was said, because the costs of defense can be based on a percentage of the "value of the case," high claims or awards can raise the costs of legal services for the insurance company.

The contingent fee appears to affect more than the cost of insurance; there was consensus among industry participants that the contingent fee prevents full compensation to the victim who engages the services of an attorney. The industry participants contended that if the insurance company pays what the claim is actually worth, 30 percent of that payment goes to the victim's lawyer. Others, however, were not as willing to place so much blame on the legal profession, citing personal experience that 98 percent of the cases never go to court, and that in some places, at least, 85 percent of the claimants never hire attorneys. These facts, they contended, make it difficult to hold the legal profession responsible for the high cost of administering payment of claims.

There were several proposals designed to reduce the cost of legal services. One law professor (not Keeton or O'Connell!) suggested the industry will have to change to a system whereby the lawyer is not as necessary, suggesting that a plan like the Basic Protection plan could accomplish that result. The majority of the participants disagreed, maintaining that the attorney will continue to be deeply involved in any system. But most advocated the use of a "flat rate" fee system based on several factors other than the amount of the recovery. A few suggested that the court set the fee at the end of the case.

Some—especially among the lawyers—defended the contingent fee, justifying it as a means of giving the poor man his day in court. They went even further and raised the problem of how to compensate the attorney for a plaintiff in a losing cause. In answer to this, one insurance participant replied:

> "Everyone gets paid. All but two percent of the cases are settled. At that point they are 50–50 [verdicts for plaintiffs and defendants]. So only in one percent of the cases do the lawyers not get a fee."

Many were disappointed at the lack of substantial discussion of the contingent fee during the conference. The failure to discuss the fee system was attributed to the power of the bar, which has created the feeling that discussion of the contingent fee is "off limits everywhere." One insurance executive pointed out that the discussion was academic for all practical purposes. "We cannot do away with the contingent fee; no legislature will abolish it. The bar associations are too powerful." The resentment of many insurance participants toward the bar—and the plaintiffs' bar in particular—was very strong. Said one: "The plaintiffs' bar . . . [has] to have jewels in the tailpipes of their cadillacs." Said another: "The contingent fee system is a cancer."

### C. *Availability of Insurance: Classification According to Area and Occupation*

Many felt that restrictive underwriting by insurers, making it difficult for individuals in a given neighborhood, occupation or age group to get insurance, has been the most strongly criticized aspect of the present system. Said one insurance participant: "In the big cities there's one half—well, a large percentage—that no one wants to insure. Like Lawndale in Chicago, for both fire and auto." Such restrictions, it was pointed out, have civil rights implications, given the fact that ghetto areas are often adversely affected. These restrictive practices, it was felt, have aroused far more interest than the question of the adequacy of compensation to accident victims, which has only very recently been exciting public attention.

There was general agreement that the main complaint today is that it is impossible to get insurance in certain areas, such as potential riot zones. The public believes that insurance companies do issue "blackout" maps to their agents. Another problem, it was charged, is that neighborhood restrictions also apply to residents who live in fringe areas which deny them the "right" to insurance coverage, either by a total refusal to write a policy on such persons or by requiring them to pay prohibitively high rates. Consequently, it was also charged, the system penalizes not only the safe driver who lives in a high risk zone but also the safe drivers on the perimeter of the zone.

Some industry participants also agreed that another source of public dissatisfaction is the occupational classification system. One insurance executive thought the system was a valid one, but admitted that it offends many people, such as lawyers and clergymen, if they learn they are not rated among the safest drivers. Another insurance participant challenged the validity of the practice, concluding that occupational classifications are used as a matter of administrative convenience only.

The consensus was that although some area and class underwriting is rational from an actuarial point of view, the public's toleration of it is sorely strained.

### D. The Collateral Source Doctrine

The collateral source doctrine was one problem which elicited a great deal of agreement among many participants. One insurance executive framed a common attitude when he said:

> "I think all special damages should be put on the same level as fire insurance. One cannot recover twice for fire loss and the same should be true of out-of-pocket expenses in the auto context; it should not be possible to recover twice. The whole process of duplicate payments should be attacked. It grew up historically and there is no justification for it. Nor can you distinguish voluntary from government sources [as was suggested]. We should go all the way and have no duplication."

Most of the participants agreed that repealing the collateral source doctrine would reduce the cost of insurance coverage significantly. Some were convinced that the collateral source doctrine must be abolished if the fault system is to be preserved.

Others cautioned against viewing the abolition of the collateral source doctrine as a panacea for the industry's ills. Implementation of a communication system adequate to prevent double recovery creates administrative problems, including the practical problems of honesty, disclosure, and job changes. At least one participant felt that the problem could only be solved by legislation. He thought the public might be reluctant to give up these excess proceeds and would view any industry attempt to eliminate payments with hostility.

There were several other suggestions made as to the method of abolishing the rule. One participant suggested that the defendant be allowed to tell the jury that the plaintiff has collateral sources of compensation. Others suggested that the judiciary could abrogate the rule, thus eliminating the necessity for legislation. But the consensus was that the abolition of the collateral source doctrine should be effected by the legislature. It was clear to most that double recoveries must be prevented, and that this would produce a substantial cost savings.

### E.   Cancellations

Although once a serious problem, most insurance industry participants believed that current cancellation practices are fair. Some pointed out that other problems are receiving more attention today. At least one insurance participant, however, thought that the problem was still present: "I've seen, and expect to continue to see, gross abuses in cancellation practices; some of the kid adjusters do get sort of uppity." It was pointed out that the notice of intent not to renew has replaced cancellation as the major device used to revoke coverage.

Several participants indicated relief that some legislatures have passed laws prohibiting abusive cancellation practices and that similar legislation is currently being considered in many other states. The industry is more or less reconciled to such legislation, said some, and several suggested that the industry should sponsor it in order to improve public relations.

Some were not convinced that the cancellation power is clearly an "evil." One industry representative complained: "A guy can be on LSD and we could not cancel him out until he is found guilty of a felony." Such differences of opinion could again be resolved, it was felt, only by defining the exact role of the insurance industry in society. Some felt that if one of the functions of an insurance system is to protect the public from "bad" drivers, insurance companies should not be able to cancel a policy because the driver is a poor risk. Others strongly resisted such a definition of the function of insurance when dealing with the underwriting and cancellation issues.

### F.   Court Congestion

The consensus was that court congestion is not caused by auto accident litigation. One Illinois lawyer pointed to the situation in Cook County: "There are 110 judges; 38 are handling personal injury cases. About 75 percent of the personal injury cases are automobile accident claims. Auto cases are not to be blamed for the congestion of the courts." Another cited the statistic that only 14 percent of Massachusetts court time is spent on auto cases. There was general agreement that there are areas of the country in which court congestion has been caused by auto cases, but participants generally felt that court congestion, where it does exist, is a problem for the bar and government, not for the insurance industry. It was also generally agreed that court congestion alone was not a reason for substantially changing the present system of auto insurance.

### G. Government Regulation

Several participants felt, as one insurance participant put it, that:

"under the present system of tight regulation, insurance companies have few alternatives. The problem is one of basic concepts; if the laws change, the industry will change. Every time a company changes a rate or establishes a new policy, the state commissioner is on its back."

Thus, governmental regulation was seen by some as the reason for the lack of reform from within the industry. Others felt that the real problem was not strict regulation, but too little regulation. The "bad" companies, such as the "fly-by-night" firms that leave consumers unprotected when they go bankrupt, are not sufficiently controlled. Inadequate regulation has resulted, it was contended, because the state agencies are understaffed, or, in some cases, because they are in the "vest pockets" of some insurance companies. There was general agreement that the agencies need better personnel and that new, more flexible schemes of regulation would be advantageous to the general public.

### H. Compensation of the Victim

There was considerable feeling that an increasing source of much of the criticism leveled at the industry is its failure to adequately compensate accident victims. Many felt, however, that there are many innocent accident victims who go uncompensated because of inadequate coverage of the tortfeasor. A number felt that the rule of contributory negligence is a prime cause of lack of compensation. Some participants pointed out that even if a victim is covered and has a right to collect, the actual payment often comes too late. Although the victim is fully compensated for his loss, he may not receive the proceeds until several years after the injury, with concomitant hardship in the interim. Others cited the companies who have sought to remedy this problem by instituting advance payment plans.[3] It was suggested that the industry should offer these plans as a matter of standard practice.[4] It was also felt that the public would use the plans more frequently if the companies would publicize them more effectively.

The focal point of the discussion of compensation was the issue of

[3] *See* Kemper, *The Basic Protection Plan: Reform or Regression?*, p. 104 n.20 *supra*.

[4] A discussion of a new experimental Guaranteed Benefit Plan announced by the American Mutual Alliance appears in Wall St. J., Nov. 14, 1967, p. 12, col. 6. According to this report, "an 'advance payments' plan . . . offers to pay at once [a victim's] out-of-pocket expenses but only if [the] . . . insured driver is clearly [liable] . . . . The Alliance proposal would theoretically pay except when the driver is clearly not [liable] . . . ."

whether the public wanted to be compensated for "pain and suffering." Most of the participants were of the opinion that the public was very strongly committed to the availability of pain and suffering awards. They contended that the public is willing to pay more for insurance coverage to retain the right to sue for general damages and the chance of recovering what some considered a "windfall." Several participants contended, however, that the public's commitment to such general damages is not very strong and that most people would be willing to forego general damages for certain recovery of their special damages and reduction of the cost of insurance coverage.

### I.  *The Industry's Public Image*

Most insurance participants seemed to agree that a major problem, if not the cause of all industry's problems, is the poor public image of the industry. Indeed, this—along with the need to ascertain consumer desires—was an ever-recurring theme. The poor public image is a result, it was said, of psychological factors. The explanation was that:

> "[S]tudies prove that there is considerable personal pleasure in buying an expensive car—you can polish it, show it off, drive it. There is no pleasure, however, in insuring it. Insurance is basically a defensive transaction, prompted by fear. People don't like it, and resent buying it."

These factors are compounded by the fact that insurance is a rather standardized product, further reducing consumer appeal. Abuses exposed by the press or spread by rumors are believed, and the net result is a basic distrust of all insurance. Most believed the general public has lost sight of the fact that the industry is dedicated to "the principles of social benefits and distribution of costs." The public does not understand insurance in general and its own individual policies in particular.

Several felt that the industry's response to the public's changing demands is almost invariably negative, and that, as a consequence, the public has become more willing to scrap either the whole system, the whole industry, or both, to satisfy its demands. The public, some contended, wants changes that will make insurance conform to current welfare concepts. Regardless of the merits, if the industry will not submit to gradual change, many felt that the system would be placed under governmental control.

There was strong sentiment for an industry program of public relations directed at improving the image of the auto insurance industry. Several suggested that the public should be made aware of the problems of the industry, and the industry's response to these problems, through massive advertising campaigns.

### J.  *Cutthroat Competition: The Antitrust Implications*

Several industry participants pointed out that the intensely competitive nature of the industry makes new programs more difficult to establish. The industry, they contended, operates under a maximum exposure to risk: "[W]e are the only industry that sells a product without knowing how much it will cost." Strong competition from over 800 companies does little to improve the situation. Thus, the risk of innovation, they concluded, becomes prohibitive. Moreover, it was stated, there is the fear within the industry that if the leaders were to get together in an effort to solve the several problems of the industry, they would probably be found guilty of a violation of the Clayton Act. There was general agreement that, as a result of this situation, the industry is suffering from a lack of both leadership and intra-industry cooperation.

## K.  General

Several participants contended that most of the problems stem from the unique social situation of the industry. The insurance industry, one insurance participant contended, "is affected by every social ill that can be imagined; alcoholism, divorce, suicide, etc. But no one would say that we're responsible [for alleviating] . . . all [these] . . . social ills." Replied a lawyer, "But you're trying. For example, if I get drunk and get in an accident, you try to price me off the road. Why doesn't the liquor industry try to price me out of the booze market—say, charge me $25 a fifth? You're really trying to legislate or enforce traffic safety; and it's not your field." Others among the insurance participants seemed to agree it posed problems for the industry to be given— or forced to accept—such responsibility.

## IV.  Suggested Solutions

### A.  Abolition of the Fault System

Several discussions centered around the validity of the contention that the fault system of determining liability must be altered or abandoned in the automobile insurance context. Some felt that the industry has performed well in the legal framework of the fault system but that "[t]he industry cannot feasibly provide an inexpensive auto insurance policy so long as the present system prevails." One statement in particular expressed the general feelings of the opponents of the fault system:

> "[T]here is something inherently wrong with the fault system. We see many instances of perjury, blown-up claims and the idea that it is perfectly legitimate to milk the insurance company for all that it is worth. We must realize that the fault concept is a relatively recent development in the law. Certainly the common law, where the tort system developed, never realized that the automobile would come along or that the number of suits would skyrocket."

One estimate that there is a party actually at fault in only 25 percent of accidents further substantiated for some the opinion that the fault concept does not result in an equitable adjudication of rights and liabilities. Since, it was argued, most accidents are due to complex situations beyond human control and are the result of highway speeds and mechanical failures, society as a whole should bear the cost of compensating the traffic victim. Most opponents of the fault system believed that most people, knowing there is insurance, tend not to think in terms of fault; rather, their only real concern is that they be compensated should a loss occur.

There was substantial disagreement as to the effect of the abolition of fault on the cost of insurance coverage. Some contended that the cost savings involved in the reduction of legal services would yield substantially lower premiums. Others, however, contended that payments of claims without regard to fault would yield a substantial increase in the number of claims, thus offsetting any cost-reducing aspects of the change. Most participants agreed that abolition of the fault system alone would do little to solve many of the other problems of the industry. For example, the fact that a number of claims go uncompensated is not always the result of the fault system. The victim may be unpaid because of no insurance.

The general consensus was that the basic concept of fault can result in a just system, if there is willingness to take action to correct the obvious flaws. Many questioned the value of a change to a no-fault system. Most cases, they argued, are not fought on the issue of liability, but on the amount of damage that may be recovered. Moreover, "people won't give up their traditional ideas about 'redressing the wrong against a culpable party.' The public is not criticizing the fault system." Several felt that the use of "fragmentary reform" would cure the problems of the public and the industry. One insurance executive, for example, contended that the industry would remove most of its problems if changes were made regarding collateral sources, judicial reform, and fraud; present problems, he stated, could be solved without changing the fault system. A few felt that the public is neutral as to the fault issue. One participant's experience was that the average person does not consider the fault problem at all, except in regard to the backlog of cases in some courts.

The general attitude of the industry participants was that the fault system, though admittedly not without problems, should not be discarded. They seemed to favor evolutionary change within the fault system. However, there was a strong and vocal minority, including some from the insurance industry, who advocated abandoning the fault system in the auto accident context.

## B.   *The Basic Protection Plan*

Since, as several pointed out, the Basic Protection plan is the only comprehensive plan for solving the auto accident compensation problem that has received much public and legislative support, it was the focal point of some workshop sessions. In general, the participants attempted to ascertain whether Basic Protection would solve the industry's problems.

One insurance participant stated: "We have the premise: the public wants cost reduction. I've taken a hard look at the Basic Protection plan, and can't dismiss it. Pain and suffering coverage is optional if the insured wants to pay for it.[5] Let each driver decide how much coverage he wants to pay for." There was, however, widespread doubt that Basic Protection would reduce costs. Although some were willing to assume that the plan would save money by eliminating overinsurance, others characterized the plan as "actuarial insanity." In fact, the cost estimates involved in implementing Basic Protection were the greatest cause for concern among industry participants. The extremely negative reaction to Basic Protection in most instances appeared to result from an extreme reluctance to abandon a predictable system and experiment with a new one; many verbalized this reluctance by asserting that no one had convinced them that Basic Protection would reduce costs.

There was general disagreement on the effect of Basic Protection on the cost of legal services and court congestion. Several were of the opinion that litigation would not be substantially reduced. They argued that most cases that reach the trial stage "can be made to look like $5,000 cases." Thus attorneys will simply allege damages over the Basic Protection tort exemption.[6] One participant theorized that the Basic Protection payments may be used to finance tort litigation, thus increasing litigation.

Others noted that the plan does not abolish the contingent fee.[7] Thus it was suggested that, in many cases, the cost of legal services to a victim will not be substantially reduced. However, most agreed that the overall effect of Basic Protection should be to reduce the importance of the lawyer in the auto accident context; all the attorneys present were convinced that plaintiffs' attorneys will be adversely affected by the plan. Most insurance participants and proponents of Basic Protection agreed that "the plaintiffs' bar has been taking too much of auto insurance pay-out." Said one participant:

> "I am a lawyer. I do not want to start something new. I have a personal economic interest in the system as it now stands. The Keeton-O'Connell plan cuts the lawyer out entirely. The lawyer has the real stake here, not the insurance companies. To them it would be a temporary inconvenience."

(To this replied an insurance executive: "Our studies show bodily injury premiums would go down 60 percent. This is more than temporary inconvenience.")

A frequently voiced criticism of the Basic Protection plan was that even if it would reduce costs, there would be a corresponding reduction in the compensation available to the traffic victim. A majority of the participants

[5] Keeton & O'Connell, *Basic Protection Automobile Insurance*, p. 61 *supra.*
[6] *See id.* at 50-51.
[7] *See id.* at 68.

seemed to assume that the public will not like relinquishing the opportunity to recover pain and suffering[8] and collateral source benefits.[9]

Some participants believed that Basic Protection would greatly increase fraudulent claims. "Instead of the adversary system we will have nothing." Others pointed out, however, that there are several techniques to avoid fraud—such as wage verification. One pointed out that the $100 deductible feature[10] will be no more susceptible to fraudulent activity than the present system.

The $10,000 limit[11] disturbed a few for reasons other than the practical problems involved in making the limitation work as designed. One insurance participant expressed the belief that the limit "is a kind of merchandising decision, with the implication that retention of the fault system above this amount was to appease those opposed to the plan." Another participant compared the limitation to the wrongful death statute's limitation, now abolished in Illinois,[12] and predicted that if the plan were implemented, political forces would operate to change or remove the $10,000 limitation on recovery without fault.

Most of the "violent" criticism (*e.g.* from one insurance participant: "I'd like to say that Keeton-O'Connell is a . . . bunch of hooey") was aimed at the underlying premises of the Basic Protection plan. Some participants found the plan to be too "shallow." They argued that the plan is based on too many questionable assumptions; for example: "pay the negligent drivers and solve the problems of the industry." They failed to see how this will reduce costs of insurance. Moreover, they questioned the validity of a plan that deals only with claims of the ordinary amount, when it is large claims that are allegedly being left unpaid. Others concluded that "Basic Protection won't end uncompensated injuries because most people won't buy liability coverage; thus once the loss is beyond the limits of coverage of his own [Basic Protection] policy, the victim will be left uncompensated for his loss."

One insurance participant noted that every coverage offered by the Basic Protection plan is presently available; the only difference is that insurance is not compulsory. Thus, several agreed that Basic Protection did not offer enough new coverage or solve enough of the problems of automobile insurance to justify adopting this untried system of loss allocation. According to one critic:

"The Keeton-O'Connell plan is a red herring being used to provide a socialized system of insurance to benefit the unfortunates. This puts the burden on the well-to-do, who would have to pay extra for insur-

[8] *See id.* at 61.
[9] *See id.* at 54-56.
[10] *Id.* at 56-58.
[11] *Id.* at 58-59.
[12] ILL. REV. STAT. ch. 70, § 2 (1967).

ance to spread the risk. The attack on the fault system is a smoke screen
for socialism."

Another participant viewed the plan as basically a tax on driving but concluded that since "driving a car is now almost an absolute right, maybe a tax
on driving is the solution."

Several insurance executives suggested that the Basic Protection plan
might well be tried out in one state to ascertain how it works. Several other
participants felt, however, that there would be a real problem if a state
scraps the fault system, adopts the Basic Protection plan, and finds that it
does not work. How, they asked, does a state return to the fault system?

Another question was whether the government should assume some
fiscal responsibility for the plan after adopting it. Some suggested that the
government might subsidize the Basic Protection plan in the first few years,
or at least subsidize any losses. Most participants, however, rejected flatly
any suggestion of governmental support of the insurance industry, fearing
that the eventual result would be state insurance.

The majority of the participants were of the opinion that Basic Protection "cannot be sold" to the public or state legislatures. They cited the
recent experience in Massachusetts where the plan passed the House but was
defeated in the Senate. A substantial minority, however, held the opinion
that Basic Protection or a similar plan would be passed in some states unless
substantial improvements are made within the present system. Most of the
participants agreed that the Basic Protection plan has value as a catalyst.

### C. *Alternate Solutions Proposed During the Conference*

According to one insurance participant: "Nobody has a better plan than
Basic Protection; but does that mean we have to accept it?" As another insurance executive said, "We were not prepared for this conference. The
industry has been caught flat-footed on many of these questions." Several
felt that the industry should collectively suggest desirable solutions and support remedial legislation to implement reforms. Because of the lack of preparation for the conference, it was said, there were no detailed proposals set
forth by the insurance industry. However, during the course of discussion,
various suggestions were made by individual participants.

One executive suggested that is would be advisable to change to a system that would be similar to workmen's compensation, administered by
private companies, on the grounds that greater efficiency would presumably
result. The main objection was that workmen's compensation benefits often
fall far short of actual loss. Moreover, although workmen's compensation
is good in the industrial context, many felt it would not necessarily be effective in the auto accident context. This conclusion was primarily based on
two factors. First, there would be greater opportunity for fraud because of
the lack of administrative control, lacking the employer-employee relationship
and a business location. Second, the system would cost much more because of

the greater frequency of accidents and the fact that there would be no employer contributions.

Another plan discussed was compulsory insurance and a concurrent return to "the basic concept of spreading the loss," without countless differentiations of rates. But as some pointed out, this would require the good driver to subsidize the bad driver. One participant noted that the industry had started with a flat insurance rate structure, but was forced to abandon it because of the rigors of competition. Another insurance participant countered with the suggestion that the insurance industry could be converted into a quasi-public utility, shielding certain practices from the rigors of competition.

Another suggestion was to establish a comprehensive plan for partial prepayments:[13] whether any other reforms would be enacted would be dependent upon the felt needs of each state. The critics of this plan were quick to point out that the change would be minor and would leave most of the problems unsolved. The proponents countered with the contention that the plan would give each state the flexibility necessary to meet the needs of the particular situation. There was considerable feeling, however, that prepayment plans would be wholly inadequate to meet the needs of the public.

One opinion voiced by many participants was their belief that if the fault system is retained, contributory negligence will have to be replaced by comparative negligence. Although they were concerned with the effect on cost, it was suggested that the change would only amount to approximately a 10 percent increase in costs and that the industry could tolerate the increased costs when compared to the resulting improvement in the system.

The one 'solution' most consistently advocated by participants from the insurance industry as one which would be simple, safe, relatively inexpensive, and "require no legislative activity" was to conduct a massive public relations campaign to convince the public that the insurance industry is serving their needs in the best possible manner. The politicians, it was felt, will respond only to public opinion polls, and favorable public opinion can be produced most easily by a publicity campaign. As one proponent pointed out: "You must give the public what they need, and convince the public that it is what they want. People have no conception of what they bought and paid for when they get insurance. We must look more reputable." This idea was greeted with much enthusiasm. However, several participants objected and insisted that there must be more to the industry's program than a publicity campaign; that any plan for the future must include more concrete steps, such as those that will reduce costs. Said one high ranking insurance executive with responsibility in his company for public relations:

"And do what [with a massive public relations campaign]? The problem is that there's a great misconception of what . . . 'public image' is.

[13] *See* notes 3 & 4 *supra* and accompanying text.

It's a reflection of what the company is, and the only way to change it is to change what you are. My company realizes it's been wrong—and that's why the image is bad; . . . the question now is how to change so that the image projected is good."

### D. *The Future of Legislation and Governmental Regulation*

One participant related the results of research done in 1954: "48 percent of those members of the public surveyed were of the opinion that more federal regulation was needed. Today the percentage in favor of greater federal regulation would probably be even larger." Others noted that the Basic Protection plan is "a natural for the federal government. It has been put into draft form and can be readily introduced in Congress." "If the various states pass such a plan in different forms, it is very probable that the federal government will step in to achieve some degree of uniformity." One participant pointed out that federal regulation would require a change in the common law of auto accident liability which is basically a matter of state concern. Thus, he concluded, the federal government cannot put a plan like Basic Protection into effect unless it can force the states to adopt it by using some form of economic pressure.

Insurance participants were confident that the industry could exist under "rational" legislative changes. Even if Basic Protection were enacted, insurance companies would find a way to write the necessary policies, *provided* the regulatory framework established by the legislation imparts the necessary flexibility, both as to rates and otherwise. Many believe the industry should write a model code and then push for passage through state legislatures. One executive suggested that the insurance industry should be legislated into a quasi-public utility: force the companies to sell to everyone, remove the direct competition and use a franchise system.

Many thought that there are several areas in which the insurance industry would welcome legislative action. Insurance participants were unanimous in appealing for stronger laws and quicker action against "bad" drivers. Insurance personnel contended that when the government fails to penalize the high risk drivers and the industry attempts to do so by pricing them out of their insurance, the result is that the insurance industry bears the brunt of the resulting resentment among both drivers and their victims.

### V. Conclusion

Several participants were convinced that industry inaction would result in the passage of the Basic Protection plan in a few states, particularly Michigan. On the other hand, most industry personnel were extremely resistant to any fundamental change. More than a few evinced a personal distrust of "social reformers" advocating drastic innovation. Finally, industry participants seemed extremely concerned with the industry's public image; a great many participants felt that the best immediate solution to current problems would be to conduct a public relations campaign.

# INDEX

In this index "B.P.p." signifies Basic Protection plan